Index to the Works of Adam Smith

THE GLASGOW EDITION OF THE WORKS AND
CORRESPONDENCE OF ADAM SMITH

*Commissioned by the University of Glasgow to celebrate the bicentenary of
the Wealth of Nations*

I

THE THEORY OF MORAL SENTIMENTS
Edited by D. D. RAPHAEL *and* A. L. MACFIE

II

AN INQUIRY INTO THE NATURE AND CAUSES
OF THE WEALTH OF NATIONS
Edited by R. H. CAMPBELL *and* A. S. SKINNER; *textual editor* W. B. TODD

III

ESSAYS ON PHILOSOPHICAL SUBJECTS
(and Miscellaneous Pieces)
Edited by W. P. D. WIGHTMAN

IV

LECTURES ON RHETORIC AND BELLES LETTRES
Edited by J. C. BRYCE
This volume includes the *Considerations concerning the
First Formation of Languages*

V

LECTURES ON JURISPRUDENCE
Edited by R. L. MEEK, D. D. RAPHAEL, *and* P. G. STEIN
This volume includes two reports of Smith's course together with
the 'Early Draft' of part of the *Wealth of Nations*

VI

CORRESPONDENCE OF ADAM SMITH
Edited by E. C. MOSSNER *and* I. S. ROSS

Associated volumes:
ESSAYS ON ADAM SMITH
Edited by A. S. SKINNER *and* T. WILSON

LIFE OF ADAM SMITH
By I. S. ROSS

ADAM SMITH LIBRARY: A CATALOGUE
By H. MIZUTA

*The Glasgow Edition of the Works and Correspondence of Adam Smith and
the associated volumes are published in hardcover by Oxford University Press.
The six titles of the Glasgow Edition and the Index, but not the associated
volumes, are published in paperback by Liberty Fund.*

Index to the Works of
ADAM SMITH

COMPILED BY
K. HAAKONSSEN
and
A. S. SKINNER

LIBERTY FUND

INDIANAPOLIS

This book is published by Liberty Fund, Inc., a foundation
established to encourage study of the ideal of a society
of free and responsible individuals.

𒀝𒄀

The cuneiform inscription that serves as our logo and as the
design motif for our endpapers is the earliest-known written
appearance of the word "freedom" (*amagi*), or "liberty."
It is taken from a clay document written about 2300 B.C.
in the Sumerian city-state of Lagash.

This reprint has been authorized by the Oxford
University Press.
Printed in the United States of America

10 09 08 07 06 05 04 03 02 P 5 4 3 2 1

Library of Congress Cataloging-in-Publication Data

Index to the works of Adam Smith/compiled by K. Haakonssen
and A.S. Skinner.
    p. cm.
    Originally published: Oxford: Clarendon Press, 2001.
    ISBN 0-86597-388-1 (pbk.: alk. paper)
    1. Smith, Adam 1723–1790—Indexes. 2. Economists—Great
Britain. I. Haakonssen, Knud, 1947– II. Skinner, Andrew S.
HB103.S6 I53   2002
330.15′3—dc21 2002066089

Liberty Fund, Inc.,
8335 Allison Pointe Trail, Suite 300
Indianapolis, Indiana 46250-1684

This book is printed on paper that is acid-free and meets
the requirements of the American National Standard for
Permanence of Paper for Printed Library Materials,
Z39.48-1992. ∞

Cover design adapted by Erin Kirk New, Watkinsville, Georgia,
based on a design by JMH Corporation, Indianapolis, Indiana

Printed and bound by Worzalla Publishing Company,
Stevens Point, Wisconsin

Contents

Introduction   vii

LECTURES ON RHETORIC AND BELLES LETTRES

Index of Subjects   3

Index of Persons   9

ESSAYS ON PHILOSOPHICAL SUBJECTS

Index of Subjects   17

Index of Persons   25

THE THEORY OF MORAL SENTIMENTS

Index of Subjects   35

Index of Persons   65

LECTURES ON JURISPRUDENCE AND APPENDIX

Index of Subjects   73

Index of Persons   95

Index of Acts of the English and United Kingdom Parliaments   103

Index of Acts of the Parliaments of Scotland   105

Original Index to Report dated 1766   107

WEALTH OF NATIONS

Introduction

In writing his introduction to the *Lectures on Jurisprudence*, Edwin Cannan recorded the extraordinary way in which the manuscript of these notes had been discovered:

On April 21, Mr. Charles C. Maconochie, whom I then met for the first time, happened to be present when, in course of conversation with the literary editor of the Oxford Magazine, I had occasion to make some comment about Adam Smith. Mr. Maconochie immediately said that he possessed a manuscript report of Adam Smith's lectures on jurisprudence, which he regarded as of considerable interest. (Cannan, 1896, p. xv.)

Cannan's reaction may be imagined.

More than sixty years later, John Lothian accidentally discovered, at an auction held in Aberdeen, two sets of lecture notes as delivered by Smith. The first set were notes of the lectures on jurisprudence given by Smith in the session 1762–63, that is in the session preceding the version edited by Cannan. Lothian observed:

The second set of manuscripts, in two volumes, similarly bound but with leather tips to protect the corners, carried on the spine of each volume in neat handwriting the inscription, 'Notes of Dr. Smith's Rhetoric Lectures'. These manuscripts proved to be an almost complete set of a student's notes on part of Smith's course on Moral Philosophy given in 1762–63. (Lothian, 1963, p. xii.)

The *Lectures on Rhetoric and Belles Lettres* were edited by Lothian in 1963. Both sets were subsequently purchased by the University of Glasgow and were to become key elements in the decision to proceed with editions of these works and the other volumes. The edition was formally embarked upon in the early 1960s and completed twenty years later with the publication of John Bryce's edition of the *Rhetoric*.

The completion of the edition was secured financially when the Liberty Fund undertook a paperback version of the entire work. This decision effectively provided access for a very wide audience.

Wider access to the series prompted the belief that it would be appropriate to produce a general index to the *Works* as a whole. As I recall, I offered this suggestion to the Liberty Fund some fifteen years ago. The Fund agreed both to support the project and to the suggestion that the indexers should include Knud Haakonssen. While we have joint responsibility for the outcome, Knud Haakonssen's main task was with Smith's ethical and jurisprudential material, while I mostly took care of the remaining areas and the task of co-ordinating the volume as a whole.

In this context we would wish to acknowledge a debt to Professor Drummond Bone, formerly of the Department of English Literature in the University of Glasgow, and now Vice-Chancellor of Royal Holloway, University of London. Professor Bone identified a colleague, Dr. Peter Cochrane, who was to give us invaluable advice with regard to the indexes to the *Rhetoric*, and to those other literary works which were first published in the *Essays on Philosophical Subjects*.

We began the work using traditional and manual techniques, before being introduced to the advantages of modern computer technology. In Glasgow University this development was the result of advice received from Professor Richard Trainor, now Vice-Chancellor of the University of Greenwich, who in turn introduced us to Dr. Thomas Munck, head of the Computing Unit in the Faculty of Arts. We are indebted to Dr. Munck and to his team who helped check the texts for keywords to be used in the index.

While we have not sought to produce a *concordance*, nonetheless the flow of information generated by responses from the Computing Unit was so great as to become almost unmanageable. We were forced to the conclusion, for example, that the fact that Smith mentioned the term 'capital' on 702 occasions in the *Wealth of Nations* might not of itself be very helpful. Accordingly, we have sought a compromise which, we hope, will give the indexes as a whole greater descriptive power.

This index is to Smith's *Works* and does not include the *Correspondence*, although there are cross-references to this material. Each index is separate on the ground that the works involved are very different in terms of focus. Each includes an index of subjects and of persons. For the sake of convenience, the indexes include the lists of statutes prepared by the editors of the *Lectures on Jurisprudence* and of the *Wealth of Nations* where the main contributors were P. G. Stein (LJ) and R. H. Campbell (WN). We have included the original manuscript index to the *Lectures on Jurisprudence* as in the Glasgow edition, on the ground that this is a document of importance in its own right. The volume also contains a copy of the index which was added to the third edition of the *Wealth of Nations*. The index may have been added as a result of criticism from Hugh Blair (*Correspondence*, letter 151) and from William Robertson who noted that:

As your Book must necessarily become a Political or Commercial Code to all Europe, which must be often consulted both by men of Practice and Speculation, I should wish that in the 2d Edition you would give a copious index. (*Correspondence*, letter 153.)

The first index is reprinted following the original, but with cross-references to the present version.

Whoever the author of the original index may have been, it is a remarkable document, notable for its sensitivity to many of Smith's major themes. Interestingly, the same quality is evident in the index to Sir James Steuart's

Principles of Political Oeconomy, which had been issued by the same publishers, Strachan and Cadell, in 1767.

We owe debts to our respective institutions, to the readers appointed by the Liberty Fund, and to colleagues in Great Britain who include Tony Brewer (Bristol), Vivienne Brown (Open University), and Donald Winch (Sussex). We are also indebted to numerous scholars who have bombarded us with random questions. The 'nicest' of these came in a telephone call from the United States where my interlocutor was in urgent need of a reference to 'pots and pans, augmentation of' (*Wealth of Nations*, pp. 439–40)!

It is hoped that the indexes will be useful, supplementing those that already exist, and that their usefulness will be further enhanced by another technical advance. An electronic version of the *Works* will be made available on the Liberty Fund's Library of Economics and Liberty website, with free access. There will be a separate electronic version published by Oxford University Press. Both will include copies of these indexes. The opportunities opened up by these initiatives are surely considerable.

We have reason to be grateful to the Principal of Glasgow University, Sir Graeme Davies, who readily agreed to these proposals on behalf of the University Court.

The technical costs involved were met by the Liberty Fund. The cost of preparing the numerous editions through which the final version has passed were borne by the Department of Economics in Glasgow. The texts were prepared by Christina MacSwan, who was involved with the Smith project from its beginnings, and completed by Lavina MacMillan. We are indebted to both for their efficiency and, above all, patience.

Andrew Stewart Skinner
Glasgow University
February 2001

REFERENCES

Cannan, Edwin (ed.) 1896. Adam Smith's *Lectures on Justice, Police, Revenue and Arms* (London: Macmillan).

Lothian, John (ed.) 1963. *Lectures on Rhetoric and Belles Lettres* (Edinburgh and London: Nelson).

Smith, Adam, 1977. *Correspondence*, ed. E. C. Mossner and I. S. Ross (Oxford: Oxford University Press).

Lectures on Rhetoric and Belles Lettres

Index of Subjects

A

abstraction 9–12, 41–2, 55–7, 174, 176, 206–7, 209, 212–15, 219, 221
  see also adjectives, generalisation, nouns, number, prepositions, verbs
Actium, Battle of 31
adjective, adjectives 6, 9–12, 17, 77, 205, 210, 214–15, 223–6
  adjectival agreement, origin of 208
  cannot qualify one another 209
  imply abstraction 206–7
  origin of 9–10, 204
admiration:
  excited by the great and the noble 43, 45, 48, 64 n., 68–9
  language of 131, 139
  rational 61
Aeneid, The (Virgil) 26 & n., 31 & n., 36 & n., 72 & n., 97, 125
Agricola (Tacitus) 83 & n.
allegories 8, 30, 52
anakoloutha 159–60
analogy:
  foundation of in language 208, 220
  love of 215
  see also language
antonomasia 204, 206
archaisms 28
architecture 143–4
Areopagus, the 149, 175
Armenian, number of cases in 211–12
artificial objects 74
arts, fine 57
Athens:
  character of citizens compared to Sparta 164–5
  compared to Cicero's Rome 158–9
  democratical 149
  education of youth 138
  growth of commerce, decline of martial spirit 149–51, 153, 156
  judicial courts of 175, 179, 180–1, 186
  as a maritime power 168
  quality of fortunes in 156–9
  seizure of Syracuse 86, 94

B

ballads 104, 135–6

Balliol, College 28 n.
barbarism 105
  and judicial oratory 174
  and poetry 136–7
  see also commerce; savages
beauty:
  of language 26
  of style 40, 126, *see also* style
Billingsgate language 34
business, prose as the language of 137–8

C

cadence 21–2, 38, 53, 59, 140, 160
Capua 167 n., 168
Cartesian philosophy 146
cartoons (of Raphael) 126
cases (in language) 6, 11–16, 210–15, 220, 223, 225
causes 91–4
  and effects 98–9, 171–72
  of events 90–5, 106–8, 113–15, 163, 165–6, 168
Cecina, army of 114
celestial motions 93
centaurs 104, 111
Centos 46
character, description of 78–84, 94–5, 130–4
character and circumstance, its effect on style 34
character of author, its effect on style 34–5
characters of writers 40–1
Cherry and the Slae (ballad) 136 & n.
child, children's speech 13, 131, 203 n., 204, 219
Clouds, The (Aristophanes) 44
comedy 44–5, 47, 81–2, 88, 121, 124–5
comic writers 47, 81, 120–1
commedia dell'arte 44–5
commerce:
  in Athens 149–51
  and prose 137–8
  see also barbarism, power
Commons, House of 175
  ribaldry in 199
compassion 22, 34, 37, 101, 186–7
  in Cicero 192, 194–5
compound words and language 3–4, 9 n., 14, 63, 69, 201, 222

Comus (Milton) 28 n.
consonants, harsh effect of 16, 22–3
constitution, British 176
constitution(s) 62, 108–9, 176, 199 n.
contractions 14
conversation 48, 23–4, 34, 36–8, 55
  in Greece and Rome 159
Corcyria 167–8
Corinth 167–8
Corinthians 141 n., 167–8
cottage, seen at a distance 68
courts, judicial 114, 141, 151, 175, 178–81,
  196–7, 222 n.

D

dancing 136–7
De Corona (Demosthenes) 33 n., 178–9 n.
declensions and conjugations 12–13, 25,
  215, 220–4
deliberative eloquence 63–4, 110, 128, 135,
  138, 142–70, 185, 187
  Demosthenes and Cicero its best
    examplars 149–62
  as inserted in Livy's histories 166, 169
  as inserted in Tacitus' histories 168–9
  as inserted in Thucydides' history 162–8
  its origin 137–8
  two main methods the Socratic and the
    Aristotelian 146–7
demonstrative eloquence 63, 128–41
  actions to be extolled in 129–30
  history of 135–41
  language appropriate to 131–2
  structure of 132–3
  style of 133–4
  virtues to be extolled in 130–1
description 62–88
  of actions of men 85–8
  of artificial objects 74–5
  of the characters of men 78–84
  of invisible objects 68
  of natural objects 76
  of passions 75–6
  of several objects 73–4
  of visible objects 65–7, 71–2
dialectic 181–2, 193–4
didactic discourse, its purpose 62, 142
  its structures 142–6
didactic writers:
  their differences from historians 35–6,
    101
  their similarities with orators 36
didactic writing 7, 89–91, 100, 128
diphthongs, softening of 16, 22
direct method of expression 67
Don Quixote (Cervantes) 34, 124 & n., 132

dramatic poetry 120
  difference between it and epic 120, 121
Drapier's Letters, The (Swift) 49
Dunciad, The (Pope) 28, 44 & n.
dunghills, descriptions of 65

E

Eclogues (Virgil) 225
Edinburgh Review 57 n., 146 n., 205 n.
education:
  a gentleman's 47
  in ancient Greece 138–9, 193
elegies 126–27
Elegy Written in a Country Churchyard
  (Gray) 127 & n.
Eloisa to Abelard (Pope) 18 & n., 77 & n.
eloquence, ancient division of 36, 63, 128
England 4, 15, 83 n., 92 n., 99, 116, 123,
  175, 196, 198
English:
  compared with French and Italian 222–3
  language 3–4, 13–16, 211, 214, 218–19,
    221–6
English pronunciation, sonority of 16
epic poem:
  difference from dramatic 120–1
  entertainment the purpose of 88, 90, 97
  reality not on the side of 97
  see also romance
epithet 77, 135, 207–8
Epistle to Dr. Arbuthnot (Pope) 24 & n.
Erse, poetry 136
Essay on Man (Pope) 5, 33–4, 117–18 & n.
Ethics (Aristotle) 144
exordium 178

F

farce 124
feelings, importance of in elocution 18–19,
  22
  see also passions
figurae 25, 33
figures of speech, *see* speech
French:
  comedians 44
  a compound language 13–15, 222–3
  manners of 198
  panegyrics in 131
  writers 122

G

gap/chasm, *see* ideas

gay:
    a gay man should not endeavour to be
        grave 40, 48–9, 55, 120
gender 12, 33, 215, 223
    loss of 221
    origin of 11, 207–9
genera 205
generalisation 9–10, 205–6, 209–11
    see also abstraction
Geneva 205
Georgics (Virgil) 61 & n., 72 & n., 74 & n.,
        145
gestures and gesticulation 4, 188, 198
Glasgow University 28 n., 162 n.
glory, goal of oratory 128–9
gods 54 n., 96 n., 104–5, 109 n., 135, 139
good writer, prerequisites of 42
grammar 12–13, 221
    ambiguity 5, 8, 18–19, 159, 205 n., 216
    rules of 6, 25–6, 211
gravity 93
Great, and the lowly 124, 133
    in Athens 149–50
    in Rome 154–9
Greece, *see* Athens
Greek (language) 12–16, 25, 154, 210–11,
        214–15, 221–4
grief 22, 37, 50 n., 69, 87 n., 101, 124–5
Gulliver's Travels (Swift) 43, 44, 49
gutturals, loss of 15

H

Hamlet (Shakespeare) 28 & n., 31 & n., 121
Hardyknute (ballad) 136 & n.
Hebrew 214, 216
historians 7, 35–6, 75 n., 86, 104–16
historical writing 50, 63–4, 70–1, 82,
        89–116, 128, 154, 159, 163, 168
    causes, relation of 91–3
    characters in 94–5
    chronology in 98
    connection with oratory 89
    design and contrivance more interesting
        than chance and instinct 90
    didactic intention out of place in 102
    exclamation out of place in 101
    history's purpose to instruct 90
    impartiality in, need for 101
    importance of intention behind 91
    legends as precursors of 104–5, 107
    Machiavelli's, scientific quality of 114–15
    modern historians 96
    'poetical connections', use of 100
    poets the first historians 104
    proofs spoil narrative 102
    reflection, place of in 103

simultaneous events, difficulty in
        narrating 98–100
    style of Greeks and Romans contrasted
        161
    suspense superfluous in 96–7
    see also Guicciardini, Herodotus, Livy,
        Tacitus, Thucydides, etc.
Hudibras (Butler) 27 & n.
humour 43–54, 124–5, 186
hymns 104
hyperboles 27, 30–2, 140

I

ideas:
    association of 9, 93
    chain of 146
    'gaps' or 'intervals' in, a source of
        discomfort 100, 105, 119, 173, 178
    ordering of 17–19, 23–4, 93, 217
    painting or describing in writing 42
    see also deliberative, demonstrative,
        didactic, historical, and judicial
        eloquence
Il Pensoroso (Milton) 70–3
Iliad, The (Homer) 30 & n., 76 & n., 97
imagination, pleasures of (Addison) 53
inflections in English and French 14–15
inhumanity 124, 131
internal objects 75
Italian (language) 14–15
    a compound language 222–3
    function of diminutives in 208
    sweetness of 224
Italy 5, 114, 138

J

jokes 39
judges, English 174–6, 196–7
judicial or civil eloquence 63, 128, 135, 138,
        144, 148–9, 170, 196
    argument from statute of precedent
        174–7
    divisions of 178–82
        exordium 178
        narration 178–80
        confirmation and refutation 181
        peroration 182
    examples from Greeks 145, 160, 182–90
    examples from Romans 160, 162, 182,
        190–6
    methods and art of 170–82
    its origin 137–8
    proof from causes 170–1
    proof from effects 171–3

state of English 196–200
subjects of 170
judiciary, how it separated from executive
174–6
juries 196–7

K

King Lear (Shakespeare) 64 & n.

L

ladies 4
see also women
L'Allegro (Milton) 70–3
language 3–29, 38–42, 53, 104, 116, 131,
137–41, 154, 168, 201–26
development of, compared with that of
mechanical engines 13, 223–4
impact of conquest on 220–1
migration, impact of 220–1
and national temper 3, 154
primitive progress of 9–13, 207, 210, 212,
214–19
role of sound in 11, 14–16, 21–2, 70,
208–9, 211, 215, 224, *see also*
sound
simplification of, its consequences 223–6
system of 218
Latin (language) 12–13, 25, 27, 154, 207,
210–11, 219–20, 222, 224
see also English, French, Greek, Italian
laughter 22, 43–6, 120, 124
law, natural 19 n.
Lochaber (ballad) 136 & n.
logic, ancient 181, 194
Lombards 220–2
Lords, House of 57 n., 175, 197, 199
luxury 92, 110, 112, 150, 157–8

M

Macbeth (Shakespeare) 121 n.
Macedon 152–3, 185 n.
see also Philip of Macedon
machine 13, 223–4
see also language
Marathon, Battle of 141
mathematical demonstration 63, 73
Memoires (de Retz) 103 & n.
merchant, life of contrasted with soldier 39
Merchant of Venice, The (Shakespeare) 67
Metamorphoses (Ovid) 65–6 & n.
metaphors 8, 27–31, 34, 52, 140
mixed metaphors 30–1

metaphysical 11, 58, 112, 145, 148, 207,
209, 212–19, 221
metonymy 27, 29–30
Mexico 204
mimicry 190
morality:
a practical science 4
systems of 51, 55
mouse:
in a chapel 45
music 14–15, 67, 137–9
English taste for 15, 198
Mytylene 164

N

narration 28, 64, 82, 86, 89–103, 105–10,
114, 116, 135 n., 173, 178, 184, 189,
193–5, 197
see also historical writing
native and familiar words, use of 3
natural, objects 73–4, 76
see also law, philosophy
neologisms 27
nobles 124, 150, 156–8
nouns 6, 8, 11–15, 21, 208
adjective 205–10, 215
gender in nouns, origins of 207–8
origin of 9, 203–6
substantive 12, 203, 205–8, 210, 212–15,
217, 220
novels 97, 111
number:
implies high degree of abstraction 214
mysticism of 143 n.
origin of 12, 213–14
three, significance of 143 & n.

O

Observations upon the United Provinces
(Temple) 39 & n.
odes 28, 126–7, 140 n., 225–6 n.
Odes, v (Horace) 225–6
Odyssey (Homer) 30 & n., 76 n., 97
On a Distant Prospect of Eton College (Gray)
127 & n.
On Poetry (A Rhapsody) (Swift) 23 & n.
On the Sublime (Longinus) 33 & n.
opera 198
oratory 7, 21, 35–6, 63, 89, 101, 103,
117–18, 128–9, 139, 145, 147–8,
153–4, 173, 178, 180 n., 186
deliberative 145, 148–69, 185, 187
demonstrative 64–5, 128–41
judicial 170–200

Orphan, The (Otway) 124 & n.
'*Ossian*' 136 n.
Othello (Shakespeare) 125

P

painting, art of 42, 45, 123, 126
panegyric 63–4, 131–5, 138, 143
Paradise Lost (Milton) 24, 27 n., 30 & n.,
    46 n., 64 n., 67 n., 69 & n., 73 & n.,
    119, 125 & n.
paranomasia 29, 32
Parliament (Westminster) 57, 175, 199 n.
Paris 175
parodies 46–7
passions 56–7, 68–9, 75, 111, 126, 139,
    186–7, 197–8
    see also feelings
passive voice 221–2
pastorals 126–7
Peloponesian War 106, 141, 150
periods, structure of 17–18, 21
Peripatetic philosophy 193
peroration 182
Persia 138 & n., 140, 150 n.
persuasion, powers of 62, 89, 145, 163–4
Pharsalia, Battle of 129–30
Philippics (Demosthenes) 149, 152 & n., 185
philosophers:
    Hobbes's system of 58
    sometimes observe that laughter proceeds
        from contempt 45
philosophical method 145–6
philosophy, natural 57, 90 n., 144–6, 181
plain man 36–41, 49, 141, 183–5
    see also style
Plataea, Battle of 150 & n., 179
pleaders 178, 196–9
poetical 74, 100, 104, 117–18, 135–6
poetry 56, 104, 117–19, 125–6, 135–7
    amusement its purpose 117, 137
    epic 120–1, 125
    and history 117
    the language of pleasure 137
    non-repetitive 117–18
    poet, as story-teller 118–19
    style of Greeks and Romans contrasted 161
    superior to prose 118
    why it predates prose 136–7
poets 19 n., 46, 50, 53–4, 68, 76–7, 97, 104,
    111, 117–27, 136, 139–40, 161
politeness, varying standards of 19
politics, Machiavellian 95, 114–15
power, and riches 149–50, 155–8
prepositions:
    come in place of old declensions 221
    development of prepositions through

mingling of nations 220–1
    imply abstraction 210
    'of' most metaphysical of all prepositions
        212–13
    origin of 9–11, 13, 205–6, 223
    their work initially done by case-endings
        210–11
Pro Aulo Cluentio (Cicero) 171 & n.
pronunciation 14–16
pronouns, use of 8, 12, 15, 38, 214 n., 218–19
propositions 101, 117, 142–4, 178
propriety 4–5, 21, 30, 41, 43, 53, 56, 59, 82,
    124, 126, 159
prose 22 n., 65, 104, 117–18, 135–9, 226
proverbs 34, 159
puns 46–7, 61
Puritans 56–7

R

rank, social 4–5, 17, 36, 45, 124, 133
    and wealth 149, 157
Rape of the Lock (Pope) 44
relation 10, 205–6, 210–13
Revenge, The (Young) 125 & n.
rhetorical discourse 26–7, 62–3, 89, 103,
    146, 148, 177, 181–2, 193–4
rhetorical style, definitions of 89, 101
rhetoricians 27 & n., 29, 40, 101 n., 172–4,
    181, 190 n., 197, 226 n.
ridicule 44–5, 121–5
Rival Queens, The (Lee) 29–30 & n.
romance 91, 96–7, 111, 130–1, 146
    see also epic
Rome:
    commonwealth, state of 154–62
    courts of, more regular than in Athens
        179
    empire and the taking of Troy 119
    empire in the period of Trajan 112
    luxury of 110
    in the period of Cicero 192–6
rules:
    of behaviour 42, 51
    of exposition 21, 24–7, 55, 64, 71, 73, 85,
        89, 117, 128, 132, 181–2, 225
    see also deliberative, demonstrative,
        didactic, historical, and judicial
        discourse; *see* grammar, language

S

Salamis, Battle of 141
savages:
    hypothetical and the development of
        language 9–12, 203–4, 214, 216

dancing and music the amusements of 136–7
see also barbarism
Saxon Heptarchy 99
Saxon language 13, 222–3
schoolmen 205
Seasons, The (Thomson) 30 & n., 31 & n., 72 & n.
sensibility, in Cicero 91–2
sentence length 7, 23, 53
   structure 5, 16–24, 72
sentiments 33, 37, 40 n., 41, 53, 55, 58, 63, 69, 71–2, 75, 97, 103, 113, 127 & n., 167, 190
separation of powers, executive, judicial, military 176
sibilance, increase in 15
similes 30, 47 n., 49, 52–3, 60, 140
sound:
   agreeable, repeated 11
   of language 16, 21–2, 211
   man's love of similarity of 208–9, 215
   in music, melody of 15
   soothing 70
Spanish Friar, The (Dryden) parts should be separated 121 & n.
Spectator, the 46 n., 52 n., 64–5 n., 125 n.
speech, figures of 25–39, 159
story-telling 34, 46, 52, 71, 88, 91, 96, 118–21, 178, 180, 184, 189, 198
style:
   perspicuity of 3–8, 16, 25, 107, 116, 197, 199
   Smith's definition of 55
   varieties of 34–43, 55–61
   see also plain man
substantives 9–11, 77, 208–9, 213, 215
surprise 65, 68–9
sympathy:
   the relation between speaker and auditor 25, 40
   for the situation of others 90
system:
   of language 218
   of morality 51
   of rhetoric 27
   in science 144–5
   of Shaftesbury 58
   see also didactic discourse

T

Tale of a Tub (Swift) 48
'*To Delia*' (Waller) 23
tragedy 44, 88, 97, 111, 119–26
   misfortunes of the great fit subject for 124

transitions, best way of making 59–60
translating, problems in 19
triangle 4
tropes 6 n., 25, 27, 33, 40
Tweedside (ballad) 136 & n.

U

unity of interest in poetry 120–1
unity of place in dramatic poetry 123
   no-one fooled by failure to observe it 123
   to be preferred 123
   Shakespeare's indifference to 123
unity of time in dramatic poetry 121
   no-one fooled by failure to observe it 122
   Shakespeare's indifference to 122

V

Venice Preserved (Otway) 125 & n.
verbs 6, 17, 21, 25
   further development of 219–20
   impersonal verbs the earliest 216
   must have been a late invention 221
   origin of 12–14, 215–25
   the substantive, verb ('to be') most metaphysical of all 13, 221, 223
   third person singular the first development 218
   'to have' a metaphysical verb 221
verse, versification 23, 41 n., 49 n., 65, 117, 118 & n., 137, 139 n., 225–6
vice 41, 78, 94, 130–1
virtue:
   amiable and respectable 130–3
   in oratorical description 130–1
vowels:
   softening of 16
   sweet effect of 22

W

Wallace Wight (ballad) 136 & n.
war, wars 50 n., 104–7, 119, 130 n., 133, 141, 145, 149, 150–3, 164–7, 169 n., 187
wit 44, 46–7, 50, 59–61, 121
women 131
   see also ladies
wonder 65, 104, 111, 131
word order, importance of 5, 19
writing:
   invention of characters 217
   origin of 217

Index of Persons

A

Abelard 18 n., 77 n.
Absyrtus 160 n.
Achilles 139, 140
Achilles Tatius 73 & n., 76 n.
Adam 64, 69, 92, 203 n.
Addison, Joseph 35, 46 n., 51–4 & n.,
    64–5 & n., 66 & n., 74, 125 n.,
    127 n.
Aeetes 160 n.
Aeneas 31, 46, 75, 119 n., 135 & n.
Aeschines 156 & n., 179, 183 & n.,
    185 & n., 186–90 & n.
Aeschylus 28, and see also Aeschines
Aetion 75 & n.
Agamemnon 87
Agesilaus 133–4
Agricola 83, 91 n., 101
Agrippina 100, 113
Ajax 30 & n.
Albucius 195–6
Alcibiades 157–8, 165, 181
Alexander (of Abonuteichos) 52 & n.
Alexander (the Great) 29 & n., 30, 32,
    75 & n., 179, 204, 229
Alonzo 125
Andocides 182 n.
Anne (of Austria) 79 & n.
Antiphon 182 & n.
Antores 72 n.
Anytus 180 n.
Apollo 115 & n.
Apollodorus 66 n., 184, 185 & n.
Appelles 75 & n.
Apuleius 46, 76 & n.
Arbuthnot, John 230
Aristophanes 44, 165 n.
Ariosto, Ludovico 96
Aristotle 7, 22 n., 23 n., 36, 80 n.,
    125 n., 140 n., 144–7, 150 n.,
    193
Arruntius 195 & n.
Artaxerxes 94
Asclepius 52 n.
Aspasia (the Milesian) 141 n.
Athena 187 n.
Atterbury, Francis 199 & n.
Augustus 101 n.
Aujac, G. 184 n.
Ausonius 46 n.

B

Bacchus 110 n.
Baliol 62
Balzac, Jean-Louis Guez de 73 & n.,
    74 & n.
Basilide 80 n.
Beattie, James 229
Beckwith, C. E. 49 n.
Blair, Hugh 136 n.
Blunt, Anthony 126 n.
Boccalini, Traiano 95 & n., 114 & n.,
    115 & n.
Bolingbroke, Henry St John, Lord 7 & n.,
    15, 19 & n., 23, 38, 53, 91 n.
Bossuet, Jacques-Benigne 132 n.
Boswell, James 64 n.
Brancas, Comte de 81 n.
Brett, S. R. 200 n.
Brisson, Barnabe ("Brissonius") 167 n.
Brown, John 137 n.
Brown, Tom 28 n., 41 n.
Bruce (King) Robert 62, 130 n.
Brutus 140, 161 & n.
Bruyere, La, Jean de 80–2, 132
    see also La Bruyere
Buccleuch, Duke of 227
Buchanan, George 230
Buckingham, G. Villers, 2nd Duke of 83 n.
Buckingham, J. Sheffield, Duke of 74 & n.
Burke, Edmund 190 n., 230
Burnett, Gilbert, Bishop of Salisbury
    83 & n., 115–16 & n.
Bute, Earl of 231
Butler, Samuel 27 & n.

C

Caelius 161 n.
Caesar, Julius 93–4, 107, 108, 130 n., 162,
    179 & n., 192 n., 229
Caligula 113
Callisto 66 n.
Calvus, C. Licinius 161 n.
Campbell, G. 228
Casaubon, Isaac 80 n.
Catiline 78, 80, 93, 109
Cato 46 & n., 153 & n., 162
Catullus 28
Cecina 114

Chalcas 87
Charicles 150 n.
Charles I 99
Charles II 83 n.
Charles Edward (Prince) 199 n.
Chevreies, Mlle 79
Child, F. J. 136 n.
Cibber, Colley 28 & n.
Cicero 21–2 & n., 25, 32, 36 & n., 58, 78 n.,
    80, 87 n., 133, 140 & n., 143, 145,
    148 & n., 149, 154, 158–60 & n., 161–3,
    171 n., 172, 173 n., 179, 180–1,
    182 & n., 183, 185 n., 186, 187 n., 188,
    190–2 & n., 193 & n., 194 & n., 195,
    196, 204
Cinna 155
Clarendon, E. Hyde, Earl of 82, 83 & n.,
    115 & n.
Clarke, Samuel 6 & n.
Clearchus 94 n.
Cleisthenes 149 n.
Cleombrotus 152 n.
Cleon 150 & n., 165 and n.
Clodius 156, 172 & n., 179, 182
Cloudeslie, William of 230
Cluentia 171 n.
Cluentius 180, 194 n.
Clym of the Cleuch 230
Coleridge, Samuel 140 n.
Collins, William 225 n.
Condillac, l'Abbé Etienne Bonnet de 203 n.
Congreve, William 47 & n.
Corneille, Pierre 125
Cornelius, L. Octavius 176 n.
Corvus, Marcus Valerius 147 n., 169
Coxe, W. 199 n.
Crassus, Appidius Claudius 147 & n., 162 n.
Crawford, Robert 136 n.
Crebillon, Prosper Jolyot (pere) 112 & n.
Creon 164
Critias 150 n.
Cromwell, Oliver 79, 92 & n.
Ctesiphon 185 n., 186 & n., 189 n.
Curll, Edmund 44 & n.

D

d'Auvergue, Henri de la Tour (Vicomte de
    Turenne) 78–9
    see also Turenne
Daves, C. W. 27 n.
Dearing, V. A. 49 n.
Decimus, Silanus 162 & n.
Defoe, Daniel 230
Demades 183 n.
Demetrius, son of Philip 167 & n., 226 n.
Demetrius of Phalerum 23 & n.

Demetrius of Tarsus 23 n.
Demochares 140 & n.
Democles 140 n.
Democritus 164
Demonicus 140 n.
Demophile 80 n.
Demosthenes 22, 33 & n., 140 n., 145 n., 149,
    150–4 & n., 156 & n., 159–63, 178 & n.,
    182–3 & n., 185–90 & n., 193–5
Desdemona 129
Descartes, René 146 & n.
Dido 26, 36 & n., 75
Dinaca 171 n.
Dinarchus 182 n., 183 n.
Dio Cassius 31 n.
Diodorus, Siculus 203 n.
Diodotus 165
Diogenes 50, 178 n.
Diomedes 30 & n.
Dionysius (of Halicarnassus) 87 & n.,
    99 & n., 105, 108 & n., 109, 154 n.,
    182 n., 184 & n., 188–9 & n., 226 n.
Ditton, H. 49 & n.
Dodsley, R. 65 n., 127 n.
Dryden, John 46 n., 77 n., 121 n., 229, 230
Dubos, l'Abbé 16 & n., 46 n., 76 & n., 226 n.
Dufresney, Charles 44 n.
Dulcinea 132

E

Edward I 62 & n.
Edward II 130 n.
Edward III 222 & n.
Elliot of Minto, Gilbert 7
Eloisa 18
Empedocles 138 & n.
Epaminondas 152 n.
Erskine, E. 28 n.
Eubulus 151 n., 152
Euclid 140 n.
Eupolis 184 n.
Euripedes 97
Europa 54
Euryalus 36, 69 & n.
Eustathius 87 n.
Evander 69 & n., 135 & n.
Eve 64, 69

F

Faber, G. C. 49 n.
Falkland, Lord 83 & n.
Fazio, S. 87 n.
Flaminius 97 n.
Flechier, Valentun-Esprit 132 & n.

Florus, Lucius, A. 101
Florus, P. Aranius 36 n.
Forbes of Tolquoun Castle, William 1
Fraser, J. 66 n.

G

Gardenstoun Lord 230–1 n.
Garrick, David 122
Gay, John 46 n., 49 n.
Geoffrey of Monmouth 105
Germanicus 100 & n., 106 n., 113 & n.,
  168–9
Giles, J. A. 105 n.
Goldsmith, Oliver 230
Gordon, Thomas 92 & n., 114 & n.
Gorgias 138 & n., 139, 140
Graves, Richard 65 & n.
Gray, Thomas 127 & n., 140 n., 230
Gregory of Nyssa 203 n.
Guicciardini, Francesco 114 & n., 115

H

Hadrian 176 n.
Hale, Sir Matthew 83 n.
Halifax, George Saville, Marquis, Lord 83 n.
Hamilton, Duke of 83 n.
Hamilton, William (of Gilbertfield) 136 n.
Hamlet 121
Hammer, J. 105 n.
Hammond, James 127 n.
Hannibal 96 n., 97 n.
Harvey, John 62 n., 67 & n.
Hay, John (2nd Marquis of Tweeddale)
  136 n.
Hegesippus 149, 154 & n.
Helen 139 n., 140
Henry IV of France 119
Herbert, Henry 81 & n.
Hercules 135, 139
Hermagoras 193 & n., 195 n.
Hermogenes 33 n., 180 n.
Herodotus 87 & n., 88, 94 & n., 98–9 n.,
  105, 106, 108, 109, 139, 161
Hesiod 50 n., 161 & n.
Hill-Powell 64 n.
Hobbes, Thomas 45 n., 57–8, 60 & n.
Homer 6, 28, 30 & n., 50 n., 54 n., 67,
  75–6 & n., 97, 104, 119, 121, 125 n.,
  126, 161 & n., 229
Horace 28, 81 n., 127, 196 n., 199 n.,
  225–6 n.
Hortensius 161 & n., 193 & n.
Howard, Thomas (Earl of Arundel)
  83 & n.

Hume, David 140 n., 229, 230
Hyperides 154 n., 182 n., 183 n.

I

Iago 125
Iphigenia 87, 122
Isaeus 182 & n., 183, 184 & n., 185
Isocrates 21, 139–40 & n., 182 n.

J

Jago, Richard 127 n.
Jensen, H. 212 n.
Johnson, Samuel
  no love of Smith 5 n., 47 n., 64 n., 127 n.,
    228–9, 230
Jouin, Henry 122 n.
Jugurtha 92, 110 & n.
Julianus, Salvius 176 n.
Juno 66 n.
Jupiter 54, 66 n., 67
Justinian 176 n.
Juvenal 6 & n., 76 n.

K

Killigrew, Mrs Anne 229

L

La Bruyere, Jean de 80–2 & n., 132
Lafitau, Joseph-François 203 n.
La Motte Aigron, Jacques de 74 n.
Latona 75
Lauderdale, Earl of 83 n.
Le Brun, Charles 122 & n., 123 n.
Lee, Nathaniel 29 & n.
Leheny, J. 52 n.
Leibnitz, Wilhelm Gothfried 43 & n., 212 n.
Lintot, B. 44 & n.
Lipsius, Justus 167 n.
Littleton, Lord 115
Livy 21, 76 n., 86, 95–7, 100–1 n., 103,
  108–9 & n., 147, 161, 166–9, 229
Locke, John 43 & n., 57 n., 58
Longinus 33 & n., 185 n., 190, 226 n.
Louis XIII of France 79 n.
Lucan 130 n.
Lucian 47 n., 48–9 & n., 50–2 & n., 54, 60,
  75 & n., 76 n.
Lucius 46 n.
Lucretius 28, 161
Lucullus 157–8

Lycon 180 n.
Lycurgus 182 n., 183 & n., 185 & n.
Lysander 179 & n.
Lysias 141, 182–4 & n., 185 & n.

M

Machiavelli, Nicolo 36, 91 n., 114–15,
    185 & n.
Macpherson, James 136 n.
Macray, W. D. 83 n.
Malpeines, M. A. L. 203 n.
Mandeville, Bernard 36 n.
Manilius 133 n.
Mansfield, Earl of 200 & n.
Marcellinus, Ammianus 19 & n.
Mardonius 150 n.
Marius 110 n., 155–7
Marivaux, Pierre 44 n., 112 & n.
Martial 217 n.
Masinissa 130 & n.
Mason, John 22 n.
Maximus, Valerius 87 n., 101 & n.
Medea 160 & n.
Medicis, Marie de 122 & n.
Meikle, J. 230
Meillet, A. 212 n.
Meleager 139
Meletus 180 n.
Meliboeus 70
Menalque 81 & n.
Menelaus 87
Menon 94 n.
Mezentius 69 & n.
Micipsa 92
Milo 172 & n., 179, 182, 194
Milton, John 24 n., 27 & n., 28, 30, 42,
    46, 47 n., 64 & n., 67 & n., 69 n.,
    70–3, 119, 125 n., 225–6 & n., 229–30
Mithridates 133 n., 160
Modius, François 167 n.
Moliére, Jean-Baptiste Poquelin 81
Montagu, Lady Mary Wortley 74 n.
Montaigne, Michel Eyquem de
    198 & n.
Montesquieu, Charles de Secondat,
    Baron of 198 n.
Montgomerie, Alexander 136 n.
Monmouth, Geoffrey of 105 & n.
Montrose, James Graham, Marquis of 79,
    115
Moses 8, 32

N

Nero 113

Newton, Sir Isaac 145–6, 204
Nicocles 140 n.
Nisius 36
Nivers, Mme de 79 n., 80 n.
Nugent, Thomas 16 n., 76 n.

O

Oepidus 225
Oldmixon, John 47 n.
Oppianicus 171 n., 180 & n.
Orrery, Earl of 42 n.
Othello 125, 129
Otway, Thomas 125 n.
Ovid 65 & n., 66

P

Palmedes 139 n.
Pallas 36 & n.
Pancha, Sancho 34, 124
Paris 140
Paterculus, Velleilus 36 & n.
Pausanians 150 n.
Pedius 196 n.
Pembroke, William Herbert (3rd Earl of)
    83 & n.
Percy, Thomas 230
Pericles 94, 141, 150, 157, 164–5
Persius 167 & n.
Phaeton 66 n.
Pheidias 187 n.
Philip of Macedon 33 n., 149, 151–3 & n.,
    154 n., 160 n., 167 & n., 178–9, 187 n.,
    190
Philips, John 46 n.
Philo 156 n.
Phocion 71
Pindar 67, 140 & n.
Plato 8, 59–60, 141, 146–7, 158, 180 n.,
    190
Plautus 217 n.
Pliny 73–4, 87 n., 101, 199 n.
Plutarch 181 n.
Polybius 93, 95, 108, 130 n., 229
Pompey 129, 130, 133 & n., 158
Pope, Alexander 5 & n., 18 n., 28, 31 n.,
    33 & n., 44 & n., 49 n., 58, 74 & n.,
    77 & n., 78 n., 83 n., 91 n., 117–18 n.,
    229–30
Poussin, Nicolas 71, 122 n., 126–7 & n.
Propertius 161 & n.
Proxenus 94 n.
Prynne, William 7 & n., 200
Pulteney, Sir William 199 n.
Pym, John 200 & n.

Pyramus 71
Pythagoras 138 & n.

Q

Quinctius Titus 147 & n., 169
Quintilian 21 n., 22 n., 25 & n., 26 n., 87 n.,
    109, 143 n., 148 & n., 161 & n., 172 n.,
    173 & n., 180 n., 182 n., 190 n., 192 n.,
    194–6 & n., 226 n.
Quixote, Don 132

R

Racine, Jean 122–3, 125–6
Ramsay, Allan 136 n., 230
Raphael 126
Rapin, Paul de 99 & n., 100, 116
Regnard, Jean-François 44 n.
Retz, Paul de Gondi, Cardinal 78 n.,
    79 & n., 80–1, 103 & n., 132
Richard III 122
Robert the Bruce 130 & n.
Roberts, W. R. 23 n., 87 n.
Rochester, Earl of 83 n.
Rosa, Salvator 70
Roscius 172, 193
Rousseau, Jean-Jacques 9 & n., 174 n.,
    198 & n., 203 n., 205 & n., 213
Rowe, Nicolas 127 n., 130 n.
Roxana 75 & n.
Rufus, M. Caelius 161 n.

S

Sacheverell, Henry 199 n.
Sallust 7, 78, 80, 91 & n., 92–3, 109, 110,
    153
Sanchez, Francisco 217 n.
Sannazzaro, Jacob 46 & n.
Sarpi, Paolo 91 n.
Saxe, Maurice Marechale de 78–9 & n.
Scarron, Paul 41, 46 & n.
Seneca 195 n.
Shaftesbury, Anthony Ashley Cooper,
    3rd Earl of 6 n., 7 & n., 8 & n., 21,
    22–3, 38, 42, 53, 56–8, 59 & n.,
    60–1 & n., 142
Shakespeare, William 28, 30–1, 46 & n., 64,
    67, 77, 121–3, 125–6, 129, 229
Shenstone, William 28 n., 65 n., 127 & n.
Sherburn, G. 74 n., 91 n.
Shrewsbury, Duke of 74 n.
Sidney, Sir Philip 28
Simon, Richard, 203 n.

Simpson, G. E. 62 n.
Socrates 44, 59–60, 141 n., 180–1 & n.
Somers, Lord 57 n.
Sophocles 121, 123, 125
Spaeth, S. 67 n.
Spenser, Edmund 28, 30, 65, 67 & n.
Staienus 180 & n.
Steele, Sir Richard 67 n.
Stepney, G. 76 n.
Stones, E. L. G. 62 n.
Suetonius 195 n.
Swift, Jonathan 4, 7, 15, 23, 38–9,
    41–4, 48–9 n., 50, 52–3, 58, 143 & n.,
    228–9
Sylla (Sulla) 155

T

Tacitus 7, 19 n., 36 & n., 78–9, 83 & n.,
    91 & n., 92 & n., 94 & n., 95, 100–1,
    103, 106 & n., 111–12, 113, 114 & n.,
    161, 168–9
Tarquins 179
Temple, Sir William 38–9, 41, 84 & n.
Thales 138 & n.
Theocles 59
Theognis 161 & n.
Theophrastus 80 & n., 81–2, 132
Theramenes 150 & n.
Theseus 139, 140
Thisbe 71
Thompson, A. 105 n.
Thomson, D. A. 136 n.
Thomson, James 28, 30–1, 42, 56,
    71–2, 77
Thrasyllus 184 n.
Thrasymachus 140 & n.
Theseus 139–40
Thucydides 6, 7, 86–8, 91 n., 93–5, 96,
    99–100, 105–10, 113 & n., 139 n.,
    141 & n., 161, 163–9
Tiberius 95, 195–6
Tibullus 28, 217 n.
Tigranes 133 n.
Timanthes 87 n.
Timarchus 87 n., 185 n., 189 n.
Tiro 192 & n.
Tirwhyt, W. 74 n.
Tissaphernes 133 n., 134
Tithonus 66 & n.
Titian 70
Titus 106 & n.
Tityrus 225 & n.
Tooke, Horne 205 n.
Trajan 76, 112
Turenne, Viscomte de 78–9 & n., 83 n.
Turnus 31

U

Ulysses 87, 129

V

Varus 113 & n.
Vernon, Edward 28 & n.
Verres 106 & n., 155, 194 n.
Vespasian 94
Vida, Marco 46
Villate, Cartaud de la 137 n.
Virgil 26 & n., 28, 30–2, 36, 46, 61, 70, 72,
    74–6, 81 n., 97, 119, 125–6, 127, 135,
    145, 161 & n., 225 & n., 230
Vitruvius 203 n.
Vittelius 94 & n.
Voltaire 119 n., 229, 231 n.

W

Waldegrave 200 n.
Wallace, William 136 & n.
Waller, Edmund 6, 22–3
Walpole, Horace 200 n.
Walpole, Robert 199 & n.
Warburton, William 5, 35, 203

Wardlaw, Elizabeth, Lady 136 n.
Warton, Joseph 225 n.
Warton, Thomas 225 n.
Warwick, Countess of 127 n.
Webb, Daniel 75 n., 87 n.
Whiston, W. 49 & n.
William (of Orange) 57 n., 78 n.
Williams, M. 127 n.
Wilmot, Sir Robert 199 n.
Winchelsea, Countess of 46 n.
Wronglove, Lord 28 n.

X

Xenophon 6, 8, 39, 94–5, 107–8, 133–4,
    146–7, 159–60, 169, 180 n.

Y

Yates, Frances, A. 143 n.
Young, Edward 125 n., 140 n.

Z

Zanga 125 & n.
Zeller, H. 212 n.

Essays on Philosophical Subjects

Index of Subjects

A

Aberdeen, University of 76 n., 90 n.
Accademia del Cimento (Florence) 139 n.
Accademia della Crusca 232
Academie Française 232
accents in English and Italian verse 223–5
acoustics 213 n.
acting, *see* music; pantomime
actors 194, 202, 210
admiration, quality of 33–4, 56, 114, 116
aesthetics, *see* system
aether, *see* ether
Africa:
    dance of 209
    negroes of 187, 189
    see also nations
air 57, 78, 102, 106–11, 118–19, 127, 138,
    146–7, 199
Alchemy 47 n.
Alphonsus, tables of, *see* tables,
    astronomical
America 174–5
    savage tribes of 187, 189
American Revolution (1775–83) 242 n.
analogy, uses of
    the 'great hinge upon which everything
        turned' 47 & n.
    of the machine 66 & n.
    of nature 84
    used by Kepler 89–91, 95
    see also machines, systems
Arabs, scientific scholarship of 46, 60 n.,
    67–9
Aristotelianism, *see* peripatetic(s)
art, Dutch 178–9
art, pleasing when it carries its own
    explication 185
arts, economic, social factors affecting the
    184, 187
    imitative 171–213, 305–6
    see also dance; music; painting
Asia 51
Asia Minor 51
astronomy 5, 53–105, 245
    Aristotelian system of 55–7, 59, 67, 69,
        74, 79, 102
    Cartesian system of 42–3, 87–8, 92–8,
        102–4
    Copernican system of 71–81, 83–5, 91–7

Eudoxus' system of 57–9
Newtonian system of 97–101, 103–5
Ptolemaic system of 59–67, 69–70, 81–2,
    84, 90
    see also air; ether; spheres
atomism 139

B

Babylon, Babylonians 51 n., 69
barbarous 51, 187
    see also savages
beauty 278, 287, 289, 292, 305, 306 n., 334,
    349–50
    of astronomical systems 74–5
    attracts admiration 33–4
    concept of, in the intellectual world 124
    and the doctrine of the Four Elements
        111–12
    and the imitative arts 176–8, 182–4,
        193–5
    of nature 56–7
    parallel with virtue 47
    see also imitative arts; systems
Bee, The, or Literary Weekly Intelligencer
    225 n.
biology, French advances in 248–9
blindness 135–6, 149–50, 153–4, 158–61

C

Cadiz (Spain) 344
calendar, Gregorian reform of Julian 76 n.
Caliphates, Islamic 67–9
camera obscura 148
Cartesianism 39 n., 42–3, 87–8, 92–8,
    102–4, 123 n., 244
    see also physics
cataract, operation for 153–4, 158–61
categories, Aristotelian 52
causation, theories of 44–7
cesura or pause in English and Italian verse
    224–5
Chaldea, Chaldeans, *see* Babylon
chemistry:
    philosophy of, crept along in obscurity 46
    requires labour and assiduity, rather than
        genius 243

children 38, 161, 163–5, 201, 313, 334–5
China, Chinese 213, 254
Church of England 272
circle:
    equalizing 61–2, 71, 86, 88
    as perfect figure 85–6
classification, principles, practice of 37–40,
        120, 126–9, 144–5, 166, 232, 248–9,
        276
cold 108–12, 140–51, 167–8
colour 149–52, 156, 158–60, 166, 178,
        181–2, 185, 193, 205–6, 251, 335
comets 33, 48, 54 n., 81
    Halley's comet 29, 103 & n.
commerce, free, desirability of 316–18, 322,
        339, 341–6
concert (musical) 145, 197, 199, 203
concerto:
    Corelli's 195
    enjoyment of, likened to that derived from
        a great system in any other science
        205
    see also philosophy, science
Corinthian order 178, 181
Critical Review 297
Croton (Italy) 52 n.
Culloden, battle of (1746) 259
curve line 86, 91

D

dance/dancing:
    addressed to the eye 189
    affects more than painting or statuary
        208
    can represent causes and consequences,
        not just a moment 208
    cannot subsist without music 190
    country dancing 209
    difference between it and ordinary
        movement 210–11
    measure essential to 207
    natural to man 187
    need not be imitative 207
    representational dancing 188–9
    Roman and Greek dances imitative,
        modern not always 208
    superior to music in representation 189,
        207
    two Greek words for 209
    see also minuet, tragedy
deities 49, 114, 117, 123 n.
Deity 113, 116–17, 120–1, 122 n., 123 n.
density 103–4, 147
dialectic 24–5, 52, 62, 65 n., 120
divisibility, attribute of 137, 144–5,
        149–50

dryness 108–12
duty 35, 280 & n., 287–9

E

Earth 54, 56–7, 60–1, 63–4, 67–8, 72–85,
        90–1, 95–6, 98–114, 117–18, 137,
        146, 246 n.
East India Company of France 340
eclectics 122 n.
eclipses 33, 43, 48, 54, 56, 64, 100
ecliptic, obliquity of 55–6, 61, 68, 72–3,
        100, 102
Edinburgh Review 96 n., 227–30, 232,
        242–54, 276, 339
effluvia 42, 146–7
Egypt, Egyptians 51
Eleatic philosophy 56
elements 12, 92–4, 118–19
    Four, doctrine of 52, 107–12, 116
ellipses, astronomical role of 86–9, 91, 95,
        100–1
emotion, emotions 34–6, 39–42, 116, 123,
        186, 189, 191, 205
Encyclopédie (Diderot and d'Alembert)
        96 n., 245–8, 250, 320, 338–9
engine (condensing) 139
    see also machines
England:
    condition of the inferior ranks of the
        people, better than in France 184
    contributions of, to philosophy 242–6,
        249–51
English and Italian verses, composition of
        217–19
epicureanism 65 n., 112 n.
epicycles 59–61, 69–70, 72–4, 81–2, 86–7
epistemology, influence of Humean, on
        Smith 320–1
equalizing circle 61, 71, 86, 88
equant 69 n., 72 n.
equinoxes 64 n., 102
essences, specific 118–29
ether 57, 62, 81, 94–6, 112, 116–17
European Magazine and London Review
        230
exhibitioner, term explained 270 n.
extension, attribute of 136–7

F

Faerie Queene, The (Spenser) 217
fellow-feeling 136, 281
fire 49, 72, 78, 94, 107–9, 112, 141, 146
flowers 113, 118, 128, 142, 181–2
fluid, fluids 62, 81, 95, 109, 138, 147, 240

fluidity 138–40, 238
Fontainebleau (France) 200 n.
France:
  condition of the inferior ranks seldom so
      happy as in England 184
  economists of 301, 304 n., 320 n., 340,
      343–4
  fashion in 184, 201
  opera in 202
  philosophy and science in 243–50
  poets in 254
  receipt of Cartesian philosophy in 104

G

genera and species 38
Geneva 254, 302
Germany 84, 243–4
Glasgow, University of 46 n., 90 n., 172–3,
    229, 265, 270, 273, 295, 297, 298, 300–1,
    302 n., 320–2, 327–9, 333, 348, 350
Glasgow Courant 259
grammar 241, 247, 272 n.
  principles of 337–8
gravity 5, 45, 54 n., 78, 98–104, 108–9, 111,
    146
Greece:
  colonies among the first to arrive at a state
      of civilisation 51–2
  dance in 208–9
  philosophy in 56, 67–8, 122 n.
  songs of ancient 190
grief 35–7, 191–2, 236, 282–3, 286
Guardian N° 167, 234

H

Halley's comet, *see* comets
Hamburg 344
hearing, sense of 135, 143–5, 147, 150, 168, 199
  see also sound
heat:
  quality of 107–12
  sensation of 140–6, 167–8
heavens 43, 54, 56–64, 69, 72–6, 78, 80–3,
    83 n., 87, 89, 96–7, 99, 102, 105–6,
    110, 112–13, 115 n., 116, 294
hermeticism 78 n.
heroic rhyme 220–2
heroic verse 219
history, theoretical 46, 293 n., 294–6, 337, 350
Holland, *see* Netherlands
House of Commons 341 n., 343 n.
Hudibras (Butler) 221, 239
human nature 121, 271, 290, 295, 301
  always constant 121

humour 230, 238–41
hypothesis 42–3, 54, 56, 58, 62, 67 n., 69–77,
    81–3, 88–91, 96, 102–4, 125, 138

I

ideas:
  association of 34 n., 41, 134, 161, 163
  chain of 41–5, 50, 58, 66, 91–2, 105, 113,
      244 n., 292
  customary association of 37, 41, 44–5,
      141
  desire for coherence 43, 62–3, 69, 76–7,
      96–7, 103, 107
  fear of gap or interval 41–5, 58, 91
  platonic 121–5
  see also imagination, sense
ignorance, pleasing wonder of 185
imagination:
  attracted by simplicity in explanation of
      phenomena 74–5
  desire to preserve coherence of the ideas
      of 77, 79
  disturbed by complexity 64, 67, 70
  disturbed by the sentiment of surprise
      34, 39, 42
  indolent 126
  intellectual systems, inventions of 105
  natural prejudices of 86, 89, 91–2, 96
  natural propensities of 58
  relieved by the 'discovery' of explanation
      42–4, 46–8, 50, 56
  repose and tranquility of, the ultimate end
      of philosophy 61–2
  see also admiration, ideas, surprise,
      system, wonder
imitation, see *Imitative arts* 171–213;
      music, painting, statuary, topiary
Inchkeith, island of 307
induction 335
inductivism 41 n.
inequality, origins of human 250–3, 339
inertia, law of 91–6
inertness, of matter 92, 98, 104
insects 38, 162, 249
instincts, of animals and human beings 151,
      161–5, 250
investigation, philosophical, scientific
      aspects of 244–9, 292–6
invisible hand of Jupiter 49
Ionic order 178
iron and loadstone 40, 42
Islam 67–9
Italy:
  Greek colonies in 51–2 & n.
  natural philosophy in 244
  poets in 254

Italy (*cont.*):
    reform of opera in 202
    school of 55–6, 107
Italian verses 215, 220–1, 223–5, 350

J

jurisprudence 247, 274, 294–5, 300, 310–11,
    327, 349
Jupiter 49, 50 n., 117, 179
Jupiter, planet 55, 72, 81, 83, 90, 99,
    101–4
justice 274–5, 284–90, 309, 311–12,
    312 n., 315, 317, 320, 322, 327,
    334, 341

K

Kirkcaldy 171–2, 269–70, 272, 307
knowledge, theory of, *see* epistemology
Königsberg 71 n.

L

language 140–3, 148, 156–61, 209–10, 213,
    220–4, 241–3, 261, 337
    ambiguity of 140–6
    *Considerations Concerning the First
        Formation of Languages* 38 n.,
        66 n., 156 n., 292, 295 n.
    Smith's theory of 276–7, 292–6
landscape 152, 198
Lapland 101 & n.
law/laws:
    natural 349
    and society 48, 50–2
    system of 310, 318
    see also jurisprudence
levity 108–9, 111
lexicography, principles of 232–41
light 138, 146, 158, 160–2
lightning 48, 50, 54 n., 106, 111, 202
logic 65 n., 120, 273–4, 320, 335, 337
looking-glasses, not objects of wonder
    44 n., 185–6
    see also mirrors
Lounger, The 260

M

machines:
    intellectual systems, analogies with 66–7,
        73, 113, 289
    see also system(s)

magnetism 42
Mars, planet 55, 72, 81–2, 85
Marischal College, Aberdeen 90 n.
mathematicians 65, 68–9, 76 n., 340
mathematics 51 n., 55 n., 56 n., 64–5, 68,
    85, 213 n., 243, 245–6 n., 293,
    320
mechanics 245
medicine 46 n., 51 n., 63 n., 243
melody 188, 190–1, 193, 200, 202–3,
    205–6
Mercury 55, 72, 74, 80–1, 83, 104
metaphysics 80, 118–29, 140, 146, 247, 249,
    274, 297, 338–9, 343
meteors 33, 48, 54 n., 102, 106, 111
metre, *see* prosody
Miletus 52 n., 56
minuet 207
mirrors 44 n., 163, 185–6
mobility, quality of 137
moisture 108–9, 111–12
Moon 43, 54–5, 57–9, 61–4, 66, 72, 81–4,
    89–90, 94–5, 98–102, 106, 108, 110,
    115, 117
    see also nodes, planets
motion, laws of 40–2, 77–80, 82–3, 89–90,
    92 n.
    see also planets; spheres
music 45, 47, 85, 252
    addressed to the ear like poetry 189
    appeals to ear by repetition 192–3
    can subsist alone 190
    may appear perfect imitation 191
    natural to man 187
    instrumental music inferior to vocal 195
    affectation detectable by improper
        modulation 212–13
    can only support other truly imitative
        arts 199–201
    cannot be supported by imitative arts
        205
    depends on memory and foresight
        204
    difference between it and ordinary
        speech 212
    excites but does not imitate passion
        198
    guides and supports vocal music 203
    imitative instrumental music needs
        explanation 195–6
    inspires original, not sympathetic,
        feelings 198
    inspires contrasting moods 197–8,
        204–5
    is its own subject 205
    precision and proportion in 211–12
    produces considerable effects without
        imitation 203–4, 205–6

time without tune is still music 211
treble more cheerful than bass 197
vocal music imitates unifying passions
    best 192–3
adds new beauty to its objects 193–4
does not imitate unsocial passions well
    192–3
musician:
    art of 199, 210, 206
    nicer ear of 45
musk, odour of 147
Muslim, *see* Islam

N

nations, barbarous, music and dancing in
    187, 189, 212
natural philosophy, *see* physics
nature:
    and art 193–4, 198–9
    connecting principles of 45–6, 48, 52,
        56–7, 67, 84, 90, 105–6, 107,
        119 n.
    early concepts of 113–15
    irregularity of 48–50
    philosophic attitudes towards 65
    see also polytheism
needle-work 182, 184
negroes 187, 209
Neoplatonism 67 n., 78 n., 144 n.
    see also Platonists
Netherlands 344–5
    see also art, Dutch
New Groat's Worth of Wit, A (1756) 230
Newcastle-upon-Tyne 206 n.
Newtonian science 103–4, 244
    see also Newton
nodes, lunar 100, 102
    see also Moon
novelty, influence of, on perception 37–40,
    56–7, 68, 75

O

observation, role of, in scientific research
    134, 156–68
    see also causation
octave, *see* music
ontology 116–21, 126–9
opera machinery of 42
    cannot be appreciated in closet 202
    comic opera needs better acting 194–5
    needs graceful actions 194, 210
    nothing more affecting than 194
    realistic scenery and effects abused in
        202–1

optics 148, 185, 245–6
oscillation, planetary 58 n., 101

P

painter 155–6, 180, 182, 200–1, 206–7
painting:
    cannot equal the perspective of nature
        160, 193
    expression of 205
    imitation frequently pleases 179–80
    more ingenious than statuary 186
    parallels drawn with painting 47
    perspective in 184–5, 186
    a plain surface in, made to resemble all
        three dimensions of a solid surface
        179, 182
    see also music, needlework, statuary,
        topiary
pantomime 189, 208–9
parallax, stellar 85 n.
passions:
    music and 190–3
    operation of 48–9, 250–1, 281–4, 288–9
    theory of 34–7
perception, unreliability of 152–5
peripatetic(s) 69, 78, 108, 120, 128, 193,
    244
perspective, rules of 151–61
Peru 101
Philological Miscellany 277 n.
philosophy:
    principles directing enquiry in 34–53
    purpose of to expose connecting links of
        nature 45, 51, 119 & n.
    see also pleasure, ideas
physics 42 n., 46 n., 48 n., 52 n., 63 n.,
    96 n., 97, 119, 249, 290, 339
    early theories of 5–6, 23, 24–7, 77,
        106–7
    modern theories of 244–5, 270–1
Physiocrats 301, 304 n., 320 n.
pity, operation of 251, 286
plagiarism 321–2, 335–6
planets:
    motion of 15–19, 55, 57–64, 66, 71–8,
        80–91, 94–101, 103–4, 106, 110,
        112, 117
    see epicycles; moon; motion; spheres
Platonists (later) 114, 122 n., 123, 128
pleasure:
    custom deadens the vivacity of 37
    in observing resemblances 37
    philosophy an original pleasure and good
        in itself 75
    see also ideas, imitative arts, philosophy,
        science

poetry:
  can subsist alone 190
  like music, addressed to the ear 189
  origins of 188
  parallels with music 47
  produces its effect by a connected variety
        192
  superior to dancing in representation 188
  of William Hamilton 259–62
polytheism 49–50
Prague 83 n.
prepositions 224, 236, 238
pressure, effects of, on substances 94,
        138–40
property:
  historical introduction of 252
  see also Rousseau
prosody 217–25
prutenic tables, *see* tables, astronomical
Ptolemaic system, *see* spheres, eccentric
        theory of 243
Pythagorians 47, 52–3, 57, 72 & n., 113,
        127–8

R

rank, desire of 284
ranks, distinction of 51 & n., 184, 187
Renaissance, the 59 n., 75 n.
resemblances:
  exact not agreeable 177–8
  imperfect more satisfying 182, 183, 185,
        191, 196
  see also imitation
rhetoric 65 n.
rhyme:
  in English, double rhymes ludicrous 221
  in Italian, verso cadente 219, 221
  single, double and triple 220–1
  single rhymes more burlesque than triple
        rhymes 221
  Smith's misreading of 221 n.
  triple rhymes more frequent in best
        writers 221
  verso sdrucciolo 218, 221
  verso tronco 219, 221
rhythmus (or rythmus) common to Music
        and Dance 187, 211
Roman Empire, ruin of, produced neglect of
        science 67

S

St Paul's Cathedral, London 176
St Peter's Basilica, Rome 176
Saracens 69

satellites, planetary 90
Saturn 15, 55, 72, 81, 90, 99, 103–4
savages:
  have little curiosity to find out hidden
        chains of events 48–9
  manners of, according to Rousseau
        251–3, 255–6
  music and dancing among 187–9
  and the origins of polytheism 49
scenery, theatrical 201–2
schoolmen 69, 102, 118, 120
science:
  Newtonian theory of 103, 244
  satisfaction of 185
  systematization of 12–13, 244–9
  see also astronomy, chemistry, physics,
        pleasure
Scots Magazine 230–1
sculpture, statuary 179–86, 193, 201, 207–8
seasons, operation of 55–6, 73, 108–12
Sennaar (Shinar), plain of 69
sense:
  prejudices of sense and education as they
        affect the reception of ideas 76–7,
        88, 91
senses, external 36, 133–68
  see also cold, hearing, heat, sight, smell,
        sound, taste, touch
sentiment/sentiments:
  influence on perception 183, 186
  of moral approbation 282, 284, 286
  natural 288, 291
shape, perception of 137
Sicily 51, 52 n.
sight, sense of 133, 135, 148–64, 168
singing:
  imitates discourse 190
  singer must be actor 194
  unnaturalness of 190–1
size, perception of 154–6
smell, sense of 135, 142–7, 164–8
solar systems 94, 103
  see also spheres, heliocentric theory of;
        sun
solidity 136–8, 144, 149–50
solstices 63
souls, transmigration of 116–17
sound, sense of 143–8, 168
  see also acoustics; hearing, sense of
Spain 69 n., 243, 344
Sparta 313
spheres:
  concentric theory of 54–9, 62–4, 69, 112
  eccentric theory of 59–70, 81–2, 84, 90
  fluid theory of 62–3
  heliocentric theory of 71–81, 84–5,
        91–7
  music of 57

solid theory of 60, 69, 81, 102
see also astronomy, Earth, Moon, music,
   planets, stars, sun
spirall, Archimedean 86 n.
spirits, doctrine of 39 n.
stars 54–6, 59, 62–4, 77, 94, 106, 115, 117,
   151
statuary:
   colouring inappropriate to 180–2
   compared to painting 186
   drapery inappropriate to 180
stoic 23, 47 n., 62 n., 63, 116 n., 128, 253
stoics 65 n., 85, 108, 116–17, 121–3 n.,
   127–8
sun:
   motion of 43, 54–64, 66, 72–5, 77–8,
      80–5, 88–91, 94–100, 102–4, 106,
      110, 112, 117, 146
   see also spheres, heliocentric theory of;
      solar systems; solstices
sunspots 94
superstition 49–50, 50 n., 112, 114
surprise, quality of 33–6, 40–1, 75
syllable counting:
   in English verse 222–3
   in Italian verse 223
   intervals between 225
sympathy 44, 198, 200, 205
system/systems:
   beauty of 75, 82
   as imaginary machine 66–7, 105–7
   mechanical theory of 65–7
   as rhythmical series 187, 205
   see also imagination, machines, theism

T

tables, astronomical 68–70, 76
tapestry, and needlework, inferior to
      painting 182
   great expense of 182
Tartary, Tartar 254
taste:
   as aesthetic discernment 230, 243–4
   economic, social factors 174, 182–4
   as physical sensation 135, 142–6, 164,
      166–7
telescopes, astronomical use of 83–4, 94
theism 114–17
thunder:
   attracts the attention of the philosopher
      54 n., 106 ff.
   see also elements
   and terror of the savage 48, 50
toleration, religious 67, 229–30

topiary, art of 174, 183–4
touch, sense of 135–42, 148–50
trade, *see* commerce
tragedy 202, 209
translation, practice of 271
transmigration of souls, *see* souls
Thrasimenus, battle of Lake (217 BC) 36
Treatise of Human Nature (Hume) 34 n.,
   39 n., 41 n., 42 n.
triangles, concept of 125
trivium (grammar, rhetoric, logic) 12–13

U

unity of place, in drama 202
universe 46, 51, 54, 56–7, 65–6, 66 n., 70,
   72, 74–5, 81–2, 85, 93–4, 102, 104,
   107–9, 113–16, 126 n., 137 & n.,
   253
universals 24, 119–20, 122 n., 123–5, 129
usury 336–7 n., 348

V

Venus 55, 59 n., 72, 74, 80–4, 96 n., 102
   see also planets
Versailles 184
verse 188–9, 219, 225
   see also Italian verses
vision 149, 153–4, 160–2, 164
   see also sight, sense of
vocalisation without meaning, the earliest
      form of music 187–8
Vortices, theory of 93–7

W

wave theory 138–9 n.
Westminster Abbey, London 180
wind, result of motion of spheres 78–80
wit 230, 241
wonder:
   as origin of philosophy 10
   see also admiration, surprise
   sentiment of 33–45, 51, 51 n., 54, 56, 75,
      86, 181, 185–6
worms, nature, characteristics of 166–7

Y

yew, ornaments in 183–4
   see also sculpture

Index of Persons

A

Addison, Joseph, English essayist 202, 234–5, 239
Aesop, Greek fabulist 179
Alembert, Jean Le Rond d' 92 n., 245, 293, 302, 339
Alexander, H. G. 137 n.
Alfonso X, King of Castile 70, 76
Allan, D. J. 55 n.
Almamon, see Ma'mūn
Amicus 225 n.
Anacreon, Greek lyric poet 52, 260
Anaxagoras, Ionic philosopher 52, 109 n., 113 & n.
Anaximander, Ionic philosopher 52
Anaximenes, Ionic philosopher 52
Antoninus Pius, Titus Aurelius Fluvius, Roman emperor 62, 67
Anville (or Enville), Marie-Louise-Nicole, Duchesse d' 303
Apollonius of Perga, Greek mathematician 59
Apuleius, Lucius, Latin satirist 57
Archelaus, early Greek philosopher 52
Archilochus, Greek elegiac poet 52
Archimedes, Greek mathematician 71 n., 86 n., 109
Archytas of Tarentum, Greek mathematician and philosopher 52
Argenson, René Louis de Voyer, Marquis d' 345 n.
Argyll, Archibald Campbell, 3rd Duke of 296, 298
Ariosto, Ludovico 220 n., 221
Aristarchus of Samos, mathematician and astronomer 17, 71–2 n.
Aristides Quintilianus, Neoplatonist philosopher 199 n.
Aristillus, early Greek astronomer 64 n.
Aristotle 43, 47, 51 n., 52–6, 57–8 n., 59, 67–9, 69 n., 71, 74, 78 n., 79, 81, 102–3, 109 n., 112 n., 113, 115–16, 120, 121–2 n., 125–8, 138, 234, 244 n., 334–5, 336–7 n.
Aristoxenus, Greek musical theorist 47
Arnauld, Antoine 213 n.
Arnold, Sir Thomas Walker 68 n.
Asgill, John, English pamphleteer 343 n.
Atticus, Titus Pomponius 65
Averroes (ibn Ruoshd), Arab philosopher 69
Avison, Charles, composer 206 & n.

B

Bach, Johann Christian, composer 200 n.
Bacon, Francis, Baron Verulam, Viscount St Albans 47 n., 233, 235, 239–40, 245–6, 271, 275 n., 311–12, 323
Baird, George 337
Balme, D. M. 115 n.
Baretti, Giuseppe Marc Antonio (Joseph) 218
Baring, Sir Francis 348
Barnard, Thomas, Bishop of Limerick 325
Beattie, James, Scottish poet 218
Beauclerk (or Beauclerc), Topham, English dandy 325
Beccaria, Cesare, Marchese de 311
Bengesco, Georges 254 n.
Bentham, Jeremy, utilitarian philosopher 348
Bentley, Richard, Cambridge classicist 236
Berkeley, George, Bishop of Cloyne 134, 137 n., 148, 150, 154 n., 156–7, 348
Besterman, Theodore 254 n.
Black, Joseph 32, 172–3, 265, 332, 350
Blair, Hugh 218
Blavet, Jean-Louis, l'Abbé 303 n., 338
Boisguilbert, Pierre Le Pesant, sieur de 345 n.
Bonar, J. 199 n., 219 n.
Boscovich, Roger Joseph, Jesuit mathematician and astronomer 139 n.
Boswell, James 231 n., 305–6 n.
Bouguer, Pierre, French physicist 101 n.
Boulliau, Ismael 88
Bower, Archibald, papal historian 298
Boyle, Robert, Irish physicist and chemist 245
Bradley, James, Astronomer Royal 246
Brahe, Tycho, Danish astronomer 75, 80–5, 90, 96–7, 102
Bramhall, John 233
Brown, John 189 n.
Bruno, Giordano, sceptic philosopher 77 n.
Buccleuch, Henry Scott, 3rd Duke of 171, 173, 298, 301–2, 306–7, 325
Buckingham, John Sheffield 1st Duke of 230
Buffon, Georges Louis Leclerc, Comte de 248
Burke, Edmund 296, 325, 345 n.
Bürkert, W. 57 n.

Burnet, John 65 n.
Burney, Charles, English musicologist 199 n.
Bushnell, Nelson S. 259 n.
Butler, Joseph, Bishop of Bristol and Durham 250, 339
Butler, Samuel, English satirist 221, 239
Bysshe, Edward 217

Craigie, Thomas 273, 322
Cratylus, Greek philosopher 53
Craufurd, *see* Crawford
Crawford, William 259, 262
Cudworth, Ralph, Cambridge Platonist 123 n., 126, 279
Cullen, William, Scottish physician 46 n.
Culpepper, Sir Thomas 347

C

Cadell, Thomas, publisher 265–6, 268
Callender, James Thomson 231
Callippus of Cyzicus, Greek astronomer 55, 58 n., 59
Campbell, T. D. 45 n.
Campomanes, Pedro Rodriguez 311
Cannan, Edwin viii, 49 n., 321 n.
Carra de Vaux, Bernard, Baron 68 n.
Cartaud de la Villate, François 189 n.
Cary, John, of Bristol 340
Cassini, Giovanni Domenico, astronomer 90–1, 95, 97–8
Chalmers, George, Scottish antiquary 259
Chamberlayne, Edward 343 n.
Chastellux, François-Jean, Marquis de 218–19, 225 n.
Chaucer, Geoffrey 188, 217
Cheselden, William, English surgeon 153–4, 158–60
Chesterfield, Philip Stanhope, 4th Earl of 231
Child, Sir Josiah 340, 344, 347–8
Churchill, W. A. 217 n.
Cicero, Marcus Tullius 47, 57 n., 65–6, 114, 116 n., 122 n., 189 n., 193 n., 318
Clarke, M. L. 26
Clarke, Samuel, English philosopher 137 n., 250, 279, 339
Cleanthes, Stoic philosopher 62
Clerk-Maxwell, James, Scottish physicist 139 n.
Coke, Sir Edward, Chief-Justice 341 n., 349
Colbert, Jean-Baptiste, French statesman 318–19, 345 n.
Condillac, Étienne Bonnot de Mably de, French philosopher 347
Condorcet, Sophie de Grouchy, Marquise de 339
Conway, Henry Seymour, General 307–8
Copernicus, Nicolas 65 n., 71, 75–6, 78–91, 94, 96–7, 102, 294
Corelli, Archangelo, Italian composer 195, 203
Cornford, F. M. 52–3 n.
Cowley, Abraham, English poet 234, 238

D

Dalrymple, Elizabeth 259
Dalrymple, Sir John 259–60
Dalzel, Andrew, Professor of Greek 272 n.
Dante, Alighieri 219, 220 n.
Daubenton, Louis-Jean-Marie, French naturalist 246, 248
Davidson, Archibald, Principal of Glasgow University 273 n., 328
Davie, G. E. 154 n.
Davies, William, publisher 266
Davy, Sir Humphry 139 n.
Delambre, Jean-Baptiste-Joseph, French astronomer 12
Democritus, Greek philosopher 53, 128 n., 140
Descartes, René 39 n., 42–3, 87–8, 92–8, 102–3, 133, 138 n., 244, 249–50, 328 n., 339
Destouches, André, Cardinal 200 n.
Destouches-Néricault, Philippe 200 n.
de Witt, John, *see* Witt, Johan (Jan), de
Diderot, Denis 245
Diels, H. 52 n.
Digges, Thomas 77 n.
Diogenes Laertius 113 n., 127 n.
Dionysius of Halicarnassus 213 n.
Dobie 224–5
Douglas, David, Lord Reston 172, 265, 331–2
Douglas, Jane 325–6
Douglas, John, of Strathenry 269
Douglas, Margaret, mother of Adam Smith 269, 325
Douglas, Robert, of Strathenry 269–70
Dryden, John 33, 188 n., 221–2, 234–6, 239
Drysdale, George 270 n.
Drysdale, John 270
Du Piles, *see* Piles
Duclos, *see* Pineau-Duclos
Duncan, W. J. 260 n.

E

Empedocles, Greek philosopher 52, 107
Enville, Mme d', *see* Anville

Epicurus, Greek philosopher 53, 128 n., 140
Eudoxus of Cnidus, Greek astronomer 55–9, 71, 102

F

Fairfax, Edward, English scholar, translator 239
Faraday, Michael 139 n.
Ferguson, Adam 294 n., 297
Filangieri, Gaetano 312 n.
Flamsteed, John, Astronomer Royal 103 n.
Forbes, D. 313 n.
Formey, Jean-Henri-Samuel 246
Forteguerri, Niccolò 221 n.
Fortescue, Sir John, Chief-Justice 341 n.
Foulis, Robert and Andrew, publishers 259, 348
Fourier, Jean-Baptiste-Joseph, Baron de, French mathematician 56 n.
Fracastoro, Girolamo *8*, 59
Franklin, Benjamin 147
Freud, Sigmund 165 n.
Fussell, Paul 217 n.

G

Galen of Pergamum, Greek physician 68
Galilei, Galileo 19–20, 80, 83–4, 87, 92 n., 96 n.
Garnier, Germain 270 n., 347
Gassendi, Pierre, French mathematician 87, 133, 140
Gee, Joshua 348
Geminus of Rhodes, Stoic philosopher 23
Gemma, Reinerus 77 n.
Gibbon, Edward 325
Gilbert, William, English physician 42 n.
Gillies, John, Scottish historian 334–6, 337 n.
Gilson, Etienne 68–9 n.
Girard, Gabriel, l'Abbé 338
Gournay, Jean-Claude-Marie Vincent, seigneur de 320, 344–7
Gray, Thomas, English poet 225
Green, T. H. 50 n., 314 n., 319 n.
Gregory, David, Scottish mathematician 245
Griffith, G. T. 59 n.
Groenewegen, P. D. 304 n.
Grose, T. H. 50 n., 314 n., 319 n.
Grove, Sir George, English musicologist 202 n.
Guillaume, A. 68 n.

Guthrie, W. K. C. 57 n.
Gutteridge, G. H. 242 n.

H

Halley, Edmund 103 n.
Hamilton, Sir William 265–8
Hamilton, William, of Bangour 259–62
Handel, George Frideric 190 & n., 195, 203
Harriot, Thomas, English astronomer 83 n.
Hartley, David, English philosopher 47 n.
Haskins, C. H. 69–70 n.
Haydn, Franz Joseph, Austrian composer 204 n.
Hazard, Paul 11
Heath, Sir T. L. 55 n., 57 n., 64 n., 67 n., 71 n., 101 n., 109 n.
Helmholtz, Hermann von, German physicist 92 n.
Helvetius, Claude-Adrien, French philosopher 297, 302, 338
Henry VIII, King of England 341 n.
Heraclitus, Greek philosopher 53, 120
Herbert of Cherbury, Edward Herbert, 1st Baron 341 n.
Hesiod, Greek poet 113
Hevelius, Johann, German astronomer 103 n.
Hill, G. B. 231 n.
Hipparchus, Greek astronomer 59, 64–9, 71, 79, 86, 88, 101–2
Hippocrates, of Cos, Greek physician 68
Hobbes, Thomas 93 n., 233, 250, 279, 339
Holt, Andreas, Danish trade commissioner 171–2
Home, Henry, *see* Kames
Homer 52, 260
Hooke, Robert, English chemist 138 n.
Hooker, Richard, English theologian 234
Hope, Charles, Lord 297
Horace (Quintus Horatius Flaccus) 234, 260
Hortensius Hortalus, Quintus, Roman orator 333
Houdar de La Motte, Antoine, French librettist 200 n.
Howell, W. S. 244 n.
Hume, David 39–41 n., 50 n., 133, 171–2, 173 n.
Hunter, John, Scottish surgeon 153 n.
Hutcheson, Francis, Professor of Moral Philosophy 48 n., 250, 271, 273, 279, 328–9, 333–4, 339
Hutton, James (Smith's literary executor) 32, 265, 327–8 n., 332, 350

Huxley, G. L. 55 n.
Huygens, Christian, Dutch physicist 138 n.

J

Jacob, Hildebrand 208 n.
James I and VI, King of England, Scotland
    and Ireland 239
Jennens, Charles, minor poet 195 n.
Jenyns, Soame, English writer 296
Johnson, Samuel 219, 225 n., 229–41,
    270 n., 276, 305–6 n.
Johnstone, William, *see* Pulteney,
    Sir William
Jones, Sir William, British orientalist 325
Jonson, Ben, English dramatist 234
Jupiter 49, 50 n., 117, 179

K

Kames, Henry Home, Lord 222 n., 229,
    259, 272, 294–5, 297, 333
Keill, John 245
Kelvin, William Thompson, 1st Baron,
    Scottish mathematician and physicist
    139 n.
Kepler, Johannes 18–20, 47 n., 84–98
Kerr, Robert 47 n.
Knox, John 299
Kranz, W. 52 n.

L

La Bruyère, Jean de 329
La Fontaine, Jean de 331
Lalande, Joseph-Jérôme Le Francais de,
    French astronomer 12
La Mettrie, Julien Offray de, French
    philosopher 47 n.
Lancelot, Claude 213 n.
Lansdowne, William Petty Fitzmaurice,
    2nd Earl of Shelburne and 1st Marquess
    of 347
Laplace, Pierre-Simon, Marquis de, French
    astronomer 147 n.
La Rochefoucauld, François, 6th Duc de
    303 n.
La Rochefoucauld d'Anville, Louis
    Alexandre, Duc de 171–2, 219 n., 267,
    303
Lauderdale, James Maitland, 8th Earl of
    341, 343 n.
Lavoisier, Antoine-Laurent, French
    chemist 47 n.
Law, John 348–9

Le Gendre, Adrien Marie 345 n.
Leibniz, Gottfried Wilhelm 92 n., 137 n.
Le Prieur, Pierre Alexandre, publisher
    254 n.
Leucippus, Greek philosopher 53, 128 n.,
    140
Linnaeus (Carl Linne), Swedish botanist
    162, 164, 166
Livy (Titus Livius), Roman historian 36 n.
Locke, John 125, 133, 136 n., 150, 153–4 n.,
    234–5, 250, 339–40, 343, 346, 349
Loewenberg, A. 200 n.
Lothian, J. M. viii, 38 n., 42 n., 52 n., 54 n.,
    65–6 n., 225 n., 244 n., 275 n.
Loudoun, Hugh Campbell, 3rd Earl of
    269 n.
Loughborough, Lord, *see* Wedderburn,
    Alexander
Louis XIV, King of France 247
Lucretius (Titus Lucretius Carus), Roman
    poet and philosopher 93 n., 128 n., 138
Łukasiewicz, Jan 26
Lully, Jean-Baptiste, French composer
    200 n.
Lumisden, Andrew 259
Lycurgus, reputed Spartan legislator 313
Lyttelton (or Lyttleton), George, 1st Baron
    296, 298

M

Macdonald, Sir James, of Sleat 301–2
Macfie, A. L. 50 n.
Machault d'Arnouville, Jean-Baptiste 345
Mackenzie, Henry, Scottish author 265
Mackintosh, Sir James 230
Maclaine, Archibald 270, 333
Maclaurin, Colin, Scottish mathematician
    83 n., 90
Maestlin, Michael, German mathematician
    84
Malebranche, Nicolas 48, 123 n., 125, 250,
    339
Ma'mūn, al-, Abdallah 68–70
Mandeville, Bernard, English satirist
    250–1, 303 n., 339
Marais, Marin, French composer and
    musician 200 n.
Marmontel, Jean-François, French author
    218, 302
Mason, John 218
Mattheson, Johann, musician and composer
    202 n.
Maurepas, Jean-Frédéric-Phélypeaux,
    Comte de 248, 345
Maxwell, James Clerk, *see* Clerk-Maxwell,
    James

Medici, Giuliano de' 83 n.
Melissus of Samos, Eleatic philosopher
 53
Metastasio (Pietro Trapassi), Italian poet
 194, 202, 254
Meyerhof, M. 68 n.
Meyerson, E. 42 n.
Millar, Andrew 296, 298
Millar, John, Professor of Civil Law 172–3,
 230, 265–6, 273–6, 295, 309 n.
Miller, David, schoolmaster 270
Miller, Thomas, Rector of Glasgow
 University, and, as Lord Glenlee, Lord
 President of the Court of Session 302 n.,
 333
Milton, John 33, 70 n., 190, 195, 217 n.,
 223, 238, 243
Mitford, William 218
Mizuta, H. 101 n., 154 n., 219 n.
Molyneux, William 153–4 n.
Monboddo, James Burnet, Lord 218
Mondolfo, R. 52 n.
Montesquieu, Charles-Louis de Secondat,
 Baron de La Brede 11, 274, 275 n., 294
Montucla, Jean-Étienne 9–11, 294
Moraux, P. 112 n.
More, Henry, Cambridge Platonist 123 n.
More, Sir Thomas 341 n.
Morellet, André, l'Abbé 267, 302, 338,
 340
Morris, Corbyn 230
Mosheim, Johann Lorenz von, German
 theologian 333
Mossner, E. C. 172
Mozart, Wolfgang Amadeus 204 n.
Müller, Johannes, *see* Regiomontanus

N

Necker, Jacques, French statesman and
 financier 302
Newton, Sir Isaac 83 n., 90–1, 92 n.,
 97–105, 133, 138 n., 140, 147, 244–5,
 246 n., 275 n.
Nichols, John 337

O

Ocellus of Lucania, reputed Pythagorean
 philosopher 52 n., 115
Orléans, Philippe II, Duc d' 349
Osiander, Andreas 76 n.
Oswald, George, of Scotstoun and
 Auchincruive 338
Oswald, James, of Dunnikier 270, 298, 300,
 333

Oswald, John, Bishop of Raphoe 270
Owens, J. 127 n.

P

Pagel, W. 39 n.
Paracelsus (Theophrastus Bombastus von
 Hohenheim), medical man and scientist
 39 n., 47 n.
Parmenides 53
Pauly, A. von 112 n.
Pemberton, Henry 218
Pepys, John, brother of Samuel 21
Pepys, Samuel 21
Pergolesi, Giovanni Battista 194
Peripatetic philosophers 69, 78, 108, 120,
 128
Persius (Aulus Persius Flaccus), Roman
 satirist 298
Peterborough, Bishop of, *see* Terrick
Petrarch (Francesco Petrarca) 219, 225
Petre, Miss 267
Petty, Sir William 348
Peuerbach (Peurbach, Purbach), Georg von
 69–71, 81, 102
Philips, Erasmus 342–3
Phocion, Athenian general 298
Piles, Roger de (Du Piles) 206
Pindar, Greek lyric poet 234, 238, 260–1
Pineau (or Pinot) -Duclos, Charles 213 n.
Pitt, William, the Younger 345 n.
Plato 51 n., 52–3, 55 n., 57, 59, 71, 93 n.,
 114, 116–17, 120–8, 193, 251, 271, 318
Pliny (Gaius Plinius Secundus), the elder
 65
Plutarch 57, 65, 71–2, 122 n.
Pohlenz, M. 116 n.
Polignac, Melchior, Cardinal de 90
Polybius 334
Pompadour, Jean-Antoinette Poisson,
 Marquise de 304 n.
Pope, Alexander 201, 221–2, 224, 234,
 239
Popper, Sir Karl 41 n.
Porphyry, Neoplatonist philosopher 120
Pouilly, Lévesque de 250, 339
Powell, L. F. 231 n.
Prevost, Pierre 218, 221 n., 223 n., 231
Prieur, *see* Le Prieur
Pringle-Pattison, A. S. 154 n.
Proclus, Greek Neoplatonist 67
Protagoras, Greek Sophist 53
Ptolemy (Claudius Ptolemaeus), Egyptian
 astronomer 59 n., 64, 67–71, 72 n.,
 73–4, 75 n., 76, 78 n., 81–2, 84, 88, 90,
 102
Pulteney, Sir William 273

Pythagoras, Pythagoreans 47, 52–3, 55 n.,
    57, 72, 113, 127–8

Q

Quesnay, François, French economist and
    physiocrat 302, 304, 311, 343 n., 344, 347
Quinault, Philippe, French poet and
    dramatist 200 n.
Quinctilian (Marcus Fabius Quintilianus),
    Roman orator 333

R

Racine, Jean 260
Rae, David, Lord Eskgrove 260
Raphael, D. D. 172, 173 n.
Ray, John, English naturalist 238
Réaumur, René Antoine Ferchault de 249
Recorde, Robert 77 n.
Regiomontanus (Johannes Müller) 71
Régis, Pierre-Sylvain 250, 339
Reid, Thomas 266, 268, 270 n., 348 n.
Reinhold, Erasmus 76
Rembrandt (Rembrandt Harmentz van
    Rijn) 179
Reynolds, Sir Joshua 325
Rheticus (Georg Joachim von Lauchen),
    German astronomer 76–7 n.
Riccoboni, Marie-Jeanne Laboras de
    Mézières, Mme 302–3
Rice, John 218, 225 n.
Richardson, William 260
Riddell, Mr 328 n.
Ritchie, A. D. 154 n.
Ritchie, James, merchant of Glasgow 300 n.
Robertson, William 266, 268, 293–4 n., 298
Roscommon, Wentworth Dillon, 4th Earl of
    239
Ross, Miss 326 n.
Ross, Patrick, of Innernethy 326 n.
Ross, Sir David 53 n., 127 n.
Rouet, William 297
Rousseau, Jean-Jacques 198–9, 200 n., 219,
    231, 246, 250–6, 339
Rowe, Nicholas 218
Rudolph II, Holy Roman Emperor 83 n.
Ruscelli, Girolamo 223–4, 225 n.
Russell, J. 87 n.

S

Salviati, L. 232 n.
Sambursky, S. 116 n.
Sappho 52

Sauveur, Joseph 213
Say, Jean-Baptiste 347
Say, Samuel, minor poet 217, 223, 225 n.
Scarron, Paul, French writer 179
Schlegel, August Wilhelm von 174
Scott, Lady Frances 217
Scott, William Robert 171–2, 173 n.,
    245 n., 302 n., 321 n., 322 n.
Selby-Bigge, Sir L. A. 39 n., 42 n.
Selkirk, Dunbar Douglas (formerly
    Hamilton), 4th Earl of 333
Seneca, Lusius Annaeus 47 n., 65, 122 n.,
    127 n.
Shaftesbury, Anthony Ashley Cooper, 3rd
    Earl of 250, 339
Shakespeare, William 233–5, 239–40, 243,
    260
Sheridan, Thomas 218
Sidney, Sir Philip 238–9
Simonde, *see* Sismondi
Simonides of Ceos, Greek lyric poet 52
Simpson, Dr, *see* Simson
Simson, Robert, Scottish mathematician 271
Sismondi, Jean-Charles-Léonard Simonde
    de 347
Skinner, A. S. 217 n., 313 n., 319 n., 349 n.
Smart, Christopher 201 n.
Smith, Edmund, classicist 233
Smith, John, Cambridge Platonist 123 n.
Socrates 53, 122 n., 124
Solon 318
Sophocles 260
South, Robert, English divine 239
Spens, H., Scottish classicist 26
Spenser, Edmund 217, 243
Speusippus, nephew of Plato 122 n.
Stanhope, Philip, 2nd Earl 302
Stesichorus, Greek lyric poet 52
Steuart, Sir James 348–9 n.
Stewart, Dugald 32 n., 133, 171, 173–4,
    219, 229 n., 230–1, 233 n., 242 n., 254 n.,
    265–51
Stoics 47 n., 62–3, 65 n., 85, 108, 116–17,
    121–3 n., 127 n., 253, 256
Swift, Jonathan 233

T

Tarn, W. W. 59 n.
Tassie, James, Scottish modeller 331
Tasso, Torquato 219 n., 224 & n.
Taylor, A. E. 52 n., 93 n., 114 n.
Temple, Sir William 239
Terrick, Richard, Bishop of Peterborough 298
Terzetti 220 & n.
Thales of Miletus 52, 56
Theon of Alexandria 67

Thomson, H. F. 13 n.
Tillotson, John, Archbishop of Canterbury
  234
Timaeus of Locri, Pythagorean philosopher,
  possibly fictitious 52, 114, 120, 125
Timocharis, early astronomer 64 n.
Timon of Phlius, sceptic philosopher 113 n.
Titian (Tiziano Vecelli) 206
Townshend, Charles, English statesman
  298, 301
Trissino, Gian Giorgio, Italian poet 218
Trudaine, Jean-Claude 347
Turgot, Anne-Robert-Jacques 302, 304,
  311, 320, 337 n., 338, 344, 346–9
Tyrwhitt, Thomas 188 n.
Tytler, Alexander Fraser, Lord
  Woodhouselee 229

V

Vanderlint, Jacob 342–3, 346
Vauban, Sébastien Le Prestre, seigneur de
  345 n.
Veblen, Thorstein 174
Veitch, John 266–7, 339 n.
Vico, Giambattista 26
Vincent, Claude 344
Virgil (Publius Vergilius Maro) 77 n., 260,
  323
Vivaldi, Antonio 203 n.
Voltaire, François Marie Arouet de 90, 247,
  254, 297, 305 n., 345 n.

W

Wackenroder, Wilhelm Heinrich 174

Waller, Edmund 236
Waller, Richard 139 n.
Walpole, Horace, 4th Earl of Orford
  296
Walzer, R. 68 n.
Warburton, William, Bishop of Gloucester
  296
Ward, Seth, Bishop of Exeter 88
Ward, William 337–8
Watts, Isaac 233
Wedderburn, Alexander, 1st
  Baron Loughborough, 1st Earl of
  Rosslyn 172, 229, 231, 242, 273,
  296
Whitehead, A. N. 41 n.
Witt, Johan (Jan) de 340, 344
Wordsworth, William 260
Wright, Patience 181

X

Xenocrates 114 n., 122 n.
Xenophanes 53, 56

Y

Young, Thomas 139 n.
Yvon, Claude, Abbé 248 n.

Z

Zeller, E. 52 n., 122 n.
Zeno, Apostolo 202
Zeno of Citium 62 n., 116 n.
Zeno of Elea 53

The Theory of Moral Sentiments

Index of Subjects

A

abhorrence:
 of self 84
 of vice 91, 117, 164, 169, 329
Académie française 126
Académie des Sciences 125
action(s):
 agreeable, or disagreeable, effects of
  101–4, 189
 deserving reward or punishment 67–74,
  78, 99–100, 105
 humane 191
 merit, or demerit, of 92–108, 170
 proceeding from affection of the heart 18
 see also intention
admiration 14, 49, 55, 58–60
 and approval 20, 25, 31, 48–9, 263–4
 desire for 114, 116–17, 259
 for exalted behaviour 192
 for Marcus Aurelius 236–7
 mistaken 114–15
 of multitude 56
 a musical passion 37
 and national pride 227–8, 232
 of noble and magnificent building 99
 of perfect virtue 152, 156, 245, 290
 for the praiseworthy 114–17
 principles of 134
 proper object of 245
 of prudence, limited 216, 263–4
 public 53, 57, 189
 of rich and great 50–4, 61–4, 144, 181–3,
  195, 201, 225–6, 253
 for sciences 189
 self- 249–51
 for self-command 45, 77, 152, 156, 189,
  238–40, 245
 for success 250–5
 for violence 217
 for virtue 61–2, 167, 178
 for wealth, wisdom and virtue 61–2
 see also ambition; applause; surprise;
  wonder
adulterer 175
adversity 43–9, 58, 166–7
affection(s) 1–4
 benevolent 25, 38–9, 102, 106, 172, 227,
  262, 267, 301–4 (Hutcheson)
 brotherly 81, 222
 conjugal 162

 for Deity 171
 domestic/familial 142–3, 221–3, 227
 and duty 171–2
 for elderly person 219
 filial/children's 171–2, 220–2
 in friendship 224
 malevolent 102, 105–6
 moderation of 271, 306
 natural 28, 171, 220–1, 223, 226, 243,
  332
 of parents 81, 142–3, 171, 219–21
 and praise or blame 92–3, 97, 101, 106,
  172
 propriety, or impropriety, of 16–26
  passim, 67, 73–4, 138 n., 266–7,
  293, 306
 and prudence 262
 selfish 227, 267, 292–3, 317
 social 38, 102, 172, 243
 and society 85–6
 and the stoic wise man 275 n., 277,
  292–3
 and sympathy 70–6 passim, 220–3, 306
 unsocial 102, 172, 243
 usefulness in moderation of 306
 and virtue 266–7
 virtue as balance of 293
 see also intention; passim
Africa 208, 286 n.
 negroes of 206
age, old, see old age
alderman, wives of 57
ambition:
 disappointment in 29, 43, 149–50
 of ecclesiastical power 318
 object of 62, 64, 66, 173–4, 186, 191, 225,
  336
 origin of 50–61 passim
 as a passion 173, 268
 of poor man's son 181–2
 and prudence 62
 speech as instrument of 336
analogy:
 of the looking glass 112
 of nature 322
 see also machine; system
anger:
 of children 145
 command of 207–8, 238, 240–1, 263
 constant features of 324
 and custom 207–8

anger (*cont.*):
　of God/heaven 77, 181
　and propriety 243
　reaction to expression of 11, 24, 35–7
animal(s) 77, 94–5, 198, 272, 336
antipathy 75–6, 312, 327
antiquity:
　remains of 283
apathy, stoical 143, 273, 292
appetite(s) 77, 165, 189, 215, 267–8, 287,
　　299
　bodily 27–8, 58, 212, 268
applause:
　in correspondence of sentiments 14
　as expression of admiration 20, 31, 49
　for just retaliation 90–1
　merited/unmerited 26, 90, 115–21,
　　　128–30, 109–11, 228, 248, 311
　see also approbation and disapprobation
approbation/approval and
　　disapprobation/disapproval:
　and admiration 20, 25, 31, 48–9,
　　　263–4
　of beneficence 78, 93, 298–9
　and custom and fashion 194
　desire of, *see* desire, of approbation/praise
　dual standard for 26
　and duty 176–8
　four sources of 326
　of grief 17–18
　in Hume 188, 327
　in Hutcheson 321–4
　instinctive 71, 77
　and intention 93 vs benevolence
　of justice 79–82
　vs justice 79–82
　and love 68
　of mankind 79–80, 85
　in moral philosophy 314–15
　of others 16–19, 109, 111, 114–17, 123,
　　　130
　principle of 314–27
　of propriety 78, 82, 93, 162, 294,
　　　309–11
　and punishment 77, 88, 90–1
　reason as principle of 318–21
　and retaliation 71
　of self 109–14, 146–8, 178, 247–8, 303
　　　and *see also* self-approbation
　of self-command 189–90, 264
　self-love as principle of 315–17
　sentiment as principle of 321–7
　Smith's theory of 326–7
　and sympathy 16–18, 46 n., 48–51, 78,
　　　317, 321, 325–7
　three theories of 314
　two standards of 25–6
　universal 129

and utility 20, 179, 187–92
approval and disapproval, *see* approbation
　　and disapprobation
Aquilian law 104
Arabs:
　regard for kin 223
architect 99
　of universe 289
architecture 36, 195–6, 197, 313
arms, laws of 342
art(s):
　appraisal of 26, 179
　beauty of 185
　contribute to conveniency 134
　determinants of excellence in 123
　and fashion 195, 197–8
　of governance 54
　and happiness 187
　human 316
　ingenious 248–9
　of intrigue and cabal 64, 125
　liberal 229, 249
　love of task for 185, 313
　poetic 249
　quackish 213
　of war 298
artists:
　perceptions of great and inferior
　　　247–9
Athenians 210, 240 n., 254
　exposition of children by 210
atom, man as 59, 276
atonement 92, 104, 107, 339, 390–1, 396,
　　　400
Author of nature 77, 105
　laws of 273
　purpose of 93, 166
　teachings of 128, 298
　see also God; Nature
Author of human nature 169
authority:
　of conscience 129, 134, 137, 164 n.,
　　　165
　of general rules 161, 176, 221
　of internal judge 245, 292
　of law 222–3, 341
　Tory principle of 233 n.
avarice 50, 57
　disappointed 149–50
　objects of 173–4

B

Barbarians:
　disregard for motives 101
　falsehood and dissimulation in 208
　laws among 341

self-command in 205–9
see also savages
Bastille 149
baubles 180, 184
beauty:
  ability to discern 110–13
  Buffier on 198–9
  and custom 194–200
  in character of men 187–93
  Hutcheson's theory of 322
  ideas of personal 111–12
  object of speculation 192
  of one's mind or face 54, 110, 112
  of poetry 123
  in political systems 185, 232–4
  of private life 242
  of self-command 238, 240, 242
  and utility 179–80, 183–8, 192–3, 298–9,
    316, 326
  taste for 327
  of virtue 198–9, 247, 298–9, 301, 304,
    307, 316
  see also arts; taste
beggar:
  and begging 10, 49, 64
  is despised 144
  security of 185
belief:
  disposition to 335–7
  in future state 169
beneficence:
  approbation of 78, 93, 298–9
  duties of 79, 81
  is free 78–81
  and gratitude 225
  and justice 78–82, 170, 218, 262, 390,
    392–4
  laws of 332
  motivation for 262
  as ornament of society 86
  towards individuals 219–27 *passim*
  towards societies 227–34 *passim*
  and utility 264
  see also benevolence; humanity; kindness
benevolence:
  in the Eclectics 300
  of God 91, 106, 166, 235–6, 277, 290,
    292, 300, 305
  in Hume 24 n., 80 n.
  in Hutcheson 24 n., 265, 301–4
  as just passion 40
  and justice 80 n., 237–8, 241
  and praise 302
  and prudence 216, 267
  and public spirit 232–3
  and self-interest 25, 137, 230, 235
  and sense of duty 172
  of statesman 230

in Stoics 300 n.
  universal 235–7, 290
  virtue consisting in 241, 265–7, 300–6
  and other virtues 24 n., 237, 241, 262
  see also beneficence; humanity; kindness
bettering our condition, *see* ambition
blame:
  assignment of 80–1
  avoidance of 126–8
  and desert 26, 80–1, 92–3, 101, 109 n.,
    111, 114, 160, 301, 304
  dread of 113–34
  see also praise
blame-worthiness:
  aversion to 113–14, 116, 119, 126,
    130–1
  avoidance of 127–8
body, the bodies:
  appetites or passions originating in 27–9,
    268
  conveniences of 212–13, 272
  external action or movement of 92–3
  eye of 134–5
  heavenly 313
  injury to 142–3
  labour of 55
  necessities and conveniencies of 212–13
  pain and pleasure of 44, 272, 295–6, 298,
    299
  sympathy for pain of 10, 13, 27–9, 71
boys, education of 222
breast, inhabitant of 137
British Library 385, 387
Buccaneers, the 240
burlesque:
  in French and English verse 196–7
business:
  God's vs man's 237, 277
  Nature vs man's 292–3
  public 65, 216
  of the world 136
bustle:
  of the world 50, 57, 146

C

cabal(s) 64
  literary 125
  political 151
  prudent man's view of 213–14
  religions 170
Cambridge 301
Carthage/Carthaginians 228–9, 286
'Castalio' 32
casuist(s), casuistry:
  and jurisprudence 329–35 *passim*
  and moral duties 227, 329–42 *passim*

casuist(s), casuistry (*cont.*):
  standard of public good used by 302
  standards for right and wrong of 304–5
Catalinarians, the 240
cause(s):
  of action, dist. end 18, 67
  efficient and final 87, 104
  and intentions 73–4, 94–7 *passim*
  in nature as distinct from philosophy
    293
centinel, *see* sentinel
character:
  civil and military 204
  of a coward 244
  and cultural difference 204–11 *passim*
  effect on other people's happiness 218
  effect on own happiness 212–17
  false 241–2
  family 224
  of professions 201–4, 209
  see also man
charity 79–80, 226
chastity 163, 242, 312, 332, 335, 339
cheerfulness 39, 41–2, 47, 59, 85, 132, 276
chess-board of human society 234
child/children/infant(s):
  credulity of 335
  death of 219
  education of 212, 222, 259
  expectations of 219
  exposure of 210–11
  filial piety of 49, 81, 142
  learning self-command 145
  of Nature 52
  and parents 39, 111, 142–3, 219–27
    passim
  unaware of the future 12
China 227, 230
  hypothetical earthquake in 136
  ladies' feet bound in 199
Christian, Christianity 24 n., 25, 92 n., 171,
    178, 238 n., 283 n., 300 n., 301, 329,
    333, 383, 387, 390–1, 396, 400–1
  see also religion
church:
  ancient fathers of 331
  casuists of 329
  Christian 301
circumspection 103–4, 166, 304
citizen:
  of Amsterdam 204
  the good 229, 231
  Roman 192
civility 163, 205, 222
civilization 223
clan 223
clergy-man 202–3, 209, 334, 399
  see also monks

colleges 222
colours, agreeable 199
  as sense-quality 322
commerce 186, 223, 229, 313
  of Europe 136
  of the world 139
commonwealth(s):
  founding of 183
  of nature 140
  power of 340
  prosperity of 81
  in Rome 286
  wisdom 218
compassion:
  for criminals 73, 118–19
  for the great 52–3, 56–7
  for imprudence 216
  Machiavelli's lack of 217
  for misfortune of others 9, 46, 49, 58, 60,
    152
  for poverty 144, 226
  as social passion 38
  and sympathy 10, 12, 22, 38, 43
  see also pity
compensation:
  for damages 103–4
competitor(s) 83, 181
composition, rules of 175
concupiscence 339; cf. 268
condemnation 128–9
condescension 23, 261
condition, bettering of 50
confessor:
  role in Catholic Church of 333–5
conscience:
  and approval 326
  authority of 129, 134, 137, 146
  and casuistry 333–4, 339–40
  danger of corruption of 141 n.
  degree of passion approved by 242–4
  erroneous 176–7
  as the impartial spectator 130–1, 134,
    137
  and moral faculty 164 n., 326
  'pangs of' 101, 115, 117–19
  of person prevented from criminal act
    101
  remorse of 119, 333–5
  see also self-deceit
constancy 30, 59, 119–20, 129, 146, 278,
    283
  in Hutcheson's system 304
constitution 185 n., 232 n., 234
  powers, privileges, and immunities 230
  and rules of justice 340–1
  stability of 230–1
  see also government; state; system, man
    of; system, spirit of

consumption:
    of rich people compared to poor people
        184
contempt 61–3, 144–6
    for coward 244
    for death 206, 239, 288
    dread of 62, 117–18
    of men of rank and power 56
    object of 138
    among savages 205–7, 288
    for those who emulate rich and powerful
        54–5
    for victim of unsocial passions 34–5
    of wise man 121
contract:
    breach of 84
    obligations of 339
contrivance:
    love of 182, 185
conveniency(-ies):
    and beauty 179–86
    and external fortune 212–13
conversation 12, 23, 41, 64, 213–15, 249, 337
corruption:
    of morals 61
    of the world 137
    of the young 89
Corinthian architecture 196
cottage vs palace 50, 181
country(-ies):
    commercial 223
    concern for/interest in one's own 98, 186,
        216, 235–7, 239, 274, 290, 297–9
    love of 171, 227–34, 238
    pastoral 222
    see also constitution; fellow-citizens;
        government; nation(s)
courage 36, 55, 99, 270–1
court(s) (judicial) 105, 126, 130, 160, 341
cowardice 244, 270–1
coxcomb:
    conscience of 115
    contempt for 54–5
    insensibility of 143
    vanity of 259, 309
Creator 92, 170
credulity 335–7
crime 65
    false imputation of 119–20, 122
    murder as 65, 84
    and punishment for 60–1, 88–92, 99–101,
        176–7
criminals 60, 69, 73, 92, 119–21, 176, 239
critic 26, 112, 175, 327
custom:
    influences judgement of beauty 194–200
    influences moral sentiments 200–11
    and utility 199

see also aesthetics
Cyrenaics 214 n.

D

damage:
    by blamable negligence 102–4
dancer on the slack rope 10
dead, the
    imaginary resentment of 71, 95
    sympathy for 12–13
death 84, 116, 138–9, 142, 144, 160, 191–2
    contempt in savage nations for 206–7,
        282, 287–8
    dread of 13, 156, 203
    in Epicurean philosophy 296–7
    penalty 90, 95, 100, 119–20, 192, 206–7
    propriety of voluntary 281–2, 284–8
    and self-command 238–9, 242, 244, 306
    stoics on 276, 278, 280, 281–8
death-song:
    of American savage 206, 282
    prepared by ancient philosophers 283
Decalogue, the 142
deceit:
    involuntary or mistaken 336–9
    wilful 336–7
decorum(s) 30, 169, 207, 214–15, 335
deduction, *see* induction
deference 52–3, 310
deformity:
    and custom and fashion 194
    distinguishing differences in 20
    and disutility 187–8, 192, 298
    ideas of personal 111–12
    of one's mind or face 110
    of injustice 137
    and vice 316, 322, 328
Deity, *see* God
demerit 93, 97, 99–101, 105, 110, 138 n.,
        168, 170, 188
    components of sentiment of 74–6
    deserves punishment 67
    disapprobation of 78
    see also merit; punishment
demigod within the breast 131, 245, 247
    see also spectator
demons 118
demonstration 123
desert 67, 74–6, 86, 91, 104
design(s) 69, 93, 96–108 *passim*
    see also piacular guilt
desire(s):
    of approbation/praise 109 n.,
        113–14, 116–17, 126–7, 129, 131,
        159, 166–7, 176, 213, 259, 309–10,
        336

desire(s) (*cont.*):
  disappointment of 51
  natural 295–300, 336
  primary objects of (Epicurean philosophy)
      295–9
  of the rich 183–4
devotion:
  as musical passion 37
  duties of 132
dialectic 145
diffidence 335, 337
dignity:
  of character 137, 239, 245
  of human nature 23–4, 28, 132
  of proud man 256
  and rank 38, 53, 239, 244–5, 268
disapprobation:
  aversion to 112, 116–17, 123
  of demerit and impropriety 67, 78, 93,
      110–11, 118, 294, 325
  foundation of 316, 324
  influence of custom and fashion on
      194–211
  object of 78–80, 130, 159
  of others 17, 109, 123, 161
  see also approbation
discipline:
  among savages 205–6
  see also self-command
  civic/social 81, 100, 103
  military 90
discretion:
  habit of 304
disease 12, 139, 182, 287
disgust:
  for appetites of body 28
  for unsocial passions 36
dishonour 49, 60, 119, 154–5
disorder(s) 132, 149, 158, 166
  of human life 158
  public 81, 231, 241, 304, 315, 318, 340
dissimulation 162, 208, 241, 339
  see also character
distribution:
  by nature 168, 218
  of necessaries 184 n., 185
  of rewards 132, 269 n.
divinities, ideas of 164
  see also religion; superstition
doctors 155
drama 107
dreams, waking 52
dress, and fashion 64, 194–7
  and vanity 256, 309, 313
drunkenness 286
Dryads, the 94
duelling 240
Dunciad, The (A. Pope) 123

duty(-ies) 33, 42, 59, 127
  active 237
  of beneficence 79–81, 178–81, 332
  of chastity 163
  Christian 333
  to the dead 71
  of devotion 132
  essential articles of 340
  of fidelity 163
  filial 172
  and general rules 161–4 *passim*, 170–8
      passim
  to God 176
  of gratitude 79, 162, 174, 332
  of justice 163
  of law-giver 81
  of man of rank 64
  moral 333–5
  of politeness 163
  to public interest 332
  of religion 170, 176–7, 334
  of restitution 64, 339
  rule(s) of 162, 176, 202, 329, 340
  sense of 109, 162, 164, 170–2, 176–8,
      192
  and society 163
  of soldier 133, 153
  in stoicism 277, 281
  of the virtues 163, 209

E

ear-picker 182
earth:
  masters of 57
  oppressors of 76
  vice-regent upon 128, 130
earthquake 136, 167
eclectics, the 300
Edinburgh 124
education 164, 245, 260, 279
  artificial and refined 139
  domestic 222
  of imagination 200
  liberal 201
  public 222 & n.
  by rules 163
  of savage 206–7
  secret of 259
  and sense of beauty 200
  of the young 222, 245, 259, 335
effeminacy:
  love as 205–6
  tears as 46
Egoism, *see* self-love
elegance 123, 175–6
eloquence:

ancient 240
  of Cicero 286
  of faction-leaders 232
  of Mandeville 308
  masculine 197
  modern 240
Elysium 91
emotion(s):
  distinguishing kinds of 324–5
  expression of 207
  flattening or bringing down of 22–3,
    26, 45
  moderation of 76–7
  variations in kinds of 324
  see also passion; spectator
emulation 50, 62, 114, 229, 309
ends:
  adjustment of means to produce 87, 179,
    185
  of deity 300
  dist. motive 18, 67
  of man 106, 267–8
  of nature 77–8, 87, 105
enemy(-ies) 48, 54, 96, 98, 100, 102, 139
  contempt for 206
  of God 166
  literary 125
  public 155
  secret 146
  sympathy with 36
England 72, 125, 208
  and France 222, 229
  and Scotland 223
  see also Great Britain
envy 41–2, 44–7, 58, 98, 140, 152, 159, 164,
    226–30, 254, 257
  defect of 228, 243–4, 246, 250, 311
  of greatness 51
  of men of rank and power 56
Epicurean(s) 281
  sage 216
  system 307
equals 63, 66, 80–2, 132, 145, 152, 212–14,
    256, 260, 297, 336
equality 184 n., 185
equipage 64, 182, 186, 256, 309, 313
equity 87 n., 323
  natural, rules of 341
  sense of 103
equivocation:
  man of, and casuistry 339
estate, forfeiture of 168
  injury to 82, 269
esteem 33, 38, 41, 58, 63, 72, 79, 90, 95, 97,
    162, 166, 168, 177–8, 189, 201, 209,
    213–14, 216, 243, 254–5, 261, 263,
    269–70, 272, 283, 294–5, 297, 316,
    334, 336
  and admiration 60, 77, 114, 238, 240,
    252, 259, 328
  and approbation 61, 68, 85, 109 n., 146,
    190, 224–5, 304, 307, 310
  due 108
  of equals 66
  of mankind 85
  mistaken 114–15
  proper, natural object of 92 n., 265, 298,
    300, 309–11
  and society 85
  universal 60
  for worthless men 239–40
  see also self-estimation
eternity 236, 290
ethics:
  Christian 24 n., 25, 171, 178, 236, 300 n.,
    301, 333
  science of 329
  Smith's lectures on 67 n., 164 n.,
    189–90 n., 265 n., 316 n.
  useful part of moral philosophy 340
eulogy 123, 197
Europe 54, 136, 230
  commerce of 136
  jails of 206
  ladies of 199
Europeans 199, 205
evil(s) 53, 59–61, 76, 77, 82–4, 96, 99, 105
  abhorrence of 200
  Epicurean attitude to 296–7
  moral 323, 325
  natural 239, 244
  positive 78–9
  returned for evil done 68
  stoic attitude to 280, 283
  without design/unintended 106, 108
execration, proper object of 137
execution 47, 49, 120, 323
expiation 107
exposition:
  of infants 210

F

faction(s) 125, 170
  civil 151, 155, 232
  contest of 245, 282
  as corrupting moral sentiments 156
  ecclesiastical 155
  injustice of 146
  laws of 155
  literary 125
  and prudence 216
  public 231
  as school for forming man's temper
    245–6

faction(s) (*cont.*):
  violence of 146, 242
  see also cabals
faculty(-ies) 19
  of mind 19, 265, 269–70, 272, 314,
    318–19, 321–3
  moral 158–9, 164 n., 165–6, 319, 323,
    326
  of speech 336
  of understanding 260–1
fair-sex, *see* woman/women
falsehood:
  abhorrence of 167–8
  in barbarous nations 208
  of candidates for highest station 63–4
  effect on those familiar with 200–1
  ignominy of 339
  involuntary 337
  of vain and proud men 257
  vice of 332
fame:
  contempt of 33
  love of just 116–17, 309
family(-ies) 39–40, 219–24
fanaticism:
  corrupts moral sentiments 155–6
  and spirit of system 232–3
fashion:
  and beauty 194–200
  man of 63
  see also custom
  and moral sentiments 200–11
fear(s):
  command of 238–41, 263
  of death 120, 156, 203, 230
  derived from imagination 30
  natural 92 n., 116, 164, 169
  religious 164
  as response to anger 36–7
  as tormentor 12
feeling(s):
  capacity/incapacity for 94–6
  command of 152
  and the dead 71
  function of 320
  natural 92 n., 148
  passive 137, 139–41, 145–6
  sense and 320
  sympathetic 152, 294
  see also sentiment(s)
fellow-citizen(s) 53, 81, 118
  welfare of 231–2
fellow-feeling 10–4, 34, 39, 43–4, 51, 58,
    70–8 *passim*, 190, 232
  for agreeable emotion 45
  for bodily passions of others 143–4
  and fidelity 163, 169, 332–3
  general nature of 90

for human misery 226
  imperfect 60
  and resentment 74–6, 78
  response to lack of 21
  with success 140
  see also compassion; pity; spectator;
    sympathy
flatterer/flatterers/flattery 56, 63, 256–7,
    309
Flanders 132
folly(-ies) 62–4, 103, 106, 115, 130, 311
fortitude:
  in Aristotle 270–1
  in Epicurean philosophy 297
  in Plato 268
Fortunate Islands 32
fortune:
  accession of 45
  conduct of man lifted by good 40–1
  external 212–16 *passim*
  influence on sentiments 11, 58, 92–108,
    252–3
  injury to 142–3
  prudence in care of 216
  road to 63–4
  of society versus individual 89–90
  see also misfortune
France:
  Court of 204
  and Great Britain compared 229
frankness 55, 201, 337
fraud:
  abhorrence of 89, 167–8
  of candidates for highest station 64
freedom, spirit of 201
French people:
  emotion expressed by 207
  natural enemies 230
French Revolution, the 229 n., 231 n.
friend(s) 48, 72, 97–8, 120–5 *passim*, 142–6
    passim
  bounds on generosity 172
  company of 22–3
  vs impartial spectator 129
  judgment of 16–17
  too generous and affectionate 40
friendship 32–3, 39–43 *passim*, 47, 56,
    90
  actions required by 174
  and beneficence 219–26, 303
  deprivation of 39
  in love 33
  obligation to 80
  and the prudent man 214
  and self-estimation 256
  as social passion 38–40
  and vanity 257
  variations in sentiment of 328

frugality:
  and custom 204, 209
  esteem for 189–90
  and the prudent man 213–15
  as virtue 242, 271
  virtue of the poor 201
fury(-ies):
  of conscience 118
  of own passions 157, 160–1, 263
  of remorse 65
  of resentment 27, 38, 105, 172

G

gaiety 42, 201–4, 246, 280
gallantry 55, 121, 332
game(s):
  of hazard 150
  of human life 278–81
  of human society 234
generosity:
  admiration for 167
  dist. humanity 190–1
  in love 33
  propriety and prudence of 137, 175, 190
  as social passion 38
  standard of impartial spectator for 137
  as virtue/duty 79–80, 172, 174–5, 190–1
  see also heroism
Germany 132
Glasgow 124
Glasgow University **29**, 124 n., 265 n.,
    301 n.
  library 385, 388
glory:
  love of 117, 259, 309
  of riches 64
God(s) 48, 59, 77, 91–2, 133 n., 164, 168
  accountability to 111 n.
  admiration for 105–6, 253
  benevolence of 166, 235–6, 277, 292, 300,
    305
  in Christian doctrine 77, 91–2, 132–4,
    387, 400
  duty to obey 171, 176
  in Eclectic philosophy 300–1
  as judge of the world 105, 128 n., 130–4,
    156, 400
  justice of 91–2
  intends universal happiness 166, 235–7
  laws of and virtue and vice 91–2, 161,
    163–70
  made man the judge of mankind 128–30
  non-existence of 118
  reason for loving virtue 91–2 n.
  in Stoic doctrine 36, 59–60 n., 156, 236,
    274, 276–8, 281, 289–90, 292

  and vanity 250–1
  wisdom of 87, 92, 106, 128 n., 166,
    169–70, 236, 253, 277, 290, 292,
    300
good 67–8, 99
  the greatest 59, 81–2, 303
  and propriety 79
  public 302
  universal 235–6
  of whole vs part 292
  see also intentions
government(s) 56, 64, 99
  administrators in 56
  authority of 340
  beauty or deformity of 187
  civil 80, 186–7, 318
  constitution(s) of 185–6, 231
  European 60
  institution of 80
  and obedience 318
  persons conducting administration in 56
  ideal plan of 234
  system of 185, 232
  and tyranny 340–1
  see also law; state
grace(s) 58–9, 63–4, 133, 242
grammar 175–6, 327
gratitude 15, 24, 28, 31, 37, 56, 93, 105
  and animate/inanimate objects 94–5
  and beneficence/benevolence 81–2, 225,
    301, 324
  duties of 79, 171–2, 174
  and fellow-feeling 70, 73, 75
  gratification of 94–8
  and justice 82
  law of 162
  object of 69–70, 94–7
  obligation of 174
  and pleasure 94–8, 101
  and resentment 67–74, 76 n., 94–7,
    171–2, 324
  and reward 67–72, 81, 101, 301
  rules of 174
  and sense of duty 162, 174
  and sense of merit 68–76, 78–9, 81, 225
  and society 85–6
  and sympathy/sympathetic 71–6, 78, 85,
    225, 238, 264, 317, 326–7
  see also ingratitude
gravity of demeanour 47, 246–7
great, the 51, 53, 55–6, 61–5
  adulation of 65
  air and manner of 53–5, 194–5
  circumstances of 179, 182–3, 186
  drawing-rooms of 63
  respect for 226
  vices of 201
  see also man, of rank

Great Britain 72
  and France compared 229
  see also England
Great Judge, *see* God
Great Superior 170
Greece:
  effect of disorder in ancient 281–2
  language of 269
  people of 283–4
  theatre of 30
  treatment of new-born infants in 210
grief:
  alleviated by sympathy 14–15
  as component of remorse 85
  for fellows 10–11, 15–17
  of fellows 70
  as musical passion 37
  painful 42
  and propriety/sympathy 16–18, 21, 24,
    27–8, 40–9, 70, 226, 317
  renewal of 15
  and self-command 145–6
  as selfish passion 40–3
  see also sorrow(s)
guilt 84, 101, 107
  conscience of man with 118–19
  see also design; piacular guilt
Guinea 199

H

habit:
  and the imagination 31, 194, 200
  virtue 270–2, 324, 329
  of visual correction 135
  see also custom
Hamlet 259
happiness 36–7, 39, 41, 45, 51–2, 58, 66,
    92, 119, 132, 139, 166, 168, 181–2,
    185–7
  ancient philosophers' views on 282–3
  and approbation 114, 326
  components of 41–5, 109, 149
  concern for 262
  constitution should promote 185–6
  eternal 133
  effect of hatred and anger on 37–8
  effect of individual's character on 212–18
  in Epicurean philosophy 295–7, 307
  and greatness 65
  and love 113
  means of 182, 184
  motive for hurting or disturbing 218
  natural state of 121
  of oneself 82–3, 139, 212–13, 262, 266–7,
    289, 304–5, 308, 315
  of others 9–13, 24, 68, 70, 106–7, 137,

    185, 218–22, 262, 267, 302–3, 322,
    327
  romantic 31–2
  of society and individual 89–91, 187, 205,
    227, 229, 232, 326
  and Stoics 147, 274 n., 277–82 *passim*,
    290
  universal 106, 185, 235–7, 289
  see also aesthetics; joy
harmony:
  with mankind 85
  of sentiment 78
hatred 34–40, 53, 68–9, 79, 83–4, 89,
    216–17, 243–4
  man's desire not to be object of 113–14,
    117–19
  national 229–30
  of self 84
  for violator of justice 84–5
hazards:
  unequal games of 150
  of war 134, 146, 152, 249
health 28, 45, 58–9, 183, 216
Heaven 101
  anger of 181
  appeal to 169
Henriade 196
heretics 155
heroes/heroism 99, 192, 242
  admiration of 173, 232
  Greek 282–4
  of history 134, 238–9
  nations of 206
  remembrance of 238–9
  school of 58, 60
Highlands/Highlanders 223
highwayman 120, 330
historian(s) 54, 56, 285
history 74, 76, 150, 160, 223, 238, 240, 284
  of jurisprudence 342
  of moral philosophy 265–327
Holland 209
honesty, best policy 63
honour(s) 23, 33, 36, 43, 51–2, 55, 57,
    72, 75, 106, 118, 265, 268, 295,
    310–11
  and ambition 65
  laws of 60
  race for 83
  sense of 23, 148, 156, 322
hospitality 163, 174, 209, 337
human form:
  beauty in 198–9
humanity:
  great society of 229
  love of 55, 137
  mankind 12, 21, 27, 40–3, 49–51, 53–4,
    56–9, 204–5, 233

protectors of 134
ranks of 50–1
union of 99
virtue of 12, 17, 23, 24 n., 25, 33–4, 38,
    40, 88, 90–1, 107, 136–7, 153,
    166–7, 171–2, 174, 187, 190–1,
    204–5, 233, 306
    see also benevolence; man/men
human life 57, 59 n., 134, 158, 280
    benevolent direction of 292
    as game 278–9
    purpose of 50, 57 n., 59 n.
human nature:
    decent and indecent passions of 27
    dread of death as principle of 13
    effect of passions of 200
    genius of 59
    hatred and resentment 34–5
    hope/fear 132, 169
    perfection of 25, 168, 296
    principle(s) of 13, 43, 128, 165, 177, 266,
        326
    rules of conduct govern 165
    selfish and original passions of 135–7
    science of 319
    and societal improvements 229
    system of 87
    weakness(es) of 26, 128 n., 146, 176–7,
        190, 273 n., 287
    see also man/men passion; self-command
human society, *see* society
humility 41, 247, 260, 305
hypocricy, hypocrites 64, 201

I

imagination:
    anticipates fame 116
    and customary connection 194, 199, 204,
        332
    of illusions 13, 51, 57, 78, 115, 256
    imitation 36–7
    and industry of mankind 183–4
    origin of vanity from 115
    passions arising from 29–34, 77
    principles of 200
    role of 135, 183
    sense of beauty dependent on 200
    of senses of others 9–13, 22
    of sentiments of the dead 71
    and the spectator 116, 118, 127, 135
    and sympathy 3, 12–13, 21–2, 29,
        31, 51–2, 75–6, 116, 219,
        317
    unsocial passions derived from 34–8
    and vision 135
impartiality, *see* spectator, impartial

impropriety 16, 18–19, 24, 37, 67, 81, 93,
    96, 188, 209, 220, 277
    of affections 74, 220
    disapprobation of 78, 118
    and disproportion 67
    and hatred 79
    of motives 71
    of other men's affections 16–23
    of own passions 110
    sense of 12, 75, 85, 138 n., 194, 200–1,
        263
    and shame 85
    see also propriety
imprudence:
    habitual 63
    combined with other vices 216–17
imputation 119–22, 127
indignation 82–4, 88–91
    divine 92
    expression of 240
    of false imputation of crime 119–20
    natural 101
    object of 118, 138, 298
    revenge as object of 77
    of spectator 73, 76, 84
    at unjust superiority 256–7, 261
    want of proper 243–4
individual:
    dist. society 89–90, 233, 323, 326
    and happiness of others 218–27
    and his/her own happiness 212–17
    principally recommended to his own care
        219
    rights of 80
induction:
    source of moral rules 159–60, 319–20
industry 215
    founded upon deception 183–4
    habit of 304
    perseverance in practice of 189–90
    rousing of 169
    and success 166–7
    as virtue 242
infants, *see* child/children
inferiors, inferiority 52, 55, 260–1
inhabitant of the breast, *see* spectator
inhumanity 15, 94, 103
injury(-ies) 15, 34–5, 38–9, 52, 71, 77, 95,
    119, 122, 153, 268, 273, 338 n.
    and justice 79, 80–1, 91, 241, 310, 330–1,
        335, 340
    mutual 81, 85
    to others 136 n., 137–8
    and punishment 69, 91, 95–6
    and resentment 16, 21, 24, 27, 99, 172,
        191, 244, 324
    response to 80–81
    and right 80–1

injury(-ies) (*cont.*):
    to self, insensibility to 244–5
    and self-restraint 263
    and society 86, 89–90
    to sovereign 99
injustice 35, 57, 63, 84, 96, 98, 128 n.,
       141 n., 249, 252, 261, 323, 330
    abhorrence of 89
    deformity of 136 n., 137
    effect on those accustomed to 200–1
    God(s) as avenger(s) of 14, 169–70
    indignation at 119–21
    and merit 269
    and negligence 102–3
    perseverance in 158
    and propriety 270
    and prudence 217
    and punishment 88, 91, 102, 120
    and resentment 79, 218
    restrained by dread of death 13
    and self-love 304
    in society 81, 86, 88
    and valour 241, 264
    as vice 299
innocence:
    injured 119–22, 131–2, 144, 167
    resentment is security of 79
innovation, spirit of 231–2
instinct(s):
    basic to speech 336
    for compassion 152
    directed by nature 77–8
    original (moral sense) 165
    of pride 260–1
    and reason 78
institution(s):
    of nature 222
    positive 318, 341
    to promote public welfare 185
instruments 35–6, 337
intemperance 152
    disapproval of 45, 299
intention(s) 184 n.
    and causes 73–4, 94–7 *passim*
    and nature 37, 87
    not object of punishment 100,
       105–6
    in praise or blame for an action 92–8,
       101–2, 106
    of providence 128 n.
    see also motive(s)
interest(s) 43
    of government 340
    of one vs many 91, 138, 140, 229
    own vs others 134–41, 172–3, 191,
       228–30, 235, 262, 275, 309
    public of society 88, 90, 184–6 n.,
       228–30, 235, 240, 332

    private 172–3, 235, 266, 304–5, 307–9,
       315, 341
    see also self-love; utility
international relations 154–5, 228–30
invisible hand:
    in distribution of necessaries 184–5
Ionic architecture 196
irreligion 118
Italy 208, 217
Italian people 197, 207

J

Jesuit 198
Jew's-box 180
joy:
    as musical passion 37
    of prosperity 139–40
    as selfish passion 40–3
    and sociability 110–11
    sympathy with 11, 14–16, 36–7, 40–1,
       43–7, 50–1, 70
    see also envy; happiness
judge(s) 60, 73, 99, 126, 147, 157, 172, 207
    appointment of and rules for 340
    functions of 340
    of hearts 105
    and jurisprudence 330
    man judge of mankind 128–30 n., 130–1
    of right/wrong (clergy) 334
    and spectator 85, 113, 129 n., 193, 227–8
    supreme 130
    within 130 n., 134, 137, 141 n., 245, 247,
       262
    of the world 121, 128 n., 131, 134, 156
judgment(s) 19–21, 25, 41, 43, 54–5, 81,
       122, 296–7, 335–6
    of another man's faculty 19
    faculty of 267
    influence of custom and fashion on 155,
       194–200 *passim*
    moral 21
    others' 110, 122–3, 128–30 n., 130–1
    own 122–3, 128–30 n., 130–1, 156, 158,
       234
    regulated by general rules 160
    regulated by maxims of morality 319–20
    of supreme arbiter/judge, etc. 130–1
    of the world 129
    see also spectator; sympathy
judicatory(-ure):
    court/s of 160
    and regular jurisprudence 341
jurisprudence:
    in Aristotle 269, 341
    history of 342
    natural 218, 329–33

and casuistry 329–33
and laws of all nations 341
and positive law 340
justice 130, 141 n., 184, 209, 217
approval of 298–9
in Aristotle 269, 341, 389, 391–2
basis of 102
and beneficence 78–82, 86, 218, 262, 390
commutative 269
distributive 269
duty of 163
in Epicurus 297
equitable 62
exact 132, 167, 175–6
and force 79–80, 88, 329–30
of God 91–2, 128 n., 131–2, 169–70, 383, 387, 389–93, 398–400
in Hume 80 n.
and international law 155, 228, 341–42
kinds of 269–70, 390, 392, 396–7
laws of 82, 84, 87–8, 154, 218, 341–2
and merit 82, 132–4, 241
motivation for 262
natural 340–1
and natural jurisprudence 218, 329–30, 340–2
necessary rule of 105
a negative virtue 82
in Plato 269–70, 341
dist. police 341
and propriety 82, 91 n., 190, 275 n.
and prudence 149–50, 217, 297–9
and punishment 86–91, 105, 217, 330, 335, 389–95
and resentment 79, 96
and reward 81–2, 166–67
rules of 63, 80, 82, 89, 105, 149, 155, 175–6, 216, 319, 327–35, 339, 340–1
sacred laws of 83–4
sense of 82, 136, 153, 339, 341
natural sentiments of 341
as pillar of society 84, 86–9
and utility 87–91, 190, 264, 297, 383, 394, 398–9
as a virtue 29, 79–82, 166–7, 175, 218, 237, 241, 262, 264, 269–70, 297
governing the world 141
justitia attributrix/expletrix 269–70

K

kindness 33, 38, 40, 72, 80–1, 107, 125, 225–6
kings:
bounty of 102
respect for 52–4
servants of people 53
knave(-ry) 167–8, 216
knowledge 53–5, 213, 237, 249, 272, 299

L

labour(s) 32–3, 50, 55, 57, 136, 183–4, 190, 205, 297
ladies, *see* woman(women)
landlord 184
landscape, seen through a window 135
language:
ambiguity of 312
English 124, 273 n.
fashionable 64
good 62
Greek 269
insufficiency of 328
Lares, the 94
laughter 60
law(s):
above the 63–4
ancient 94 n., 95 n.
Aquilian 104
of barbarous nations 100, 341
of Christianity 25
civil 87 n., 190, 218, 318–19
of civilized nations 81, 100
condition for being above 63–4
of the Deity 28, 161, 163–70
discipline of 100, 103
English 100 n.
European 100 n.
of faction 155
and general rules 165–6, 340–1
and government 342
human 28, 168
of honour 60
of justice 82, 84, 87–8, 154, 218, 341
of motion 165
of nations 155, 228, 341–2
and natural jurisprudence 340–2
of Nature 82, 148, 273
and negligence 102–4
perfect system of 233–4
philosophy of 341–2
positive 318–19, 340–1
of retaliation 71, 82–4
Roman 102 n., 104, 190
and sanctions 166
Scots 100, 103
and security 222–3, 242
sentence agreeable to 128
and sexual love 28, 33
of society 9, 33, 76
and sovereign/superior 166

law(s) (*cont.*):
   as standard of morals 318–19
   as standard of right and wrong 318,
      340
   and station of life 63–4
   unalterable 148
   of war 90, 155, 342, 389, 391
law-giver(s) 81, 134
lawyer(s) 341
leader(s) 336
   political 231–4
   in science and taste 20
legislator(s) 63, 216, 232, 242, 250
legislature 185, 234
letters, men of 124–6, 228, 285
levees 257
liar, conscience of 115, 336–7
liberty 32, 151, 290
   barter of 57
   cause of 238
   defence of 297
   loss of 51, 81
   lovers of 286
   personal 150
   of Rome 192
   of states 230
   of suicide 279
licentiousness 89, 200–1, 306–14, 339
life(-ves):
   according to nature (stoics) 273,
      279–81
   amusements of 202, 246
   animal 87
   to come 91, 132–3, 169, 170
   common 18, 41, 48, 145
   contemplative 236
   contempt of 288
   director of 59
   disorders of 158
   enjoyments of 246
   a game of skill (stoics) 278–9
   happiness in 132, 185
   human, *see* human life
   labours of 57, 183
   last dregs of 181
   and laws of justice 84
   love of 77
   of mortification 133
   necessaries of 184–5
   of neighbour 153
   peaceable 242
   periods of 201–2
   pleasures of 246
   poetic imagination of 32
   precariousness of 136
   private 57, 150, 181, 202, 242, 252
   proper business of 292–3
   public 150, 181

   purpose of 50
   ranks/states of 50, 56, 181, 185, 201–2,
      209, 222
   respect for 339
   of repentance 133
   sacrifice of millions of 137
   stations of 63
   taking of 60
   a two-penny stake in 279
linen manufacture 185
lions, den of 86
looking-glass/mirror analogy 110, 112
love 29, 31–2, 37, 39, 90, 94, 97
   as agreeable passion/sentiment 15, 39
   and ambition 57
   and approbation 68
   of art and contrivance 185
   of children 142
   in Christian ethics 24 n., 25, 171,
      300 n.
   of country 171, 227–34, 238
   deserved 113
   desire for 113
   of dignity 137
   disappointment in 29
   of distinction 182
   effect of 39–40
   of equals 66
   of fame 117, 309
   in the family 39–40, 142–3, 172, 202,
      205–6, 219–23
   and fellow-feeling 73
   dist. friendship 225
   of God/neighbour/self 171
   and gratitude 68
   of the honourable 137
   and the imagination 31–3
   of life 77
   of mankind 55–6, 137, 171, 229
   of music 37
   of neighbour 25, 137
   objects of 91, 113, 245
   passion of 49
   of Phaedra 33
   and pity 40
   of pleasure 78, 312
   of praise 126–7
   as principle of action 300
   of propriety 59
   Rochefoucauld on 57
   of the sexes 28, 31–3, 49, 52, 78, 225,
      312, 335
   and society 85–6, 88
   and sympathy 70, 75, 85
   of system 185
   and virtue 91, 117
   weakness of 205
loyalty 53

lust 164, 312
luxury 35, 184, 312–13

M

machine(s) 7, 19, 179–87, 192, 316, 326–7
  see also system
magistrate 81, 231, 318, 340
magnanimity 47–9, 53, 58–60, 108, 138,
    244, 252
  according to Aristotle 258, 271
  admiration of 58 n., 167
  approval of 298–9
  in Plato 268
  vs pride 255, 258, 310–11
  and prudence 216, 298–9
  and resentment 38
  Roman 56, 65
  of savages 205–6
  and self-command 238–9, 310–11
  stoical 136 n., 141 n., 293
  virtue of 25–6, 176, 268, 271, 306–7, 310,
    328–9
Mahomet (Voltaire) 177
malice 42, 77, 96, 146, 235, 243, 301
man/men:
  made for action 106
  brave 59 n., 60
  of honour 163
  of letters 123–4
  mean spirited 34–5, 56–7, 243–4, 246
  poor 51, 64, 138, 181
  proud 255–9, 261
  prudent 207–16, 264
  of public spirit 185, 190–2, 232–3
  of rank 50–5, 62–6, 197
  rich 50, 184–5
  solitary 110–11
  of system 231 n., 233–4
  weak and imperfect 77, 106, 117, 121,
    131, 145, 148, 151, 156, 237,
    252–3, 273 n., 281, 305
  wise 58–9, 87, 117, 121–2, 126–7, 146–8,
    151, 156, 231, 234–6, 245, 247,
    249, 253, 259, 275–9 n., 281,
    289–91, 306
  of woman 28
  see also humanity; human life; human
    nature; spectator
manners 35, 125, 146, 201–11, 224, 240,
    251, 329, 334, 341
manufactures 185, 229
market, bidder in 282
marriage 47, 205–6
masters:
  artistic 26
  of the earth 57, 185

  of fashion 197
  political 53
  of property 179, 182
  of self 23, 59 n., 145, 278
  of slaves 206, 288
*Mathematical Principles of Natural
    Philosophy* 124
mathematicians/mathematics 124–5, 189
maxims 89, 92–3, 163, 172, 174–5, 210,
    233–4, 299, 319–22, 332
means 77–8, 87, 179–86
Meditations, The (Marcus Aurelius)
    236–7
melancholy 13, 32, 94, 287
merchants 86, 185
merit 18, 31, 41, 54, 62–4, 67–108 *passim*,
    121–2, 126–7, 134, 170, 247–9
  see also actions; demerit; intentions
metaphor 268
military profession 203–4
mind, the:
  and body 87
  composure of 37–8, 245
  constitution of 323
  elevation of 41, 131
  eye of 135
  faculty of 19, 265, 269, 314, 319, 321–2
  harmony of 337
  natural state of 45, 273 n., 312, 318
  perception of own 110
  tranquility of 22–3, 37, 131, 166, 181,
    208, 244, 273 n., 296–7, 307
ministers 56, 98, 154, 217, 257
Minorca 192
mirth, effect of 14
miser 173–4
misery:
  and compassion 73, 226
  in Epicurean philosophy 295–6
  fellow-feeling/sympathy with 9–10,
    12–13, 51, 220, 235, 322
  of others 68, 86, 138–9, 219–20
  source of 149–50
misfortune:
  compassion with 46, 56
  of evil without design 106
  external 144
  malicious pleasure in 68
  private 141–56 *passim*
  with remedy 150–2
  sympathy with 51–2, 60, 78, 83, 139–40
mob 10, 35, 47, 62, 226, 253
moderation 238, 268–9, 271
monarchies 56
monks 120, 133–4, 401
  see also clergy-man
moralists 62, 139–42, 237–9, 328–9,
    340–1

morality:
  books of 340
  divine 300
  lessons of 139
  obligations of 170
  rules/maxims of 89, 159, 161, 164,
    319–20, 327, 329
  stoic 288, 292
  system of 265, 293
moral philosophy:
  ancient moralists treatment of rules of
    327–9, 341
  authority of rules of 161–70
  ethics and jurisprudence as useful parts of
    340
  formation of rules of 159–60, 319–20
  jurisprudence and casuistry writers'
    treatment of 329–31
  principle of approbation in 314–15
  purpose of all systems of 293
  sense 321
  systems of 265–342
  see also Hutcheson
mortality 12, 131–2
mortification 41, 53, 133–4, 279
motive 18, 38
  and propriety 71–8, 82–5, 129 n., 218
  for virtue 115, 131, 171–8 *passim*, 300,
    302–5, 308–9, 311
Muscovy 186
Munster, treaty of 230
murderer(s) 52, 71, 73, 86, 90–1, 100,
    103 n., 159, 177, 217
music 35, 37, 195, 197, 248, 313

N

nation(s) 56, 154–5, 184, 228
  civilized 81, 100–1, 199, 204, 207–9, 341
Nature/nature 28, 47, 52, 58–9, 65–6, 71,
    77, 79, 86, 105, 108, 116–17, 122,
    128–30, 137, 140, 142, 159, 168–9,
    188, 219, 225–7, 289, 298
  anticipations of 92, 164
  Author of 77, 93, 105, 128, 166, 169, 273
  and benevolence 137
  and care of individuals 212, 219
  commonwealth of 140
  constitution of 85
  deception by 183
  dignity of 132
  Director of 78, 235
  discipline of 145
  doctrine of 53, 91
  economy of 77, 321
  ends of 37, 77–8, 87, 105, 142, 148, 166,
    198

intention and gratitude of 37, 105, 225
judge constituted by 130
law dictated by 82
and laws of God 87, 163–4, 273
necessities of 50
oeconomy of 77, 321
vs philosophy 91 n., 163–4, 287, 292–3,
    399
precept of 25
purposes of 87
and retaliation 71, 82
rewards of 128–9, 147–8, 168
rules of 128–9, 168
ruling principle in 141
and self-preservation 77, 82, 212, 287
and society 37, 86, 116–17, 148
state of 318
in stoicism 58, 272–5, 289
system of 36, 292
teaching of 11, 22, 47, 53, 58, 86, 91, 106,
    128, 130, 134, 274, 292–3
voice of 212
wisdom of 107, 220, 226
works of 166
see also human nature
necessaries 184
necessities 50, 205, 212–13, 268
negligence 102–3, 107
negotiation/s 154, 230
negro 206
neighbour(s) 81, 122
  resentment against 218
  dependence upon 63
  hurt to 79, 82–3, 175
  and justice 84, 269, 330, 339
  life of 153, 339
  love of 25, 137, 171
  relations with 224
  states or nations as 229–30
nobility 72, 234
nobleman/men 43–4
  French 207
  Polish 204
North America 199
North Americans 208

O

oaths 339
obedience 81, 166, 236, 250, 302, 305,
    318–19
obligation(s) 68, 75, 274
  to beneficence 79–80
  of contracts 339
  to friendship 80
  of gratitude 174
  ground of 305

to justice 79–80, 330, 333, 339
of morality 170
to obedience 305
society without 86
oblivion 65
obloquy 144
obscurity 51, 128, 149, 338
odes 124
oeconomy 50, 173, 209, 321
of greatness 183–4
habit of 304
of nature 77
office(s):
(mutual) good 39, 70, 72, 79, 81, 85–6,
95, 106–7, 153, 172, 218, 221,
224–5, 235, 256, 264, 297, 301
of the mind 269–70, 319
moral 28, 172, 174, 270, 297
of the moral faculties 165
officer(s) 54, 60, 95, 101, 132–3, 191, 202–3,
209
Offices (Cicero) 291–2, 329, 340–1
old age 42, 182, 201–2, 219, 246, 260
Olympia 250
opinion, public 123–5, 257
oracle:
and Socrates 251
orators:
Roman 207–8
order 58–9
and beauty 185, 327
and frugality 204
natural, of beneficence 218–30
of Providence 288
of society 52, 61, 88, 91, 226, 253, 316
of universe/world 36, 168, 253, 274–5,
316
order(s) (social groups) 196, 230–1, 234–5,
267, 341
Origen 288 n.
Orphan of China (Voltaire) 227
ostentation:
in display of piety 142
of vain man 255–7, 259

P

pain:
of body 29–31, 44, 295–6, 299
and constancy 59, 244, 278, 283
and custom 206–7
depends on sense and feeling 320
Epicurus on 295–9 *passim*
of mind 44
and resentment 94–7
and sympathy 14, 16, 24, 29–31, 44, 61,
143–4, 156

see also pleasure; sympathy
painting 26, 35, 248, 313
palace(s) 35, 50, 179
paradoxes, of stoics 289, 291
parasite 257
parent(s) 39–40, 81, 142–5, 171–2, 202, 210,
219–27 *passim*, 233
parliament, member of 173
parsimony 173, 204, 213, 215, 256
particle, man as 59 n., 276
partners, in trade 224
party(-ies) 155–6, 215, 232–3, 250, 286, 307
passion(s) 10–13, 15–16, 21–8, 37–59
ancient division of 237
benevolent 76 n., 172, 301
bodily 27–31, 143, 295
and self-command 205, 237–43, 278
degrees consistent with propriety 27–43,
141, 273 n.
gratitude and resentment as 68–9
proper duty of each 269
gratification of 262–3
honourable 122
of the imagination 29–38, 77
malevolent 172
and moral sense 322–6
musical 37
original 9, 16, 34, 42, 44, 46 n., 48, 135
partiality of 156–8
pitch of 338
Plato on 267–8
presumptuous 137
public 187
secondary 33
selfish 40–3, 135, 140, 141 n., 156 n., 157,
172–4, 244–5, 262, 290–3, 308–10,
312, 317
social/unsocial 34–40, 42, 46 n., 110, 172,
243–4, 262
see also emotions; pleasure
patience 30, 34, 53, 56, 156, 205, 283
patriot(s)/-ism 35, 60, 75 n., 155, 185, 228,
232, 282
people 53, 56–7, 60, 65, 101, 207, 233,
341
perception and moral judgement 134–5,
165, 187–8, 192–3, 266, 320–5, 327
perfection:
divine/infinite 91–2 n., 132, 164, 166,
235, 300, 305
in Epicurus 296
of human nature 25, 51–2, 60, 105, 168,
274, 300
in Hutcheson 303
moral 145, 175–6, 216, 303, 324, 327
in Plato 268, 270
of policy and law 185, 234
and propriety 25–6, 247–9

perfection (*cont.*):
  in Stoic doctrine **8**, 36, 58 n., 60 n.,
      141 n., 274, 277, 290–1
  of the world/universe 274
Pharsalia 65, 252
Philippics (Demosthenes) 240
philosopher(s) 18, 34, 187, 210, 228, 237,
      258 (Aristotle), 297 (Epicurus), 299,
      307, 326
  Academic 216, 282
  of former ages 28, 134, 306–7, 316, 340
  and casuists 340
  contemplative 237
  cynical 276
  Eclectics 140, 281–5, 300
  great (Socrates) 238
  ingenious (Hutcheson) 322
  indulgent (Aristotle) 329
  an ingenious and agreeable (Hume) 179
  a late (Butler) 43
  natural 124–5
  Peripatetic 216, 273, 282
  profession of 33–4
  splenetic 127
  stoical 59 n.
  superficial (Price) 229 n.
  two sets of 139
  virtues of 63
philosophy 12, 53, 136, 139, 248
  ancient 91, 281, 294
  atomical 299
  Epicurean 294, 296–9
  humble 120
  of law 341
  moral 21, 57, 313–14, 340
  two useful parts of 340
  two questions of 265–6, 314–15
  natural 313–14
  vs nature 91 n., 163–4, 287, 292–3, 399
  Platonist 301
  splenetic 183
  stoical 58–60, 141 n., 277–8 n., 280–1,
      292–3
  system(s) of 21, 265–342, 313
  and theology 133 n., 171
  of vision 135
  see also moral philosophy
physic 150
physician 151, 288–9
piacular guilt 107, 338
piety 142, 301
pilot (ship's) 59
pistol 100
pity 9, 10, 14 n., 20, 40, 43, 84–5, 88, 178,
      226, 243, 304
  see also compassion
place, *see* aldermen, wives of
plagiarism 122, 309 n.

plan 36, 98–9, 166, 169, 173, 230, 232, 234,
      268, 289, 292
  see also system
plant, mechanism of 87
Platonists 300
pleasure(s):
  and ambition 65, 150
  and beauty 179–85 *passim*
  causes of 94–6, 101
  and desire 320
  Epicurus on 295–7, 299
  and gratitude 94–8
  vs honour 65
  Hume on 46 n., 179
  love of 78, 238, 268, 312
  in misfortune of others 68
  and pain 44, 78, 121–2, 295–7, 299
  and praise-worthiness 114–17
  of self-approbation 303
  and self-command 145–8 *passim*, 189–90
  and self-love 308, 312
  sensibility to 246
  of society/solitude 148, 337
  of sympathy 13–16, 46 n.
  sympathy with 44, 219
  and temperance 59, 278, 297
  of utility 88 n., 179–80, 182, 327
  and vanity 50, 150, 182
  see also pain
poet(s) 32, 58, 131, 134, 143, 228
  character of 123–6, 248–9
  society of 126
poetry 26, 123–4, 195, 248
police 3, 90, 102, 185–6, 341–2
policy 63, 90, 187, 234
politeness 15, 42, 54–5, 163, 201, 204–7,
      256, 258
politics 186
poverty 43, 50–1, 59, 61–2, 91, 138–9, 144,
      149, 151, 205, 256, 272–4, 276, 283,
      295, 297, 306
power(s):
  balance of 230
  of civil magistrate 81, 318
  of the Commonwealth 340
  Infinite/superintending/superior 170,
      277, 281, 300, 305
  of man over mankind 128, 130
  national/military 228–9
  pursuit of 50
  of social groups 230–1, 233
praise(s) 25, 45, 59, 77, 80, 92–3, 101, 106,
      126
  due/merited/deserved 20, 25, 77, 92–3,
      101, 106, 109 n., 127, 160, 270,
      290, 303–4, 330
  love of/desire for 113–15, 126–7, 131,
      308–10, 336

unmerited 45, 80, 114–19
praise-worthiness 64, 80, 117, 134, 308–10, 336
  love of 113–15, 126–8, 131
preferment(s) 41, 63, 83, 102, 106, 132, 257
preheminence/pre-eminence 50, 54, 57
prejudice 195, 228–30, 233–4
presumption 55, 62, 81, 167, 247, 249–54 *passim*, 261
pretensions 115, 191, 223, 249–50, 255–61 *passim*, 309
pride 41, 65, 131, 147, 154, 223, 246, 255–61 *passim*, 308–9
prince(s) 54, 60, 63, 72, 173, 217, 226, 234, 285
principle(s):
  active/of action 137, 139, 165, 219, 300, 304–7
  of approval/disapproval 76–7 n., 91, 314–27 *passim*
  of human nature 9, 13, 43, 58–9 n., 76–7 n., 87, 128–9, 134, 141 n., 165, 177, 266, 278
  or instinct 152
  of judgment 128–9
  of laws in all nations 341–2
  man of 163
  of morals 265
  of motion 234
  of religion 170–1
  ruling/governing (reason) 267–8
  of self-approbation/disapprobation 109
prison 35, 151, 284
privileges 230–1, 233–4, 302
profession(s) 63, 201–4, 209, 213, 239, 245, 317
profligacy 63–4, 224
promise(s) 84, 330–3, 339
property 184 n., 297
  and laws of justice 84
  of neighbour 153, 339
Prophets:
  great men as 251
proportion(s), *see* propriety
propriety(-ies) 57–9, 61, 64, 91–2, 105–6, 139, 207
  of affections 16–26 *passim*, 67, 73
  approbation of 78, 82, 93
  and beneficence 79
  and benevolence 301, 304
  and beauty 179–80
  bounds of 141, 273 n.
  customary vs natural 194, 196, 202–4, 207–11
  exact 53, 142, 247–8, 270, 332
  or fitnesses (in stoicism) 291
  and force 79–80
  of generosity 137, 190

of indignation 240
and justice 82, 89, 275 n.
law of 87 n.
love of 59, 278 n.
of machine 179
and merit 18, 67–9, 74–5, 78, 105
and motives 71–8
of other men's affections 16–23
of own sentiments/conduct 110, 112, 116–17, 122, 129, 152, 154, 156, 244
of passions 27–43 *passim*, 242–3, 263
perfect vs common 25–6, 48, 80, 117, 141 n., 247–9
and proportion 67
and prudence 54, 263, 276, 298–9
of punishment 88, 172
recommends self-command 262–4
of resentment 38, 240
rules of 63
propriety of observing rules of justice 89
sense of 38, 67, 74, 76, 88, 136, 143, 159, 170, 172, 188, 190–2, 245–6, 262–4, 308, 338
standard of 139
as standard for self-estimation 247–9
in Stoical philosophy 141, 272–94
and suitableness 67
supported by self-interest 170
and sympathy 16–26, 74
of system 179
and utility 188–9, 264, 305–6
and vanity 308–9
as account of virtue 244, 266–73, 293, 305–7
vs virtue 25–6, 294
prosperity 43, 47, 56, 58–9, 146, 149, 183, 187, 226–31 *passim*, 252–4, 308
  of commonwealth society 81, 88
  effect of 40–1, 45
  external 166, 287, 307
  joy of 70, 139, 226, 254
  of nature 36
  pursuit of 50
  of state and individual 227, 231
  and sympathy 70, 73
  of whole vs part (Stoics) 236–7, 274–5, 289–90
  of the universal world 106, 236
Protestants 177
Providence 36, 59, 128, 166, 185, 274, 276, 278 n., 281, 288–9, 326
  see also God(s)
provinces 173, 256
  privileges of 234
Prudence/prudence 28, 55, 59, 105, 128, 212, 337–8
  effect of exercise of 264

Prudence/prudence (*cont.*):
  in Epicurus 294, 296–7
  and justice 297
  and moderation 47, 263
  objects of 213, 216
  office of 174
  in Plato 268
  in Stoics 59 n., 219
  virtue of 149, 166–7, 173–6, 187, 189,
      192, 212–17, 237–8, 249, 262–4,
      267–8, 270–1, 276, 294–5, 304–7
  and wisdom 216, 299
public, the 35, 41, 50, 69, 95, 98, 116, 123–5,
      132, 162, 189, 208, 214, 251, 311
punishment(s) 67–82, 87–91, 95, 99–103,
      163–70, 172, 176–7, 330, 334–5,
      389–95, 398, 400
  actions as objects of 104–5
  and approbation 77, 88, 90–1
  and beneficence 81, 86
  capital/by death 88, 90–1, 95, 100, 103,
      192, 284 n.
  and contempt 138
  cruelty of 120
  degradation by 60–1
  distribution of 132
  dread of 85–8, 335
  fitness of 78
  of God 163–70
  in imagination 76
  infinite 128
  and intention/motive 99–103, 105
  and justice 79, 84, 87–8, 120
  in life to come 91, 132
  and merit/demerit 86–91, 99–103, 105
  of Nature 168
  and negligence 102–3
  objects of 67, 69–70, 78, 91–2, 105
  propriety of 88, 172
  and resentment 67–72, 74, 77–9, 84, 88,
      99, 102, 105
  and rules of casuistry 334–5
  and shame 60–1
  of suicide 287
pusillanimity 16, 271, 299
Pythagoreans 269

                          Q

quacks:
  civil/religious 249
Quaker, a 178

                          R

raillery, delight in 42–3

rank(s) 38, 50–7, 60, 61, 64, 144, 185,
      194–5, 197, 201–2, 205, 212–22, 226,
      228, 249, 253, 256
rape 100, 332
rationalism, *see* reason
reason:
  artificial refinement of 91, 164
  and conscience 137
  and ends 77–8, 87
  human, weak eye of 128
  and the moral faculty 135 n., 164–5, 189,
      266–70, 315, 318–21
  vs natural principles 87
  and passions 59, 267–72, 275 n.,
      278 n.
  and philosophy 52, 53, 91, 164
  utility of 189
rebel(s)/rebellion 65, 155, 318
rectitude:
  approximation to 248
  of conduct, casuists on 302
  of judgement 156
  perfect 273–4
  of religious man 170
Reformation, the 301
reformer 232–4
regiment 133, 207
religion:
  ancient 107, 164, 184 n.
  authorizes expectation 91
  consolation of 120–1, 400
  duties of 170, 176–7
  and ethics 91–2, 131–4, 163–71, 176–8,
      202–3, 383, 387
  false notions of 132–4, 176–7
  hypocrites of 64
  modern 251
  natural principles of 170
  and rules of morality 163–71
  sentiments of 287
  and superstition 91
  terrors of 164
  see also Christianity; conscience; Roman
      Catholicism
remorse 33, 82, 101, 119–20, 177, 228, 334
  and breach of veracity 338
  fury of 65
  horror of 118, 161
  nature of 85
  see also grief; pity; resentment; shame
repentance 92 n., 101, 133, 158, 161, 244,
      247, 332
  life of 133
republic(s) 267, 277, 281, 285–6
reputation 82, 170, 213, 216, 250, 298
  loss of 33, 54, 61, 125, 132, 142–4, 207,
      269
  love of 309

resentment:
  actions as object of 104–6
  causes and conditions of 94–7
  circumstances engendering 34–5
  when replaced by compassion 53
  of crime 84, 100, 118
  and defence 79
  and demerit 93–107 *passim*
  and design vs event/outcome 104–5
  functions and consequences of 79–80
  furies of/furious 105, 160
  gratification of 68–70, 94–6
  for injury/injustice 218, 244
  and justice 79, 83–4
  moderation of 76–7
  natural 79, 83–4, 90, 107
  and negligence 102, 104
  and pain 94–7
  as passion derived from imagination
    34–8, 71–6
  and propriety 38, 74–5
  and punishment 67–9, 72, 74, 77–9, 84,
    88, 90, 160, 171–2, 218, 389
  and remorse 85
  and revenge 90
  and society 86
  sympathy with/sympathetic 15, 34–8,
    68–79, 83–4, 90, 188
  tormentor of human breast 119
  and treason 99–100
resistance 155, 302
respect 56, 61–4, 97, 128, 130, 160–1, 226,
  233, 245, 263, 269, 272, 298, 310
Restoration, the 53
retaliation 71, 76, 82, 88, 90–1, 94–5, 128
revelation 92, 128, 383, 389–90
revenge 35, 38, 77, 90, 94, 96, 164, 240,
  243, 263, 268, 294
revenue 342
Revolution, the (of 1688–9) 53
revolution(s) 40, 195, 250, 313, 342
reward(s) 18, 163–70, 172, 193, 265, 315,
  334, 400
  actions deserving 67–78, 85–6, 113
  of Deity 128 n., 163, 166, 169–70, 305
  and good behaviour 147–8
  and beneficence 78, 81, 86, 301
  distribution of 132, 269
  infinite 128
  and justice 81–2, 91, 269
  of nature 147
  and virtue 91–2, 108–32, 302
  see also punishment
rhetoricians 196
rich, the
  esteem/admiration for 50–4, 61–4, 140,
    144, 181–4, 186, 195, 201, 225–6,
    253, 295

and poor 50–1, 61–2, 64, 138, 144, 184–5,
  201, 225–6, 276
  selfishness of 184
  see also Invisible Hand; man
riches 58–9, 91
  pursuit of 50
  see also rich, the; wealth
ridicule:
  sense of 322
right, the:
  and amelioration of wrong 233
  dist. fact 77
  and (the) wrong 160, 165, 200, 209, 234,
    315, 318–20, 324, 334
right(s):
  to defence 80
  of individuals 80
  and injury(ies) 80–1
  personal 84
  of resistance 302
robber(s) 217, 239, 331
  society among 86
Roman Catholicism 333–4
  false sense of duty in 177–8
  romance 10, 32, 34, 58, 143, 160
romance(s) 10, 32, 34, 58, 143, 160, 222,
  226
Romans 56, 197, 207–8, 224, 285–7
Rome 192, 207–8, 229, 280, 288
rudeness 35, 163, 204, 214, 341
rule(s) 18, 58, 102
  adherence to by inferior ranks 201
  of approbation/judgement 109 n., 115,
    128–30 n.
  of architecture 196
  breach of 335
  casuistic 227, 330, 340
  of chastity 335
  of composition 175–6, 327
  of Deity/God(s) 111 n., 165, 170, 274 n.,
    277, 280–1
  distortion of 340–1
  of duty 161–3, 171–2, 176, 202, 329, 340
  general 90, 121, 156–76 *passim*, 220–2,
    243, 273, 319–20, 326–34 *passim*
    as laws of God 163–70
    limitations of 226–7
    origin and use of 109 n., 156, 159–60
  of good offices 81
  of grammar 175, 327
  and induction 159–60, 319–20
  of judgement 128–9
  Jupiter's 274
  of justice 63, 80–2, 89, 105, 138, 149, 155,
    175, 216, 241, 319, 327, 329, 330,
    333, 335, 339–41, 390–4
  of justice fulfilled by doing nothing 82
  as laws 161, 163, 165–6, 170, 218

rule(s) (*cont.*):
  of merit/demerit 170
  Nature's 128
  of prudence 149, 175–6, 237
  of temperance 63
  utility of 89, 138, 160–1
  of veracity 335
rulers:
  and unjust war 155
Russia 60, 204

S

sacrifice(s) 92 n., 170, 177, 228, 274 n.
sage 216
sailor 94, 282
St Bartholomew massacre 177
St James's 132
Saints, inheritance of 133
savages 199, 205, 209
  see also Barbarians; North Americans
school(s) 222
schoolmen 268–9, 390, 392, 396–7
science(s):
  abstruse 189
  academy of 125
  and arts 183, 213, 229
  of casuistry 333
  of ethics 329
  of human nature 319
  liberal 229
  of natural jurisprudence 218, 333
  superior 213
  and taste 19–20
  virtue as species of (Plato) 272
Scotland 100, 103, 223
self-applause 106, 148, 193
self-approbation 48, 59, 114, 116, 249–50
  degree of 147
  love/desire of 117, 303
  principle of 109
  triumph of 129
  and virtue 117, 143, 177–8
  see also approbation and disapprobation
self-command 24–5, 77, 237–64 *passim*
  acquiring highest degree of 152–4
  in acquisition of fortune 189–90
  beauty of 238
  in civilized and barbarous nations 205–8
  discipline of 146–7, 156, 163, 279
  fear and anger mislead 237–42
  foundations of 245
  gives lustre to all other virtues 241
  gradations of 145–7, 273 n.
  means to acquire and use 151–3
  among North American Indians 205–6
  perfect 141

  proper 189, 215, 216, 262–4
  and prudence 215, 263
  and resentment 77
  in respectable virtues 25
  role of perfect knowledge for 237
  in unjust cause 241–2
  utility of 25, 156, 189, 264
  of less violent passions 242
  see also moderation; resentment;
      spectator; virtue(s) of self-
      command
self-deceit 156–61
self-denial 23, 53, 191, 205, 312
self-estimation 246–62 *passim*
  see also self-love
self-government 23, 25
self-interest 148, 270–1, 303
  avarice and ambition as objects of
      173–4
  in philosophy of Mandeville 308
  supports propriety 170
  want of attention to 304
  see also man
selfishness 9, 25, 78–9, 135, 137, 140–1,
      184, 290, 302, 308, 317
  see also passion(s)
self-love 59 n., 96, 135–9, 157–161, 170,
      172–4, 262
  and benevolence 137, 302–4
  circumstances for modifying 83–5,
      131
  ethics of 13–14, 266–7, 294–9, 308–13,
      315–17, 321
  misrepresentations of 137, 158–61
  preference for 83
  principle of 272
  and public interest 235, 275
self-preservation 77, 82, 272, 304, 318
self-satisfaction 23, 113, 147, 166
senate 63, 65 n., 207, 228, 251, 286 n.
sense(s):
  common 115, 171, 176, 331
  direct/antecedent (Hutcheson) 322–3
  of duty 109, 161–2, 164, 170–2, 176–8
  and feeling 320
  functions of 320
  of guilt 84, 101, 107
  of justice 82, 136, 153, 339, 341
  of merit/demerit 67, 74–6, 78, 97–8, 101,
      105, 138 n., 159, 225, 238, 248,
      249, 264, 302
  moral 158, 164 n., 165
    a peculiar faculty/power (Hutcheson)
      158, 266, 321–6
  objects of 29, 165
  of others 9–10, 22
  people of 57
  of propriety 9, 74–5, 88, 136, 143, 170,

172, 188, 190–2, 245–6, 262–4,
  301, 304–8, 338
public 322
of seeing 323
of hearing 323
see also conscience; demerit; impropriety;
  merit; propriety; sentiment
sensibility 118–24 passim
defect/excess of 143, 243–6
of feelings of others 47–9, 152
and habit 201–2, 207, 209
to interests of others/self 139–40, 143–5
and manhood 152
in poetry 123–4
and self-command 25, 143–7, 156
virtue of 25
sensuality 206, 312–13
sentiment(s):
causes of corruption of 61, 154–6
concerning beauty 194–200
end/effect of 67
foundation of moral concepts 320, 397
of the heart 18, 328–9
influence of custom and fashion on
  200–11
influence of fortune on 92–3, 104,
  252–3
irregularity of 104–6
moral 132, 134, 194, 323
utility of 106, 253
  corruption/corruptors of 61–4, 154–6
  and custom 200–11
  disorder in 252
  origin of 265, 313
  plurality of 324–6, 397
  propriety of 154
  theory of 265, 397
  two systems 321
natural 76, 91–2, 103, 119, 168, 209,
  314
as principle of approbation 321–7
prompting reward or punishment 67–9
religious 170
variety of 328
and vice/virtue 67
see also approbation
sentinel 90–1, 389, 391, 394–5
servant(s) 53, 132, 180, 181, 236
sex(es) 28, 31, 33, 42, 78, 177, 206, 208,
  312, 332, 335
shame 33, 49, 59 n., 60, 118, 120, 149, 278,
  333, 335
dread of 261, 268
furies of 65
horrors of 84–5, 129 n., 161, 166
inward 193
of poverty 297
sense of 322

sympathy with 61
and violation of faith 332
ship 59 n., 276
shipwreck(s) 94, 282
sickness 59 n., 142, 145, 174, 183, 249, 272,
  274, 275, 276, 283
slave(s)/slavery 104, 130 n., 282, 285, 288
snuff box 94
sobriety 148, 269, 307
sociality 214
society(-ies):
ages of, see nations
and beneficence 86, 218, 227–34
as a chess-board 234
civil 40, 340
civilized 207, 209
foundation for (justice) 85–91
game of 234
and civil government 318
happiness of 89, 91 n., 186–7, 227
harmony of 22
Hobbes's theory of 315–18
human need for 84–5
laws of 9, 33, 76
a great machine 316
of mathematicians and natural
  philosophers 125
among merchants 86
a mirror 110–12
morals of 63
order of 52, 61, 88, 91, 226, 253, 316
pleasures of 148, 337
of poets 126
preservation of 77
refuge in 315
among robbers 86
security of 138
stability of 52, 61, 226, 230–1
state(s), ages of 209–10, 223, 342
universal 235–7
utility of 86–90
soldier(s) 138, 153, 191, 236, 239, 245, 284,
  389, 400–1
see also officers; warrior
son, poor man's 181
sophisms(-try) 143, 233, 312
sorrow(s) or grief 283
comforter of 169
affects imagination 183
moderation of 142–54 passim
and resentment 102
silent and majestic 24
in solitude 110–11
sympathy with 9–18 passim, 22, 40,
  43–50, 61, 70, 317
see also grief
soul(s) 13, 106, 108, 171, 206, 267–9
sound(s), harmony of 46 n., 165, 322

sovereign(s) 56, 81, 191, 227, 228
earthly 132
and law 166
obedience to 99–100
of passions 326
and unjust war 155
of civilized world 288
see also man of rank; power
sovereignty(ies) 217, 227, 235
see also state(s)
species:
beauty of 198–9
happiness and perfection of 105
propagation of 77, 87, 142, 185
spectator(s) 10–12, 16, 21–3, 27, 37–8,
45–9, 56, 60, 76, 78–9, 81–5, 91,
103, 111–13, 127, 143–4, 146,
153–4, 160, 169, 179, 182,
189–91, 209, 246, 273, 306, 312,
323, 327
abstract 153
accommodation to sentiments of 190–1
admiration for rich and great 182–3
approval of restraint by 189–90
and the beauty of utility 179, 182
candid 148
and compassion for the great 52
fellow-feelings of 190–1
generous 81
human 169
in Hutcheson and Hume 327
ideal 153
imagination of 127
imagined 129–1, 134, 137–8, 141, 145,
147–8, 153, 157–8, 215, 225–7,
245, 247, 262, 287, 292–3
impartial 24, 26, 27, 38, 45–6, 69,
78–9, 82–3, 90–1, 97–99, 104,
110, 114, 116, 118, 129–131, 134,
137, 145–8, 154–8, 161, 191,
215, 218, 225, 226, 228, 240,
242–3, 246, 249, 252, 261–4,
269–70, 283, 287, 292, 294, 330,
338, 397
in Hume and Hutcheson 327
indifferent 39, 85, 154, 157, 158, 238
indulgent 154
intelligent 283
partial 154
the only precise criterion of propriety *17*,
294
real 131, 145, 147, 153–5
revered 155
of self/own behaviour 112–14, 116
and self-command 26, 145–8, 153–4, 215,
240, 242–3
of self-esteem 246, 249, 252, 261–2
sentiments of 60, 90, 191, 323

sympathy of 21–2, 48–9, 60, 76, 78,
143–4, 179, 273 n.
as theory of conscience 114, 116, 118,
128–32, 134, 137
well-informed 130
see also conscience
speculation 21, 23, 136, 187, 192, 237, 315
speculators:
political 234
spirit
and flesh 133
public 168, 185–6, 190–1, 232–3, 302,
309
see also freedom; innovation; system
stage 12, 123, 323
state(s) 90
constitution of 230, 340
law of 218
little 267
natural/of nature 45, 318
of orders/societies in 230–4
protection by 222–3
sovereign 227–8, 230–4, 235
well-governed 186, 340
wisdom of 218
see also government, civil; sovereignty
statesman/men 57, 63–4, 134, 151, 173,
216, 228, 230, 234, 242, 250, 285, 298
statuary 313
stile; *see* style
Stoics/stoics(-ical) 58–60 n., 138, 147, 156,
272–93, 300 n.
apathy 143
criticized 143, 147, 156, 291–3
on happiness 147, 149
on justice 138
magnanimity 136 n.
man recommended to his own care 219
paradoxes of 289–91
on perfection of nature 36, 141 n., 274,
277, 289
and self-command 141 n., 290
and self-preservation 219, 272
and self-sacrifice 140–1, 274–5
style 38, 64, 195, 197, 208 n., 209, 211, 339
subject(s) of state 99, 155, 166, 186, 229,
232
subsistence 134, 184
superintendent of universe 59, 277–8,
289–90, 292
cf. power
superior(s) 41, 47, 52–3, 56, 63–4, 79, 81,
152, 154, 166, 170, 181, 191, 201,
226, 228, 248, 253, 256, 257, 297, 319
superstition(s) 71, 91, 94, 164, 331, 333–4
surprise and admiration 14, 20, 31, 48
sword 60, 168
syllogisms, abstruse 145

sympathy 10–19, 21–4, 27–52
  agreeable and disagreeable forms of 46
  and approbation 46 n., 48, 71, 73, 110,
    321, 325
  artificial 47
  and the beauty of utility 179, 182
  and benevolence 38–9
  for children 12, 219
  complete 44, 46, 48, 49
  conditional 18
  consolation of 84
  vs contempt 58–61
  and custom 205, 209
  with the dead 12–13, 71
  defined 10 n., 43
  degrees of 42–3
  direct/indirect 74–6, 317
  disagreeable 46 n.
  and disapprobation 71, 74, 110
  double 38–40, 74–6, 301, 326
  for elderly person 219
  and envy 44–7, 140
  expressions exciting 11
  exquisite 191
  extreme, absurd/unreasonable 140
  and family 219–21
  general 57
  and gratitude 69, 71–6, 78, 317
  habitual, and affection 220–5
  and hatred 34–6, 68
  healing consolation of 15
  and humanity 190–1
  in Hume 88 n., 144 n., 179, 327,
    397–8
  illusive 71, 78
  and imagination 9, 12–13, 21–2, 29, 31–4,
    51–2, 75, 116, 219, 317
  indulgent 146, 154
  with joy vs grief 15, 40, 51, 70, 139–40,
    152
  and justice *13*, 83–5
  for man oppressed or injured 70–1
  and merit 69, 74–6, 78, 225
  with misfortunes 60, 103
  misinterpretation of 317
  mutual 13–6
  natural 71, 224–5
  with bodily passion 27–31, 143–4
  as derivative of passion 10–6, 31–2, 34, 36
  for pain and pleasure 27–31, 44, 61
  with passions of imagination 29, 31–4
  and pity 9–10, 43
  a principle of human nature 266
  and propriety 16–27, 74, 78, 242–3, 263,
    306
  with public good 185
  and resentment 15, 34–8, 69–78, 83–4,
    99, 235, 317

  with rich/great 50–3, 57, 140, 144 n.,
    179
  satisfaction with others' 15
  and self-approbation 110, 116, 145–7,
    193
  and self-love/selfishness 40–3, 317
  and situation 11, 21–4, 28, 45
  with social passions 38–40
  with sorrow 14, 43–9, 50, 61, 70, 317
  with suffering 70, 74
  system of 317, 327
  and utility 88 n., 179, 185, 306, 327
  for victim of negligence 103
  see also fellow-feeling
system(s):
  of benevolence 306–7
  Epicurean 307
  fitness/harmony of 179, 183, 185
  of government 185–6, 232–5
  of human nature 87
  ideal, imaginary beauty of 232, 283,
    293–4, 313–1
  of laws 233, 340
  licentious 306, 308–9
  love of 185
  man of 231 n., 233–4
  of moral approbation 314
  of morality 188, 265, 293, 306
  of philosophy 2, 199, 265–342
  of police 186
  of propriety 306
  of prudence 307
  society as 183, 185–6, 231–4
  spirit of 185, 231 n., 232
  of splenetic philosophers 127
  universe/world 59 n., 140, 236–7, 276–7,
    289
  of utility (Hume) 327
  see also machine

T

talent(s) 54–5, 98–9, 132, 181, 204, 213–14,
    216, 256, 259
Tartars 223, 227
Tartarus 91
taste 19–21, 24–5, 99, 123, 175, 189, 193,
    194–5, 197, 252, 291, 313
  for beauty 327
  in determining degree of excellence 123
  objects of 195
  see also arts; beauty
temperance 28, 59, 63, 192, 214, 238, 242,
    269–71, 278, 297–8
  in Hutcheson 304
  in Mandeville 312
  in Plato 268–9

tenderness 25, 46, 142, 190, 202, 208, 219–20, 227
theatre 30, 32–4, 46, 52, 58, 107, 123, 177
theologians 318
thief/thieves 100, 120, 175, 217, 331
Tholouse 120
Time, future 151, 189, 215
toleration 176
tooth-pick 182
Tory principle of authority, *see* authority
toys 180–1
trade 136, 155, 185, 201, 204, 213, 224
tradesmen 173
tragedy(-ies) 10, 29–30, 32–34, 43, 46, 52, 107, 123, 177, 196–7, 222, 226, 227
traitor(s) 10, 52, 168, 228, 254
tranquility 37, 48, 120, 131–2, 136, 146–53 *passim*, 166, 208, 215–16, 219, 230–2, 238, 241, 244–5, 273 n., 288, 293, 296–7, 307
remedies to restore 22–3, 150–2
role of 149–51
sacrificed 181
in sorrow 24
source of inward 113
treachery 331–2
treason 99–100
treaty(-ies) 154, 230
tribunal:
of confessor 335
of conscience 128–32
God's 105, 131
trinkets 180–2, 184
truth:
desire/love of 166–7, 337–8
duty of 163
law of 331
resemblance to 313–14
violation of 335
tumult 57, 65, 153
Turkish Spy, the 95
Turkomans 223
tweezer-case(s) 181–2
tyranny 106
tyrant(s) 169 (God), 280, 288 (Domitian), 323

U

understanding 189, 260–1
universe 87, 274–8, 314
God as director of 59, 235–7
great/immense machine of 19, 236
Judge of 156
means adjusted to ends in 87
order and perfection of 274–7
physician of 289

plan of 36
Superintendent of 277–8, 289–90, 292
system of 237, 277
upstart(s), generally disagreeable 41
utilitarianism:
in Hume 87–8 n.
theological 166, 235–7, 277, 305
utility:
and approbation 179
and beauty 179–80, 183–8, 192, 199, 238, 316, 326–7
of class distinction 52
in ethical theory 20, 35, 235, 400
frivolous 180–2
of government 185–7
of intellectual virtues 20
in irregularity of sentiments 106, 253
pleasure of 179
public 210
and punishment 71, 87–91, 391, 394, 398
and science 189
and society 85–6, 88, 148
in Smith's ethics 166, 169, 188–9, 304–5, 326, 394–5, 398–9
of trinkets 180–2
and virtue 264, 296–7, 305–6, 315–16, 327

V

vain-glory 149–50, 228
valour 54, 58 n., 99, 216, 241, 264
vanity 33, 50, 52, 59 n., 62, 64, 89, 115, 117, 127, 130, 149–50, 169, 182, 223, 246, 251, 255–9, 263, 286–7
affinity to love of true glory 310–11
anger as object of 240
characteristics of 257–8
and insanity 250
of man's labour 136
pleasures of 150
with self-admiration or pride 255–7, 261
in system of Mandeville 308–12
vengeance 24, 70–1, 76, 84, 94, 105–7, 118, 166, 172, 201, 208, 335
veracity 335, 337–40
Versailles 132
verse(s) 196–8, 248
vice(s) 18, 33, 61–4, 76 n., 81, 188, 319–30
abhorrence of 36, 117, 164, 169, 329
capricious 225
of Cato 286
characters of 113, 188
deformity of 316, 322, 328
effects of 91
and impropriety 294, 306
and imprudence 216–17, 298

insensibility to 118
of lying 115, 122
political view of 316
private/public benefit 312–13
and punishment 91–2, 113, 167–9
and religious restraint 171
and sentiment 67
and society/social order 315–16
temptations of 171
torments of 113
triumphant 121
dist. virtue 306, 308
viceregent(s) 128, 130, 165–6
victory(-ies) 36, 47, 49, 59 n., 99, 102, 232,
254, 268, 278
vigilance 304, 307
virtue(s):
affectation of 117
and affections 262, 293
amiable 23–5, 35, 113, 152, 216, 242,
306–7
of ancestors 253
according to Aristotle 23, 25, 267, 270–2,
299, 329, 341
according to Augustus 300
awful 23, 25, 63, 152, 306
beauty in 299, 316, 322
of beneficence 78–9, 81, 174, 262, 264
as benevolence 241, 265–7, 300–6
cardinal 269
practice of 329
character(s) of nature of 113, 212, 314
passim
according to Church Fathers 301
according to Cicero 307, 341
of circumspection 304
among civilized nations 204–5
according to Samuel Clarke 265, 293
classified 237, 241
as conformity to reason 320
of constancy 304
contemplative 134
according to Ralph Cudworth 301
cultivated 204–5
and custom 200–11 *passim*
and desert 113, 117
devout 134
discouragement of 105
divine 137
duties of 209
according to the eclectics 300
according to Epicurus 294–300, 307
as excellence 25
of firmness 304
as fitness 293–4
and fortune 63, 132
of frugality 242, 271
gentle 152, 306

and habit 324
and happiness 91, 266, 291, 307
of heroism 58, 228
according to Hutcheson 265, 267, 301–4
imperfect 291
insensibility to 118
intellectual 20, 216
and interest 235
of justice, *see* justice
according to La Rochefoucauld 308
and life to come 132
love of 91, 117, 164, 169, 225, 310–11,
329
man's vs woman's 190
according to Mandeville 308–14
monkish 133 n.
and moral sense 266
according to Henry Moore 301
nature of, *see* character(s) or nature of
negative 82
offspring of flattery and pride 309
perfect 91 n., 152, 178, 216, 237, 272,
291, 324
of philosopher 63
philosopher's view of 282
in Plato 267–70, 299, 300, 341
according to Platonists 300
of politeness, *see* politeness
political view of 316
and pride 258
and propriety 25–6, 262, 266–94, 299,
305, 306, 320
as prudence 189, 212, 262, 264–7,
294–300
see also prudence
according to Pythagoras 300
public 186
as quality of action 271
as quality of person 271
reality of 306, 309, 312–13
and reason 266, 319–21
as relation 265, 293
and religion 64, 171
and resolution of mind 324
respect and admiration for 62
respectable 23–5, 152, 258, 306–7
and reward 91–2, 108, 121, 132,
166–9
road to 63–4
among rude and barbarous nations 205
general rules of 174–6, 327–30
and science of ethics proper 329
depends on sense and feeling 320
and self-approbation 117, 178
of self-command 25, 61, 153, 237, 241–2,
262, 264, 306
of self-denial 205
and self-love 262, 266

virtue(s) (*cont.*):
  and sentiment 67, 113, 328–9
  according to Shaftesbury 293
  according to John Smith 301
  social 80, 270
  and social ranks 53–6, 61–4
  and society/social order 315–16
  soft 152–3, 306
  in Stoic doctrine 272–93
  superiority of 99
  and sympathy 266
  three systems of 266–7, 305
  and talents 54–5, 99, 132, 214, 256, 259
  theories of 266–7, 305
  as truth of things 293
  unfashionable 64
  as utility 305–6, 327
  utility of 264, 296–7, 315–16
  vice 306, 308
  of vigilance 304
  of warrior 63
  and will of Deity 305
  and wisdom 61–2, 216, 226, 253
  according to William Wollaston 293
  woman's vs. man's 190
  in Zeno's system 267, 272–3, 299
  see also morality
vision, philosophy of 134–5
voice
  of anger 36
  of divine Being 281
  of human life 41
  of human weakness 26
  of the impartial spectator 137
  of misery 36
  of Nature 212
  of wretchedness 48
vortices 313

W

wages 50
waggoners 185
want(s) 183, 205
war(s)/warfare 152–5, 191, 236, 252, 298
  civil 52, 55, 65, 155, 232, 242, 286
  foreign 55, 232
  hardships and hazards of 134, 146, 152, 249
  instruments of 36
  laws of 90, 342
  Mysian 280
  Peloponnesian 281
  two principles of 245
  prisoner of 206, 282
  as school 239, 245–6
  self-command prospers in 153

  in state of nature 318
  triumph of 65
  unjust 155
warrior 63–4, 208, 250–1
watch(es):
  as means or end 180
  wheels of 87
weakness:
  in anxiety about praise 127–8
  of benevolence/soft virtues 301, 303, 306
  of childhood 219
  contempt for 62
  and custom 205–7
  gradations of 145–6
  of humanity 26, 31, 48, 92 n., 106, 117, 121–2, 128, 132, 134, 146, 158–9, 169, 176–7, 190, 237, 253, 273 n., 280
  of love 205–6
  of man lacking proper indignation 243–5
  self-deceit as fatal 158–9
  of sorrow 15, 49–50
  of sovereigns 132
  war and faction as remedy for 245–6
  of women 33, 151
wealth:
  admiration for 61–2
  hypocrites of 64
  magnificence of 182
  pleasures and limitations of 183
  Princes' 72
  pursuit of 50, 181
  race for 83
  recompense for industry 166–7
  respect for 253
welfare:
  public 185
  of society 89, 231, 304–5, 315–16, 318
will(s):
  of Deity 128, 170–1, 176, 236
  freedom of 79
  of magistrate 318
  and virtue 305
window, landscape seen through 135
wisdom/the wise:
  admiration for 61–2
  affections of 275 n., 277
  anticipation of tranquility 151
  approbation of 253
  directing life 59, 229, 276, 292
  of God/Author of Nature/Superintendent of the Universe 36, 87, 92, 106, 166, 236, 253, 274, 277, 290, 298, 300
  see also God(s)
  governing the world/universe 141, 277
  Infinite 170
  of nature 107, 218, 220

in Plato 268 n.
political 231–2
and prudence 216
relation to impartial spectator 146–7
sacrifice of private interest by 235–6
of Socrates 251
of state 218
in Stoic doctrine 58–9, 147, 156, 275 n.,
     276–8, 281, 289–93
study of 62
and virtue 61–2, 187, 216, 224–6 *passim*,
     253, 282, 298–9
woman/women:
  in Bengal 287
  in China 199
  of fashion 287
  feelings for infants 12, 40
  of gallantry 121
  humanity as virtue of 190
  lack generosity 190
  lamentations of 244
  laws of society and 33
  vs man/men 28, 190, 317, 324, 328
  "a woman who paints" 115
  seduction of 100
  see also education
wonder 20, 20 n., 31, 48, 99, 189, 217, 228,
     323
woollen manufacture 185
world: the
  affairs of 128

another 91, 121, 132, 283
applause/acclamations/approbation of 58,
     106, 129–30
attention of 51, 62
being the whole w. to oneself 83
censure of 112, 129
citizen of 140–1
civilized part of 288
commerce of 139
corruption/depravity of 45, 137
Director of 274
disorder of 169
fatherless 235
government of 54, 141
great Genius of 59
happiness of 166
Judge of 121, 128 n., 131, 134
judges of event, not design 104–5
in the moon 140
order of 168
prosperity of 106
trade of 136
writer(s) 77, 125–6, 143, 197–8, 248, 330
writings 124, 176, 196–7, 210, 217, 252,
     307, 339

Y

youth 42, 142, 182, 201–2, 206, 209, 214,
     225, 246, 259, 260, 288, 329

Index of Persons

A

Accursius, Franciscus 190 n.
Acton, H. B. 184 n.
Addison, Joseph 15 n., 125 & n., 198
Aemilius Paulus 56
Ajax 284 & n.
Alexander the Great 58 n., 99, 214–15, 250, 253–4 n., 284 n.
Anne, Queen of Great Britain 230
Antigonus 284 & n.
Antimachus 253 n.
Antipater 254 n.
Antoninus, Marcus 236–7, 288
Apollonius of Tyre 285 & n.
Aristides 75 & n.
Aristippus 214, 294
Aristodemus 284 n.
Aristomenes 284 & n.
Aristotle 196 n., 210, 258 & n., 267, 269–73, 269 n., 271 n., 272 n., 282 n., 299, 329, 341, 385, 387, 392, 396–7
Armenia, King of 102
Arria 286 n.
Arrian 275 n.
Arundel, Earl of, *see* Howard, Thomas 2nd Earl of 257
Athenaeus 254 n.
Attila 253
Augustine of Hippo, St 331 n.
Augustus 285, 300
Aurelius, Marcus 236 & n., 237, 288 n., 300 n.
Avaux, Claude de Mesmes, Comte de 230
Avidius Cassius 237

B

Barbeyrac, Jean 331
Bathurst, Bishop Henry 385
Berkeley, George 135 n.
Birch, Thomas 238
Biron, Charles, de Gontaut, Duc de 49
Boileau-Despréaux, Nicolas 125 n., 248–9
Bonar, James 80 n., 241 n., 287 n., 385, 397
Borgia, Cesare 76, 217
Brissenden, R. F. 85 n.
Brutus, Lucius Junius 192
Brutus, Marcus Junius 58 n., 292

Buffier, Claude 198–9
Burke, Edmund 283, 293
Butler, Joseph 14 n., 42–4 n., 164 n.
Butler, Samuel 198
Byng, Admiral John 192 n.

C

Cadell, Thomas 231 n.
Caesar, Julius 23 n., 58 n., 65 & n., 99, 251–2, 252 n., 253, 286 n., 292 n.
Calas, Jean 120 & n.
Callisthenes 254
Camillus, M. Furius 75 & n.
Cannan, E. 385
Cardinal de Retz, *see* de Gondi, Jean François Paul, Cardinal de Retz
Catiline 240 n., 252 & n., 316
Catinat, Nicholas 133 & n.
Cato, Uticensis 23 n., 48, 50 n., 58 n., 252 & n., 286 & n., 316
Cato the Censor 208 & n., 228 & n.
Celsus 288 n.
Chalmers, Alexander 385
Chalmers, George 229 n.
Charisius, Flavius 292 n.
Charles I, King of Great Britain 52, 53
Charles II, King of Great Britain 201
Charles V, Emperor 152 n.
Chrysippus 143 & n., 291
Churchill, John (1st Duke of Marlborough) 230 n., 251–2
Cicero 65 n., 128, 134 n., 207–8, 233 & n., 240–2, 252 n., 253 n., 272 n., 281 n., 286 & n., 291–2, 295 n., 307, 329, 331 & n., 340–1, 401
Cineas 150 n.
Clarendon, Earl of, *see* Hyde, Edward (1st Earl of Clarendon)
Clarke, Samuel 265 & n., 293 n.
Claudius I (Tiberius Drusus Nero) 200
Cleanthes 291 & n.
Cleitus 254 n.
Cleomenes 284 & n.
Clermont, Bishop of 133 n., 169
Clytus 254
Colman, George 124 n.
Condé, Louis II de Bourbon, Prince de 251 & n.

Condorcet 30
Cooper, Anthony Ashley (1st Earl of
    Shaftesbury) 241
Cooper, Anthony Ashley (3rd Earl of
    Shaftesbury) 293 n.
Corellius Rufus 286 n.
Cornielle, Pierre 197 n.
Cowley, Abraham 32
Crassus, Lucius, Licinius 208 & n.
Crassus, Marcus, Licinius 241, 242 n.
Cudworth, Ralph 301 & n., 318–19
Cunningham, Mrs W. B. 385, 397
Cunningham, Rev. W. B. 385, 387–8, 396
Curtius Rufus, Quintus 250 n., 254 n.

D

Daoyz, S. 190 n.
d'Alembert, Jean le Rond, Baron 124 n.,
    125–6, 231 n.
d'Auvergne, Henri de La Tour, Vicomte de
    Turenne 251–2
d'Avaux, Count 230
Davila, Enrico Caterino 241 & n.
de Gondi, Jean François Paul, Cardinal de
    Retz 61, 174, 230, 286
de Gontaut, Charles (Duke of Biron)
    49–50
Demetrius the Cynic 276 n.
Demosthenes 240
Descartes, Rene 313 n.
Despréaux, *see* Boileau-Despréaux, Nicolas
Digby, Lord George 2nd Earl of Bristol
    241
Diogenes Laertius 272 n., 285 & n., 295 n.
Domitian 288 & n.
Douglas, David, Lord Reston 385
Dryden, John 150 n., 198
Du Bos, Jean-Baptiste, l'Abbé 207 & n.

E

Eckstein, W. 44 n., 80 n., 87 n., 100 n.,
    197 n., 204 n., 233 n., 276 n., 281 n.,
    286 n., 287 n.
eclectic philosophers 300–6
    see also Platonists
Elliot of Minto, Sir Gilbert 3rd Bart.
    46 n., 398 n.
Epaphroditus 288 & n.
Epictetus 59 n., 136 n., 141, 143, 275–6,
    280, 288 & n., 300 n.
Epicurus 294–9, 307
Epirus, King of 150
Eugène of Savoy, Prince 251
Eumenes 284 & n.

Euripides 30 n., 284, 285 n.
Expilly, Jean-Joseph, l'Abbé 229 n.

F

Fitzmaurice, Thomas 29 n.
Fontenelle, Bernard, le Bovier, Sieur de
    125 & n.
Frederick the Great, King of Prussia 60 n.,
    251
Frederick, William I 60 n.

G

Gaius, Emperor 276 n.
Gellius, Aulus 288 n.
Genghis Khan 253 & n.
Gracchus, Gaius 208
Gracchus, Tiberius 208 n.
Gray, Thomas 123–4, 124 n., 143
Grotius, Hugo 87 n., 269, 341–2, 342 n.,
    398
Gustavus Adolphus 251

H

Halsband, R. 124 n.
Hannibal 75 n.
Henri IV, King of France 49 n.
Hercules 30
Hesoid 32 n.
Hippolytus 30 & n.
Hobbes, Thomas 14 n., 315, 318–19
Home, Henry, *see* Kames
Homer 125 n., 134 n., 241, 284 n., 401
Horace 32, 124 n., 196 n.
Houbraken, Jacobus 238 n.
Houdar de la Motte, Antoine 125 & n.
Howard, Thomas (2nd Earl of Arundel)
    [Howard line] 257
Hume, David 23–4 n., 44 n., 52 n., 80 n.,
    144 n., 179 n., 283 n.
  criticized by Smith 20, 87–8 n., 135 n.,
    137 n., 188, 265 n., 287 n., 305–06,
    327, 388–9
  influence on Smith 110 n., 133 n., 135 n.,
    137 n., 243 n., 287 n., 320 n., 383–5,
    397, 399–401
  praised by Smith 179, 188, 383, 400–1
Hutcheson, Francis 44 n., 157 n., 331
  criticized by Smith 137 n., 158 n., 164 n.,
    265 n., 304–5, 322–4
  his theory of ethics 24 n., 265, 301–4,
    320–3
  praised by Smith 301, 320–2, 397

Hyde, Edward (1st Earl of Clarendon) 241 & n., 256–7

I

Isabella 107 & n.

J

James I, King of Great Britain 72, 186
James II, King of Great Britain 53 & n.
Jesus Christ 133 n.
Joanna of Castile 151–2
Jocasta 107
Johnson, Samuel 124 n.
Jupiter 59–60, 164, 185 n., 274, 277–8, 289
Justinian 104 n.

K

Kames, Henry Home, Lord 80 n., 85 n., 123 n., 164 n.
Koser, R. 60 n.

L

Lactantius, Firmianus 285 & n.
Laelius, C., Sapiens 208 n.
Laelius, C., the elder 208 n.
La Fontaine, Jean de 125 & n.
La Motte, Antoine Houdar, de 125 & n.
La Placette, Jean 331 n.
La Rochefoucauld, François Duc de 57, 127 n., 308–9 n.
La Rochefoucauld d'Anville, Louis Alexandre, Duc de 308–9 n.
Lauzun, Comte de 149 & n.
Leliuses 208
Lémery, Nicolas 126 n.
Leonidas 58 n.
Livy 75 n.
Lloyd, Robert 124 n.
Locke, John 241 n., 322
Lothian, J. M. ix
Louis XIII, King of France 64
Louis XIV, King of France 54, 149 n., 230 n.
Lucian 285 & n.
Lucullus, L. Licinius 99, 102 n.
Lysander 241, 242 n.

M

Macedon, King of 56

Macfie, A. L. 184 n., 185 n.
Machiavelli, Niccolò 217
Mackenzie, Sir George 100 n.
Magee, Archbishop William 383–4, 398, 400
Malebranche, Nicolas 157 & n.
Mandeville, Bernard 14 n., 127 n., 182 n., 184 n., 308–13, 315 n.
Marana, Giovanni Paolo 95 n.
Marcellus, Marcus Claudius 65 & n.
Marcus Crassus 241–2
Marivaux, P. C. de C. de 143
Marlborough, Duke of, *see* Churchill
Mason, William 124 n.
Massillon, Jean Baptiste, Bishop of Clermont 133 n., 169 n., 400
Maxwell, J. C. 46–7
McCulloch, J. R. 398 n.
Medici, Catherine de 241
Meek, R. L. 23 n., 396 n.
Millar, Andrew 25–6, 36–8
Millar, John 67 n.
Milton, John 123, 197 n., 283
Mitford, John 385, 387, 396
Mithridates 99 n.
Mizuta, H. 402
Molière 125 n.
Mominion 32, 107
More, Henry 301 & n.
More, Thomas 239 & n.

N

Necker, Jacques 229 n.
Nero 76, 200, 276 n., 288 n.
Newton, Sir Isaac 124

O

Oedipus 107
Othello 34
Otway, Thomas 32 n.
Ovid 32

P

Paetus, Caecina 286 n.
Palmira 177
Parmenides 253, 254 n.
Parmenion 254 & n.
Pascal, Blaise 139 n.
Pausanias 284 n.
Peripatetic philosophers 216, 273 & n., 282–3

Perrault, Charles 125 n.
Persaeus 285 & n.
Peter the Great, of Russia 186 n., 214
Petrarch 32
Phaedra 33, 123
Philip I of Castile 151–2
Philip of Macedon 214, 240 n., 254 & n.
Philoctetes 30 & n.
Philopoemen 284 & n.
Philotas 254 n.
Phocion 284 & n.
Pindar 32 n.
Plato 48 n., 134 n., 210, 233–4, 251 n., 253,
    254 n., 267–70, 267 n., 272, 282 n.,
    299–300, 341, 401
Platonists:
    Cambridge 301 n.
    later 300 & n.
Pliny the Younger 286 & n.
Plutarch 20, 56 n., 99 n., 102 n., 150 n.,
    228 n., 233 n., 254 n., 284 & n.
Pompey 65, 98, 99 n., 252 & n.
Pope, Alexander 123 & n., 124, 125 n., 198,
    289
Pradon, Nicolas (or Jacques) 123 n.
Price, Richard 229 n., 231 n.
Priscianus, Caesariensis 292 n.
Propertius 32 n.
Pufendorf, Samuel 315 n., 331
Pyrrhus 150 n.
Pythagoras 300
Pythagoreans 269

Q

Quinault, Philippe 125 n.
Quintilian 197

R

Racine, Jean (son of Louis) 33, 123–4, 143,
    196, 197 n.
Racine, Louis 123, 125 n.
Rae, John 46 n., 124 n., 143 n., 204 n.,
    309 n., 383–7, 398, 400
Raleigh, Sir Walter 239 n.
Regulus, M. Atilius 285–6
Retz, Cardinal de 61 & n., 174, 230,
    286 & n.
Riccaboni, Marie-Jeanne 143
Richardson, Samuel 143 & n.
Richelieu, Cardinal de 174
Robertson, William 152 n.
Rousseau, Jean-Baptiste 197 n.
Rousseau, Jean-Jacques 183–4
Russell, William, Lord 239 n.

S

Sallust 23 n., 197
Santeul, Jean de 248–9
Scipio Aemilianus 208
Scipio Africanus Major 75 n., 208 n.
Scipio Nasica Corculum 228 & n.
Scott, W. R. 385–8, 395–6
Seneca 48, 156, 197, 276 n., 278 n., 286,
    291, 292 n., 300 n., 307
Shaftesbury, Anthony Ashley Cooper, 1st
    Earl of, *see* Cooper
Shaftesbury, Anthony Ashley Cooper, 3rd
    Earl of, *see* Cooper
Shakespeare 123 n., 259 n.
Sidney, Algernon 239 n.
Simson, Robert 124
Sinclair, Archdeacon John 384, 387, 400
Sinclair, Sir John 384
Smith, Adam:
    Captain of Edinburgh City Guard 204 n.
    final illness and death 385
    lectures at Edinburgh 80 n., 385–6, 388,
        396
    lectures on ethics 67 n., 164 n., 189 n.,
        190 n., 265 n., 316 n., 395–7
    lectures on justice 43, 385–98
    Lord Rector at Glasgow 301 n.
    Professor at Glasgow 80 n., 301 n.,
        385–6, 396, 399
    on religion 383, 399–400
    student at Glasgow 124 n., 301 n.
    translations from quoted authors 54 n.,
        57 n., 61 n., 128 n., 133 n., 141 n.,
        169 n., 183–4 n., 270 n., 273 n.,
        276 n., 280 n., 298 n.
    use of amanuenses 388, 398
    visit to France 308 n.
Smith, John 301
Socrates 48, 214 & n., 238, 251, 254 n.,
    284 & n., 298, 401
Solon 233 & n., 242 n.
Sophocles 30 n., 107 n.
Southerne, Thomas 107–8 n.
Southwell, Edward 301 n.
Stein, P. G. 190 n.
Stewart, Dugald 67 n., 124 n., 231 n., 309 n.
Stewart, Matthew 124
Suetonius 251 n.
Sully, Maximilien de Béthune, Duc de 64 n.
Sulpicius Rufus 208 n.
Swift, Jonathan 197 n., 198, 214

T

Tacitus 197
Tamerlane 253

Tarquinius Superbus 192 n.
Themistocles 75 n., 241, 242 n., 284 & n.
Theramenes 284 & n.
Thomson, James 139 n.
Thucydides 284 n.
Tibullus 32
Tigranes 102
Timoleon 75 & n.
Timotheus 285 n.
Tronchin, Theodore 29
Turenne, Henri de 251 n.

U

Ulysses 241, 242 n.

V

Venus 251
Vertue, George 238 & n.
Vespasian 276 n.
Voltaire 54 n., 120 n., 123 & n., 134 n., 143, 177, 196, 197 n., 214, 227, 401

Vulcacius Gallicanus 237 n.

W

Walker, D. M. 100 n.
Wedderburn, Alexander, 1st Earl of Rosslyn 283 n.
William of Orange, King of Great Britain 230
Wilson, T. 32 n.
Wollaston, William 293 n.

X

Xenophon 298 n.

Z

Zamti 227
Zeno 143, 143 n., 267, 272, 284–5, 285 n., 291 & n., 299

Lectures on Jurisprudence and Appendix

Index of Subjects

A

Aberdeen 355, 528
accession, as title to property 11, 13–14,
    27–32, 459–61
accumulation 387, 510, 520–2, 577
    see also money, property, stock, wealth
actions, legal 10, 12, 32, 71–2, 75, 77–8, 80,
    90, 94–100, 103, 126, 203, 262, 276,
    282–3, 307–8, 424–5, 432–3, 456,
    472–5, 483, 528, 546
adoption 40, 64, 169, 448, 466
adscripti glebae 189, 191, 418, 454, 579
adultery 124, 133, 146–7, 170, 438–9,
    440–2, 448, 457
adventitious 8 n., cf. rights, acquired
aesthetics:
    role of the four distinctions between
        colour, form, variety and imitation
        335–7, 488
affinity, degrees of 58–9, 163, 166–7, 447
    see also consanguinity
affront 19, 53, 92, 118, 122–4, 303, 312–13,
    329, 373, 480–1, 527, 552
    see also libel, reputation, slander
Africa:
    areas of the coast, thinly inhabited 158
    a barbarous country 212, 214
    conquests by Carthage 233, 240
    corn, imported by Rome 525, 581
    numbers of slaves exported to America 193
    prices of slaves in America 178
    rules of succession in 38
    seraglios in 443
    slavery in 181
    testamentary succession unknown 65
African company 516
agnates 42
Agnus Dei, papal bull 42
Agra (India) 152, 156
agriculture:
    advantages of 337, 488, 522
    improvement hindered by right of
        primogeniture 466
    profits from 70–1, 185, 190–1, 194–6,
        353, 466, 491, 494, 498–9, 522–6,
        579–81
    and seasons 342, 490, 565–6
    as stage of society 14–16, 20–3, 28, 107,
        213, 219, 221, 223–4, 229–30,
        244–5, 459–60, 469, 488, 542, 584

    with respect to the trade 5
    see also labour, division of
Alexandria 91, 243
alienation:
    of dominions 324, 435
    of property 28, 52, 56, 73–5, 79–80, 425,
        468–70
aliens, rights of 7, 304–11, 317–18, 321,
    399, 403, 431–3, 528, 545
allegiance, principle of 318, 321,
    433–4
    see also homage
allodial, *see* government, land tenure
alluvions 29, 461
ambassadors 212, 539, 545, 549, 551–4
amercements 250, 260, 274, 419
    see also fines
America:
    manners in savage nations of 16, 106–7,
        185, 201, 204, 212, 214, 239, 380,
        439, 476, 483–4
    see also society
American colonies:
    commerce carried on with paper money
        504, 521
    use and treatment of slaves in 178, 181,
        183, 193, 239, 453, 524
American Indians, *see* Indians, American;
    Peru; Brazil
Amphictyons 553
Amsterdam 289
  Bank of 504–5
Andes mountains 380
angles, abrupt and irregular 336
Anglo-Saxons, *see* Saxons (in England)
animals, wild, domestic 14–18, 18 n.,
    19–20, 23, 27, 177, 334–5, 487–8,
    492–4, 497, 499
    see also derelict goods, game laws
annuities 384, 416, 536–7
Antioch 364
Apennine mountains 380
appeals:
    of blood 109–10
    decennery 247
    to House of Lords 271, 383
    legal aspects of 272, 280–1, 283, 417, 423,
        477, 480, 484
    see also common law
apprenticeship 84, 192, 231, 353–4, 357,
    456, 495, 529

Arabia, Arabs:
  Eastern Empire of Rome, fell by the
    incursions of 240
  limited opportunities for growth in 223
  manners of 97, 158, 213–17, 219, 229,
    242, 408, 522, 529
  merchant of, the price of water in the
    desert 358, 496
  in the shepherd state 15, 219, 414, 460,
    583
Archimedean spiral 336
architects, architecture 50, 196, 336
Areopagus, court of the 407
Argos, Argives 204 n., 221
aristocracy, government by 7, 109, 125–6,
    200, 222, 225–8, 236, 244, 253, 255,
    257–9 *passim*, 263, 274, 287–8, 291,
    319–20, 323, 404, 409–10, 413, 418,
    426, 470, 481, 524
arithmetic 226 n., 337, 354, 495
Armenians 97
armies:
  Roman 233–8, 415
  standing 54, 157–8, 231–8 *passim*, 246,
    265–6, 269–71, 331, 399, 412–15,
    421, 541–4
  see also mercenaries, militias, wars,
    warmaking
arms 398–9
  firearms 114, 550
  see also wars
arson 126, 481
artisans 232, 341, 343–4, 352, 355, 490, 492,
    539, 564, 566–7, 583
artist(s) 336 n., 337, 340, 347, 489, 539
art, and contrivance 334, 337
art, of war 232–5, 412, 540
arts, *see* commerce
ascendants 44, 48–9, 62, 163–4, 166, 446,
    463–4
Asia:
  commerce carried on by caravans 528
  conquests of 219–20
  government, purely military 414
  manners of 65, 156–8, 213–15, 306
  ravaged by Mahomet 408
  savage nations of, shepherds 65, 219
  slavery in 181
Asia Minor 219
assassination 105, 108, 118, 201, 204, 207,
    291–2, 428, 549–50
assault and battery 119, 122–3, 479–80
asylum, rights of 553
astronomy 354, 495
Athens:
  courts of 116, 206, 314, 407
  citizens went to war at their own expense
    530

democracy in 227–33, 235–7, 304–5
exposure of children in 173
females not allowed to succeed 49, 62
fortification of 409–13
marriage in 165, 446
origin of city of 222, 225–6
sedition in 197
sparing in granting citizenship 431
testamentary succession introduced by
    Solon 38, 64, 462
Attica 204, 222, 408–9
Augsburg 289
Austria, Austrians 189, 543
authority:
  in family 143–4, 146, 154–5, 162, 165,
    172–4, 176, 204, 449–50
  hereditary 204, 212, 215–16
  hereditary, elective compared 189
  love of domination and 192
  of masters 176, 181–2, 186–9, 452
  principle of 57, 215–16, 318–22, 401–2,
    407, 434
  of superior age 57, 321–2
  see also family, power
authorship:
  exclusive privileges of 11, 83
  rights of 11
avoirdupois, *see* weights and measures
Azov, Sea of 218, 221, 408

B

bailment 99, 471 n.
baker(s):
  exclusive privileges of 84
  give their labour to provide food for men
    337, 489
  serve not from benevolence, but self-love
    493
  a very profitable business 364
balance:
  of trade, *see* commerce, trade
  of property 49–50
  of industry 365, 498
  of power 552
balance, or weighing machine 370–1, 500
Baltic Sea 26, 245, 532
banishment 127, 204, 461, 466–7
  see also outlawry
bankruptcy 131–3, 234, 471, 475, 483, 505
banks, banking 132, 377–80, 384, 386,
    502–7, 515–21, 576
Bantam (Java) 154–5, 443
Barbados 453, 579
Barbarians:
  land and property rights under 49–53
  migrations of 408

power of father among 175
punishment for murder among 106
role of chieftain among 212
slavery among 182
treatment of aliens among 306, 309
Baron(s) 107–8, 254–5, 258–9, 261, 274,
      276, 279 n., 283, 295, 417–19, 422,
      448, 476, 481
barter 336, 347–8, 351–2, 488, 492–3, 503,
      527, 570–4
   see also exchange
Bartholomew Fair 528
bashaws 157, 242, 414, 444
bastards 158–72, 310, 438–9, 447–8
battle(s) 50, 54, 60, 130, 198 & n., 205,
      210, 211 n., 219, 231–2, 234,
      239, 248, 256, 262, 264, 283 n.,
      411
Bdelli, *see* Delhi
bear, *see* Stock Exchange
Bedriacum, battles of 198
beggars 9, 348, 493
beneficia 52–3, 249, 251–3, 464
benefit of clergy, *see* clergy, benefit of
benevolence 172, 449, 493, 571–2
Bengal 344, 586
Berne, canton of 289, 306
bigamy 133 n., 457
Birmingham 351, 540
Black Sea 221
Boetians 204
Bohemia 181, 189, 455
bona fides 10, 33, 35–6, 81, 461
bon marché 5–6, 331
bonds 74, 80, 102, 106, 132–6, 162, 445–6,
      474, 480, 484
boroughs, burghers 48, 84, 255–60 *passim*,
      270, 273–4, 288, 322, 418–20
   see also succession
bounties 364–6, 382, 498–9, 526, 529, 575
Brandenburgh, House of 59, 263
Brazil 388, 391, 577
brewer(s) 84, 196, 327, 337, 348, 363–4,
      489, 493, 498, 501, 514, 533
bribery 260, 273–4, 279
   as source of wealth 206, 212
Britain 130, 236, 238–9, 272, 307, 360, 398,
      406, 415, 429, 460, 463, 489, 503,
      524, 530, 546, 562, 581
   aliens cannot purchase land 432–3
   appointment of judges in 187
   civil list in 263, 269
   compared to Germany in terms of size
         and population 263
   computation of cash in 381–3
   constitution of banks, differs from that of
         Amsterdam 505
   crown of, a feminine fief 60, 435
   doctrine of original contract peculiar to
         316, 323, 434
   government of Saxons in 247–8, 351
   how established 264–70
   liberty of the subject well provided for
         121
   maintains her allies 243
   milled and unmilled money in 385
   mixed government of 402
   no need for a standing army in 421
   Pope, sends legates to 301
   prohibition on the export of bullion
         510–18, 578
   proportion of population available for war
         230–1, 411, 508, 542
   richer than France 392
   should be made a free port 512, 514
   sovereign power in 319
   see also armies, civil list, Commons,
         Lords, contract, election, juries,
         England, Saxons
Brussels lace 195
bull, papal 296, 301, 429–30
bull, *see* Stock Exchange
bullion 295, 299–300, 385–6, 388, 430, 509,
      511
burgess 120 n., 306
burghers, *see* boroughs
burglary, *see* theft
Burgundy(-ians) 247, 441
butcher 84, 337, 348, 363, 368–9, 383–4,
      472, 497, 500
   see also bakers
butcher's meat 344, 366, 383, 499
buttons 343, 351, 491, 539, 566, 568

C

Cairo 152
Calais 529
Canada(-ians) 21, 516
canon law 36, 46–7, 68, 72, 89–90, 95,
      98, 112–13, 147–8, 163, 166, 170–1,
      279, 282, 310, 441–2, 447–8, 468, 474
Canton 289, 306, 585
Cape of Good Hope 204 n., 212, 243, 352,
      583
capital punishment, *see* punishment
Cappadocia 179, 193
caravans 528
   see also commerce, trade
Carovingian dynasty 252
carriage, *see* transport
carriages 10, 214
cartel treaties 548
Carthage, Carthaginians 443, 446, 468 n., 551
   would have shared the fate of Rome had it

Carthage, Carthaginians (*cont.*):
  not been conquered by 219, 233,
    236, 240, 411, 541
  marriage in 446
Catti, German tribe 184
Caucasus mountains 213
Celts 523
cess 416
  see also land, allodial
cessio bonorum 109 n., 455
Chaeronea, Battle of (388 BC) 230–1, 411
Champagne 371 n., 501, 528
chance, risk of 211, 262, 304, 357, 491, 495
Chancellor, office of 80, 278, 281–3, 286,
    295, 423–5, 428
chance medley 111, 114–16, 290, 427, 477–8
  see also homicide
Chancery, Court of 98–9, 275, 278–83
    passim, 286, 423–6, 474, 540
Change Alley 537–8
  see also Stock Exchange
chattels 99 n., 445
  see also property, real, personal
Chatti 184
cheapness, a necessary consequence of
    plenty 333, 358, 362, 364, 370, 487,
    496–7, 575
  see also dearness
Chester, county of 249
chieftains 54, 129, 158, 211–15, 217, 225,
    227–8, 233, 240, 243–4, 405, 407,
    409, 415–16, 426, 464, 543
children:
  authority of father over 449–50
  care of 438–9, 442–4
  employment at early age of 539–40
  illegitimate 168–9, 447–8
  learn discipline from their parents 142
  neglect of 193
  not liable for criminal punishment 139
  in order of succession to property (Rome)
    40–1
  in polygamous marriage 151–3, 157, 159,
    442–4
  practice of exposing 172–3, 175, 449, 457
  property in 27–8, 540
  of second marriage 160
  see also authority, infants, minors, legal
    status of
China, Chinese 219, 352, 374, 491, 541,
    576, 585–6
  emperors of Tartarian descent 242
  exposure of children in 173, 449
  Great Wall of 221, 408
  metals used as currency 374
  polygamy in 154, 158, 444
  populous 158–9, 444
  seraglios in 152

Chironea, *see* Chaeronea
Christ Church, Oxford 328
Christianity:
  and children 173, 175, 540
  and civilization 540, 574
  and contracts 90–8
  and homicide 112
  and marriage 47, 146–50, 161, 438,
    441–2, 447
  and power of the father 173, 175, 449
  and slavery 180, 191, 198, 451, 454, 456
  and succession 68
  and war 549–50
  see also canon law, clergy, Protestantism,
    Roman Catholicism
Church, *see* Protestant, clergy
Cimbri 218, 408
Circassia 156
citizen(s) 7–8, 196–9, 235, 304–10, 409,
    431–3, 455
citizenship 40 n., 235, 304–10, 412, 431–3
city guard 230, 331–2, 486–7
city-states 228–9, 409
civilians 86, 102, 399, 401
civil list 263, 267–9, 271, 274, 421
Civil War (England) 429
clan(s) 54 n., 129, 214, 216, 219, 221,
    224–5, 287–8, 409, 426, 463 n.
  see also government, tribal, Scotland,
    Highlanders, Tartary
clare constat 33
clergy:
  benefices of 52–3, 464
  benefit of 110–16, 127, 478
  and capital punishment 112–13
  constitutional role of 397–8, 429, 436–7,
    448
  and divorce 150
  legal role of *39*, 89–90, 278, 280, 423, 426
  and marriage 146–8, 150, 441
  and property 282, 425
  and slavery 189, 255, 454–5
  and testamentary succession 68–9, 468
  see also canon law, Christianity, Papacy,
    Protestantism, Roman Catholicism
Clyde, Firth of 26
coemption 66, 143, 148, 440–1
cognates 42
coin(-age):
  debasement of 100–2, 295, 301, 373–7,
    474, 501–3
  export of 299–300, 377, 379, 385–92, 430,
    504, 506, 509–11, 518, 577
  as medium of exchange 499–504
  offences concerning 295–6, 299–302,
    385–8, 429–30, 501, 509, 511
  origin of 367–73, 500–1, 575–6
  overseas circulation (foreign exchange) of

299–300, 377, 379, 385–92, 430,
    504, 506, 509–11, 518, 577–8
without seigniorage 360, 385–6, 430,
    509–11
stamp on 371, 373–4
see also banks, money, stock
collaterals 43–4, 48–9, 58–60, 62, 165, 446,
    463–5, 564–6 *passim*
see also succession
colliers 29, 191–2, 453, 579
colonies, *see* Africa, America, Greece/Rome,
    Spain/Portugal, East/West Indies,
    slaves
colour 335–6, 488
combat, trial by 58, 123, 210–11, 283, 312,
    406, 425
comitia calata 64 & n.
comitia centuriata 227
comitia curiata 38
commerce, trade:
  advantages, disadvantages of 5, 83–6,
    91–2, 96–7, 235–6, 238, 242–3,
    289, 333, 337, 377–8, 386–94,
    486–8, 494, 503–4, 507–14, 526–9,
    535, 538–41
  arts, sciences, and 335–9, 410–12,
    414–15, 542
  balance of 300, 387–9, 392–3, 506 n., 507,
    510–13, 515, 535, 578
  free 6, 8, 256, 363–4, 390–2, 511–12, 514,
    578
  jealousy in 390–1, 512
  lawlessness and 230–2, 245, 256, 416,
    528
  profits of 343, 349–50, 354–5, 360,
    365, 373, 380–94, 532, 564, 566–7,
    574
  slow progress of 526
  as stage of society 14–16, 459
  subsidies in 243, 259–61, 267, 270, 419,
    524
  see also banks; labour, division of;
    contracts; exchange; fairs and
    markets; free trade; monopolies;
    transport
commodatum 96, 100, 473
common law (England):
  alienage 307–9
  appeals 12, 137, 424, 484
  arson 126, 481
  capital punishment 109–10, 135
  contracts 98, 424–5, 474
  debt 131, 134, 163, 425
  forgery 132
  inheritance 64–5, 310, 425
  pledges 79–80
  property transfer 73, 75–6, 310, 425
  retaliation 118

succession 46–9, 462, 466
theft 127, 482
treason 298
trials 284–5, 425–6
wrongous imprisonment 119–20, 480
Common Pleas, Court of 27, 95, 275–8
    passim, 279 n., 280, 422–4, 540
community, *see* society
competition, *see* price
compositions, for crimes 106–10, 112,
    117–18, 128, 130–1, 208–10, 213,
    245, 260, 274, 416, 419, 476–7,
    479–80, 483
compurgation 425
confarreation 66, 143, 148, 440–1
confederacies 289–90
conquest:
  Norman 52, 68, 110, 251–2
  rights of 411, 466, 550
consanguinity and affinity, degrees of 41,
    146, 163–7, 441, 446–8, 462–3
conscience, courts of 36 n., 282, 425
  liberty of 397, 426, 436
Constantinople 152, 156, 191
consuls:
  modern 554
  Roman 67, 228, 234 n., 319, 410, 414
contempts 291, 301–3, 313, 430–1
contracts:
  as basis of personal rights 9, 12, 78,
    86–102, 134, 400, 424, 472–4
  disputes arising from 105–6, 280, 282
  exceptions in 98, 474
  original/tacit 207, 316–18 *passim*, 321–4
    passim, 397, 402–4, 434–5
  quasi- 12, 86, 102–3, 400–1, 472, 474–5,
    484, 546
  see also marriage, by contract
copyholders 188, 454
  see also feudal
copyright 11, 83, 400, 472
Corinth 227
corn 85, 183, 342–3, 365–7, 380, 382,
    496–9, 507–8, 526, 575
  see also bounties
corporations 22, 84–6, 90, 256, 258–9, 282,
    363–4, 419, 472, 497–8, 529
Corsica(-ns) 323
cotton 337, 344, 491
counterfeiting 87
  see also coinage
Courland 288, 290
courts of justice 258–9, 274–87, 407,
    422–6
  barons' courts 254–5, 257, 259, 283
  county courts 418
  decennery courts 247–8, 254, 417–18
  hundred courts 246–7, 249, 254, 417–18

courts of justice (*cont.*):
  see also Chancery, Common Pleas,
      exchequer, justiciary, King's
      Bench, Session, Star Chamber
Coventry Act (1670) 118–19, 479
cowardice, as punishable offence 130,
    209–10, 406
Crete, Cretans 37, 204
crime 5–6, 103–40, 208–13, 245–6, 422–3,
    426, 475–87
  see also compositions, delinquency,
      murder, piracy, punishment,
      robbery, theft, treason
Crusades 549
Culloden, Battle of 60 n.
culpa, see negligence
customs and excise 6, 235, 238, 263–4, 268,
    325–7, 344, 362–4, 375, 390, 421,
    431, 497, 511–12, 514, 529, 531–4,
    567, 575–6
  see also exports, imports
Cyprus 37

D

dearness 333, 362, 497
debt:
  national 381–2
  personal 133–6, 162–3
  public 268, 421, 514–17, 519, 535–7
decemviri 227, 292, 410
de donis, statute (1285) 69
deductio in domum 144, 440–1
deer-stealing, *see* game laws
defence 6–7, 209, 265, 407, 528, 540, 542
  see also armies, fortification, wars
defence, self- 111, 114–15, 127, 477
Delhi 152
delict, *see* delinquency
delinquency 12–13, 86, 103–4, 400–1, 472,
    475
  see also crime
delivery (legal) 72–3, 469–71
Delos 193
Demesnes 6, 250, 253, 259, 266, 270,
    419–21
Democracy, democratical 109, 125,
    185–6, 200–4, 209, 211, 222,
    225–8, 236, 242, 244, 258, 273,
    287, 289, 291, 303, 318–20, 402,
    404, 407–8, 410–11, 413, 427, 434,
    470
denization 308, 310, 432
Danes, depradations of 245
  alliance with France 552
deodands 116–17, 139, 478–9, 485
depositum 72, 88, 91, 96, 99–100, 473

derelict goods 24, 460
  see also treasure trove
descendants, *see* succession
detinue, writ of 99
Deuteronomy 118 n., 478
dexterity 345–6, 350–2, 491–2, 495, 567–8,
    570, 572, 574, 583
  see also labour, division of
diamonds, *see* gemstones
discipline:
  civic 245, 443, 452–3, 483
  military 231–3, 238, 260, 266, 412, 542–3
dispossession 126–7, 481
division of labour, *see* labour, division of
division of land, *see* land, division of
divorce 44, 47, 66, 141, 143–51, 156–61,
    166, 438, 440–2, 444–5
  see also marriage, monogamy, polygamy
Doctors' Commons 148
Domesday Book 527
domination, love of 186, 192
dominium 10, 21, 26, 470
dominium directum 28–9, 74, 77–8, 250–1, 470
dominium utile 28–9, 74, 250–1, 470
dower, dowry 66, 89, 154, 161–2, 168,
    251–2, 299, 429, 446
drink, drunkenness 363, 497, 514, 533, 540
duck, lame 538
  see also Stock Exchange
duels 112, 122–4, 210, 480
Dutch, *see* Netherlands
duty, *see* customs and excise
dyes 337

E

East India Company 363, 497, 516
East Indies 88, 150, 167, 191–2, 443, 447,
    541, 586
  trade with 243, 363, 415
  see also Java
Ecclesiastical Courts 36 n., 90, 95, 98, 113,
    124, 148–9, 170, 426
Ecclesiastical Law 89–90, 98, 171, 437, 441
Ecclesiastics 89, 113, 148–9, 301, 397,
    429–30, 437, 441, 454, 468
  see also Clergy
Edinburgh:
  frequency of capital crimes in, as
      compared to Glasgow 333, 486
  Court of Session at 120, 480
  John Law, proposed erection of a
      land-bank at 515
  travellers made testaments before setting
      out for Aberdeen 528
  sixpence a day allowed to French
      prisoners 548

education:
  children, learn discipline from their
      parents 142, 172, 174
  expense of, should be recompensed 355
  neglect of in commercial society 539–40
  children, set soon to work 539–40
Egypt:
  polygamy in 150, 444
  the Nile 158–9
  every man bound to follow the profession
      of his father 192
  export of corn to Rome 525, 581
  early cultivation of 586
election 50, 197, 222 n., 227–8, 238, 273,
    410, 422, 431
elections 197, 273–4, 290, 410, 422
  see also representation, right of; votes,
      voting
emancipation 40, 43, 45–6, 48, 63, 188–9,
    256, 454–5, 462, 464, 527
engine(s) 232, 347, 349
England 35–6, 46, 48–9, 64, 68, 73, 75–6,
    79–80, 94–5, 118, 127, 157–8, 239,
    246, 292, 300, 329, 330 n., 332–3, 336,
    340, 366, 372, 376–7, 392–3, 397, 418,
    435–6, 445–8, 466, 468–71, 477–8,
    486–7, 506–7, 512, 519, 524, 526,
    546–7, 550–3, 556, 575–6, 579, 581
  abolition of slavery in 189, *see also* slavery
  benefit of clergy in 113, *see also* clergy,
      benefit of
  children of 6 or 7 years set early to work
      540
  corn of France as good and cheap as that
      of England 342–3, 490
  distribution of fortunes in 196
  divorce in 147, 149, 442
  habeaus corpus in 120, 480, *see also* habeas
      corpus
  judicial combat in 211, 406, *see also*
      judicial combat
  law governing treasonable practices
      137–8, 295, 297–8, 302, 429–31
  laws of in regard to marriage 161–3,
      168–70
  libels and abusive papers circulated in
      125
  and the Normans 245, 257–8, *see also*
      Normans
  payment of rent in 185, 383, 522, *see also*
      rent
  population of, exceeds 9 million 305, 382
  present form of government, unique to
      261–7, 269, 270–90, 323, 327, 374,
      420–7, 502
  primogeniture in 61, *see also*
      primogeniture
  rights of aliens 307, 309–11, 433
  seeds of democracy sown earlier than in
      Scotland 109
  statute of bankruptcy 131, 134–5, 483
  taxes in 530–5, *see also* taxes
  turnpikes of, have increased the opulence
      of the inland parts 356, 494
  value of coinage 374, 502
  wool, considered to be the source of
      public opulence 475
  see also education; commerce
entails 61, 65, 68–71, 467–9, 524–5, 581
equity 42, 119, 316, 436, 546–7
  courts of 136, 281, 424–5
  law of 24, 134
  natural 82, 100–1, 105, 130
  rules of 23
  see also Chancery
error, writ of 278, 280–1, 424
Erse 245
escheat 54–5, 250, 417
escuage 60, 78, 259–60
estates, landed, *see* land, property in
Este family 244 n.
Euboea 221
Europe, *see* individual countries
Euxine Sea, *see* Black Sea
exception (defence at law) 98, 474
exchange(s) 15–16, 91, 324, 355, 368–71,
    374–6, 379, 386, 390–2, 459, 490,
    495, 507, 511–12, 514
  bills of 100, 135, 516–21 *passim*
  medium of 336, 347–9, 351–3, 367–77,
      488, 492–4, 499–504, 506 n.,
      509, 519–21, 524, 527, 529, 570–6,
      582
  propensity to truck, barter and 355, 493,
      570
  see also fairs and markets, money
exchequer 95, 268, 275, 531–2
Exchequer, Court of 95, 275, 278, 279 n.,
    280–1, 421–4
  see also revenue
exclusive privileges, *see* privileges,
    exclusive
executive power, *see* power, federal
    (federative)
exiles, *see* banishment
exports, imports 498, 504, 510, 512–13,
    525, 529, 534–5, 576–8
  see also coin, commerce, customs and
      excise, trade

F

fairs and markets 256–7, 528–9
family:
  biological foundations of 141–2

family (*cont.*):
 and early society 39–48, 201, 207, 213,
  313, 404–8, 467
 laws, rights relating to 7–8, 141–75, 200,
  399, 438–50, 485
 relationships 438–50
 respect, authority in 216–17, 449–51
  passim
 see also power succession
famine 195, 197, 359, 364, 496, 498, 525
fealty, *see* homage
federal (federative) power, *see* power, federal
  (federative)
felony 105 n., 110, 113–15, 258, 294–5,
  299 & n., 301 & n., 302–4, 385, 429–31
feu 51–4, 250, 253, 418, 465, 470
feuda 51–2, 60–2, 249–50, 252, 417, 470
feudal, feudally, *see* land, law, government,
  lord, feudalism
feudalism, feudal system:
 customs of 332–3, 481
 duties of 54–5, 78, 85, 244, 417, 464–5,
  469–70, 542
 holdings 28, 33 n., 77, 237, 250, 418
 jurisdictions 253, 435
 laws of 28, 48, 251, 287, 422, 454, 464,
  470, 524
 legislative powers under 254–5
 succession in 42, 48–9, 435
 vassalage in 29, 416–18, 530
 see also government, feudal; land tenure,
  feudal; primogeniture
feudum 51–2, 250, 470
feus 52, 60, 70, 252
fideicommissum 66–8, 468
fidelity, infidelity 54, 89, 99, 146–9, 160,
  166, 178, 310, 438–9, 441–2, 457,
  464, 504
Fife, likened by James VI to a coarse woollen
  coat, edged with gold lace 585
figures:
 geometric 336
 importance of uniformity, proportion,
  and comprehension in 335–7
 see also aesthetics
fines 19, 24, 69, 104, 106–9, 112, 119,
  121–4, 127–34, 178, 210, 250, 255,
  260, 272, 275–6, 279, 296 n., 302–3,
  416, 419, 423 n., 441, 476, 479–80
fire 5, 114, 312, 331, 334, 351, 487, 505
fire arms 114, 550
fire engines 347, 349, 492–3, 570, 574, 582
 see also inventions
fire-raising 126, 481
fishers 14, 406–7, 498
fishing:
 age of, *see* hunters, societies of
 fishing rights 14, 18, 24–7, 260, 460

 see also game laws, sea law
Florence 231, 244
Florida **8**, 435
Fontainebleau, Peace of (1762) 435 n.
forest laws, *see* game laws
forestallers 528
forgery, forgers 131–3, 429, 481, 483–4
forisfamiliation 45–6, 48, 63, 464
 see also emancipation
Forth, Firth of 26
fortification, forts 26, 219, 224, 288, 295,
  407, 409, 428, 531, 551
 see also wars, warmaking
fortune, *see* succession, wealth
France 55–7, 60–2, 80, 122, 124, 157–8,
  216, 331–3, 342, 371–2, 374–7,
  388–93, 430, 435, 465–6, 469, 474,
  502, 511–19, 521, 531, 539, 575,
  577–9, 581
 the oldest enemy 234, 547
 disorder in, until the time of Capet 252,
  276, 288
 sovereigns absolute in 263–6, 292
 rich, rather than the poor, sent to Bastille
  272
 little drunkenness in 363, 497
 licentious manners of 439
 police, a French name 486
 corn, better and cheaper than in England
  490, 566
 English, better financiers than the French
  534
 see also Franks, Gauls
frank-guild 108–9
Franks 245, 247, 416
fraud 101, 105–6, 131–3, 156, 282, 326,
  368, 372–6, 425, 476, 483, 500, 502,
  504, 510, 519, 539, 548, 576
 see also coinage, debasement of; South Sea
  Company; weights and measures
free commerce, *see* commerce, trade
freedom, *see also* freemen, liberty
freeguild, *see* frank-guild
freehold(-ers) 24 n., 33 n., 253, 274 n., 285,
  419, 524
freemen 180–4, 191–2, 194, 196–8, 226,
  231, 242, 246, 256, 273, 286 n.,
  292 n., 305–6, 410, 417, 419, 431–2,
  448, 453–4, 456, 484, 524, 526
free towns 288–9
 see also boroughs
free trade, *see* commerce, trade
fur manifestus nec manifestus 128–9, 482

G

gambling, gaming 179, 538

game laws 11, 16, 19, 23–4, 82, 114, 127,
    252 n., 407, 460, 471, 482
Ganges, river 29, 158–9, 444
Gaul(s) 218, 221, 223, 227, 234, 239, 245,
    247, 287, 415–16
gavelkind 57, 62
gemstones 333, 335–6, 358–60, 487–8, 496–7
genius 348–9, 352, 493, 572–3
Genoa, Genoese 226, 243, 289, 323
geometry 156, 337, 354, 488–9, 495
Georgia (Asia) 156
German(s), Germany 51–2, 55, 59–60,
    129–30, 158, 189, 191–2, 205, 210,
    212, 218, 230, 239, 251–3, 314, 324,
    427, 433–5, 465, 476, 514, 522, 549,
    579
  nations, over-ran Europe 68, 218, 243–4,
    287, 415–16
  nobles unaffected by the introduction of
    commerce 263–5, 287–9, 420
  slaves, treated with humanity 183–4
  see also Rome; Saxony; Teutons
Glasgow:
  exchange between Glasgow and London
    520
  fairs of, much talked of in antiquity 528
  few capital crimes in 333, 486
  merchants, stock Irish, Scots and
    Hamburgh Linens 355
  and the Virginia trade 483
gold and silver 29, 31–2, 32 n., 100–2,
    229–300, 336, 344–5, 357–9, 367–77,
    379–81, 381 n., 385–91, 391 n., 430,
    491, 494–6, 500–4, 506 & n., 507–11,
    515–16, 518–20, 575–7
  beauty of, a source of value 370
  see also gemstones
Goths 49
government(s) 5–6, 17 n., 20 n., 23, 34, 45,
    49, 51–4, 237, 252, 268, 372
  absolute 237–8, 241–2, 262–5, 319–20,
    420, 422, 429, 435
  allodial 45, 60, 128, 244–8, 252, 283, 288,
    417–18, 425
  feudal 11, 23, 28, 34, 42, 49, 51–61, 73–5,
    77, 128, 187–9, 244–5, 249–52,
    254, 258, 260–1, 263–4, 283, 288,
    290, 324, 332, 417–20, 470, 486,
    520, 581
  forms of 49, 53, 125, 200–330, 401–2,
    404–5, 407, 416, 426
  foundation of 5, 55, 201, 228, 318, 398
  free 186, 452, 480–1
  military 237–41, 414
  objects of 5–8, 331, 338, 489
  origins of 201–8
  powers, rights of 200, 209, 217, 222,
    291–304, 403, 405–6, 433–4, 522

republican 181, 200, 287–8, 293, 318,
    408, 428
  tribal 224–5, 287–8, 408, 426
  see also aristocracy, confederacies,
    democracy, monarchy, power,
    republics
Great Britain, *see* Britain
Greece, Greeks 88, 149–50, 204, 214,
    232–3, 258, 287, 428, 553, 579
  all the necessary circumstances for
    improvement occurred in 223–5,
    408–9
  cattle, the measure of value 367, 499
  cultivation by slaves 185, 188–9, 255,
    451–2, 579
  defensive republics of 228–9
  ease of defence 222
  exposure of children 173
  first inhabitants of, similar to the Tartars
    221
  hardships inflicted upon conquered
    peoples 549
  lands set aside for the maintenance of
    government 530
  loss of martial spirit 235, 411–2
  no resident ambassadors in 551
  polygamy in 157–8
  women, attitude towards 439
  see also Athens, Sparta
Greenland whale fishery 18
guardians 20–1 n., 65 n., 162–3, 174 n., 175,
    399, 439, 445–7, 464
  see also minors, wardship
Guernsey 272
Guinea, coast of 22, 91, 154–5, 443
Gunpowder Plot (1605) 294, 428

H

Habeas Corpus
  Act of (1679) 122, 272–3, 422, 480
  writ of 120
Hamburg 289, 355, 427, 434, 540
Hanover 59, 330
Hanseatic League 372
Helveti 218, 243, 408
Heptarchy 239, 415
  see also Saxons (in England)
Heraclidae 221
hereditary 77, 157, 189, 192 n., 204,
    212, 216, 249, 252, 254, 263, 288–9,
    319, 322, 405, 410, 417–18, 427, 444,
    464
  see also authority, nobility
High Commission Court 286, 296, 329,
    426, 429, 436
Highlands, Highlanders, *see* Scotland

Hindustan 219
Holland, *see* Netherlands
Holy War, *see* Crusades
homage 54, 58, 74 n., 77–8, 464–5, 470
    see also oaths, of allegiance
homicide 110–17, 245 n., 290, 427, 456,
    477–9
    see also manslaughter, murder
hostis 306–7, 432
hotch-pot 46
Hottentots 529, 583–4
House of Commons, *see* Parliament
House of Lords, *see* Parliament
housebreaking, *see* theft
Hudson's Bay Company 363, 497
hundred courts, *see* courts of justice
Hungary:
    alliance with England 552–3
    freemen employed in the mines of 526
    often conquered by the Turks 158
    slavery still persists in 455
Huns 49, 220–1, 408
hunter, societies of 14–16, 18–21, 27, 39,
    107, 201–3, 207–8, 210, 213–14,
    216, 228, 244, 326, 348, 351, 400,
    404–8 n., 459–60, 476, 493, 498, 521,
    542, 572–3, 583
hypothecs, *see* mortgages

I

idiots 139, 320, 323, 457, 485
illegitimacy, *see* bastards
impeachment 272, 302 n., 315, 422, 434
incest 40–1, 163–6, 446, 448
    see also consanguinity and affinity,
        degrees of
India, Indians 338–9, 488–9, 562
    see also Mogul, Moguls
Indies, East:
    goods brought from, conveyed up the Red
        Sea 243
    polygamy in 150, 167, 443
    rules of affinity in 447
    sons follow the profession of their fathers
        191–2
Indies, West:
    and the balance of trade 392
    female slaves in a state of prostitution
        178, 451
    use of slaves in 181, 183, 185, 187, 193–4,
        455–6, 523
    wages of labourers in 350
Indians, American:
    some notion of agriculture among 15–16,
        459
    in the state of hunters 107, 185, 201, 204,

212, 214, 239, 380, 439, 476, 563,
    583–4
Indus, river 215, 219
industry 6, 25, 85, 190, 196, 223, 235, 238,
    242–3, 248, 262, 335, 337–8, 340,
    343–5, 353, 356, 360–2, 364–5, 374,
    378–83, 385, 387–8, 390–2, 394, 409,
    415, 453, 467–9, 494, 497–8, 502,
    507–8, 510–14, 520, 522–6, 531,
    533–5
    balance of 365, 498–9, 529, 575, 578
    see also labour, manufactures
inequality of fortune, *see* wealth, inequality
    of
infangthief 128
infanticide, *see* children, exposure of
infants 57, 142, 156, 444, 457, 465
infeftment 73, 75, 469
infidelity, *see* fidelity
infidels 549
inheritance, *see* succession
injury(-ies) 5–9, 12–13, 16–18, 56–7, 86–8,
    92–4, 103–6, 116–17, 119–27, 130–1,
    141, 147, 151, 160, 166, 178, 201,
    208, 248, 291, 294, 299, 312,
    397–402, 424, 439, 442, 461, 467,
    472, 474–6, 480–1, 483, 485, 539,
    546–7, 552–3
    injury, wilful 103–4, 477
    see also crimes; rights: natural, perfect,
        personal, real
instrumenta dotalis 66
insurance 132–3, 389, 510, 521
    see also fraud
interest 79–80, 100, 135–6, 144, 197, 268,
    357, 484, 519
inventions (mechanical) 11, 83, 337, 340,
    345–7, 349–51, 472, 491–3, 563, 567,
    569–70, 574, 579, 582
Ireland 305, 355
    balance of trade against Britain 392–3
    composition of juries in 285
    price of butchers-meat in 366
Iroquois 106
    see also Indians, American
Isfahan (Ispahan) 152, 154
Israel, children of, *see* Jewry, Jews
Italy 34, 52, 129, 185, 218–19, 223, 236,
    252, 265, 427
    birth does not make a citizen 304
    causes of depopulation in ancient 525,
        581
    a high country 29, 367
    loss of courage in 231, 243, 411–12, 415
    modern, continually improving 393
    sheep used as a measure of value 367, 499
    slavery in 81
    standing armies in 543

weak government of 288–9
see also Rome, Romans
iura ad rem, personalis, see rights, personal
iura in re, see rights, real
ius albani 309–10
ius postliminii 550
ius vitae et necis 449, 451
iustus titulus, see title, just

J

Jacobite rebellions (1715, 1745) 54, 138,
    273, 328, 464, 484, 540–1
see also rebellions
Jamaica 453
Japan 155, 443
Java 154–5
jealousy, *see* marriage, polygamy, trade
Jeophail statutes of 279
Jersey 272
jetsam, law on 102–3
jewels 162, 333, 335, 358–9, 488
    see also gemstones, gold and silver
Jewry, Jews:
    laws and customs 116, 118, 167, 217, 229,
        442
    religion 180, 451, 527
    and trade 527–8
    see also Mosaic law
judges 108, 115, 119–23, 147, 187, 200, 203,
    205, 207, 241, 248–9, 271, 274–87,
    291, 302, 311–15, 322, 325, 407,
    413, 422–3, 425–6, 428, 433–4, 531,
    544
judicial combat 123, 210–11, 283, 312, 406
judicial power, *see* power, judicial
jurisprudence, defined 5–6, 9, 397–9, 401,
    485–6, 541
jury, trial by, *see* trial, by jury
justice 49, 83, 121, 172, 237–8, 250, 252,
    255, 272, 279, 286, 315, 399, 442,
    480, 545
    administration of 5, 7, 16, 88, 237–8,
        241–2, 246–9, 253, 302, 322, 331,
        402, 413–14, 416–17, 422–3, 454,
        464, 486
    commutative, distributive 9
    courts of 274–5, 279, 281, 314, 407,
        422, 428, 431, 433–4, 481, 545–6,
        553
    feeling of 314
    natural 100
    for neutral nations in war 550
    object of 398
    principle, rules of 172, 197, 285, 442,
        460, 550, 597
    study of 141, 200, 398–9, 541, 544

three parts of 200
violation of 7–8
see also equity
Justices of the Peace 149, 242, 259, 277,
    286, 322
justiciary 274–7, 287, 422–3, 427

K

Kalmucks 229
king:
    feudal 28–9, 188, 256
    revenues of 259–60
    role of *colloquium* for 254
    vassals of 253–5, 259
    see also dominium, dominium directum,
        dominium utile
Kings, divine right of 319–20, 402
King's Bench, Court of 89, 95, 247–8, 254,
    258, 275, 277–8, 279 n., 280–1,
    422–4, 480, 540
knight-service 54, 61 n., 64 n., 78 n., 237 n.,
    251 n., 259–60, 419, 542
Korea 306

L

labour, division of 86, 339–53, 355–6,
    374, 390, 392, 400, 411, 489–95,
    500, 512, 521–2, 529, 539–42,
    562–86
    advantages of rich versus poor
        countries arising from 344, 491,
        566–7
    disadvantages of 527, 539–41
    the disposition to truck, barter and
        exchange 347–9, 352, 570–2
    and the extent of the market 355–6, 494,
        582
    as measure of value 503
    natural price of 355–61
    and pin-making 341–3, 349–50, 490,
        564–5
    in rude states of society 348, 351, 493,
        495, 572, 583–4
    see also dexterity, exchange, inventions,
        mechanization, transport, price,
        pin-making
Lacedaemon, Lacedaemonians, *see* Sparta,
    Spartans
laesa maiestas 291, 298, 303, 308, 428
    see also Regalia
lame duck, *see* Stock Exchange
Lancaster, house of 58–9
land:
    division of 20–3, 28, 45, 56, 224, 244–5,

land (*cont.*):
 257, 369, 408–9, 416, 460, 465,
  500, 522–3
 property in 20–3, 28, 161–2, 432–3, 435,
  465
 public 22–3, 460, 530
 tax 6, 268, 366, 382–3, 421, 531–4
 transference of 70–6, 524–5
 see also agriculture, land tenure
land banks, *see* revenue
land rents, *see* revenue
land tenure:
 allodial 28–9, 51–7, 61, 246–54 *passim*,
  257, 416, 418, 464–5
 feudal 28–9, 34–5, 73–5, 77–8, 188–9,
  237, 249–54 *passim*, 261–2, 417–18,
  454, 469–70, 524, 580–1
 forcible entry 126–7, 481
 Saxon law of 251
 see also knight-service
language 21 n., 51, 88–9, 91, 94, 201, 245,
 441, 472, 553
larceny, *see* theft
law:
 agrarian 195, 197
 civil 10–12, 23, 28, 36, 62, 68, 81, 90, 95,
  98, 100, 134, 148 n., 166 n.,
  169–70, 279, 287, 310, 397, 400–1,
  413, 442, 448, 471–4
 criminal 277, 328
 feudal, *see* feudalism
 of nations 37–8, 311, 399, 544–54
 of nature 93, 134, 154–5, 167, 404, 443,
  544, 554
 objects of 331, 338, 397
 private 295, 311, 459, 484, 545
 processes of 276–81, 283–7, 423–76
 public 290, 311, 326, 353, 433, 542, 545
 of war, peace 7, 310, 331, 397
 see also canon law; common law
  (England); courts of justice;
  ecclesiastical law; feudalism, law
  of; judges; power: judicial,
  legislative; Roman law; Scots law;
  Twelve Tables
lawyer, education and compensation of
 354–5
lease(s) 24, 70–1, 75–6, 189, 261–2, 274,
 282, 308, 327, 417, 432, 454, 473, 520
legal tender, *see* coinage
legates 301, 430, 549, 551–2
legislative power, *see* power, legislative
legitimation of offspring 144, 168–72, 440,
 447–8
Leipzig 528
Leith 585
Leyden 216 n.
libel 122, 124–6, 130, 227, 284, 304, 481

see also affront, reputation, slander
liberty:
 personal 119–22, 531–3
 political 262, 264–75, 280, 313, 420–33,
  444
life expectancy 354
Lincolnshire 26, 29
linen 243, 339, 342, 344, 355, 364, 370, 384,
 394, 490, 498, 522, 528, 534–5, 540
liquors, strong, *see* drink, drunkenness
Litchfield man-of-war 307, 432
livre tournois 516
Lombardy, Lombards 18, 117, 218, 219 n.,
 479
London 344, 355, 480, 520, 585
 Bishop of 329, 436
 the largest city in Europe 332, 486
lord, allodial 51, 53, 55, 57, 61, 245, 250–4,
 417–18
lord, feudal 53–4, 60–1, 187, 253–7, 259,
 261–4, 418, 530
 see also Parliament
lords 23, 51–5, 128, 188, 219, 236, 245–9,
 251, 255–9, 262, 264, 296, 329,
 416–19, 464, 470, 482, 528
love, a ridiculous passion 442
lunacy 34, 139–40, 167, 320, 323, 329, 457,
 461, 485, 487
luxury 189, 202, 227, 233, 235–6, 238, 240,
 261–6, 307, 332, 340–1, 405, 410,
 412, 414, 416, 420, 489, 540–1

M

Macao, *see* Meaco (Japan)
Macedon 292
 see also Alexander, Amyntas, Philip
machine(s):
 patents on invention 11, 83
 advantages of 85, 345–7, 349–51, 491–2,
  521–2, 526, 562, 564–70
 see also inventions (mechanical); labour,
  division of
madmen, *see* lunacy
Magdalen College, Oxford 328
Magna Carta 215, 259, 278, 286
maiming 118–19
malice propense, see injury, wilful
Manchester 351
mandatum 91, 100
mankind, an anxious animal 363, 497
manslaughter 110–15, 120, 290, 427, 477–8
 see also homicide, murder
mansuefactae, mansuetae (of animals)
 distinguished 20
manufacturer 342, 344, 351, 365–6, 392,
 411, 526–7

manufactures 5–6, 196, 202, 205, 223, 229–30, 238, 243, 245, 256, 262, 333, 342–4, 351, 353, 355–7, 361, 363, 365–6, 381, 387–92, 405, 410, 414–15, 454, 487–8, 490–1, 494, 497–8, 508, 510, 512, 521–2, 526–7, 529, 535, 539, 542
    profits from 194–6, 342–5, 486–7, 510, 564–8
Marathon, battle of (490 BC) 230
marriage:
    in allodial society 249
    in ancient times 66
    in barbarian European nations 146
    Christian and Roman 47–8, 143–6, 440
    by contract 144, 146, 148, 282, 440–2, 445, 467–8
    effect of 447
    under feudal law 52–5, 249–50, 464
    by force 120–1, 457, 480
    four different sorts of 159–60
    incestuous 41, 163
    introduction of passion of love into 149–50, 442
    love, jealousy in 147, 149–50, 164–5, 167, 438–9, 457
    laws, customs relating to 39–40, 47–8, 141–72, 176, 178–9, 329–48, 441–2
    liberty for salters and colliers of 191
    relation of husband and wife in 141–3
    rules prohibiting 163–6
    see also divorce, monogamy, polygamy, Rome
Marriage Act (1753) 149, 442
martial law 302, 310, 433, 543
    see also wars
martial spirit 260, 540–1
master-servant relationships 141, 175–99, 399, 438, 450–1, 456
Meaco (Japan) 155
measures, *see* weights and measures, value, measures of
Media, Medes 220
Mediterranean Sea 152, 172, 585–6
Megara 229–30
mercenaries 232, 234, 236, 238–9, 243, 260, 412, 414–15
    see also armies, standing
merchant(s) 54, 91, 224, 243, 256, 300, 307–8, 325, 337, 339–41, 344, 349, 355, 358, 364–5, 372, 375, 379, 384–9, 394, 432, 471, 483, 490, 496, 500, 504, 505 n., 506, 509–11, 515, 517, 520, 525, 527, 529, 532–4, 537, 539–40, 542, 546, 549, 552, 554
Merovingians 252
Messenia 221
metayage, metayers, see steelbow, tenants by

Mexico 374, 510
Milan 226, 231, 243–4, 289, 410
military 43 n., 56, 60–1, 73, 77, 105, 118, 128, 192 n., 205 n., 216, 224, 228 & n., 230–3, 237–8, 240–1, 243–4, 248–50, 253, 255, 257, 260, 266–7, 286 n., 305–6, 328, 331, 410, 412–15, 437, 464, 466, 468–9, 479, 527, 540, 542–3
militias 7, 233 n., 265, 331, 399, 542–4
miner 339, 349, 489, 491
mines, mining 28–9, 243, 341, 345, 349, 357, 380, 387–8, 488, 491, 495–6, 507–8, 510, 526, 575, 579
    see also colliers
minors, legal status of 34, 53, 57–8, 65, 78, 103, 250, 316, 399, 440, 457, 464, 467
    see also guardians, wardship
mint, mintage 300–1, 373, 377, 385–6, 430, 502, 509, 511
miser 384, 509
misprision 295, 301–3, 430
Mississippi Company (Bubble) 516–19, 521
Mogul, Moguls 25, 152, 154, 182, 206, 212, 242, 323, 344, 350, 491, 541, 576
    see also India, Indians
monarchy:
    and courtesy in war 550
    duties, and rights of ruler in 291–304, 311–14, 324–30, 397, 427–31, 544–5, 547
    duties, rights of subjects in 152, 272, 291–3, 297, 304–30, 397, 402, 429, 431, 433–6, 452, 547
    as form of government 7, 37, 158, 200, 212, 222, 225, 287–8, 291, 293, 397, 402, 404, 407, 409, 413–15, 466
    hereditary, elective 322, 420, 455
    military 237
    republican 258, 287, 410–11
    and slavery 182, 186, 255, 452
    see also government; kings, divine right of; regalia
money:
    accumulation of 507, 510, 577
    bills 269, 271, 421
    a dead stock 387, 576
    doctrine that opulence consists in 104–5, 378, 381–8, 430, 504, 506–9, 511, 513, 515, 519, 576, 578
    doctrine occasions errors of policy, and hurtful regulations 384–5, 388–94, 509–13, 577–8
    as measure of value 100–2, 367–80, 384–6, 393, 499–504, 507–9, 518–19, 524, 575–8

money (*cont.*):
    see also coinage; exchange; opulence;
        paper credit, currency; stock
monogamy 159–60, 171, 444–5, 448
    see also divorce, marriage, polygamy
monopolies 11, 83–6, 363–4, 386, 444, 472,
        497, 505–7, 517, 529, 532, 575–6, 579
Moors 157
Moray Firth 26
Morocco 306–7, 432
mortality:
    bills of 154–5
    causes among children of 193
mortgages, *see* taxes, mortgages
mortgages 11, 72, 77 n., 78–81, 162, 383,
        400, 421, 471
mosaic law 166–7
munera 52–3, 249–53 *passim*, 464
murder 87–8, 94, 106–18, 124, 129–30, 133,
        135, 138–40, 175, 182, 191, 199, 210,
        240, 245, 290, 294–5, 331–2, 399,
        427, 456–8, 476–9
    see also homicide, manslaughter
murderers 56, 88, 105, 109–10, 114, 292,
        476
Muscovy, *see* Russia
mutilation 117–19, 479
mutuum 91, 96, 100, 473–4
Mycenae 221

N

nail-making 345–6, 350–1, 491
Naples 156
nations, barbarous 66, 72, 164, 172, 206,
        215, 219–20, 238, 240, 243, 247, 306,
        309, 405, 408, 414–16, 446, 476, 482
    see also rich countries
natural, *see* industry, price, rights, wants,
        justice, liberty
naturalization 308–9, 403, 432–3
    see also denization
nature, laws of 93, 134, 154–5, 167, 398,
        404, 443, 544, 554
    state of 398, 404
    see also contract, original
Navarre 37
navigation 25–7, 237, 339, 393, 488, 528,
        586
Navigation Act (1651) 237
negligence 13, 100, 103–4, 117, 126, 401,
        450, 471, 475, 481, 484
negroes 91, 181, 451, 456
Netherlands, Dutch 118, 125, 226, 292,
        340, 479, 517–18
    alliances in the sixteenth century 552
    artisans well paid 344

birth does not make a citizen 304, 306
confederacy in 289–90
elections in 410, 427
exchange with France 521
influence of commerce upon manners:
    probity and punctuality 538
    stupidity of the vulgar, a consequence of
        the division of labour 539
loss of martial spirit 541
numbers of who came to England with
        King William 309, 433
painting, pleases by resemblance 336
proportion of population available for war
        230, 411
taxes in 523–3
use of foreign mercenaries 235, 415
    see also Amsterdam
neutrals 545, 550–1
New England 580
New Jersey 580
Newcastle-upon-Tyne 192, 453
Nile River 158–9, 243, 586
nobility 8, 48, 170, 200, 225, 227, 242, 309,
        325, 329, 333, 410, 435, 454–5,
        486–9, 525
    feudal 261–4
    hereditary 157, 216, 289, 410, 418, 427,
        444
    political role of 157–8, 258–64
    privileges of 416–19, 420
nobles 23–5, 51, 60, 90, 125, 182, 187–8,
        200, 225–7, 241, 244, 251, 256–62,
        264–6, 270–1, 283, 288, 291, 294,
        304, 319–20, 339, 359, 410, 454
nomads 214–15, 218–22, 408
Normandy, Normans 52, 110, 212, 245,
        252, 579
Norway 356
nuda pacta 97–8, 100, 474

O

oaths:
    of allegiance 296, 303, 321, 327, 329, 403,
        423, 431
    blood 97
    and contracts 91, 95, 99
    and juries 283, 285, 425
    and marriage 148, 441–2
    of purgation 113
    of witnesses 119, 133
    see also clergy, benefit of; contracts,
        homage; perjury; promises; trial,
        by jury
obligations:
    in canon law 72
    to the dead 63

of husband/wife 172, 178
of parents/children 172
in Roman/civil law 72
and servitudes 76–7, 85
three sources of 86
    from conduct, *see* contract
    from quasi-contract, *see* quasi-contract
    from injury (delict), *see* injury, delict
of subject 318, 321, 403
see also promises; rights, personal;
    stipulation
occupation, as title to property 13, 14–27,
    32, 71, 192, 459–60
officers, rights of commanding 549–50
Old Testament 405, 467
oligarchy, *see* aristocracy, government by
opulence:
    historical causes of slow progress of 353,
        363–6, 388, 394, 497–8, 513,
        521–8, 578–81
    see also luxury, money, wealth, national
ordeal, trial by, *see* trial, by ordeal
original contract, *see* contract, original
orphans, *see* guardians, minors, legal status
    of, wardship
Ostrogoths 221, 408
Ottoman Empire 242
outfangthief 128
outlawry 280, 301, 303, 430–1
ownership, *see* accession

P

painting 30–1, 336, 360
Palus Malotis, *see* Azov, Sea of
Papacy, political influence of 296, 301, 427,
    430, 442, 447–8, 478, 549, 551–2
    see also Roman Catholicism
paper credit, currency 31, 132, 378–9, 384,
    503–7, 515–21, 576, 578
    see also coinage, money
parabola 336
pardon, royal prerogative of 109, 135, 272,
    422, 477
parent-child relationships 142–3, 151–3,
    167, 172–5, 179, 402, 438, 444, 450,
    462–4
    see also children, minors
pares 254–5, 257–8, 418
Paris 287, 331–2, 486–7, 518
    parlement 98, 287, 426
    patriotism 218
    police 332, 486–7
    Treaty of 435 n.
Parliament:
    financial powers of 266–71, 275, 323,
        325–7, 374, 377, 385, 430, 509

House of Commons 118, 257, 259, 261–2,
    266–7, 269–72, 274, 283, 309, 315,
    319, 377 n., 419, 421–2, 434, 524
House of Lords 257, 261, 266, 269–71,
    283, 309, 315, 421
    judicial role of 271–3, 277, 286, 424, 479
    legislative role of 315, 403, 426, 432–6
        passim, 448
    political role of 236, 254, 262, 264, 297–9,
        308–9, 310–11, 327–9, 413, 421, 581
    privileges, rights of members 303, 306,
        418–19
    Scottish 515
Parthians 220
partnership 91, 97, 473
    see also commerce, trade, contracts
parole 548
patents 11, 83, 472
    see also inventions
patriarchs 202, 405
patricians 227–8, 240, 410
patriotism 218
pawns, *see* pledges
peculium castrense 43, 175, 450, 463
peers 254–5, 259, 266, 280, 285–6, 303, 419,
    421, 423
    see also House of Lords; nobility;
        Parliament; trial, by peers
Pennsylvania 580
perduellio 291, 293, 303–4, 428
peregrinus 304, 306, 309, 431
perjury 131, 133, 147, 283–4, 441, 484
Persia:
    arbitrary government 154, 182
    conquered by barbarous nations 414
    defeat of by Macedon 431
    over-ran Media 220
    part of the empire of Tamberlane 219
    polygamy in 150, 152, 157–8
    respect for family in 216–9
    seraglios, tranquility of 152
    slavery still takes place in 198
persuasion, power of 192, 352, 493–4
    see also exchange
Peru 374, 380, 388, 510
Petersburgh 195
Petition of Right (1628) 327, 436
philosophers:
    benefits of speculation of 570, 574, 582
    contrasted with the porter 348–9, 493,
        572–3, 582
    a separate trade which increases output
        347, 492, 570
    stone of 301, 430
    see also inventions
Picts 239, 415 n.
pigeon-stealing, *see* game laws
pignus 10, 91, 473

pillory, *see* punishment
pinmaking 341–3, 345, 349–51, 490–1, 539, 564–8
  see also labour, division of
piracy, pirates 82, 127, 131, 172, 224, 234, 245, 310, 482–3, 527–8
Pitt diamond 358
Plataea 283
pledges 11, 72, 78–81, 85, 96, 400, 459, 469, 471
plenty, *see* police
Poland, Poles 189, 266, 288, 290, 309, 579
police:
  Glasgow and Edinburgh 333, 486
  London and Paris contrasted 332, 486–7
  nature of 5, 331–2, 486
  role of, in government 5–6, 54, 139, 150, 167, 192, 215, 300, 331–94, 398, 447, 538–42, 544, 567, 575, 581
politicians 539
  see also Parliament
polygamy 150–61, 171–3, 442–5, 448–9
  jealousy in 151–3, 157–60, 442–3
  see also divorce, marriage, monogamy
polytheism 451
  see also infidels
Pope 148, 165, 171, 288, 296, 301, 427, 429–30, 436, 441–2, 447–8, 454, 478, 549, 551
popery 329, 436, 549
population:
  of British Isles 231
  circumstances promoting growth of 158–9
  effect of slavery on 192–9
  regulations for increasing 159
porter, *see* philosopher
Portugal, Portuguese 16, 59, 243, 264, 386–8, 391–2, 430, 509–13 *passim*, 577–8
post offices 553
possession, *see* accession, occupation, prescription, rights, real
poverty:
  causes of 197–8
  law relating to 305
  political effects of 401, 579
power:
  balance of 49, 552
  federal (federative) 200–2, 204, 206–7, 209, 211, 213, 217, 222, 237, 241, 312–16, 326, 405–7, 413, 434
  judicial 119, 121, 187, 200–1, 203–7, 213, 217, 222, 241, 275–6, 278–80, 290, 312–14, 316, 326, 405–6, 433–4
  legislative 187, 200, 202, 205, 207, 213, 222, 237–8, 241, 269–71, 313–16,

326, 405–6, 434, 545
sovereign 145, 200, 311, 319–21, 323, 326, 545
  see also authority, family, government
Praemunire, Statutes of (1353, 1392) 296 n., 298, 301, 430–1
praetor 42, 67, 175, 463, 468, 479
praetors 130, 174, 228, 237
praetorian 457
praetorship 228 n.
prescription 14, 25, 32–7, 66, 133, 135–8, 143–4, 440, 459, 461–2, 472, 484
Pretender 431
  see also Jacobite Rebellions
price:
  market 356–9, 494, 496
  natural 355–7, 360–4, 387, 389, 494–8, 510, 528, 533
  interdependence of 359–61, 496–7, 575
  of labour 192, 354–5, 528, 533
  raised by monopolies 363
  see also labour, division of; monopoly; taxes; value
priest, priests 66, 68, 146–7, 180, 296 & n., 406, 429
priesthood 145
prima seisin, *see* seisin
primogeniture 49–61, 70–1, 157, 204, 324, 435, 444, 456, 465–6, 524–5, 581
prisoner(s) 122, 198, 216 & n., 251, 417 & n., 422, 548
  see also punishment, war, warmaking
privileges, exclusive 11, 81–6, 400, 459, 471–2, 497, 516, 529
Privy Council 82, 272, 328, 374, 436
probity 333, 338, 487, 489, 528–9, 538–9
  see also fraud
proditio 293, 295, 303, 428
production, *see* manufactures
profits:
  from land ownership 73, 78, 274, 394, 417, 464, 579
  of master, merchants, dealers, etc. 85, 181, 343, 350, 354, 355, 372, 564, 566–7
  under monopoly 84, 363–4, 580
  of trades 357, 360, 365, 567, 576, 578
  see also fairs and markets, feudalism, manufactures, revenue, stock, taxation
promise 12, 67, 87, 89, 92–4, 180, 316–17, 400, 468–74
  see also oaths
property:
  common 22, 25–6
  as foundation of government 208–9
  inequality of 245, 262–3
  legal aspects of 13–86, 213, 400

loss of 30
offences against 126–33
real, personal 21–2, 29–30, 445–6
rights 5, 10, 13–14, 161–2, 459–70, 545
transfer of 13, 71–6, 282, 459, 469–80, 581
see also aliens, land, marriage
prostitution 178, 193, 451
Protectorate (Commonwealth) in Britain 237–8
Protestantism 165–6, 267, 296–8, 299, 301, 327, 329, 432, 436, 442
see also reformation
Prussia 550, 552
courage of 543
does not pay subsidies to its allies 243
great size of estates in 263
proportion of population available for war 230
subsidy provided by Britain 546
vast army of 267
punctuality and commerce 528, 538–9
punishment:
capital 106, 109–10, 112, 120–1, 129–32, 134–5, 272, 299
fines as 106–9
imprisonment as 480
legal aspects of 422
moral aspects of 136–40, 209–10
pillory as 124–5, 132–3, 482–3
resentment as regulator of 104–5, 422, 475–6, 484–5
see also banishment, war
pupils, *see* minors, legal status of
pupillary substitution 65, 467
puritans 267, 297

Q

quasi-contract, *see* contract
quo minus 280, 424

R

rank, social 8, 22, 24, 59, 107, 123, 145, 153, 161, 175, 178, 200, 226, 278, 302, 333, 360, 362, 426, 443, 492, 495, 520, 542, 566
rape 120–1, 156, 457, 480
reading, knowledge of, in Scotland 540
reason, natural 11, 82–3, 525, 538
rebellions, *see* Jacobite rebellions (1715, 1745), treason, contract
recognizance 95, 98, 473
recoinage:
circulation of 100, 385, 502, 509–10

see also coinage, debasement of; coinage, overseas
recovery 69 n.
Red Sea 243, 415
Reformation 148, 166, 303, 429–30, 436
regalia (royal privileges) 246, 252–3
Regent diamond, *see* Pitt diamond
Regiam Majestatem (1609) 58, 89
relief, *see* feudalism, duties of
religion 112, 155, 173, 179–80, 191, 296–7, 299, 328–30, 429, 432, 436, 440, 443, 451, 453, 540, 549–50, 574
see also Christianity, clergy, Jewry, Papacy, polytheism, Protestantism, Roman Catholicism
rent 24, 30, 50–2, 54, 61, 71, 77–8, 80–1, 185, 248–50, 262, 274, 276, 366, 382, 445, 498–9, 515, 522
aggregate, of England 382–3, 522–3, 530
in kind 185–6, 190, 195, 248, 454, 523–4, 580–1
land 530–1, 533–4, 575
for liberty of trade 257
see also revenue
representation, right of 48–9, 57–9, 61, 257–8, 260–1, 306, 463–4, 524
see also elections, votes, voting
republics, republican government 7, 181, 200, 223, 225–38 *passim*, 240, 242–4, 258, 288–93, 297, 299, 304–6, 318, 404, 408–14, 426–8, 431, 550
little, in Europe 288–90, 427
see also Rome
reputation 8–9, 13, 122–6, 480–1
see also affront, libel, slander
resentment 74, 88, 92, 104–6, 116 & n., 127–9, 131–2, 136–40, 160, 201, 208, 263, 277, 294 n., 399, 404, 422, 439, 475–6, 478, 482, 484–5, 546–8
res nullius 419
resistance 111, 115, 298, 311–30, 429, 433–6
see also monarchy, duties and rights of subjects in
restitution, *see* contracts, quasi-
Restoration of Stuarts (1660) 237, 267, 297, 421 n., 429
retainers 246, 248–9, 261–2, 265, 332–3, 410, 416, 420, 486, 528, 563
see also servants
revenge 94, 104–5, 108, 118, 124, 149, 154, 221, 277, 314, 476
revenue:
of king or government 6, 25, 108, 212, 225, 238, 260, 266–70, 274–6, 289, 305, 322–4, 326–7, 353, 376, 398, 402, 407, 409, 414, 419–22, 435, 502, 514–17, 529, 541, 544, 567

revenue (*cont.*):
  see also customs and excise, taxation
revenue-farming 516–17, 534
Revolution of 1688 218–20, 299, 303, 311,
  323, 325, 328, 344, 380, 429, 436, 535
revolutions 218–20, 323, 408
rhetoric, Smith's lecture on 165
Rhodes 102
rich countries:
  can afford to undersell poor ones 344,
    491, 566–7
  see also labour, division of
Riga 195
Right, Petition of, *see* Petition of Right
rights:
  acquired, adventitious 8, 105, 399, 401,
    459, 476
  natural 8, 13, 105, 398–9, 401, 459, 476
  origins of 8, 13–14
  perfect, imperfect 5, 7, 9, 200, 326–7, 545
  personal 9–10, 12–13, 14 n., 37, 71, 75,
    78, 85–140, 309, 399–401, 459,
    470–2, 475–6, 485, 580
  real 9–11, 13–86, 90, 133–5, 287,
    399–400, 459–72, 476, 481, 524
  see also citizenship, contract, prescription,
    primogeniture, representation,
    resistance, servitudes
risk 387–9, 495, 509–10, 520–1, 528, 534,
  536
rivers:
  navigable 26–7, 29, 159, 219, 528
  rights in 460–1
roads, advantages of 356, 378, 494, 503,
  528, 576
  see also transport
robbery 16, 82, 87, 94, 105, 127, 129–31,
  210, 224, 272, 332, 356, 482–3, 494
  see also theft
Roman Army 233, 239–40, 314
Roman Catholicism 113, 165, 296–7, 299,
  301, 327–30, 429, 436
  see also Christianity, clergy, Papacy
Roman Empire, fall of 49, 52–3, 232–5,
  240, 247, 288, 380, 415, 476, 508,
  522, 526, 530, 541
Roman law 59, 68, 79 n., 80, 92, 314, 441,
  457 n., 479
  arson in 126
  children in 169–70, 172–5, 448
  citizenship 304, 306
  contracts in 98, 100, 103, 473–5, 546
  hypothecs in 81, 471
  libel in 125, 481
  marriage in 47, 66, 143, 148–50, 161, 164,
    169, 438, 440, 446
    divorce in 145–6
  noxal surrender in 547

personal injury in 122, 479
on pledges 80–1, 471
property transfer in 73, 462
representation in 59
servitudes in 76–8
slaves, treated with humanity 184
slaves in 179–81, 188, 191, 193, 198, 255,
  306, 451, 452, 455, *see also* slaves
senatorial power of 206
succession in 38–45, 49, 62, 64, 144, 448,
  462–5
theft in 128, 132, 482
treason in 291, 303, 428
on wills 64–7, 466–8
see also Twelve Tables, law of
Russia:
  alliances of, in the sixteenth century 552
  frequency of revolutions in 323
  slavery in 181, 189, 198, 579
  succession in 435
  trade with England 535
  see also Siberia

S

Salic law 60, 107, 325, 435, 479
salters 191–2, 453, 579
Sardinia 37, 298
satire 481
savage nations 15, 65, 106–7, 146, 156–8,
  201, 204, 207–8, 239, 244, 313,
  334–6, 338–41, 346, 348, 351, 380,
  426, 443, 451, 460, 487, 489, 493,
  508, 521–2, 530, 563, 572, 583
Saxons (in England) 37, 57, 59, 62, 212,
  239–40, 244, 247–52, 309, 380, 415,
  467, 523, 579
Saxony 265, 309, 433, 546, 550
Scandinavia 146
  see also Denmark, Norway, Sweden
schools, *see* education
Scotland:
  abolition of slavery in 189
  banks of, encouraged trade and
    manufactures 380, 503
  change from allodial to feudal government
    252–3
  common people less honest as compared
    to England 333, 487, 538–9
  Dutch recruit in 238–9
  few have a vote for members of
    Parliament 323
  Highlands of 54, 56, 129, 261, 464, 524,
    540–1, 582
  invention of machines by common
    workmen 351
  Lowlands of, richer than France 392

neither rich nor well cultivated 218
payment of rent in 185, 515
reduction in the power of the nobility 262
Roman Wall in 415
united with England 265
see also Union, Act of
Scots law 35–6, 98–9, 110, 113, 126–9, 132,
135, 466, 469, 478
on appeals 271
on arson 126, 481
courts of justice in 274, 285, 287, 426
on debt 131, 135, 163, 475, 484
on discharge 134
English law compared to 49, 62, 64, 69,
73, 75, 95, 110, 113, 127, 132, 161,
166, 480, 482
on forgery 132
frankgild in 54–5, 108, 168–9, 446
land tenure in 161–2, 469, 581
on marriage 159
on pledges 79–80
on retaliation 118
rights in 35, 471
theft in 128–9, 482
thirlage in 85
on treason 298, 429
wrongous imprisonment in 120, 122
see also Session, Court of
scutage, *see* escuage
Scythia, Scythians 97, 193, 220, 238–9, 441
sea law 25–7, 29, 460
Rhodian 102–3
see also ships
seasons and agriculture, *see* Agriculture
seisin, prima seisin 33, 250, 417
self-command 352, 533
self-interest 50 n., 348, 352–3, 493, 538
self-love 347–8, 493
Senate 182, 228, 236–7, 427, 435
powers of 206, 211, 213, 241, 290, 407,
413
seraglios 152–3, 156, 443
Sertorian War 234
servants 50–3, 61, 73, 113, 152, 159, 261,
297, 301, 333, 339, 361, 385, 486,
492, 553
laws relating to 141, 162–3, 166, 175–99,
399, 438, 446, 450–6, 458, 483
see also retainers, slaves
servitudes 10–11, 25, 76–8, 81, 85, 90, 162,
400, 455, 459, 470, 472
servitus, *see* servitudes
Session, Court of (Scotland) 81, 95, 98, 109,
120, 136, 279, 286–7, 423, 426, 456 n.
see also Scotland
settlement, *see* citizenship
Settlement:
Act of (1701) 297–8

Law of 431
Seven Years' War (1756–63) **8**, 238 n., 324,
384, 411, 415, 543, 546–8
sexes:
inclinations of 141–2, 527
proportions between 154–6, 193, 443
Sheffield 351
shepherds, societies of 14–16, 20–1, 27–8,
39, 107, 202–4, 208–10, 213–22,
228–30, 244–5, 248, 287, 326, 369,
404–8, 411, 426, 459–60, 500, 514,
521, 542, 572–3, 583
sheriffs 54 n., 68, 120, 122, 242, 247, 271–2,
274–5, 277, 279–80, 284, 422–3, 425,
480
ships:
as deodands 479
insurance of 132–3, 483
see also sea law, war, warmaking
Siberia 216, 219
Sicily 581
sieges 232–3, 235, 359, 412, 548–9
see also war
Silesia 37
silk 84, 243, 337, 344
silver, *see* gold and silver
sinking fund 268, 421, 538
slander 122–4, 399, 480–1
see also affront, libel, reputation
slave, slavery, slaves 80–1, 143–4, 176–86,
187–93, 194, 196, 197–9, 226–7, 231,
234, 242–4, 255–6, 306–7, 410–12,
450–6, 476, 523
abolition of, claims of the clergy 454–5
in modern times 181, 187, 191
no encouragement to industry 523, 526,
579–80
probable invention of the spindle by 346,
492, 569
universal in the beginning of society;
man's love of domination 186–7,
192, 388, 451
see also villeinage
Smyrna 152, 156, 219
socage 61–2, 74, 237
societas (partnership) 91
society:
stages of 14–16, 27–8, 106–7, 129–30,
187, 201–21, 459
see also agriculture, commerce, hunters,
shepherds
soul, immortality of 63–4
South Sea Company (Bubble) 519, 538,
578
sovereign 55, 264, 266–7, 276, 296–7,
318–21, 323–6, 330, 376, 397, 420,
427, 430–3, 435, 454–5, 465, 544–8,
552–3

sovereign (*cont.*):
crimes against subject by 291, 293–4,
296, 304, 311
in European republics 427
three branches of supreme power of 200,
311–14, 322
see also government, kings, monarchy,
power, regalia, treason
Spain:
ambassadors of 551–3
causes of the poverty of 535
conquered by Carthage 233, 240
derives great riches from colonial mines
243
elimination of slavery in 189
ill effects of such riches 387–9, 391–2,
510–13, 577
kings of, promoted agriculture 525
little drunkenness in 363, 497
sovereigns absolute 263–5, 311, 323–4,
435
Sparta, Spartans 128, 173, 182, 221, 228,
231, 236, 292 n., 314, 369, 411–13,
439, 482
spectator 17–19, 32, 87, 104, 142 n., 422,
459, 461, 475
see also sympathy
speech, freedom of, *see* liberty, political
spiral, Archimedean 336
stampmaster 529
standard of value, *see* value, measures of
staple (market) town 473, 529
Star Chamber, Court of 95, 286–7, 426
steel-bow, *see* tenants
stipulation 89, 94–7, 472–3
stock:
accumulation of 519–22, 527, 579–80
agricultural 189–90, 454, 471, 523–5,
580
common (family) 39–43, 45, 47, 463–4
dead 378, 385, 387, 389, 503, 509–10, 577
education as 357
jobbing 518, 535–8
manufacturing, trading 344, 366, 514–15
national 365, 381–4
tax, interest on 519–20, 531–2
of the whole kingdom *34*, 365, 381–4
Stock Exchange, bears and bulls in 537–8
subjects, duties of, rights of, *see* monarchy
subsidies, *see* commerce, trade
substantia cedet formae 30–1, 461
succession:
Borough-English 63, 466
by descent 59–60, 62, 163, 435, 446,
463–4
by election 263, 265
feudal 249–50, 252, 254, 464
rights of 10–11, 37–71, 81–2, 171–2, 246,

253, 294, 297–8, 325, 400, 462–6,
471
successio perstirpes 43, 48–9, 57
testamentary 14, 27, 37–8, 40, 43, 63–71,
90, 204, 275, 282, 308, 448, 466–9
see also bastards, collaterals, salic law
sugar trade (N. America) 181, 183–4, 193,
491, 523
Sweden, Swedes 216, 266, 349, 370, 544,
552
Switzerland 125, 289, 292, 304, 306, 427,
431
see also Helvetti
sympathy 17, 130, 142 n., 184, 294, 401,
438, 475, 484
see also spectator
Syria 179, 193

T

tabula 30, 461
taille 581
tallage 251, 253, 581
tanners 84, 348
Tartary 16, 23, 38
absolute authority of chiefs in 244
conquests of 157–8, 219–21, 522, 541
early inhabitants of Greece in the same
state as 221, 223, 409
expeditions of, involve the whole
community 215, 229, 408
German nations had better notions of
property 416, 460
incapable of improvement 409
lack of agriculture in 15
princes, hearing of causes requires a
gratuity 206, 212–13, 529
respect for age in 57, 465
and for descent 216
a savage nation 157–8
the shepherd state of 218, 409, 414, 514,
583
see also Germans, shepherds
tax, taxes 6, 238, 241–2, 251–2 n., 257–8,
263, 266–8, 270, 272, 299, 323–4,
326–7, 344, 353, 362–6, 371, 373,
382–3, 398, 404, 421, 428, 431,
435–6, 491, 497–9, 502, 511, 514–16,
526, 529–36, 542, 550, 553
canons of 531–3
farming of 234, 256, 517, 534
see also customs and excise; land, tax;
revenue; stock
tenants 29, 48, 51–2, 60–1, 70–1, 246,
248–51, 284, 340, 383, 416–18, 420,
449, 464, 466, 486, 499, 530, 532–3
tenants at will 261, 454

see also land tenure, feudalism
tenants, free 185–6, 189–90, 196, 454
tenants, steelbow, 80–1, 189–90, 454, 471, 523–4, 580
Test Acts (1673, 1678) 327–8, 436
Testament, Old 405, 467
testaments, *see* succession, wills
Teutons 218, 408
Thebes, Thebans 231 n., 235
theft 16, 82, 87–8, 94, 105, 114, 127–32, 210, 481–3
see also robbery
Theodosian Code 97
Thessalians 220
thirlage 85
Thrace 305
Tiber River 181
tithes 190, 246, 524, 534, 581
title, just 33–6, 461–2
Tory party 319–20, 402, 532
Tours 516 n.
towns 6, 10, 76, 84, 201, 203, 245, 273–4, 295, 333, 346, 355, 409, 412, 453, 470, 473, 526, 529, 534, 550
toys 343, 488, 490, 566
trade, *see* commerce
tradition, and property law 13, 27, 71–6
traitors 210 n., 310–11, 317
transference, voluntary, *see* property, transfer of
transport:
  cost of 344, 356, 366, 378, 491, 494, 499, 510, 528, 575, 585–6
  land, water 223, 339, 356, 366, 494, 528, 562, 585–6
  see also roads
treason 113, 129, 130–1, 137, 206 n., 209, 291–9, 301–4, 310–11, 330, 403, 406, 427–31, 433, 458, 483–4
  petty 453, 483
treasure trove 25, 260, 460
  see also derelict goods
trial:
  by combat 58, 123, 210–11, 283, 312, 406, 425, 434, 465
  by jury 99, 105, 108, 115–16, 271, 276, 280, 283–7, 401, 425–6, 475
  by ordeal 210–11, 312, 406, 434
  by peers 255
tribunes 41, 227–8, 410
tribute 212, 431
trigonometry 354
Trojan War 149, 204, 221, 224–5, 228, 232, 287, 409, 412
trouver and conversion 99, 280
Troy 204 n., 412
troy weight 300, 371–2, 374, 501
  see also weights and measures

Troyes (France) 42, 501, 528
truck, barter and exchange 347–8, 351, 355, 493, 527
  see also labour, division of
Tudors 262–6, 270, 297, 420
Turkey, Turks:
  conquered Hungary 158
  incursions of, led to the fall of the Roman Empire in the East 240
  military government of 241, 414, 435
  polygamy in 150, 157, 443
  seraglios in 151–4, 439
  slavery in 182, 198, 306, 526
  sovereign, absolute power of 311, 323
  treasures in 25
Turkey (Trading) Company 363, 516
Turkomans 242
Tuscany, Tuscans 367, 499
turnpike 356
Twelve Tables, law of 34, 38, 42 n., 64, 79 n., 118, 125, 130, 132 n., 173–4, 227, 449, 462, 463 n., 467, 483
  see also Roman law
tyrants, tyranny 25, 152, 222, 236, 272, 292–3, 297, 311, 314, 339, 428, 524
Tyre 182

U

Union, Act of, between England, Scotland (1707) 265, 298, 429
United Provinces, *see* Netherlands
universities, privileges of 436
upstart 217, 225, 263, 267, 321, 402, 444
Uses, statute of 75
usucapio, *see* prescription
utility 104, 338, 407, 438, 460, 484–5, 500
  principle of 318–22, 401–2, 404, 407, 434, 475
Utrecht 505
  Peace of (1712) 326, 517

V

value:
  measures of 344, 350, 353, 367–77, 494, 499, 500–1, 503, 575
  paradox of 333–6, 358–9, 361–2, 487, 496
  affected by scarcity 258, 370, 380, 496–7
  see also price
Vandals 49, 220
vanity 71, 380
vassals 24, 35, 51, 53, 55, 60, 73–4, 74 n., 75, 77–8, 128, 187–8, 246, 250 & n.,

vassals (*cont.*):
    253–5, 259, 284, 409, 452, 454, 464,
        469–70, 477, 481–2
    see also feudalism, vassalage in
Venice, Venetians 37, 217, 226, 228 n.,
        242–3, 289, 290, 410, 427
villeinage, villeins 48, 80, 107, 185–7,
        189–90, 211, 246, 255–6, 259, 331,
        418–19, 454, 523, 542, 579
virtue, Hobbesian doctrine of 397–8
Visigoths 72, 221, 247, 408, 469
Voconian law 67, 468
votes, voting 50, 197, 227–8, 274, 289,
        290–1, 306, 323, 410–11, 427, 435,
        455, 524, 581
    see also elections; representation, right of

W

wafes, *see* waifs
wager of law 99, 283
wages 101, 333, 342–3, 350, 354–6, 360–2,
    375–6, 456, 473, 487, 490–1, 494–7,
    565–7, 574–5, 583
    of colliers 192, 453
waifs 260, 419
    franchise of 24, 35
Wales, Welsh 245
wants, natural 334–7, 340, 487–9
war:
    Carthaginian 229, 233, 236, 240, 411,
        541
    Civil 429
    Peloponesian 225, 229, 232 n., 233
    Trojan 149, 204, 221, 224–5, 228, 232,
        287, 409
war, 'the last', 'the late', 'this', *see* Seven
    Years' War (1756–63)
wardship 53–4, 244, 249, 256–7, 286, 413,
    416–17, 419, 426, 464
    see also guardians, minors
warehouses, *see* commerce, trade, customs
    and excise, labour, division of
watch-maker, education required for trade
    as 354, 495
water, *see* value, paradox of
water-carriage, *see* transport
water-mill 85, 346–7, 492

wealth:
    accumulation of 387–8
    as index of social rank 183–7, 202–4, 206,
        262–3
    individual 194–7
    inequality of 184, 202, 208, 262–3, 338,
        401, 404–5, 453, 464, 489, 563–4,
        566
    national 262–3, 343–4, 350, 353–5,
        358–9, 361–6, 381–94, 472, 486,
        494, 497, 503–15 *passim*, 519,
        521–41, 562–81
    respect for 401–2, 409
    social effects of 411–12
    see also cost of living, fairs and markets,
        luxury, money
weights and measures 367–70, 372, 374–5,
    475, 499–500, 501
West Indies, *see* Indies, West
Westminster 272, 278, 286, 422
Westphalia, Treaty of (1681) 37
Whig party 319–20, 327, 402
wills 63–71, 168–71, 174, 203, 205, 282,
    309–10, 324, 406, 425, 432–3, 448,
    451, 462, 464, 466–9, 528, 545
    see also succession
Wingild 107–9
Witenagemot 246–8, 417
woman, women 21, 24, 49, 53, 59–62, 66–7,
    120–1, 143–7, 156, 160–2, 167, 169,
    171–4, 176, 193, 222, 229–31, 247,
    411, 438–44, 457–8, 465–6, 479–81
    liberties of and respect for 439
    maintenance of young by 142, 152–8,
        438
    property rights 59–61, 465–7
    see also children, divorce, marriage,
        prostitution, rape, slavery
wool, woollen 104–5, 336–8, 342, 344, 383,
    387, 389, 475, 489–90, 522, 529, 562,
    565
writing 337, 431, 488–9

Y

York:
    city of 54, 256
    house of 58–9, 260

Index of Persons

A

Abraham 180, 216, 405, 451
Abrincus, Hugh de 249 n.
Abu Bakr 215 n.
Abu'l-Ghasi Bahadur Khan 216
Achilles 108
Adrian, see Hadrian
Aeneas 149
Aetius, Flavius 239–40, 415
Afranius, Lucius 180
Agamemnon, ruler of Mycenae 214
Ajax 108 n.
Alaric I, King of the Visigoths 221
Alcibiades 236
Alexander the Great, of Macedon 158, 233, 235
Alfred the Great, king of the English 51, 59
Alfric, Earl of Mercia 57 n.
Amyntas III, of Macedon 305, 431
Anastasius I, Byzantine emperor 170
Anne, Queen of England 114, 131, 298, 326, 330, 393, 478, 513, 519, 536
Antoninus Pius, Roman emperor 452
Antony, Mark (Marcus Antonius) 145, 156, 234
Arcadius, Flavius, Roman emperor 240–1, 468 n.
Archimedes 336
Argenson, Marc René de Voyer, Comte d' 5, 331
Aristides the Just 228
Aristogeiton 292
Aristotle 22–3, 88, 192 n., 197, 371 n., 530
Attila, the Hun 164, 220
Atticus, Titus Pomponius 196 n.
Augustus (Gaius Octavius), Roman emperor 43, 174 n., 234, 241, 413
  and Cleopatra 444
  and fidei commissum 67, 468
  and libel 481
  and property rights for sons 43 n., 450
  and slavery 177–8, 452
  and Twelve Tables 125
Aurelius, Marcus (Antoninus), Roman emperor 241
Austria, House of 189
Ayesha, wife of Mahomet 156

B

Bacon, M. 80 n., 471 n., 473 n. (Q)
Balliol, John de 58, 465
Barbarossa, see Frederick I
Beaufort, John 171 n.
Becket, Thomas, a saint, martyr 51
Biefeld, Baron J. F. von 5 n., 230
Blair, Hugh 573 n.
Bolingbroke, Henry St John, 1st Viscount 270
Bosman, W. 154
Bouquet, Pierre 52 n., 251–2
Brandenburg, House of 59, 263
Bruce, Robert, King of Scotland 58, 465
Brunswick, House of 59
Brutus, Marcus Junius 292
Burnet, Gilbert 118 n., 325 n., 327 n., 328–9 n.
Bute, John Stuart, 3rd Earl of 546 n.

C

Caesar, Gaius Julius 145, 236, 292 n.
  and administration of justice 238
  dictator 413
  in Gaul 218, 227, 234
  and property rights for sons 43, 175, 450, 463
Caligula, Roman emperor 320, 323, 525
Callis, Robert 26 n.
Calvin, John 436
Cameron, Archibald 138, 484
Cameron of Lochiel, Donald 54
Cannan, Edwin 552 n.
Canterbury, Archbishop of 329
Cantillon, Richard 354 n.
Canute, King of England 110, 112
Capet, Hugh 252, 276, 288, 427
Cappadocia 179, 193
Caracalla, Roman emperor 174 n., 240
Cassius (Gaius Cassius Longinus) 30
Catherine II, of Russia 243
Catiline (Lucius Sergius Catilina) 97
Cato, Marcus Porcius, the elder 66, 181, 525, 581
Ceres, Roman deity 132
Catullus, Gaius Valerius 180
Chambers, E. 342 n.

Charlemagne, Holy Roman Emperor 37,
    221, 263, 288, 372, 427
Charles I, of England 211, 273, 286, 327 n.,
    327–9, 397
    and Parliament 266–7, 269–70, 297
Charles II, of England 35, 118, 231, 237,
    297, 300 & n., 393, 413, 513
    and Court of Wardship 286, 426
    and extravagance 267, 421
    and Parliament 269, 325–8
Charles V, Holy Roman Emperor 265,
    288
Charles XII, of Sweden 216
Charles Martel, King of France 276
Charlevoix, P.-F.-X. de 20–1, 21 n., 106,
    201
Cicero, Marcus Tullius 41, 67, 145
    and agriculture 525, 581
    and aliens 306–7
    De officiis 174, 197 n., 306 n., 525,
        548 n., 581
    orations of 414
    and the poor 196–7
    and war 548
Cimon, Athenian Commander 447
Cincinnatus, Lucius Quinctius 229
Cinna, Lucius Cornelius 234
Claudius, Roman emperor 525
Cleopatra 156, 444
Clovis I, king of the Franks 239
Cocceii, Heinrich, Freiherr von, German
    jurist 28 n., 36, 39 n., 324 n., 398,
    552 n.
Cocceiis, Samuel, Freiherr von, German
    jurist and Chancellor 36
Columbus, Christopher 455–6
Comyn, family of 262
Conrad II, Holy Roman Emperor 52, 252
Constantia, Queen of Naples 156, 444
Constantine (Flavius Valerius Constantius
    Augustus), the Great, Roman
    emperor 79 n., 170
Cortez, Hernando 455–6
Coventry, Sir John 118, 479
Craig, T. 52 n.
Crassipes, Furius 145
Cromwell, Oliver 34, 236–7, 240, 267,
    292–3, 297, 397, 413, 428–9
Cromwell, Richard 297
Cumberland, William Augustus, Duke of 60
Cyaxares, King of Media 220
Cyrus, Cicero's architect 196
Cyrus the Great, of Persia 158, 220

Dalrymple, Sir John 41 n., 51–2 n.,
    58 n., 65 n., 69 n., 74 n., 249 n., 257 n.,
    274 n., 417 n., 420 n.
Darius 220 n.
Davis, H. 393 n.
Demetrius Poliorcretes 233
Demophon, son of Theseus 222
Demosthenes 49 n., 123, 193, 197 n., 232
Descartes, René 399
Dicaearchus 192 n.
Dido, of Carthage 149
Dio Cassius 177 n.
Diocletian, Roman emperor 240
Diomedes, Argive commander 204, 367
Dionysius I, of Syracuse 240
Dionysius II 292 n.
Dionysius of Halicarnassus 173 n.
Dolabella, Publius Cornelius 145
Domitian, Roman emperor 283, 320, 414
Douglas, family of 262
Douglass, William 214 n.
Draco, Athenian legislator 64, 130
Dutot, C. de F. 101 n., 516–17 n.
Du Verney, J. 516–18 n.

E

Echard, Laurence 299 n.
Edgar, king of the English 51
Edward I, of England 46, 95, 230, 372,
    429
    and Baliol 58
    and judicial power 275–9, 281, 283,
        422–4
    and liberty 260
    and representation 257
Edward II, of England 281
Edward III, of England 35, 58 n., 260, 281,
    295–6, 298, 424
Edward IV, of England 262, 294 n.
Edward V, of England 294–6, 298
Edward VI, of England 264, 296
Elizabeth I, of England 211, 332, 406, 486
    and absolute power 262, 264
    alienation of demesne land by 266, 270,
        420
    and Catholic treason laws 296, 429
Elliot, Sir Gilbert 561 n.
Elpinice, sister of wife of Cimon 447
Erskine, J. 33 n., 168, 191, 475 n.
Esca, daughter of Attila 164
Euripedes 149 n.

D   F

Daire, E. 101 n., 516 n.   Farmer, Anthony 328 n.

Ferdinand, of Aragon 455, 551–2
Ferrara 244
Fitzherbert, A. 524 n.
Florus, Roman chronicler 313
Forbes, W. 133
Francois I, of France 287
Frederick I, Barbarossa, Holy Roman
    Emperor 18, 127 n., 129, 288,
    482
Frederick, Prince of Wales, father of
    George III of England 60
Frederick II the Great, of Prussia 243, 263,
    267, 546 n., 550

G

Gaius 30 n.
Galba, Servius Sulpicius 198
Gee, Joshua 392, 506–7, 513, 576
Gellius, Aulus 64 n., 122 n., 145 n.
Genghis Khan 158, 215–16, 219–20
George I, of England 24, 536
George II, of England 24, 127, 131
Gilbert, G. 275–7 n.
Glanvill, Ranulf de 89, 256 n.
Glaucus, Lycian commander 204, 367
Godolphin, Sidney Godolphin, 1st Earl
    513
Gothofredus, Dionysius 18 n., 129 n.
Gratian, Flavius 68 n.
Grotius, Hugo 26 n., 32 n., 36, 38 n.,
    72, 93 n., 104, 136, 138, 150, 292 n.,
    397, 469, 545 n., 548 n., 550 n.,
    552

H

Hadrian, Roman emperor 44, 241 n., 450,
    452
Hale, Sir Matthew 110–12 n., 114 n.,
    117 n., 295 n., 299 n., 385 n.,
    456 n.
Hannibal, Carthaginian general 236
Hanno, Carthaginian leader 236
Hanover, House of 59, 330
Harmodius 292
Harris, J. 333 n., 348 n., 371 n., 385 n.,
    506 n.
Hawkins, W. 109 n., 111 n., 114–15 n.,
    117 n., 127 n., 131–3 n., 137 n., 284 n.,
    294–6 n., 299–303 n., 430 n., 456–8 n.,
    481 n., 483 n.
Heineccius, J. G. 38–9 n., 42–3 n.,
    64 n., 166 n., 169 n., 173 n., 440 n.,
    463 n.
Helen of Troy 149, 439

Hengist, Teutonic leader 239, 415
Henley, Lord Chancellor 456 n.
Henry I, of England 35
Henry II, of England 35, 51, 89, 262,
    283–4, 419, 425
Henry III, of England 35, 170 n., 257, 259,
    265, 278, 301, 419, 430
Henry IV, of England 260
Henry V, of England 278
Henry VI, of England 58 n., 262
Henry VII, of England 23, 51, 171 n., 264,
    420, 524
Henry VIII, of England 287, 329
    and absolute power 262, 264, 270, 272,
        290
    and benefit of clergy 113
    breaks with Roman church 296, 329
    and Court of High Commission 286, 296,
        426, 429
    and Court of Wardship 286, 426
    and premunire 430
    and regulation of alien tradesmen 308
    and regulation of prescription 35
    and Star Chamber 95, 286, 426
    and testamentary succession 64
Henry IV, of France 263, 266
Hercules 221
Herodotus 97, 123 n., 220
Hipparchus (of Athens) 292 n.
Hippias (of Athens) 292 n.
Hobbes, Thomas 397–8
Holt, Lord Chief Justice 456 n.
Homer:
    and civilization 573
    and commerce 527
    and development of government 221–2,
        224–5, 409
    and division of land 22
    and expiation of crime 108
    and love, jealousy 149, 439
    and measure of value 367, 499
    and piracy 224
Honorius, Flavius, Roman emperor 240–1,
    415, 428, 468
Horace 125 n., 145 n., 180 n., 182 n.
Horsa, Teutonic leader 239, 415
Hume, Baron D. 109 n.
Hume, David 25 n., 31 n., 51 n., 87 n.,
    93 n., 153 n., 180–2 n., 193–4 n.,
    197 n., 239 n., 240 n., 245 n., 248 n.,
    249 n., 255 n., 257 n., 261 n., 266 n.,
    270 n., 275 n., 276 n., 279 n., 307 n.,
    316–17 n., 320 n., 332 n., 334 n.,
    387 n., 390 n., 393 n., 506 n., 507,
    519 n., 541 n., 548 n., 550 n.,
    576
Hutcheson, Francis 8 n., 9, 10 n., 87 n.,
    93 n., 102 n., 133 n., 141 n., 290 n.,

Hutcheson, Francis (*cont.*):
    324 n., 335 n., 401 n., 542 n., 545 n.,
    547, 550 n., 553 n.

I

Idomeneus, Cretan commander 204
Innocent III, Pope 148, 442, 454
Isaac, son of Abraham 205
Isabella of Castille 455

J

Jacoby, F. 88 n.
James I, of Great Britain (VI of Scotland)
    24, 266–7, 374, 421, 585
James II, of Great Britain 69, 267, 297,
    325, 327–30, 421, 436
James I, of Scotland 257
James II, of Scotland 524 n.
James III, of Scotland 524
James V, of Scotland 95, 287
James VI, of Scotland, *see* James I, of Great
    Britain (VI of Scotland)
Jeffreys, George Jeffreys, 1st Baron 328
Jesus Christ 478
    see also Messiah
John, King of England 170, 259, 265 n.,
    275–6, 278, 301, 419, 430
John of Gaunt 171 n.
John III, of Portugal 59
Julian, the Apostate 364
Jupiter, Roman deity 179
Justin II 219 n.
Justinian, Roman emperor 18, 30 n., 31, 43,
    44 n., 46–7, 49, 68 n., 72, 97–8, 144–5,
    170, 241 n., 448, 450
Justinus, Marcus Junianus 220

K

Kaempfer, E. 155 n.
Kames, Lord (Henry Home) 32 n., 46–7 n.,
    58 n., 64 n., 69 n., 81 n., 87 n., 97 n.,
    107 n., 109 n., 116 n., 253 n., 259 n.,
    261 n., 283 n., 475 n.
Knox, John 436
Kolben, Peter 352–3 n., 583

L

Lafitau, J. F. 106, 201, 439 n.
La Mare, Nicolas de 332
Lancaster, House of 58–9

Lavinia (Aeneid) 149
Law, John 333 n., 387 n., 515–19, 521, 578
Lea, H. G. 211 n.
Leibniz, G. W. 63 n.
Lentulus, Lucius 67 n.
Leofric, Earl of Mercia 57
Leviticus 166–7
Libanius 364 n.
Livy 41 n., 206 n., 228 n.
Locke, John 17 n., 20 n., 142 n., 200,
    208 n., 316, 317 n., 323, 338 n., 370,
    381, 435, 506 n., 508, 519 n.
Longinus 123
Lot 405
Louis VIII, of France 265 n.
Louis IX, of France 265 n.
Louis XIV, of France 516–17, 539, 550 n.
Louis XV, of France 358
Luther, Martin 436
Lysias, Greek orator 165, 229–30

M

Mackenzie, Sir George 82 n., 106 n.,
    122 n., 129 n., 133, 284 n., 298 n.,
    483 n.
Madox, T. 275 n.
Magens, Nicholas 505
Mahomet 156, 158, 180, 215, 219, 242, 408
Malcolm III, Canmore, of Scotland 252–3,
    418
Mandeville, Bernard 339 n., 348 n., 355 n.,
    393, 513, 576
Mandeville, Sir John 393 n.
Manlius Capitolinus Imperiosus, Lucius
    174 n.
Mansfield, Lord 456 n.
Marcellinus, Ammianus 364 n.
Marcianus, Aelius 174, 449–50
Marius, Gaius 233–4, 236, 412–13
Mars, Roman deity 179
Mary I, of Great Britain (Mary Tudor)
    264, 296, 429
Mary II, of England (consort of William of
    Orange) 296–7, 330
Massey, John 328 n.
M'Douall, A. (Lord Bankton) 38 n., 46 n.,
    74 n., 127 n.
Medici family 244
Meek, R. L. 561
Melon, J.-F. 101 n.
Menelaus, legendary king of Sparta 439
Menestheus, Athenian commander 204, 222
Messiah 180, 451
    see also Jesus Christ
Meursius, J. 49 n., 116 n.
Milo (Titus Annius Milo Papinianus) 145

Minerva, Roman deity 179
Mithridates VI, of Pontus, the Great 234,
    413
Monmouth, James, Duke of 118, 327–8,
    479
Montesquieu, C. L. Secondat, Baron de la
    Brede et de 38 n., 41 n., 67 n., 128,
    145 n., 147 n., 151 n., 154–5, 156 n.,
    164–5 n., 167 n., 173 n., 182 n., 200,
    210–11 n., 245 n., 306 n., 312–13 n.,
    443–4, 447 n., 519 n.
Montfort, Simon de 265 n.
Moses 166
Muller, C. and T. 192 n.
Mun, Thomas 300, 381, 506, 508, 576
Mure, Elizabeth 171

N

Nabis, Tyrant of Sparta 292
Nepos, Cornelius 447 n.
Nero, Roman emperor 238, 320, 414
Nestor 108
Newman, W. L. 197 n.
Newton, Sir Isaac 399
Nicholas of Damascus 88
Noah 462
Numa Pompilius, Roman ruler 173, 449

O

Octavia, wife of Mark Antony 156
Omar, second Mahometan caliph 215
Oppius, Gaius 66
Orange, Prince of, *see* William III, of Great
    Britain
Orleans, Philippe, Duke of, regent of France
    298, 358 n., 515–16, 519
Ossian, legendary Gaelic bard 239, 573
Otho 198 n., 288, 427
Otto I, the Great, emperor of Germany
    288, 427
Ovidius Naso, Publius 180 n., 452

P

Palatine, Count, of the Rhine 263
Paris, of Troy 149, 439
Paterson, William 515
Paulus, Julius 30 n., 31
Paulus Diaconus 173 n.
Pausanias 116 n.
Peisistratus, Athenian tyrant 292
Pelham, Henry 393
Perizonius, Jacobus 67

Peter I, the Great, of Russia 189
Phaedra, legendary wife of Theseus 149
Philip II, of France 260
Philip of Macedon 231 n., 233, 235 n., 305,
    412, 431
Philip I, of Spain 258
Philip IV, of Spain 525–6
Piso, Gaius 145
Pitt, Thomas 358 n.
Pitt, William, 1st Earl of Chatham 393
Plato 123, 197 n., 320 n.
Pliny 369 n.
Plutarch 38 n., 41 n., 128, 130 n.,
    181 n., 198 n., 222 n., 226 n., 233 n.,
    369 n.
Pompey (Gnaius Pompeius), the Great 145,
    234, 413
Pomponius, Sextus 432
Pope, Alexander 399
Potter, J. 228 n.
Pretender, *see* Stewart, James Francis
    Edward
    the Old Pretender
    the Young Pretender
    see Stuart, Prince Charles Edward
Price, Richard 93 n.
Proculus, Roman jurist 18, 30, 31 n.
Pufendorf, Samuel von 8, 9, 18 n., 29,
    36 n., 38 n., 63, 93, 100 n., 104 n.,
    136 n., 290 n., 324 n., 367 n., 371 n.,
    398, 466

R

Radevicus 18 n.
Ramsay, A. M. 550 n.
Raphael of Urbino 360
Raphael, D. D. 93 n.
Rapin, P. 118 n., 330 n.
Ratcliffe, Charles 138
Regulus, Marcus Atilius 229
Richard I, of England 35
Richard III 294 n.
Richard of York 58 n.
Robert II, of Scotland 170, 171 n.
Robert III, of Scotland 170, 171 n.
Romulus 173

S

Sabinus, Masurius 18, 30, 31 n.
Sallust (Gaius Sallustius Crispus) 97, 145
Sancroft, William, Archbishop of
    Canterbury 329 n.
Sarpedon, Lycian commander 204
Scott, W. R. 561

Sebastian, King of Portugal 59
Selby-Bigge, L. A. 25 n., 31 n., 93 n.,
    197 n., 334 n.
Semiramis 164
Seneca, Lucius Annaeus 149 n., 177 n.,
    181, 182 n.
Sesostris 31, 192, 351, 492
Severus, Lucius Septimius 174 n.
Sforza, Francesco, Duke of Milan 244
Sharp, John, preacher 329, 436
Shechem, Prince of Canaan 205
Sidney, Algernon 316
Sinclair, J. 393 n.
Skinner, A. S. 561
Socrates 123, 481
Solon 38, 62, 64, 130, 228, 231, 410,
    462
Spelman, H. 51 n., 68 n., 251
Stair, Lord (J. Dalrymple) 18 n., 24 n.,
    33 n., 35 n., 74 n., 82 n., 93 n.,
    466 n.
Stewart, James Francis Edward (the Old
    Pretender) 303, 431, 436
Sthenelus 204 n.
Stilicho, Flavius 240, 415 n.
Stobaeus, Joannes 88
Strabo 193 n.
Strahlenberg, Philip John von 216
Stuart, House of 266–79, 270, 289–9, 302,
    330, 429
Stuart, Prince Charles Edward (the Young
    Pretender) 54 n.
Suetonius (Gaius Suetonius Tranquillus)
    238 n., 241
Sulla, Felix, Lucius Cornelius 145, 233 n.,
    234, 236, 412–13
Swift, Jonathan 393
Swynford, Catherine 171 n.

T

Tacitus 41 n., 125 n., 184 n.
    and administration of justice 241, 313,
        434
    and contracts 97
    and Jewish religion 180
    and leadership 205–6, 212
    and marriage 145
    and ownership of land 22
    and punishment 130, 210
    and treatment of slaves 182–3, 198
Talbot, Charles 456 n.
Tamerlane 158, 215, 219, 220
Telemachus (Odyssey) 108, 224 n.
Theodoric, Ostrogth leader 221
Theodosius I, the Great, Roman emperor
    125, 144–5, 240 n., 468

Theseus, legendary king of Athens 221–2,
    225, 409
Thucydides 224, 226 n., 236
Tiberius, Roman emperor 125
Tigellius 182–3
Tigranes I, of Armenua, the Great 234
Timoleon of Corinth 292
Tournefort, Joseph Pitton de, botanist
    153–4, 443
Toynbee, Mrs Paget 302 n.
Trajan, Roman emperor 68
Trebatius Testa, Gaius 18
Tribonian, Roman jurist 31
Tudor, House of 262–4, 266, 270, 296–7,
    420
Tullia, daughter of Cicero 145
Tullius Hostillius 206

U

Ulysses (Odysseus) 224, 527

V

Valentinian III, Roman emperor 68, 125,
    144–5, 240 n., 468
Valerius Corvus, Marcus 174
Valerius, Maximus 174 n.
Varus, Publius Quintilius 313–14, 434
Vattel, E. 309 n.
Vedius Pollio, Publius 177, 452
Vespasian, Roman emperor 198
Villani, J. 156 n.
Virgil (P. Vergilius Maro) 149 n., 525
Visconti, Fillipo Maria 244 n.
Visconti, Gian Galeazzo, Duke of Milan
    244
Vitellius, Aulus, Roman emperor 198

W

Walpole, Horace 302 n.
Walpole, Sir Robert, Earl of Oxford 515,
    532
Warwick, Richard Neville, Earl of, the
    Kingmaker 51, 261, 420
Wicquefort, H. van 551–2 n.
William I, of England, the Conqueror 37,
    249, 251–2, 256–7, 261, 418,
    468
William II, Rufus, of England 51, 419
William III, of England (William of
    Orange) 272, 436, 468
    called to the throne 330
    and coinage 385, 389, 509

dependence of on taxes 421
and import of bullion 300, 510–11
and land tax 382
and naturalization 309, 433
and royal assent 269
and stocks 536
and succession to throne 197–8
and treason laws 296
Willis, Chief Justice 302 n.
Woodville, Elizabeth 294 n.

Y

York, House of 58–9, 260
Yorke, Sir Philip 456 n.

Z

Zeno, Emperor 170
Zoroaster 180

Index of Acts of the English and United Kingdom Parliaments

20 Henry III, c. 6 (1236) 419
20 Henry III, c. 8 (1236) 35
20 Henry III, c. 9 (1236) 170
3 Edward I (Westminster I), c. 39 (1275) 35
13 Edward I (Westminster II), c. 1 (1285) 69
13 Edward I (Westminster II), c. 19 (1285) 46
13 Edward I (Westminster II), c. 24 (1285) 424
14 Edward III, st. 1, c. 6 (1340) 279
25 Edward III, st. 5, c. 2 (1352) 294, 295, 296, 298, 429
34 Edward III, c. 1 (1361) 259
5 Richard II, c. 7 (1381) 481
15 Richard II, c. 2 (1391) 481
5 Henry IV, c. 4 (1404) 301
8 Henry VI, c. 7 (1429) 274
8 Henry VI, c. 9 (1429) 481
18 Henry VI, c. 15 (1439) 105
3 Henry VII, c. 14 (1487) 301
4 Henry VII, c. 24 (1490) 69, 420
11 Henry VII, c. 17 (1495) 23
22 Henry VIII, c. 14 (1531) 284
23 Henry VIII, c. 1 (1532) 113
26 Henry VIII, c. 1 (1534) 296
27 Henry VIII, c. 10 (1536) 75
32 Henry VIII, c. 1 (1540) 64
32 Henry VIII, c. 2 (1540) 35
32 Henry VIII, c. 16 (1540) 308
33 Henry VIII, c. 12 (1541) 302
34 & 35 Henry VIII, c. 5 (1543) 64
1 Mary, st. 2, c. 6 (1553) 295, 430
1 & 2 Philip and Mary, c. 10 (1554) 302
4 & 5 Philip and Mary, c. 5 (1558) 529
5 Elizabeth I, c. 1 (1563) 296, 430
5 Elizabeth I, c. 14 (1563) 132
13 Elizabeth I, c. 2 (1571) 296
14 Elizabeth I, c. 3 (1572) 302, 430
23 Elizabeth I, c. 1 (1581) 296
27 Elizabeth I, c. 2 (1585) 296
31 Elizabeth I, c. 4 (1589) 430
31 Elizabeth I, c. 11 (1589) 127
1 James I, c. 11 (1589) 127
1 James I, c. 11 (1603) 457
1 James I, c. 27 (1603) 24
21 James I, c. 3 (1623) 83
21 James I, c. 16 (1623) 135

3 Charles I, c. 1 (1628) 327, 436
16 Charles I, cc. 10, 11 (1641) 286
12 Charles II, c. 23 (1660) 327
12 Charles II, c. 24 (1660) 237, 286
13 & 14 Charles II, c. 18 (1662) 105
15 Charles II, c. 7 (1663) 299, 385
18 & 19 Charles II, c. 5 (1666) 300, 385
22 & 23 Charles II, c. 1 (1670) 118, 479
22 & 23 Charles II, c. 10 (1670) 46, 47, 49
25 Charles II, c. 2 (1673) 327
30 Charles II, st. 2, c. 1 (1678) 327
31 Charles II, c. 2 (1679) 120, 272, 480
1 James II, c. 17 (1685) 49
1 William and Mary, c. 12 (1688) 365
1 William and Mary, c. 30 (1689) 301
6 & 7 William and Mary, c. 17 (1695) 300, 301, 386
7 & 8 William III, c. 3 (1695) 137
7 & 8 William III, c. 19 (1696) 300, 377
7 & 8 William III, c. 28 (1696) 105
8 & 9 William III, c. 30 (1697) 305
12 & 13 William III, c. 2 (1701) 297, 325, 330
4 & 5 Anne, c. 8 (1705) 298
5 & 6 Anne, c. 6 (1706) 114, 478
6 Anne, c. 7 (1707) 298
7 Anne, c. 21 (1708) 131, 298
7 Anne, c. 25 (1708) 299
8 Anne, c. 19 (1709) 83
9 Anne, c. 14 (1710) 538
9 Anne, c. 16 (1710) 301
1 George I, st. 2, c. 4 (1714) 309, 403
1 George I, st. 2, c. 38 (1716) 273
3 George I, c. 11 (1716) 24
4 George I, c. 12 (1717) 132
8 George I, c. 19 (1721) 24
9 George I, c. 22 (1722) 24, 127
5 George II, c. 30 (1732) 131, 483
7 George II, c. 8 (1734) 538
10 George II, c. 32 (1737) 127
20 George II, c. 50 (1747) 74
24 George II, c. 34 (1751) 127, 482
26 George II, c. 33 (1753) 149, 442
29 George II, c. 15 (1756) 364
29 George II, c. 17 (1756) 238
31 George II, c. 42 (1758) 24, 127
12 George III, c. 72 (1772) 135
59 George III, c. 46 (1819) 211

Index of Acts of the Parliaments of Scotland

[*Note*: The first reference is to the 1681 edition of Scots Acts or (for Acts after 1681) to editions of individual years.]

1449, c. 18 (A.P.S.II.35, c. 6) 524
1469, c. 29 (A.P.S.II.95, c. 4) 135
1469, c. 37 (A.P.S.II.96, c. 12) 81
1474, c. 55 (A.P.S.II.107, c. 9) 135
1551, c. 19 (A.P.S.II.486, c. 11) 133
1587, c. 50 (A.P.S.III.451, c. 34) 129
1587, c. 82 (A.P.S.III.460) 483

1617, c. 12 (A.P.S.IV.543, c. 12) 35
1672, c. 16 (A.P.S.VIII.80, c. 40) 284
1681, c. 20 (A.P.S.VIII.352, c. 86) 100
1681, c. 21 (A.P.S.VIII.353, c. 87) 274
1685, c. 22 (A.P.S.VIII.477, c. 26) 69
1686, c. 11 (A.P.S.VIII.595, c. 21) 23
1701, c. 6 (A.P.S.X.272) 120

Original Index to Report dated 1766

A

Authority when in perfection 402
Aliens 403, 432–3
Aristocracy 404, 410
Arts 411, 526–7
Artists original 411
Administration Mal 422
Assassination 428
Adoption 448
Accession 460
Ascendants 463
Act Coventry 479
Apprentices 456, 529
Agriculture 488, 522–3
Annuities 536
Arms 542
Ambassadors:
  Rights 551
  Resident 551–2
  Person and goods 552–3
  first established 552–4
  Extraordinary 553
  Ordinary 553

B

Bastards 448
Bigamy 457, 480
Bail 480
Bankruptcey 483
Barter 493
Banks 503
Bullion 510
Brokers 537–8
Besieging 551
Balance of Power 552

C

Contract:
  foundation of 400
  original 402
  who capable of 431
  breach 472
  Reales 473
  Consential 473
  Quasi 474
  render'd Real Rights 524

Chieftans 405
Crimes:
  in general in Origin 406
  of London and Paris 486
Citizenship origin 412
  British 432
Citizens according to Law of Nations 431
Courts popular 418
Courts of Justice established 422
  Chancery 423
  Exchequer 424
  High Commision 426
Commons House allowed freedom of speech 421
Corruption in Judges 423
Colliers 453
Curators 456
Collaterals 463
Coin debased 474
  and Money 499
Chance Medley 478
Children not objects of punishment 485
Carriage 494
Commodities 494
Cultivation by slaves 523
Corn it's cheapest Mercat 526
Commerce by what retarded 527
  its influence 538
  inconveniences attending 539–41
Collectors 531
Customs French 534
Capitulations 548
Captives 548
Cartel treaties, ib.
Captures 551
Consuls 554

D

Delinquency 401
Democracey 404
  Solon's 410
Demesnes Royal 420
Divorces 440–2
Derelict 460
Descendants 463
Delivery, symbolical 469
Duty of Vassals 470
  and taxes 531
Delicts 475

Division of labour encrease Opulence 489
   of lands 523
Debt public 514
Dearths 525

E

Empire fall of the Roman 415
Entails 467
Entry forcible or Willfire 481
Expence of Sea and Land War 514
   of British Government 530
   of Levying English Tax 531
Exchange 520
English Land Rent 522
Expedition of the Highlanders 540
Escape better for Guilty than Innocent to
   suffer 548
Effects of Enemies policey to secure 549
European Balance of Power 552
Envoys 553

F

Family Injuries to Man as a Member 399
   Jealousy 439
Forms of Original Government 404
Fishers in 1st periods of Society 407
   Conduct in Peace and War 407
Fall of the Roman Empire 415
   and decline of Republic Government 408
Fortifying 409
Feudal System 417
   subsists 524
Farmers 419
Felony 430
Filial independencey 450
Forcible marriages 457, 480
   Entry or Willfire 481
Fiefs 465
Forgery 481
Fairs 528
Funds 536

G

Government, its general principles 398
   original forms 404, 416
   powers 405
   Republican 408
   Military 413–14
   Turkish 415
   Modern 415–16
   Allodial 416
   Arbitrary 420

British Annual expence 530
   Expence Levying Land Tax 531
Government Annuities 535
Guardians 440
Goods and Treasure Derelict 460
   of Ambassadors 553
Guilty better to escape than Innocent to
   Suffer 547–8
Gallantry in killing Generals of Armies 549

H

Hunter's their original State 404, 407
   Conduct in Peace and War 407–8
Human Species 438
Husband and Wife 445
Humanity 452, 458
Hypothecs 471
Homicide 477
Highlanders their Expedition 540

I/J

Jurisprudence definition of 397
Justice 399
Injuries to Man as Man etc 399
   verbal 481
   written 481
Inducements to obey Magistrates 402
Judges independency 421
   rendered incapable 422
   corruption 423
Justiciary Grand abolished 423
Juries, their Origin 425
Judicial power became absolute 433
   restrained 434
Importation 436
Institution of Rome's marriages 440
Illegittimacey 432
Infidelity in a wife 457
Inheritance indevisible 464
Ideots not objects of punishment 485
Invention of machinery 491
Interest of money 520
Innocent not to suffer 548

K

Killing Generals of armies a gallantry 549
King cannot pardon Mal-administration 421

L

Law, its general principles 398

of Nations 431, 545
Cannon Law 441
Domestic 438
Private 459
Lords Hereditary 418
Legislative power 405, 437
Legittimacey 447
Labourers 453
    wages 491
Leases introduced 454
Luxury 489
Labour encrease opulence 490
Land-Rent of England 522
    of Brittain 530
Lands, their division 523
Levying English Land Tax 531
Legates 551

M

Magistracey 402
Magistrates performing without reward 529
Monarchy 404
Mal-Administration 422
Marriages 440, 457
Masters and servants 450
Manumitting 452, 548
Mortgages 471
Murther 475–6
Manslaughter 478
Medley, chance 478
Maiming and mutilation 479
Madmen not objects of punishment 485
Money and coin 499
Measures and weights 501
Mandeville Doctr's System 513
Mercats commenced 528

N

Nations barbarous 408
    neutral 550
    belligerent 550–1
Natural Rights 399–400
Natures produce 487

O

Œconomy 421
Office of origin of Chancellors 423
    public 529
Offences 430–1
Occupation 459
Opulence:
    encreased by division of labour 489

consists not in money 515
Outrages 548

P

Priviledges exclusive 400, 471
Pledges or pawns 400
Power Senatorial 407
    balance of in Europe 552
Parliament Representatives 419
    Right 435
Prisoners and cases detain'd renders a Judge
        incapable 422
Premunires 430
Polygamy 443
Parentage 449
Property how acquired 459
Prescription 461
Primogeniture 465
Promises verbal 472–3
Pignus security 473
Piracey 483
Perjury 484
Policey 486
Price of commodities 494
Possessions 531–2
Politicians 539
Pope's legates 551
Power Balance in Europe 552
Person of Ambassadors 553

Q

Quadrupeds 438

R

Rights 399
    origin 401
    of resistance 434
    Parliamentary 435
    accession 460
    Testamentary 466
    representatives 419, 463
    personal 471
    Ambassadors 551
Revenue 420–1
Republic origin 427
Religion 429, 436, 540
Rapes 457, 480
Robbery 483
Resentment 485
Rent of England 522
    of Brittain 530
Refinement modern 549

S

Society 401
State of hunters in origin 404
Shepherds Patriarchs 404–5
    in 1st periods of Society 407
    conduct in Peace and War 407
Senatorial power 407
Speech freedom allowed, House of
        Commons 421
Subjects distinction from aliens 433
Succession, Royal 435
    legal and testamentary 462
Species, human 438
Servants 450
    to Ambassadors 553
Slaves, Roman 451
    British 453
    Cultivation 523
Slavery 454
Salters 453
Steel Bow Tenants 454, 524
Symbolical delivery 469
Servitudes 470
System Doct. Mandeville's 513
    Grotius 397
    Hobbes 397
    Baron de Coccei 397
Subsists feudal 524
Sciences 526
Staple Towns 529
Stocks 537
Stockholders 537
Stockjobbers 537
Satisfaction from Sovereigns difficult
    548

T

Torry and Whig 402
Treasons 428, 484

Tests 436

Tests 436
Tenants 454, 524
Treasure derelict 460
Transferrance voluntary 469
Theft 481
Towns Staple 529
Taxes 531–2
Tittles of London Brokers 537–8
Treaties Cartel 548

U

Utility in Society 401

V

Villani the ancient farmers 418
Voluntary transferrance 469
Vassals duty 469

W

Whig and Torry 402
War 408
    expence 514
    honourable in rude Society 527
    arms 542
    outrages 548
    when lawfull 545
    holy 549
    jus post Liminii 550
Woemen when marriagable 444
Wife and husband's interest 445
Wife's infidelity 457
Willfire 481
Wealth 487, 497, 529
Wages 491
Weights and measures 501
Walpole, Sir Robert's ruin 532

Wealth of Nations

Index of Subjects

A

Abbeville, monopoly of, woollens in 461,
  462 n.
Abyssinia, salt used as money in 38 & n.
Academy, French 143
Academy, of Plato 778
Acapulco ships, sailing between America
  and the East Indies 222 & n., 225,
  227
accumulation of stock:
  annual 130, 277, 366
  early state of society preceding 65, 82,
    276
  first possible in cities 405, see also cities
  frugality, affected by the system of
    funding 925–6
  lowers the rate of profit 145, see also
    profit
  and the monopoly of the colony trade
    608, 612, see also America, colonies
  parsimony, requisite for 908–9
  passion for, offsets extravagance of
    governments 929
  precedes the division of labour 276, 277,
    see also labour, division of
  and productive and unproductive labour
    330–49, see also labour
  see also capital, labour, stock; condition,
    bettering of
actor(s), paid for public contempt of
    profession 124
  although indirectly productive of benefit
    796
  as unproductive labour 331
  see also labour, disadvantages of
Adriatic, favourable to commerce 36
adulteration, of coin 40–1, 932
adulterine guilds 141
advancing (stationary or declining), state of
    53, 72, 80, 87, 99, 106–10, 114, 151,
    159, 194, 209 & n., 211–12, 237, 258,
    424, 509, 517
  see also society
advantages, net, doctrine of 116–35
  see also employments, labour
adventure, see lotteries, risk
Aegean sea 556
Aeolian colonies 556
Africa:
  causes of barbarous state of 35–6, 634

gum seneca exported from 657
importation of slaves from 571, 578, see
    also slavery, slaves
music and dancing in 776
necessity of forts for the protection of
    commerce 731
African company 734, 737 n., 739, 741,
    742–3 & n., 745 n.
African king, authority of 24
age, as foundation of authority 711–12
age, of shepherds 29 & n., 422 & n., 689 n.,
    692 n., 710 n., 714 n., 715, see also
    shepherds
age, of hunters 689 n., 709 n., 711–12 & n.,
    713 n., see also hunters
age of agriculture 689 n., 695, see also
    agriculture, husbandmen
age of commerce 37, 689 n., see also
    commerce
ages and nations, different 11, 36, 205,
    413 n., 428, 430 n., 710 n., 777
Agen, land tax in 854
agio 328 & n., 479 & n., 480–1, 484–7
agriculture, capable of absorbing more
    capital than has been applied to it
    374
  development of 409–10, 423–4, 511–27
  discouragement of 381–96, 854
  injudicious projects in 341
  limitation of division of labour in
    16 & n.
  principal instruments of 206, 280, 364,
    568
  prior to manufactures 377–80
  productivity of investment in 363 & n.,
    366 & n.
  the proper business of new colonies 609
  stage of 692–5, 697
  see also bounties, capital(s), colonies,
    labour, pasture, rent, tax, original
    index
agricultural system 663–88
  see also economists
Agrigentum 566
aides 861, 904
Aix la Chapelle, treaty of 922
Alcavala (Spanish tax) 899 & n.
ale:
  a common drink in the American colonies
    936
  a gentleman drunk with, rare 493 & n.

ale (*cont.*):
  licences to sell 852
  a luxury 870
  poor suffer from taxes on 260 & n., 863,
    877–8
  taxes on 888–93, 938
  see also Assize of Ale
alehouse:
  drunkenness, gives employment to 362
  a losing trade carried on with 491–2
  ornament of, in Dunfermline 347
alien merchants 144 & n., 494 & n., 499,
  660, 879
aliens, duty 463, 464 & n., 879
alkaline salt 161
allodial:
  government 382 n., 384 & n., 416 & n.
  restricted by the feudal law 417
  see also government, original index
alloy 63, 482, 552, 932
Alsace 901
ambassador(s) 262, 429 & n., 732 & n., 736
ambition, undiscerning eye of 628
America, Thoughts on (*Memorandum* 1778)
  605, 615–17, 622–3, 625, 707
America, discovery of 91 n., 219–20, 225 n.,
  256, 429, 437, 447–8 & n., 569, 591
America, mines of 49, 52, 199, 205, 210–11,
  214, 217, 220, 221–2, 227–32, 234 n.,
  254–5, 258, 429, 437, 447, 512 n.,
  563, 829, 940, 944
America, British colonies of:
  the discovery of America, and of the
    passage to the East Indies, the
    two greatest events in history
    626–7
  acquisitions of, extends the market 448
  no colonies in which progress has been
    more rapid 571
  plantations follow the sea-coast 34 & n.
  rent seldom heard of in 70, 565
  not so rich as England, but growing more
    rapidly 87
  rapid progress unforeseen 597–8
  complaint of scarcity of hands in 88
  high levels of wages and profit 87,
    109 & n.
  encourages marriage 565
  high level of propagation in 88, 98, 423,
    565
  population of 495–6, 937, 939
  understocked 109, 601
  acquisition of and the level of profit 110
  cultivation of tobacco in 174–5, *see also*
    tobacco
  price of timber in 179, 577
  husbandry in 240–1, 246
  paper money in 323, 326–7, 940

Northern Colonies typically owe a balance
  to Great Britain 942
and the carrying trade 373, 375, *see also*
  carrying trade, trade
returns on trade with, slower than with
  Europe 495
but more advantageous than with the
  East Indies 448–9
enforced concentration on primary
  products, allied to the cheapness of
  land, as an explanation for rapid
  growth 366 & n., 422–3, 573
agriculture, the proper business of new
  colonies 609
no manufactures for distant sale 378–80
  prevented by legislation 582
  a violation of natural liberty 582
British administration less oppressive
  than others 590
relative freedom of trade in 574–5, 610,
  614
policy with regard to enumerated and
  non-enumerated commodities
  577–9, *see also* enumerated
  commodities, navigation acts
drawbacks on colonial produce 588
institutional advantages; colonists carry
  with them a knowledge of
  agriculture and of other arts 564
political institutions 572–4, 585–6
benefits from distance from Great Britain
  567
policy towards, dictated by merchants
  584, 661
colonial relationship sacrifices the
  interests of consumers to that of
  producers 661–2
regulation of trade involves a distortion in
  the use of resources 627–32
see also industry
mercantile strategy fit for a nation whose
  government is influenced by
  shopkeepers 613
has raised the mercantile system to a
  degree of splendour otherwise
  unobtainable 627
advocates a gradual relaxation of the laws
  with respect to the exclusive trade
  606–8
colonies contribute no force to the mother
  country, and little to her revenue
  593–4, 615
cost of defence 661, 929
colonies should contribute to the costs of
  empire 617–18, 944
they should be taxed, but not on the
  authority of the colonial assemblies
  618–19

taxation, by requisition, rejected 620
should be taxed by Great Britain 944–5
if not should be given up 946–7
advocates application of British taxes to
the American colonies 944
taxation and representation 622–4
advocacy of union 625–6
anticipated transfer of the seat of
government 626
revolt of 500
see also disturbances, colonial
slender authority over 502, 621
possible loss of, strikes people of Great
Britain with terror 605
five effects which mitigate the
consequences of the
non-importation agreement
606–7
colonial militia become in effect a
standing army 701
political constraints affecting voluntary
withdrawal 616–17
loss of, confirms folly of the mercantile
system 647
see also original index, *Correspondence*
America (North), savage nations in 32 n.,
178, 344 & n., 448, 634–5, 690 & n.,
691 n., 692, 711, 716 n.
see also hunters
Amsterdam 209, 454, 477 n., 479–81,
486–7 & n., 613 & n., 652 & n.,
818
see also original index
Amsterdam, Bank of 37 n., 327 n., 328 & n.,
479, 480 & n. 481–2, 484–7 & n.,
818 n.
see also agio
Ancient Physics 770
Angola 558 & n., 635
animals:
tribes of the same species; differences
between, but scarcely of use to one
another 29–30
see also dogs
every species, of, multiples in proportion
to subsistence 97 & n., 162
animosity, national 267 n., 429 n., 464 & n.,
474–5, 493–6, 921
see also jealousy, mercantile
annual produce, *see* labour
annual revenue, *see* revenue
annuities 70, 108 n., 318, 320, 522, 746,
749, 858, 877, 912, 914, 915–16 & n.,
917–24, 928
Antigua 595, 943
Antwerp 427, 479
Aperea of Brazil 560
anophthegms 768

apothecary:
profits of 128–9
shops a source of revenue to Hamburgh
817–18
apprentices:
considered as skilled labour 119
idleness of 119
limitation on numbers in particular trades
136 & n.
aversion to 142
apprenticeship, statute of:
and distortion of the use of resources 79,
119, 135, 138–40, 151–2
duration of 136–8
gives no assurance of quality of work 138
no tendency to form young people to
industry 139
unknown to the ancients 139
as a means of gaining a settlement 154,
see also Settlement, Laws of,
Correspondence
an encroachment on natural liberty 470,
660, *see also* liberty
privileges of graduates as a sort of
762 & n., *see also* colleges,
graduates, universities
in regulated companies 734
Arabia, Gulf of, as favourable to commerce
36
Arabs:
a nation of shepherds 36, 422 & n., 690
military power of 690–2, 700–1
administration of justice, a source of
revenue 716 & n.
sources of revenue of chiefs 816–17
hospitality of 414
authority of scherifs 713
histories full of genealogies 421–2
riches, remain long in the same families
422
see also shepherds, state of
Aragon 561
Archipelago 607
aristocracy, natural 622, 707
aristocracy, oppressive 944 & n.
absence of in American colonies 944
Armada, Spanish 569, 605
arithmetic 140 n., 767 n., 777, 882
arithmetic, political 95, 534
army(-ies):
lottery of 126
unproductive labourers 331
discipline of 699
and use of fire-arms, ibid.
standing compared to militia 698–701,
703, 705
in classical times 702–3
modern, valour of 705–6

army(-ies) (*cont.*):
  a danger to liberty 705–6
  but source of support to the sovereign
      706–7, 798
  see also original index
art, and industry 14 n., 15–16, 23, 24 n.,
      34–5, 117 n., 140 n., 143, 180, 193,
      224, 262, 265, 395 n., 436 n., 447–8,
      456, 510, 656, 670–1, 681, 686, 748,
      768 n., 790
art, works of 117 n.
artificer(s), considered to be skilled labour
      119–21
  see also original index
artillery 615, 708
arts, fine 143
As, Roman 42, 56, 930
Asia 35–6
Asia Minor 556
Assembly, houses of, in the British
      colonies, *see also* colonies,
      government
Assiento contract 745
Assize of bread 158
Assize of bread and ale 43 n., 158, 196,
      201–2
Athens, fees of teachers 149
  artisans of slavery 683
  paid soldiers of 695
Atlantic 625, 627
attorneys, mode of payment of 721, 781
augmentation of coin defined 932
Aulnagers 40
Austria 36, 705, 934
author(s), temporary monopoly of, defended
      754
authority, sources of 711–14
  see also subordination
Ayr Bank, history of 313–17
Ayrshire, demand for labour in 94
Azores 558

B

Babylon 388
Bahamas 559
bakers, incorporation of, in Scotland 158
balance, natural, of industry, *see* industry,
      balance of
balance of annual produce and consumption
      497–8
balance of payments 545–6, 941–3
balance of trade, absurd speculations
      concerning 377
  see also original index
Balista 708
Baltic trade 36, 180, 365, 602, 627

bank(s), in Edinburgh, have no exclusive
      privilege 756–7
bankers 292, 298, 329
  see also original index
Bank of Amsterdam, *see* Amsterdam
Bank of England, *see* England, Bank of
Bank of Scotland 297–8
Bank, the Royal 297
bank-money 479–80
bank notes 292–4, 300–1, 318 & n., 313–14,
      322–6, 329
bankruptcy 128, 308–9, 342, 929–30
banks, sometimes pay in sixpences to save
      time 61, 320
  sometimes allow no interest 107
  judicious operation of, creates a
        wagon-way through the air 321
  see also original index, *Correspondence*
bar (metals) 483 n., 579, 580 & n., 582,
      643
Barbadoes 598, 943
barbarians, overthrow the Roman Empire
      112, 380, 427
barbarous nations:
  ancient Scythia and modern Tartary and
        Siberia as 36
  shepherds in Africa and the East Indies:
        hunters in America 634
  power of militia in 703–6, 821
  affected by the introduction of fire-arms
        708
  sources of authority in 711–17
  music and dancing as amusements in 776
  varied occupations in, an advantage
        782–3
  see also hunters, shepherds, society,
        Arabs, Hottentots, Tartars
Barbary 406, 738
bargain 26 & n., 27 n.
bargaining 49
barley 201–2, 212 n., 536 n., 541–2,
      891 & n., 892–3
barn 97 n., 242
barons, feudal:
  oppression of, explains the rise of cities
        401–4
  feudal power of 413–18, 800–1
  and loss of authority 417–21, 803–4
  see also lords, allodial, feudal, clergy
barter, disposition to 25 & n., 27, 29–30,
      437
  see also original index
Basil 851
Batavia 635
Bath, Road Inn 347
baubles 193, 346, 421, 712
Bavaria 36
Bayonne 901

beauty:
    of precious stones 189–92
    of systematical arrangement of ideas
        768 & n.
    see also utility
beaver:
    rate of exchange with deer 65
    an enumerated commodity 579, 658,
        744 n., 881
beef 49, 167–8 & n., 205 n., 243
beer 23, 37, 49, 96 n., 260, 466 n., 492,
    501 n., 870, 871 n., 872 & n., 878,
    887–90, 891 & n., 892–3, 936,
    938–9
beggar:
    depends on benevolence 27 & n.
    once synonymous with scholars 149
benefice(s) 148, 760 n., 789, 798, 800,
    804–5, 807, 809 & n., 810,
    812
    see also original index
benefit, of clergy 649, 765, 802 & n., 826
benevolence, does not give us our dinner 27
Bengal:
    subsistence wages 114
    piece goods exports 223
    ratio of silver to gold 229
    regulations lead to famine 527
    revenue from land 637, 838
    see also original index
Benguela 558, 635
Berne 108 n., 395 & n., 403, 806, 812,
    813 & n., 819–20, 860, 909
    see also original index
bettering, of condition, *see* condition,
    bettering of
bills, of exchange 298–300, 303–5, 307,
    309–10 & n., 311–12, 313 & n.,
    314–16, 319 & n., 320, 324, 326, 328,
    433, 441, 444, 477, 479–81, 483,
    488 n., 602, 750, 820, 849 n., 861,
    911–12, 941 & n., 943
Birmingham 20 n., 89 n., 131 & n., 137,
    225–7, 260, 409 & n., 785 n., 897
birth, authority of 384, 713, 714 & n.,
    761 n., 944 n., 870 n.
birth-right 421
blacksmith 117
black cloth, price of 76, 132
Black Sea 36
Blanc, Cape 737
blood-vessel 604, 605 n.
boat-fishery 521
body, natural and political 604–6, 673–4
Bohemia 384–5, 387 & n., 390 n., 834,
    835 n., 836, 866
Bombay 751
bondmen 334, 387, 854 & n., 857, 879

Boston, work done by freemen, cheaper
        than slaves 99
    less populous than Lima 568
bounty(-ies):
    on the exportation of corn 212–13,
        215–18, 424, 461, 509 & n., 510,
        524 & n., 535, 538, 541–2, 875
    on fishing 405 n., 519, 520 & n., 521–2
    disadvantageous 489 n., 517, 523, 545,
        605, 882
    upon the production of money 555
    upon the importation of naval stores
        579–80, 583, 644–5
    public tenders receive a sort of 780
    reasonable, upon the transportation of
        coal 874
    on articles formerly charged with export
        duties 880, 896
    abolition of, proposed 885, 933 n.
    see also corn, colonies, original index,
        Correspondence
Bourbon, house of 740
Bourdeaux 335–6, 918
bow(s) 27 & n., 691, 708
bowsprits 579, 644
boy(s):
    employed in the manufacture of nails
        18 & n.
    and invention 20–1
    earnings of 89 n., 785 n.
    as apprentices 139
    education of 764, 773 n.
Braganza, family of 569
Brazil:
    aborigines in 221
    gold of 256 n., 370, 436, 491, 547, 564
    aperea of 560
    Portuguese Jews, banished to 589
    see also original index
bread:
    price of, generally the same in all parts of
        the United Kingdom 92, 129–30
    assize of 158, *see also* Assize of bread and
        ale
    relative values of bread and meat, vary in
        the different periods of agriculture
        164–5, 167 & n., 230
    of oatmeal a heartier food than wheaten
        177
    home market for extended by means of
        the trade to America 609
    see also America, British colonies of
    tax on in Holland 875, 878
Breslaw 834
brewers, brewery, taxes on 878, 888–93,
    936
bricklayer(s) 23, 87, 120, 378
brickmaker(s) 23, 84 n., 283

bridges:
    taxes levied on in ancient times 397
    how maintained 821
    as public works 724–5
Bristol 738, 754 n.
Britain:
    reformation of the gold coin in 58
    increase of population in, compared to
        America 88 & n.
    capital stock of, undiminished by the late
        war 100
    poacher considered a poor man in 118
    uniformity of pay accruing to those who
        sail from the various ports of 127
    kelp grown in 161
    relative value of meat and bread in 165,
        see also bread
    cultivation of the finer fruits in 170
    real recompence of labour in 94, 218–19
    price of articles of subsistence in 241–3
    legal rate of interest in 357, see also
        interest, rate of
    inhabitants lack sufficient capital to
        improve all their lands 365
    restraints on importation to 452, 882–3
    acts of navigation, a proper support to the
        mercantile marine 463, see also
        navigation acts
    taxes upon necessaries of life in 466,
        874–5, see also taxes, brewers
    absurd to expect restoration of freedom of
        trade in 471
    bounties upon exportation, frequently
        petitioned for 505, see also
        bounties
    average quantity of grain imported by
        534, see also corn
    security for the individual in 540
    abuse of tolls in 726–7, 894, see also tolls
    reparation of highways in 731
    regulated companies in 734–8
    taxes on beer and spirits 887–93, see also
        taxes
    national debt of 930–3
    recommends extension of British taxes to
        Ireland and the colonies 933–8
    see also corn; original index,
        Correspondence
British:
    constitution, protects America 91 & n.
    settlements in the East Indies 111
    constitution, not hurt by union with
        America 624–5
    Empire, states-general of 933–4, 946
    Linen Company 758
    see also America, Britain
Brittany 854
broad-wheeled wagons 32–3

brocades 407
Bruges 427
buccaneers 247
buckles, diamond, frivolous 419, see also
    baubles, diamonds
buffoons 331
bullion 59–60 & n., 61, 62 & n., 63,
    164 & n., 205, 213 & n., 227 n.,
    233 n., 247, 302–3, 320, 429 n.,
    432 n., 434, 443, 478 & n., 482 & n.,
    483–7, 550 & n., 551–5
Buenos Ayres 164 & n., 205, 227 n., 247
Burcester 249
burghers, and taxation 398–402, 404–5, 879
    see also cities
burgo-master(s) 486, 814
Burgundians 382 n., 705
Burgundy 171, 705, 814
bursaries 146, 762 & n.
buss(es), bounty, fishery 519–20, 521 & n.,
    522
butcher(s) 27, 31, 37, 49, 92, 117, 129–30,
    167, 207 & n., 230, 237, 242, 244,
    251, 283, 361, 378, 425, 492, 509,
    873 n., 876 n.
butcher, brewer, baker 27, 31, 37, 49, 378
butcher's meat 49, 92, 93 n., 129–30, 138,
    164–5, 167–8, 207 & n., 230, 237,
    242–4, 246–8, 251–2, 259, 425, 452,
    461–2, 509 n., 609, 652–3, 876 & n.
button 15 n.
    division of labour in making 18
bye-law(s) 135–7, 142, 145, 401–2, 416,
    557, 735–6

C

cabbages, cheaper than in the past 96
    cultivation of 167, 243, 259
cabinet-maker 32, 117 n., 260, 283
Cadiz, annual importation of precious
    metals 227
    exorbitant profits of merchants 612
    merchants, less parsimonious than the
        Dutch 613, 627
    importation from: competition with the
        South Sea Company 746
Calcutta:
    land carriage to 33
    ratio of gold and silver at 229
    council of 641, 751
    recovery of during the French War 749
    treasury of 753
callicoes 500, 503, 583
calves 249–50
cambricks 473, 500
Campus, Martius 696, 774

Canada:
  French colony of, under the government
      of an exclusive company 571
  and the 'late distrurbances' 617 n., 623 n.
  conquest of by Great Britain 881
canal(s) 163, 331 n., 724–5, 726 & n.,
      756–8
  in Lower Egypt 35 & n.
  effect on commerce 36
  near Canton 89
  maintenance of, in China 729–30, 838
  tolls on 894
  see also original index
Canaries 558
candles:
  taxes on 96 & n., 260 & n., 466, 873–4,
      878
Cannae, battle of 702
Canton, China:
  silver will buy more commodities than at
      London 55
  poverty in 89
Cape, Blanc 737
Cape Coast Castle 739
Cape de Verd islands 558
Cape, Finisterre 502, 578 n., 579, 614, 935
Cape, of Good Hope 26 n., 406 n.,
      448 & n., 558, 591, 626 & n., 635,
      737
Cape, Rouge 737–39
capital(s):
  employment of capital stock in support of
      productive labour 11, 266
  see also labour, productive
  manufacturers 66–8
  great, reduces the rate of profit 107
  see also profit
  see also accumulation, interest, stock,
      taxes and trade
capitals, circulating 270–80, 282–3 & n.,
      284–6, 288, 291–2, 295–6, 307, 363,
      438 n.
capitals, fixed 280–3, 287–92, 307, 363,
      369 n., 659 n.
  see also original index
capitation, taxes 857 n., 867–8, 869 & n.,
      904
caravans 36 n., 223
Carlisle, exchange between London and
      326
Carnatic, wars of 749
Carolina(s) 176, 573–4, 597, 936–7
carpenter(s) 16, 29 n., 31, 32 & n., 87, 100,
      117 n., 120, 260, 283, 348, 378, 429,
      695
carriage, cost of, reduced by good roads and
      canals 163
  see also canals, roads, rivers

carriage, by land and water 32–3 & n., 34–6,
      163, 372
  historical significance of 405, 408–9
  economic potential of England, related to
      fertility and ease of communication
      424
carriages, taxes on 724–5, 728–9, 877
Carron 94
carrots, cheaper than they were forty years
      ago 95–6
  cultivation of 167, 243, 259
carrying trade:
  Dutch retain a large share of that of
      France 108, 632
  defined 294, 368
  prohibition of, in Great Britain 540
  favoured by the mercantile system 583
  monopoly of the colony trade, forces some
      part of the capital of Great Britain
      to 604, 607
  see also corn; original index
Carthage, fall of 702–3
Carthagena 705, 746
Carthaginian army, superior to that of Rome
      702
Carthaginians, skilled navigators 34
cash accounts 299–300, 305, 307, 313, 324
Caspian Sea 36, 346 n., 703
Castile 559, 561
casuistry 771–2
catholic(s), English treated with injustice
      589, *see also* Roman Catholic;
      established Maryland 589
cattle:
  as an instrument of commerce in rude
      nations 38, 430 & n.
  desert moors in Norway and Scotland
      provide pasture 163
  Union of 1707 opened the English
      market for highland cattle 165
  price of, rises with improvement 234
  and affects the rent of land 264
  labouring cattle as fixed capital 280,
      287
  as productive labourers 363, 586–7
  prohibition on the importation of live
      cattle, raises prices 424, 452, 875
  American cattle, dead or alive, allowed an
      extensive market 577
  see also original index; Scotland, butchers
      meat
Ceded, Islands 570 n., 578 & n., 923 & n.,
      943
Celebes 635
Celtes, cultivated music and dancing 776
certificates:
  parish, designed to improve the
      circulation of labour 155–6 & n.

certificates (*cont.*):
  see also graduation, universities
chairmen, in London employed as
      bricklayers in the summer season
      120
  drawn from the lowest rank of people in
      Ireland 177
chance, of gain, frequently over-valued
      125–6
  see also risk
chancery 720–1
channel, of circulation (a novel expression)
      293–4, 441–2
  precepts of the mercantile system force
      industry into less advantageous
      channels 516, 604, 605 n., *see also*
      mercantile system
Channel Islands 174 n.
characters, dissimilar 28
  no two characters more dissimilar than
      trader and sovereign 819
  character of the merchants, affected by
      high profits 612–13, 637
  character of the people 668
  character of the labourer, predominates
      over that of the soldier in militias
      698, *see also* militia(s)
  see also philosopher, porter 29 n.
chiefs:
  usurp lands after the fall of the Roman
      Empire 382 & n., *see also* Roman
      Empire, proprietors
child, children:
  one half die before the age of manhood 85
  labour of each child computed to be
      worth £100 in America 88 & n.,
      565
  destruction of, in China 90 & n.
  conditions unconducive to the production
      of 96–7
  and the liberal reward of labour 98,
      565 & n.
  earnings of 89 n., 785 n.
  see also education, infants
Chili:
  takes Spanish iron 185
  rent of gold-mines 188
  price of horses in 205
  growth of towns 222
  cattle killed for tallow 247
  conquest of 562, 589–90
China:
  a stationary state 89, 98, 111
  country labourers higher paid than
      artificers 144
  price of silver in 185, 254, 448
  richer than any part of Europe 208, 255
  accounts of wealth in 367

  never excelled in foreign commerce 367,
      379–80, 495
  better off than Mexico and Peru 448
  replacement of capital employed 490
  importance of Batavia to trade of 635
  sovereigns of, derive considerable part
      of revenue from land-tax, or
      land-rent 683, 730
  executive power in, responsible for roads
      and navigable canals 729
  see also Canton, original index
chocolate:
  demand for in Europe 591
  a luxury of the poorest Spaniards 871
  duty on 886
church:
  of Rome, claims merit in the abolition of
      slavery 390 & n., *see also* slavery
  benefices of 799, 802
  see also benefits of clergy
  ancient constitution of 799
  power of 800, and causes of decline in, of
      Roman 803–13
  see also clergy
churchmen, rewards of 146–8
  as unproductive labourers 331
  universities instituted for the education of
      765
  see also clergy, universities, religion
Cibao 559
Cipango 559 & n.
circulation, money as great wheel of 288–9,
      291 & n., 292, 296, 298–9, 301–4,
      308, 322, 340, 439 n., 441, 442 & n.
circulation, between dealers and
      consumers 322–4
  in Pennsylvania 820
  see also capital, money, water-level,
      analogy of, original index
cities:
  of Italy, the first to be improved 406,
      426
  commerce and manufacturers of caused
      the improvements of the country
      422
  the poor in, sunk in obscurity and
      darkness 795 & n.
  see also towns
civil discord 344, 807
civil government, *see* government, civil
civil law 415, 720, 765, 778
civil list 404 n., 444 n., 923–4
civil magistrate:
  masters call for protection from 85
  power of necessary for the protection of
      property 709–10
  and clerical disputes 789
  see also government, civil

civil society 807
civil war:
 in England, effect on price of corn 212,
  214
 of Flanders 427
 see also war(s)
clamour(-ous):
 of masters versus labour 85, 157–8
 and sophistry of merchants and
  manufacturers 144
 importunity of partial interests 472,
  648
 see also masters, manufacturers
clergy:
 promote the emancipation of slaves
  390 & n., *see also* slaves
 as members of the general assembly of a
  kingdom 404
 breakdown in the temporal power of
  419 n., 802–3
 among the greatest engrossers of land 574
 see also original index
clergy, benefit of 649, 765, 802 & n.
climate 10, 17, 97, 111–12, 188 n., 206, 222,
  466, 586, 635, 646, 661, 664, 681,
  689 n., 902, 905
cloathing:
 cheaper as a result of improvements in
  manufacture 96
 cloathing and lodging, two great wants of
  mankind; more plentiful than food
  in primitive countries 178–180
 materials of, normally become dearer with
  the advance of industry 193
 reduction in the real price of 261–2
 as part of the stock of society 281–4
 clothing of the greater part of the people,
  the product of their own industry
  407
clock-cases, exportation of, prohibited 655
 as beautiful machines 139; *see also*
  machines
clock-makers 139–40
cloths:
 stampmasters of 40 & n.
 black, variations in price of 76 & n., 132
 wages of journeymen engaged in, little
  more than the day wages of
  common labour 119
 England noted for the manufacture of fine
  cloths 410
 woollen or linen, not the regulating
  commodities by which the value of
  others is determined 516
 price of, in ancient Rome 685
 see also linen, wool, woollen
clothiers 250, 462 n., 655, 734 & n.
clove, *see* spices

coach(es):
 poor man does not have an effectual
  demand for 73, 93
 trade of coach-maker, not within the
  Statute of Apprenticeship 137
 taxes on 725, 852–3, 876–7
 see also carriages, taxes
coal, *see* original index
coalheavers, in London exercise a trade
  equal in hardship to colliers 121
 drawn from the lowest ranks of the people
  in Ireland 177
 colliers, earnings of 117, 121
 as example of slave-labour in modern
  times 387 n.
coal-mine(s), *see* original index, mines, rent
coals, a less agreeable fuel than wood 182–3
 price of 183–5, 189, 874–5
 not exempted from duty 656
 duties imposed upon exportation 658
 but not upon inland navigation 875,
  900
 as an instrument of trade 658, 874
coal-trade, *see* original index
coast, *see* sea coast
coasting, trade 366, 368, 371, 463, 650, 900,
  935
Cochin-china 173 & n., 635
cod, used as money 38
cock fighting 907
coffee, an enumerated commodity 579
 general use of in Great Britain 883
 duties on, fall principally upon people of
  middling fortune 886
coin(-age) 56–60
 Britain, reformation of coin in 58,
  442 & n., 482, 478–9
 gold and silver had the qualities which
  gave them value before they were
  coined 191
 amount of Scottish 232, of British 298,
  442
 quantity of, regulated by the value of
  commodities to be circulated by it
  440
 expence of coinage, defrayed by
  government 478
 melting down of 480
 see also original index, gold, silver, money,
  seignorage
college(s):
 constitutions of should be more
  reasonable 151, 773, 780
 Eton, accounts of 204, 211, 214, 217, 267,
  272 n.
 see also original index; universities
colony, assemblies, governments, in 326,
  585, 587, 619–21, 940–1

colony, trade 362 n., 367 n., 436 n., 449,
    463, 584, 595–8, 600, 602, 604–10,
    616 n., 626 n., 661, 947
colonies, British/English, in North America,
    see America, British colonies of
colonies, British West Indian 38, 70, 109,
    128 n., 173–4, 373, 380, 386, 388 n.,
    389, 437, 442, 500, 502, 556, 558,
    570–1, 578 n., 581, 586 & n., 588,
    594, 661, 937, 942
    see also India
colonies, European 221, 227, 240, 426 & n.,
    448–51, 496, 512 & n., 556, 558–62,
    564, 567–8, 570–2, 574–7, 580–1,
    584 & n., 586, 588, 590 & n., 592–5,
    601, 609, 615 & n., 621, 657, 660,
    883, 934
    see also Denmark, France, Portugal,
        Spain, Sweden
colonies, Greek, Roman 556 & n.,
    558, 566 & n., 567, 590 n.,
    593 & n.
    see also Greece, Rome, *Correspondence*
colonies, new, acquisition and performance
    of 109 & n., 221–2, 240, 363 n.,
    366 & n., 556, 564–6, 570–3, 577,
    601, 609, 634
    see also original index
combinations:
    merchants/manufacturers disposed to
        against the interest of workmen
        83–6, 158
    ease of in towns 142–5
    geographical dispersal (of farmers/traders)
        militates against 142–3, 462, 526,
        577, 644, 655
    see also manufacturers, merchants,
        monopoly
comets 767
    see also wonder, thunder and lightning
commerce, policy of Europe more
        favourable to as compared to
        agriculture 11, 377–80, 397–410,
        411–27
    neglect of foreign limits industry 112
    establishment of new branches of, a
        speculation 131
    money, the great instrument of 291, *see
        also* circulation, money
    of Scotland, not very great 299
    suspended upon the Daechalian wings of
        paper-money 321
    Chinese have never excelled in 367, *see
        also* China
    great commerce of civilized society
        carried on between town and
        country 141, 284, 376 & n., 686
    no regulation of, can increase the quantity
        of industry beyond what the capital
        can maintain 453
    acts of navigation unfavourable to 464
    see also navigation acts
    treaties of 450–1, 545–5, 617, 661
    project of, gave occasion to the first
        discovery of the West 564
    public works needed for the facilitation of
        724–31, 731–58
    improvements in, destroyed by power of
        the barons and of the clergy 803,
        see also barons, cities, clergy, towns
    see colonies; companies; original
        index (commerce); risk; towns
commerce, freedom advocated
    see also free competition, trade
commercial system 428–9, 451, 472–4, 488,
    497, 517, 627, 642–3, 704 n.
    see also mercantile system
commodities, enumerated, non-enumerated
    251, 502, 577–80, 592, 594, 602,
    657 & n., 658, 935–8
Commons, House of 218, 404 n., 585 & n.,
    624, 722 n., 734 n., 738–9, 750,
    751 n., 752
commonwealth 331, 428, 688–90, 696, 723,
    817, 824, 830
companies, mercantile:
    government of, oppressive 91, 570–1,
        575, 637, 819, 840
    economic policy of 575–6, 632–6
    seldom successful without an exclusive
        privilege 741
    justified to recompense risk 754
    account of several 741–53
    see also monopolies, East India Company,
        etc., original index
compass:
    ignorance of, made navigators reluctant to
        leave the coast 34
competition:
    among buyers 73
    among sellers 74 & n.
    encourages good management 164
    narrowing of, against the interest of the
        public 267, 362, 494
    among banks, increases the security of the
        public 329
    see also banks, combinations,
        corporations, free
        competition/trade, monopoly,
        price(s), profits, wages
Compiegne 335
conceit:
    man's overweening 124
    of landlords in prescribing the conditions
        of leases 831
Concordat, in France 804–5

condition, bettering of:
  plentiful subsistence encourages the
    labourer in the hope of 99
  desire to, and the pursuit of status 338 n.
  prompts man to save 341–2
  desire to, uniform and constant 343,
    345
  security of property, essential to 405, 540
  a principle, capable of correcting the
    errors of policy 674
  see also frugality, prudence, labour
Condom, election of 854
Congo 558 & n., 635
Congress, American 623, 625 n., 937
Connecticut, expence of civil establishment
    573
  election of governor in 585
Conquest, Norman 197, 199, 344
  authority of Saxon lords as great before
    the Conquest, as the Norman lords
    after it 416
  see also barons, lords, feudal
Constantinople:
  Turkey Company establish an
    ambassador there 732
  turbulence of the Greek clergy 798
  violent and furious government of 799
Constitution, British, protects North
    America 91, 585 n.
  would be completed by union with North
    America 624
  principles of require representation of
    regions taxed 933
  see also union, empire, America
consumable goods:
  taxes on, finally paid by the consumer
    826
  in Holland 857
  paid from three different sources of
    revenue 867
  incidence of 869–906
  see also taxes
consumption, the sole end of production
    660
contracts:
  in rude periods, left to the faith of the
    contracting parties 112, 309
  role of the Court of Exchequer in
    enforcing 720
conveniences:
  desire of, has no limit or certain boundary
    181
  abundance of food the cause of demand
    for 192, 409
  and security 405
  see also consumable commodities, taxes
conversion price 200–1
copartnery 740–1, 744, 756–7

Copenhagen 336
copper:
  an instrument of commerce among the
    Romans 39, 42
  in commercial nations 56
  not at present legal tender 57
  price of 60–1
  of Japan, an article of commerce in
    Europe 185
copy-holders 854
copy-right 754
Cori 560
corn:
  of Poland as cheap as that of France, and
    England 16–17
  same quantity of industry may produce
    different quantities of 132–3,
    234
  a corn field of moderate fertility produces
    more food than the best pasture of
    equal extent 164
  importation of, to Rome 166, 236
  rent of land used for, compared to others
    171–7
  price of 56
  varies most in turbulent societies 203–4
  equal quantities of, require equal
    quantities of labour 206, 228
  effect of bounty upon the exportation of
    218, *see also* bounties
  less productive than rice 233
  corn trade and corn laws, digression
    524–43
  laws concerning may be compared to
    those governing religion 539
  high price of, distresses the poor 259
  exportation of, encouraged by bounties
    424, 517
  bounty on, worse than a tax on necessaries
    875
  duties upon the importation of 452,
    875
  free importation of could little affect
    farmers in Great Britain 461
  real value of 516
  cost of bounty, to the public 523
  see also original index, dearths,
    Correspondence
Cornwall 186–7 & n., 188
corporations:
  as a sort of enlarged monopolies 79, 135
  establishment of 140
  regulated companies resemble 733–4
  see also monopoly, apprenticeship;
    original index
Correspondence (Smith) 8, 25, 47–8, 62, 72,
    87–8, 122, 137, 140, 171, 173, 200–3,
    205, 216, 240, 249, 267, 293–4, 312,

Correspondence (*cont.*):
> 314–15, 321, 327, 351, 357–8, 362, 370, 386, 414, 452–3, 457, 461, 507, 515–16, 518–20, 523–4, 535–6, 551, 594, 599, 601–2, 605, 613–16, 626, 651, 663, 673–4, 700, 722–3, 731, 740, 754–5, 758, 761–3, 765, 768–9, 773, 793, 817, 861–2, 867, 871, 882, 886, 933, 935

corvée 731
Cossacks 446
cottagers, cotters 133 & n., 134, 243
cotton 158 n., 560–1, 643, 659
country, the charms of attract capital 378
country-gentlemen:
> a declining proportion of the legislature 215
> imposed on by merchants 266, 434
> borrow upon mortgage 350
> use resources on items of expence 411–13
> least subject to spirit of monopoly 461–3
> imitated manufacturers 462, 516
> mistakenly support duties on corn 515–16
> office of JP an object of ambition to 719
> *see also* gentlemen

courage 127
> decline of, in modern times 782
> *see also* martial spirit, militia; risk

court(s), of justice, *see* justice, courts of
coward, mental mutilation of 787, 788
> *see also* labour, division of

credit:
> of a frugal man 130
> granted by banks 299–300, 308, 483
> might supply the place of money 437–8
> *see also* banks, paper money

Creoles 569
Crown, lands 404 n., 411 n., 423 n., 821, 823, 824 & n.
Cruttenden, East Indiaman 750
Cruzades 406
Cuba 185, 192, 589
Curaçoa 571
Cursitor, Baron of Exchequer 739
customs, and excise, arithmetic of 882
> *see also* original index, duties, taxes, *Correspondence*

custom, and manners:
> effect of on dissimilar characters 29
> everywhere regulates fashion 113
> of Europe, regulates apprenticeship 119, *see also* apprentices
> affects house-rent in England 134
> and the mercantile system 145
> and the cultivation of rice 176

of merchants 309
> in ancient times, prepared the citizens for war 811
> and necessities of life 870
> *see also* frugality, prudence; martial spirit

cutlers, in Sheffield, restricted to one apprentice 136
> reduction in the price of 260

cyder tax 890, 936
Cyprus, Brutus, lent money in 111

D

daedalian, wings of paper money 321
dairy 244–5
> *see also* original index

dance, teaching of 764
> and music, as amusements of barbarous nations 776 & n.
> as a desirable public diversion, *see* music

Danes, East India trade of 223, 449
> colonies 564, 570

Dantzick 209, 477, 488 n.
Danube 36
> *see also* original index

Darien, Isthmus of 560, 562
Dauphiné 854
dearth(s), unknown in North America 87
> years of, are generally years of sickness 101
> hardship of; role of the merchant 524
> never arise from combination among inland dealers 526
> unrestrained trade in corn prevents 527, 532, 538–9
> *see also* corn, original index
> uncommon in Ancient Egypt and Indostan 682

debasement, of coin 37 n., 43–4 n., 213
debt, public 12, 43, 107, 108 n., 345 & n., 442, 541 & n., 597 n., 615, 621, 661, 822, 824, 906, 909, 911–12, 914–15 & n., 918, 920–4 & n., 926–8, 929–33, 937–8, 941, 944–6
> *see also* original index

defence:
> of Great Britain depends upon the number of sailors and shipping 371, 463–4
> in Athens, required 5,000 idle men, according to Plato 388
> of cities in feudal times 401–4
> of more importance than opulence 464–5
> bounties to fisheries contribute to 518 & n.
> bounties upon the export of gun-powder and soil-cloth, support 523

colonies have not contributed to the
defence of Great Britain 573–4,
593, 614–16 n., 619, 946
expence of 689–708
protection of trade considered as essential
to 733
and regulated companies 737–8, 740
costs of, offset by public debt 909
see also army, bounties, colonies, labour
(unproductive), navigation acts
Deity 770, 772
Delphi 150 & n.
demand, effectual 73–80, 172–5, 435–6,
548, 893
demesnes 41 n., 398, 403, 415
democracy(-ies) 406 n., 625, 818, 945
democratical 625, 945
denarii 241 n., 685 & n.
deniers 43 n., 552
Denmark:
advance of since the discovery of America
220
East India trade of 223, 449
marriage bed of James I brought from 347
gold not discovered in the colonies of 564
attempted to colonize the New World
570
granted commerce of colonies to an
exclusive company 575, 632–3, 735
Reformation in 806
a protestant country 811
transit duties 894
dependency:
in feudal times 412, *see also* feudal system
monopoly, the principal badge of in the
American colonies 615, *see also*
colonies
dependent(s):
occupiers of land as 414
reduction of, with the growth of
commerce 420–1, 712
see also authority, barons, clergy,
subordination
depenses, annuelles, foncieres, primitives
665
desert(s):
the Highlands of Scotland as 31
moors in Norway and Scotland, produce
pasture 163
Moors delivered ivory and gold-dust,
across the 558
despotism:
progress of, and dominance of the
executive power 729
respect for the privileges of the clergy in
799
diamonds:
have scarce any value in use 45 & n.

demand for, arises from their beauty 191,
193 n.
the greatest of all superfluities 224, 419
price of, may be close to the lowest price
at which it is possible to bring
them to market 231–2
see also beauty, value, paradox of;
gems
diocese 761, 799–800, 804, 807
discipline, military 401–2, 700, 701 & n.,
702, 704–5
disease:
induced by excessive application 100
loathsome and offensive, require the
attention of government 788
dismemberment, of empires 616 n., 623 n.,
740
Dissenters 789
distillery 891, 938
distribution, of employment, stock 77 n.,
104, 260, 277, 279, 343, 499, 504,
530–1, 630–2, 673, 684
distribution, of riches 496
disturbances, colonial 87 n., 498, 573–4,
578, 585, 615, 937, 945–6, *see also*
colonies
diversions, public 702 n., 796–7
division of labour, *see* labour, division of
division, of stock 104, 260, 279, 343, 499,
504, 530–1
dog(s), do not exchange 26
doge 814
Domesday Book 398 & n., 834
Domingo 185, 559, 560–2, 571
see also original index
Dominica 943
Dorian colonies 556
drawback(s) 308–12, 315–16, 450, 499,
500–1 & n., 503–4, 519 n., 523–4,
540, 583, 584 & n., 655 & n., 658,
880, 882 n., 882–3, 885, 896
see also original index, *Correspondence*
drugs 23, 24 n., 129, 643 & n., 656–7,
743
drunkenness 362, 492, 493 n., 794, 795 n.,
891 n.
Dumfries 326
Dunfermline 347
Dunkirk, treated as foreign by France 901
Dutch:
coinage 60
trade upon lower profits than any people
in Europe 108
burn spices 175, 525, 631, 636, 638
and the East India trade 222–3, 449, 632
inferior ranks, generally industrious 335
and the carrying trade 370–1, 475
importation of tea from 436

Dutch (*cont*.):
   and the woollen manufacture at Abbeville
      461
   burden imposed upon supply of fish to
      Great Britain 464
   prosper despite taxation 467
   bounty upon exportation of corn, enables
      the Dutch to acquire corn more
      cheaply than Great Britain 514
   no gold discovered in the colonies of 564
   attack Brazil 569
   establish colonies in the New World
      570–1
   settlements at the Cape of Good Hope
      635
   tax upon successions 859
   have a considerable share in our public
      funds 927 & n.
   see also Holland, original index
duty(-ies), excise 17, 29, 59, 62, 144,
      187 n., 227 n., 248 & n., 250–1, 256,
      263–4, 320, 397–8, 406 n., 424,
      425 n., 431, 450, 452 & n., 454, 459,
      463, 464 & n., 465–9, 473 & n.,
      474–5, 478 & n., 492, 494 & n.,
      497 n., 499–500, 501–2 & n., 503–4,
      511 n., 515, 518 n., 519, 521–3,
      536 & n., 537–8, 540–2, 545–7,
      550 n., 551–4, 579–84, 605 n., 610,
      642–3 & n., 644, 647, 648 n.,
      655–6 & n., 657, 658 & n., 659, 661,
      670–1, 687, 721, 722 & n., 725,
      732–3, 735, 742 & n., 746, 750, 815,
      818, 822 n., 824, 826–7 n., 843 n.,
      846, 857 n., 858–60, 861 & n., 862–4,
      871, 875–9, 880 & n., 881, 882 & n.,
      883–90, 891 & n., 892–3, 894 & n.,
      895–8, 899–900 & n., 901, 903–4,
      906, 911, 913–14, 927, 929, 933 n.,
      934–9
duty(-ies), of the sovereign 687–9, 707–8,
      723, 733, 814
dye 190, 685 & n.
dyers 16, 20 n., 655–6

E

East India:
   native governments did not encourage
      foreign commerce, but derived
      opulence from inland navigation
      35
   shells used as money 38
   great fortunes easily acquired there 111
   market for American silver 222
   trade of, to Europe, a roundabout trade of
      consumption 373

   expense of last French war laid out there
      442, 615
   richer and better cultivated than Mexico
      and Peru 448
   commerce with, less advantage to Europe
      than that with America 448–9
   re-exportation of goods from, brings back
      gold and silver 475
   goods mentioned 490, 558, 560
   drawbacks on exportation of goods from,
      to America 563, 583–4
   Columbus tried to find a western passage
      to 559, 564
   origin of the name 560
   North-west passage to 564
   Dutch settlements under an exclusive
      company 570
   advantages to Europe of the Cape passage
      591, 631–41
   its discovery one of the two most
      important events in history 626
   countries which trade directly with, enjoy
      the show 627
   mercantile regulations concerning trade
      with, derange the natural
      distribution of stock more than
      others 630
   poor countries should not trade with
      632–4
   no colonies there thriving like the
      American 634
   the Cape the halfway house 635
   see also original index
East India Company:
   oppresses and domineers 91
   servants' profits eat up rent 113–14
   import tea worth £1,500,000 223
   tea dearer than that of Dutch and
      Gottenburg companies 436
   envy of its privileges and consequent
      arguments as to the trade carried
      on 449
   restraints on the rice trade imposed by,
      caused a famine 527
   their interest as sovereigns that European
      imports should be sold cheap and
      Indian exports dear, and the
      reverse as merchants 638
   originally established to maintain forts
      732
   exclusive privilege 742
   brief review of their history 746 (-53)
   may trade after expiration of exclusive
      privilege 755
   Bengal land tax before their domination
      838–40
   a modus converted into a payment in kind
      840

its advance to government 914, 923
see also original index, *Correspondence*
East India Company, Dutch 436, 632, 747
East India Company, French 223, 732
East India Company, the Gottenburg 436
East India, fund 914
East Indiaman (Cruttenden) 750
East India trade 222–3, 225, 229, 373, 406 n., 448–9, 475 & n., 490, 558, 560, 584, 630–5 636 n., 685, 734–5, 742, 747, 749, 755, 799, 883
East Indies, *see* Indies, East, West
Eastland Company 734–5
ecclesiastical, institutions:
benefices, support the dignity of the church 148, 800
cost of, frugal in the American colonies 574
universities, originally ecclesiastical corporations 765 & n., 772
plan of government 793
restraint on collation of the benefices of the church, limit the power of the clergy 805, 807
and the presbyterian form of government 809
see also clergy, presbyterian, Reformation
economy, of the rich 98
habits of 338 n., 412, 526, 727, 781, 907
of private people 346
government of England, not famous for 818
economy, political:
different theories of 11
the mercantile system 255, 429–30
the object of, to increase the riches and power of a country 372, 434
as a branch of the science of a statesman 428
agricultural systems of 663 ff.
partial and oppressive 674
the Abbé Morellet, a man of great knowledge of 755
see also commercial system, mercantile system, economists, original index
economists, French 663–79
Economical table 672–3, 679
eclipses 767
Edinburgh:
cost of carriage between Edinburgh and London 32–3
wages of labour in 92, 94, 127
rate of interest paid by private bankers 107

cost of lodging in, compared to London 135
the new town of, contains no Scotch timber 183
public banks in 297, 299–300, 315, 756
drawing and re-drawing on London 309–10
little or no trade or industry in, prior to the Union 336
British Linen Company of 758
Edinburgh Review 243 n., 560 n., 811 n.
education:
difference between dissimilar characters attributed to 29–30
in the ingenious arts and liberal professions, expensive 119
and monetary rewards 123
apprenticeships, increase the expence of 136
few churchmen are educated at their own expense 146
rewards of teachers in 149
as a contribution to the fixed capital of society 282
institutions for the education of youth and for the people of all ages 723, 758–814
beneficial to the individual and to society at large; to be defrayed by both 815
see also colleges, universities, labour, division of, original index
Egypt(-ians):
the first country on the Mediterranean Sea to be cultivated 34–5
everyman bound to follow the occupation of his father 80
wonderful accounts of the wealth of 367, 379, 406
disliked the sea 367, 495
goods purchased by Venetians 558
policy of, favoured agriculture 681
distinguished for the exportation of grain to Rome 683
militia of, made a feeble resistance to the armies of Rome 703
land tax in 838
good roads 838
ejectment, action of 392, 721
Elboeuf 102
Eldorado 563
election(s) 102, 393 n., 419 n., 557, 722 n., 752, 799–800, 804, 808–9, 854–5, 931
eloquence 566 & n., 806 & n., 811 n.
Empire(s):
aim at immortality 830
founded for the sole purpose of acquiring customers 613, 661

Empire, British:
British system of taxation should be
extended to the colonies 900,
933–5, 937–9, *see also* colonies,
Union
Empire, Greek 406, 408 n.
Empire, Chinese 448, 681, 838
Empire, Persian 702, 705
Empire, Roman 11, 56, 112, 211 n.,
396, 381–2 & n., 396–7, 407, 412 n.,
427, 703–6, 716–17, 722, 765, 798
Empire, Russian 705–6, 857
employment(s):
inequalities arising from the nature of
116–35, 159
inequalities occasioned by the policy of
Europe 135–59
emulation:
mutual, provokes over-work 100
and the constitution of courts of justice
720
renders excellency an object of ambition
759–60
benefits of, among teachers 763, 780
see also condition, bettering of
enclosure(s):
advantages of greater for pasture than
corn 167
and kitchen gardens 170
improve productivity 665, 927
endowments:
bad effect of on education 758–9, 780,
811
see also teachers
enemy(-ies), mercantile 500
monopoly an enemy to good management
78 n., 163
prodigals as public enemies 340
engines, *see* machine(s), mercantile,
commercial system
engine(s), of the mercantile system
450 & n., 630 & n., 642, 900 & n., *see
also* mercantile system
England:
corn lands better cultivated than in
France 17
wages in and price of subsistence
compared to Scotland 92–4, 99,
107–9
improvements in agriculture,
manufacture and commerce earlier
than in Scotland 94
market rate of interest, lower than in
Scotland 107
difference in the dress and countenance of
the common people, as compared
to Scotland 108, 177
meaning of dwelling house in 134

apprenticeships in 135–7, *see also*
apprenticeship
pay of the clergy in 147–8
linen manufacture in open 152
unequal price of labour in, attributed to
Laws of Settlement 156–7, *see also*
Poor Law, Settlement, laws of
markets of, opened to Highland cattle by
the Union 165, *see also* Union
disorderly state of under the Plantagenets
204
export of corn to Scotland 208–9
price of cattle in 167, 238, 242, 259
price of English wool fallen since the time
of Edward III 248
Queen Elizabeth, the first to wear
stockings in 262
circulating money in, computed at 18
millions 289
perhaps the second richest country in
Europe 373
respect for the yeomanry of 392
cities in, exempt from suit to the hundred
and county courts 401, *see also*
cities, towns
authority and jurisdictions of Saxon lords
as great as the Norman 416
export of gold, prevented in ancient times
431
confined to coin 434
Kings of, had no accumulated treasure
442, 445
act of navigation, the wisest of all
commercial regulations of 465, *see
also* navigation acts
reformation of gold coin in 482, *see also*
coinage
regulation of engrossers 528
relative freedom of trade with the colonies
576
naval power of, in the reign of Charles II
597
parliament of 619, 799, *see also*
Commons, House of, Lords,
Parliament
consist in a great measure of proprietors
and cultivators 668
produce of agriculture, largely consumed
at home 682
milita in, attached to a particular body of
troops 699, *see also* militia(s)
valour of soldiers uncorrupted by peace
705
fees of Court, originally the support of the
different courts of justice in 720
public schools less corrupted than the
universities 764, *see also* colleges,
universities

a common custom to send young people
abroad 773
the establishment of charity schools
beneficial 785, *see also* schools
restraint on the power of the Pope in 804
the church drains the universities of their
ablest members 811
turnpike tolls in 815
government of, not famous for good
economy 818
land tax in 828
taxes upon houses 845–6
taxes upon particular employments in
852
stamp duties in 863
poll taxes in 868
taxes upon luxuries 871 ff.
ancient customs in 879
expense of collection of 896
merchants generally the people who
advance money to government 918
people of the lowest rank in poorer
circumstances than their
counterparts in America 939
see also barons, feudal system; colonies;
corn, dearth; justice,
administration of, emulation; land
tax, taxes; original index, Britain;
roads, administration of
England, Bank of 302–4, 308, 311–12 & n.,
318 & n., 319–20 & n., 322 n.,
487 n., 552, 554–5, 741, 756 & n.,
818, 911–12, 914, 916 n., 923, 942
English Copper Company 758
engrossing of land 382, 572–3
engrossing, and forestalling 528 n.,
532–4 & n.
entail(s) 381 n., 382, 384–5 & n., 393, 572
entrepot 335–6
enumerated commodities (colonial) 251,
473, 502, 577 & n., 578, 579 & n.,
580, 594 & n., 602, 657 & n., 658, 935
Ephesus 566
epicés, the chief part of French judges'
emoluments 720
equity:
and those who feed the whole body of the
people 96
ethics:
in ancient Greek philosophy 766, 770
Eton, College, accounts of 52 n., 204, 211,
214, 217, 267 n., 272 n.
Europe:
commercial advantages of the Baltic and
Adriatic seas 36
value of gold and silver in, following the
discovery of mines in America 49,
52

the value of goods generally computed in
silver 57
river fisheries in 69
twenty workmen serve under a master for
one that is independent 83
population, not supposed to double in less
than 500 years 88
propagation in 98
pecuniary wages and profits in 116
policy of, considers the labour of
mechanics, artificers as skilled
labour 119
seven years, the usual term for
apprenticeships 136
industry carried on in towns more
advantageous than in the country
142, 144–6
the greater part of the learned, educated
for the church 148
policy of, obstructs the free circulation of
labour 151–2
corn the principal produce of land which
serves for human food 175
the greater part of, approached a more
settled form of government at the
end of the 15th century 199
through the greater part of, commerce
and manufactures have encouraged
agriculture 422, 529
different notions of, encourage the
accumulation of gold 431
inhabitants of wine countries, the soberest
in 492
universities of, originally ecclesiastical
corporations 765, 772–3
teaching in 770
see also original index
Eustatia island 571
Euxine Sea 36, 703
exchange, bills of 298–300, 303–4, 309 & n.,
310 n., 311–16, 324, 328, 480–1, 483,
849 n., 861
exchange, course of 326, 353 n., 432–4,
475–9, 488 & n.
see also original index
exchange, medium of 37–9, 40 & n., 49,
57–8, 61, 190 n., 194, 208, 210, 219,
291–3 n., 325, 429, 430 n., 438, 514
exchange, the propensity to truck, barter,
and 25 & n., 27 n., 28–30, 31 n., 37
see also labour, division of, coin, metals,
money
exchangeable value 44–5 & n., 46–9, 55,
65–7, 69, 71, 189
see also value, diamonds
exercise, military 698–700
in Greece and Rome 683, 696, 698, 774,
776, 779, 786

exchequer 41, 318, 400, 650, 720, 722 n.,
    739, 753, 916
exchequer bills 319 & n., 320, 441, 911–12
excise, *see* duty(-ies), excise, original index
executioner, pay of 117
executive power:
    authority of the Commons over 585
    should be separated from the judicial
        722–3
    protection of trade by, essential to the
        welfare of the commonwealth 733
    see also defence
expences, private, and the national capital
    341, 346–9, 666–7
export trade
    see also original index, trade

F

faction(s):
    colonial 622–3, 945
    spirit of 741
    good temper and moderation of, and the
        public morals of a free people 775
    an educated people, more capable of
        seeing through the interested
        complaints of 788
    among the clergy 791, 808
    see also sects
family(-ies):
    the necessary expence of a labourer's
        family of the time of Charles II 95
    poorest, can maintain a cat or dog 243
    pride of, supported by the law of
        primogenitive 384, *see also*
        primogeniture
    nine hundred, driven out of Lucca 407
    old, rare in commercial countries 421
    old, common among the Tartars 422
    prudence in the conduct of a private
        family, can scarce be folly in that of
        a great kingdom 457
    all families equally ancient 713
    families revered in the age of shepherds
        714
    see also birth, authority of, shepherds
famine(s), *see* dearth
fanatical, fanaticism 793, 796 & n., 806,
    808–9
    see also sects
farm, taxation 399–402, 404, 901–4,
    919 & n.
farmer(s), agricultural:
    profits of 68, 76, 169, 332, 334
    farmers, properly so called 391
    see also original index, agriculture, cattle,
        corn, rent

fashion:
    increases the value of plate 62, 551, 553
    in Holland, unfashionable not to be a man
        of business 113
    manufactures, dependent upon are
        seldom long-established 131
    people of, in Sicily 364
    Rome 685
    drunkenness not the vice of people of 493
    people of, embrace liberal systems of
        morality 794
    vanity and, affects the demand for houses
        841
fermented liquors 96, 492, 887–8, 936
Fernambuco 575–6
fertile, fertility of land:
    of land, affects rent 72, 163
    planting and tillage regulate more than
        they animate the active fertility of
        nature 363
    natural fertility of the soil in England 424
    see also rent
fertile, fertility of mines:
    affects the value of gold 49, 220, 229,
        258, 510
    rent, affected by fertility and situation
        182
    of coal mines 184–7
    price of precious metals determined by
        the most fertile mine 191
    fertility of, may have no connection with
        the state of industry in a particular
        country 254
    see also gold/silver, rent
feudal:
    anarchy 204 n., 386, 854 n., 878
    government, *see* government, feudal
    law 415–16 & n., 417, 694, 859–60
    system 256 & n., 349 n., 381 n., 382 & n.,
        394 n., 402 & n., 412 n., 417 n.,
        418, 421 n., 511 n., 680 n., 693–4 n.,
        704 n., 705, 821
    merchants despised 859
    see also government, original index
fiars 94, 200 & n., 201 n., 257 & n.,
    324 n.
fideicommisses 384 & n.
fines, payable to corporations 138
    and to the king in respect of adulterine
        guilds 140–1
    payable in respect of the instruments of
        trade 659
    payable by traders 732–6, 738
    landlords take for the renewal of a lease
        831
    under feudal law 860
Finisterre, Cape 502, 579, 614, 935
fire 18, 184, 409 n., 481, 486, 682

arms 178, 699, 707 & n., 708
communication of 324
engine(s) 19 n., 20 & n., 21 n., *see also*
    engine(s)
insurance 125–6, 756
of London 344
First Formation of Languages 21, 768.
fish, abundant in the neighbourhood of
    Shetland 161
salt, may be subject to aliens duty 464
a non-enumerated commodity 577–8
see also original index
fishery:
produce of, contribute to the circulating
    capital of societies 284, 360
usual effect of bounties on, is to
    encourage rash undertakers
    522 & n.
British Greenland 643
tax on, in Holland a discouragement 905
see also original index, hunters, age of
Flanders:
onions imported from 96
wool exported to 179
manufacture of wool 263, 408
English wool exchanged for fine cloths
    407
importation of lace from, prohibited 468
industry augmented by colonization of
    America 591
supplies linen to America 627
flax:
component parts of the price of 68,
    114–15
imported from the Baltic 365
of Riga 369
imported from the colonies, under
    advantageous terms 583, 645
importation encouraged by exemption
    from duties 643, 881
fleece(s):
estimated at two-thirds of the value of the
    whole sheep in Saxon times 247
owners of in Kent and Sussex, obliged to
    report numbers and location of
    650
quality of in England 653
see also wool
fleet(s), naval:
fleets and armies maintained, not with
    gold, but consumable goods 440,
    494
of Venice, confined to the Mediterranean
    569
expence of 573
Russian 607
Florence:
a Roman colony 567

paid Lorenzo's trading debts 819 & n.
Florida, French settlers in, murdered by
    Spanish 569
flota, Spanish, extraordinary demand of,
    offsets loss of American market 607
flour:
component parts of price of 68
duties on 875
foncieres 665
Fontainbleau 335
food:
desire of, limited in every man by the
    narrow capacity of the human
    stomach 181 & n.
see also original index
footman, footmen 420, 720
forestalling and engrossing, fear of 534
forge, erected at great expence 280, 307
foris-familiated 859
forts 732, 737–9, 742 & n., 743–4, 754–5
fortune(s):
birth and 714 & n., 761 n., 944 & n.
confidence in good 123–4, 292, 559,
    562–3, 623, 918
equality/inequality of 346, 396 n., 557,
    689 n., 710–13, 715 & n., 867
see also property
rank and 357 n., 711, 784–5, 795–6, 799,
    808, 867
upstart 585, 902, 919 n., *see also* upstart
Foundling hospitals 97
France:
quality and price of corn and other goods
    compared with Poland and
    England 16–17
debasement of coin 53
ratio of gold to silver 60
seignorage in 62, 551
rent of vineyards in 78
fall in the price of grain in, since
    seventeenth century 94, 216, 257,
    506–7
market rate of interest higher than in
    England 107–8
richer than Scotland, ibid.
carrying trade, taken by Dutch, ibid.
definition of dwelling house in 135
corn cultivated in the wine provinces
    171
vineyards, need not be envied by Britain
    175
labouring poor seldom eat butcher's meat
    207
fall in the price of corn 216, 507
improved since the colonization of
    America 220
silver pre-ponderates in the coinage of
    230

France (*cont.*):
exports poultry to England 242
prices of pork and beef 243
corn as cheap as in England 324–5
Versailles, an ornament to 347
attempt to reduce the rate of interest in 358
market rate of interest, higher than in England 359
entails in 384
five parts out of six, cultivated by metayers 391 & n., *see also* metayers
loss of authority over barons in 402–3
authority of Kings not destroyed by the development of cities 404
corn of Poland exchanged for luxuries of 407
breeding of silk worms, introduced in the reign of Charles IX 408
allodial ownership preceded feudal 416
cultivation and improvement, inferior to that of England 425
prohibition on the export of coin 434
exchange of wine for English hardware 439
last war with, cost ninety millions 441–2
Merovingian Kings had treasures 446
established exclusive company for the East India trade 449
par of exchange 476–7, 479
invasion of Holland 485–6
advantages of trade with 490
cheap wine does not encourage drunkenness 492
wine, discouraged by the English in favour of Portugal 493
more populous than the American colonies, and therefore a better market 495–6
England unwilling to carry French goods 500
no drawback allowed on the export of French wines to America 503
rarely necessary to restrain the export of corn 539
provisions of the Methuen Treaty 546–9
no gold or silver mines in the American colonies 564
settlements in America 569–71
plenty of good land there 572
no revenue from colonies 574
policy of establishing exclusive companies 575
refining sugar, flourishes in colonies 581
slaves better managed there 587
capital accumulated there 588
industry augmented by colonization of America 591
tobacco dearer than in England 595
navy, at least equal to that of England in the reign of Charles II 597
tobacco imports 602
invasion of England 605
supplies linen to America 627
East India trade now open 631
English import duty on yarn 643
English prohibition on linen imports 644
indigo 645
exclusive trade in gum Senega taken by England 657
restraints imposed by ancient laws of on the internal transportation of corn 664
consist in a great measure of proprietors and cultivators 668, 682
agriculture and the corn trade, relieved of constraints 678
veterans defeated by English standing army 701
fees in parlement 720
cost of Languedoc canal 726
great roads only attended to 730
tyranny of the *corvée* 731
South-Sea company ruined by the slave trade 745
Reformation in 806
Voltaire, the only professor in, whose works are worth reading 811
treasures of Berne, invested in the funds of 812–13, 819
a tax upon the rent of land, recommended by the economists 830, *see also* economists (French)
taille in 865–6
leather shoes, not necessaries 870
tax on tobacco 871
silk manufactures, could be under-sold by English 886
péages in 894
might levy three times the British revenue 912
more debt in annuities than in England 918
more wealthy bachelors 919
oppressive public debt 928
augmentation of coin 932
see also original index, *Correspondence*
Franciscans 790
free:
governments 324, 412 n., 540 n., 585–7, 622, 788, 813
see also commerce, freedom of, competition, trade
free-burghers 400
freedom, in the present sense of the word, defined 400

see also liberty

free-hold 154, 391 n., 392, 393 n., 798

freeman/freemen 98–9 & n., 121 n., 386 n., 388–9, 391 n., 398 n., 400, 405, 494, 557, 587, 683 & n., 684 & n., 696, 738, 774–6, 857

friars 574, 771 n.

frugal(-ity) 10, 24, 130, 239, 316
  of the poor 98
  the frugal man, likened to the founder of a public workhouse 338–9
  as public benefactor 34
  and the desire to better our condition 341, 345
  principle of, predominates 342
  increases the public capital 346
  sudden frugality of the rich, acknowledges previous bad conduct 348
  frugal man, said to love money 429
  high rates of profit, destroy 612
  pretended frugality of the civil magistrate 791
  frugality of the poor, enforced by taxes 872, 896 n.
  see also condition, bettering of, government, parsimony, prodigality, prudence

fruit-garden, rent of generally higher than that of a corn-field 169, 712

fruit-wall 170

fuller's earth, prohibition on the export of 654

funds, British:
  Dutch holding in 108
  Bernese treasure invested in 819
  see also original index

fur trade 178

furnaces, in an iron-work, require great expence 280
  encourage the consumption of wood 580
  and in the American colonies, ibid.
  prohibited in the American colonies 582

furniture, household:
  as part of the stock reserved for immediate consumption 281
  a durable object 281, 347

G

gabelle 901, 904

gain, the end of all improvement 245

Gallican Church 559, 805

game, can be acquired with a small quantity of labour 205
  grows dearer with improvement 234

games, athletics 774 n.
  Olympic 786

Ganges 35 & n., 560, 682

gardening:
  garden stuff has become cheaper 96, 259
  see also original index

Garonne 336

garrisons 549, 636, 737–40, 742–4, 754–5

gems, *see* stones

genealogies 421, 422 n., 714 n.

Geneva:
  moderate benefices in 148
  respectable clergy of 810
  eminent men of letters are professors in 811

geniuses, dissimilar 30

Genoa:
  why corn is dear in 209
  shipping encouraged by Crusades 406
  obliged to use foreign corn 480
  bank of, ibid.
  Columbus belonged to 339
  tax on bread 875
  enfeebled by debt 928

gentleman, gentlemen:
  everyone fond of being 25 n.
  farmer 70
  taille in France, degrading to 394
  drunk with ale, rarely seen 493
  English university education not proper for 772–3
  would be better educated in the absence of public institutions 781
  and the foreign tour 773
  trade, disgraceful to 907–8
  see also country gentlemen

Gentoo 681–2

geometry:
  knowledge of required by watchmaker 139–40 n.
  invented to facilitate the arts 767–8 n.
  the common people should be instructed in the elementary parts of 785–6 & n.

Georgia, (N America):
  cost of civil establishment in 573–4
  not planted at the time of the Navigation Acts 597

German:
  nations, over-ran the Western Empire 381 & n., 382 n.
  use of silver money in 56

Germany:
  improved since the discovery of America 220
  slavery still exists in 387
  purveyance in 394
  free towns of 403

Germany (*cont.*):
  expence of last war laid out in 442, 615
  foreign trade 475
  linen exported from England to the
      colonies 584, 591, 604, 627
  drained by the Spanish Flota 607
  trade with America 627–8
  could have been conquered by Rome 703
  justice a source of revenue 716
  just beyond the shepherd state when
      Rome fell 717
  Reformation in 806
  eminent men of letters, often professors in
      811
gegaws 349
Ghent 427
Gibraltar 34, 740
Glasgow:
  recent rise in the demand for labour 94
  see also original index
glass:
  windows, a happy invention 23
  kelp, useful in the making of 161
  grinding company 758
  coal, necessary in the manufacture of 874
Goa 635
gods, superstition and the phenomenon of
      nature 767 & n.
Golconda 191
gold:
  and silver, common instruments of
      commerce in rich and commercial
      nations 39–41
  vary in value 49–51
  value diminished as a result of discoveries
      in America 52, 220–1, 354,
      510
  rose in price as compared to silver 232,
      233–4
  forced abroad by the operations of
      banking 295
  that wealth consists in, a popular nation
      429, 503, 588
  distributed by Spain and Portugal 510,
      567
  St Domingo, represented by Columbus as
      abounding in 561, 563–4
  Americans, lack gold and silver money
      940–4
  see also original index, coin, silver
goldsmith(s) 122, 283, 550
Gottenburg:
  tea smuggled from 223
  Company 436
government:
  more settled at the beginning of the
      sixteenth century 199
  absolute/arbitrary 586, 587 n.

allodial, *see also* allodial 382–3 n.
  order and good, introduced by commerce
      412
  art of draining subjects, pockets 861
  British colonial 326, 556, 565 n., 574,
      585–90, 615 n., 820, 940–2,
      945
  civil 44 n., 48, 222, 415–16 n., 541,
      573–4, 593, 614, 679, 693 n., 706,
      709 n., 710 & n., 715 & n., 802–3,
      807, 809, 817, 937
  ecclesiastical 574, 793 & n., 807
  expenses of 817, 821–3 & n., 920
  extravagance of 343 & n., 345–6, 818 n.,
      909, 925 & n., 928–9
  feudal 285, 334, 383 n., 386 n., 388 n.,
      412 n., 414 n., 416 n., 418 n.,
      421 n., 610 n., 695–6, 854, *see also*
      feudal
  merchants, formidable to 471, 613
  origin of 710, 715
  republican 387 n., 395, 906, 909
  see also original index; shepherds
Gracchi 775
graduates, graduation:
  privileges of, likened to statutes of
      apprenticeship 762
  honours of, should not require a
      certificate of attendance 765
  no equivalent of in ancient Greece 778
  privileges of, convenient to men of
      learned professions 780
  see also colleges, universities
grain:
  food of the common people 93
  and the price of labour 100–4, *see also*
      labour
  and the statute of labourers 195
  see also corn
grapes:
  could be grown in Scotland 458
  in countries which produce no grapes,
      drunkenness a common vice 492
grazier(s), of Great Britain have a monopoly
      of butcher's meat 452, 459
  see also original index
Greece, Greeks:
  ancient, had no work for apprentices 139
  slavery harsher than in the middle ages
      386
  cultivation of corn degenerated 388
  citizens consisted of landed proprietors
      397
  opulent and industrious 406
  trade and industry carried on by slaves
      683–4
  citizens served in war without pay 693
  military exercise in 698

militias defeated by Macedonian and Roman armies 702–3

militias defeated Persia 704–5

just beyond the shepherd state at the time of the Trojan War 717

sanguinary factions 775

education in 776–7

abilities of people, equal to those of modern nations 779

great men of letters were teachers 811

public revenue largely obtained from state lands 821

lacked linen, but lived comfortably 870

see also original index

Greek colonies:
  reasons for sending them out 556, 558

  plenty of good land 567

  sometimes contributed military force, but seldom revenue 593

  England, might imitate the tie between mother country and the American colonies 593–4

Greek language 766

Greek philosophy, the branches of 766
  schools of, established in the colonies 566–7

Greenland:
  seal fishery 643

  whale fishery 745

Grenada:
  sugar refinery 581

  new field for speculation 943

Guastalla 876

Guernsey 620

Guienne 171

greyhound(s) 25, 26 n., 30

grocer(s) 129, 361

ground-rent(s) 134, 840–44, 862

Guinea(s), coin 57 & n., 58–9, 61, 63, 127, 132, 134, 213, 226, 229, 235, 261, 290–1, 322, 326–7, 436, 520, 550–1

Guinea, coast 37 n., 492, 558, 739, 743 n.

gum, Senega 657, 658 n., 881

gunmetal 656 n.

gunpowder 465 n., 518 n., 523, 699, 708
  see also original index

gymnasia/gymnasium 696, 774, 786

H

hackney, coaches, chairs, taxes on 852–3

Halifax, city of 409

Hamburgh, credit of supported by the Bank of England 320
  goods of, paid with bills upon Holland 477, 488 n.

  agio of the bank 480

indirect trade to America 628

composed chiefly of merchants and artificers 668, 670

revenue of, derived from mercantile projects 817–18, 820

taxes in 850–2

Hamburgh, Company 734–5
  see also original index

Hanseatic League, *see* original index

harbour(s), cost of, should be defrayed by port-duties 724

hardware 17, 439, 457 n., 469, 491, 897

hare, run down by greyhounds 25

harvest 83, 132, 391 n., 431–2, 533, 602 n., 675, 693, 694 & n., 821

hatter 136

hawkers 397 & n.
  taxes on 852 & n.

hazard, profit the reward for incurring 66, 127–8
  and private co-partneries 741

  see also profit, risk

health, affected by piece-work 100–1
  trusted to the physician 122

  and the conceit which men have in their abilities 124–5

  potatoes and 177

  can be enjoyed under an unwholesome regimen 466, 673–4

  see also disease

hearth-money, *see* original index

heaven, earned only by penance 771

heavenly, bodies 767 & n., 770 n.

Hebrew, language 766

Hebrides 94, 520

heptarchy, Saxon 344

Hercules, pillars of 34

herdsman, herdsmen, *see* shepherds

Hereditas, Luctuosa 859

Hereditatum, Vicesima 859

herring(s), *see* original index

hides, used as an instrument of commerce 38, 907
  exportation of from the Highlands of Scotland 179

  human industry, limited in the production of 252

  an enumerated commodity 577, 579

  taxes on the importation of 643

  and the price of butchers-meat 652

  prohibition on the export of 654

  see also original index

higgling, and bargaining 49

Highland(s), Scottish 31–2, 93 n., 94, 96, 97 & n., 165, 179 & n., 237–40, 414, 417 n., 421, 519 n., 696 n., 701 & n.

  see also original index

highway(s), *see* roads
Hispaniola 247
hog(s), price of 243 & n., 244, 259
hogshead(s) 173 n., 372–3, 500, 546, 602–4, 606, 646, 890, 936
Holland:
    water carriage afforded by the Maese 35
    ratio of silver to gold 14 to 1 60
    richer than England, wages high, profits low, gained carrying trade of France, holds large amount in French and English funds, not decaying 108–9
    corn chiefly imported 166
    spices burnt to keep up the price 175, 525, 636
    improved since the discovery of America 220
    expelled the Portuguese from India 222, 449
    tea smuggled from 223
    houses supported by Bank of England 320
    operation of carrying trade 370–1
    farmers not inferior to those of England 395
    legislature attentive to commerce and manufactures 424
    exchange with 433
    East India Company's tea smuggled into England 436
    imports lean cattle 460
    Dutch undertaker of woollen manufactures at Abbeville 461
    supplied other nations with fish 464
    bad terms with England, ibid.
    French wine smuggled 475
    computation of state of credit and debit 477–8
    market price of bullion above the mint price 482
    buys English corn cheaper and can sell manufactures cheaper in consequence of the British corn bounty 514
    must carry on herring fishery in decked vessels 520
    position in regard to the Methuen treaty 547
    no gold, silver or diamonds in the American colonies 564
    attack on Brazil 569
    settlements in seventeenth century 570
    Curacoa and Eustatia free ports 571
    exclusive company for colonial commerce 575
    naval power in 1660, 597
    possessed New York and New Jersey, ibid.
    tobacco imports 602
    linen exported to America 604, 627
    maintains monopoly of trade to the spice islands 631
    settlements at the Cape and Batavia the most considerable in Africa and the East Indies 635
    destructive policy in the East Indies 637, 638
    English duty on yarn 643
    gum senega clandestinely exported from England 658
    type of mercantile state 668
    subsistence drawn from other countries 677
    great cities the capitals of little republics 808
    respectable clergy 810
    eminent men of letters often professors 811
    monopoly of madder owing to existence of tithe elsewhere 838
    rate of interest 845
    two per cent tax on capital paid voluntarily 851–2
    a tax intended to fall on capital 852
    servants' tax 857
    tea and sugar luxuries of the poorest 871
    taxes on bread and necessaries ruined manufactures 875–6
    tea taxed by licence to drink 878
    expense of preserving from the sea 906
    wise republic of, has been obliged to levy inconvenient taxes 928–9, 936
    see also original index, Netherlands
Holstein, cattle of, exported to Holland 677
Holy Land 406
honoraries, fees 760, 764, 778, 790
    see also original index
hop garden, profit of 169
hose 262
    see also original index
hospitality, profuse 348–9
    and the ancient clergy 801–4
    see also original index, clergy, feudal system
Hottentots 32 n., 634 & n., 716 n.
hotwalls, and the cultivation of grapes 458
house:
    definition of 134–5, 180
    as part of the national stock 281–2
    see also tax, original index
Hudson's Bay Company, *see* original index
human nature:
    and the propensity to exchange 25
    levity and inconstancy of 92–3
    character of, and the division of labour 788, 795 & n.

see also labour, division of

Hungary, Danube little use to 36
  serfs still exist in 387
  industry encouraged by colonization of
    America 591–2
  mines worked by freemen 684
hunters, age, nations of 178, 634, 692–3,
    782
  see also original index
husbandman/men, nations of 692–4, 697,
    704, 717, 782
  see also original index, agriculture, stage
    of
husbandry 75, 143, 169, 170 n., 240, 262,
    395 n., 697, 783
  see also agriculture
  instruments of 68, 160, 280, 387, 389,
    665, 856
hussars, no plunder, no pay 790

I

idleness:
  unfashionable in Holland 113
  why greater among our ancestors 335
  prevails where revenue pre-dominates
    336–7
Iguana 560
Illyrians 702
impartial spectator 945 & n., *see also*
    spectator
importation, restraints on, imposed by the
    commercial system 472–3, 488, 494
  statistics of, untrustworthy 833
  see also original index, commercial,
    mercantile system
improvers 160 n., 170, 386 n., 395, 411 & n.,
    423 & n.
incorporation(s) 136, 140 n., 141, 145, 158,
    797
independency 399, 557
Independents, the principles of that sect
    793
India, Gulf of 36
  value of gold and silver in 225, 229
  governed by merchants 637–8, 640 & n.
  not eminent for foreign trade 367
  see also Bengal, Indostan, East, West
    India
Indian Prince, authority of 24 n.
Indian Sea 631
Indiaman 750
indigo 577 n., 579, 583, 645
Indostan:
  violent police compels every man to
    follow the occupation of his father
    80

country labourers better paid than most
    artificers 144
labourers' real wages less than in Europe
    224
quantity of gold and silver affected by
    American mines 254
treasure commonly buried in 285
wonderful accounts of its ancient wealth
    and cultivation 367
its wealth obtained though exportation
    was in foreign hands 379–80
more advanced than Mexico and Peru
    448
operation of foreign commerce 490
Vasco de Gama arrived by the Cape in
    1497 559
revenue chiefly from land tax 683
silk exports to Rome 685
roads and canals 730
land tax revenue stimulates the
    sovereign's interest in such works,
    ibid.
supposed necessity for forts to protect
    commerce 731–2
silk should be admitted free to Britain
    886
see also East Indies and East India
    Company, original index
industry, *see* original index
industry, balance of 429 n., 453 & n.,
    454 n., 457, 465, 504, 506 n., 516,
    523, 604 & n., 606, 610, 630, 632, 897
industry, human 14, 47 n., 99–101, 130,
    132, 139, 154, 156–7, 206, 209,
    234–5, 237, 239, 245–6, 252, 276–7,
    335, 337, 338 n., 339, 341 n.,
    394–5 n., 405 & n., 435, 470, 687,
    781, 782 n., 788–91, 826, 833, 866,
    925
industry, of country, towns 11, 31, 141–5,
    320–1, 336, 376, 411, 427, 627, 664,
    679
industry, security of 199, 345 & n.,
    405 & n., 540–1, 610
inequality of fortune, *see* fortune, inequality
    of
infant(s), exposition of 10, 90 & n.
ingot(s) 40 n., 41, 483 n.
innkeepers, do not exercise a creditable
    trade 118
Inquisition 589 & n.
insurance, in land and water carriage 33
  and the rate of interest 114
  moderate profits in 125–6, 128
  trade of, may be carried on successfully
    by a joint stock company 756
  gives security to private people 757
  see also original index, risk

intemperance 674, 794
Intendants 731
interest, private, public 11, 26–8, 29 n.,
        89 & n., 116, 139 & n., 144, 181 n.,
        265–6, 267 & n., 338, 350, 456,
        471–2, 474–5, 525, 529, 531, 630,
        687–8, 725, 754 n., 760, 783, 790,
        796, 803, 833, 905
interest, rate of 131 n., 160, 169, 292,
        304 & n., 307, 309, 314, 316,
        318 & n., 334–5, 337, 341 n., 395,
        399 n., 423–4, 602, 611, 621, 721–2,
        745, 813 & n., 840 & n., 845, 852,
        857–8, 908, 911–12, 913 & n., 914,
        917, 918 & n., 920 & n., 926 & n.,
        928, 931, 937–8, 940
    defined 69–70
    regulation of legal 106–7, 109, 137 n.,
        356 & n., 357–8 & n., 849
    see also original index, profit
invention(s) 14, 17, 20 & n., 21 n., 23, 32 n.,
        139, 263
    see also machines
inventor, temporary monopoly should be
        granted to 754
Invisible Hand 181 n., 456
    of Jupiter 767 n.
Ionians, colonized Asia Minor 556
Ireland:
    land not cultivated by factors 174
    supplies strong porters and beautiful
        prostitutes, fed on potatoes, to
        London 177
    exports salt meat 246
    may not export wool except to England
        248
    may export raw hides to England duty
        free 251, 643
    may export hides to other countries 251
    only lately allowed to export cattle to
        England 424–5
    discharged soldiers and seamen may
        exercise any trade in 470
    bounty on hemp imported into Britain 646
    able to pay land tax 934
    extension of British custom duties to,
        proposed 935
    would get rid of an oppressive aristocracy
        and a spirit of party 944–5
    see also original index, *Correspondence*
iron, a common instrument of commerce in
        Sparta 39
Isthmian games 786
Italy:
    corn chiefly imported during Roman
        prosperity 166
    question whether a new vineyard would
        be profitable 170

olive plantations not to be envied by
        Britain 175
    not gone backward since discovery of
        America 220
    introduction of wind and water mills
        263
    artistic genius decayed by monuments
        remain 347
    cultivation degenerated when abandoned
        to slaves 388
    prohibition of exportation and
        encouragement to importation of
        corn obstructed cultivation 396
    ancient inhabitants were proprietors 397
    cities became independent 403–4
    cities the first which commerce raised to
        opulence 406
    silks and velvets exchanged for corn of
        Poland 407
    breeding of silkworms introduced 408
    sober, though wine is cheap 492
    in little states restraint on export of corn
        may sometimes be necessary 539
    Roman colonies 556–8, 567
    Greek colonies, ibid.
    school of philosophers in a Greek colony,
        ibid.
    result of admission of inhabitants to
        Roman citizenship 624
    ancient republics derived larger part of
        revenue from state lands 821
    silk manufacturers might be undersold by
        English 886
    small states levy transit duties on the Po
        894
    republics all in debt 909
    republics began the practice of funding
        928
    see also original index
Ivana 560
ivory 558

J

jack, of all trades 530
Jamaica, trade with more uncertain than
        with North America 128
    circuitous 369
    improvement of 578
    desert in 1660 597
    returns from trade irregular 943
Japan, copper exported to Europe 185
    rate of silver to gold in 229
    no gold mines, but richer than Mexico or
        Peru 448
    Batavia on the route to 635
    trade with China 680

affords an example to China 681
  see also 112 n., 225 n., 367 n.
jealousy, mercantile 493, 495–6, 500, 578–9,
    582, 640, 660
  see also manufacturers, mercantile
Jersey, island of 620
jeweller(s) 117 n., 122, 283
jewels 193 n., 346, 349
  see also stones, precious
Jews, anciently considered as vagabonds
    399 n.
  paid respect to genealogies 422 n.,
    714 n.
  Portuguese, persecuted by the Inquisition
    589
judges:
  usually men of integrity 123 n., 719
  Ius majoratus 572
justice, and equity 112, 145, 157, 307, 539,
    654, 664, 687, 910
justice, courts of:
  administered by feudal lords 383, 401,
    415–16
  in Athens 778–9
  in England 721
justice, administration of:
  anciently subservient to the purposes of
    revenue 717–18, 821
  never *gratis* 718
  payment for judicial services 719–20,
    814–15
  competition between the different courts
    of, in England 720–1
  see also public works
  decisions vary with authority of
    government 747
  equal and impartial administration of in
    Britain 610
  and equality of treatment owed by the
    sovereign to all subjects 654
  see also justice and equity
  commerce and manufactures cannot
    flourish without regular
    administration of 910
Jutland, cattle exported to Holland 677

K

kelp, rent demanded for 161 & n.
Kent, restrictions on the removal of wool
    650
Khan, Tartar 713
  see also Gengis Khan, Tartars
kidders of corn 528–9
Kings, feudal, and encouragement to cities
    399–400 & n., 401–5
  see also cities, feudal, government, feudal

Konnigsberg 454

L

labour, annual, produce of land and 10–12,
    69–71, 208, 253–8, 265, 278, 286,
    292–5, 297–8, 320, 332, 337, 339–40,
    343–5, 349, 351, 360, 362–7, 371–4,
    439, 444–6, 489, 498, 511–13, 600,
    602–3, 608, 637, 664, 675–7, 687–8,
    724, 865
  see also land, labour, original index
labour, division of:
  sources of increased productivity 13–20,
    260–1, 492
  see also pinmaking and dexterity 10–11,
    13–19, 22, 27, 50, 65, 118, 127,
    138, 140, 260, 282, 523, 530, 699,
    755, 782
  and arms 697
  and exchange 25–38, 276, *see also*
    exchange
  embarrassed by the barter economy
    37–9
  and invention 20–2, *see also* invention
  and machines 17, 19–20, 104, 287, *see*
    also machines
  and the extent of the market 31–4, 134,
    376–7, 446–8, 680
  depends on prior accumulation of stock
    276 & n., 277
  disadvantages of 781–8
  limited in agriculture 16 & n., 143 & n.,
    see also agriculture
  the propensity to truck, barter, and
    exchange 25–30
  and self-love 26–7
  sources of universal opulence 22–4 & n.
  see also carriage, land, water; transport;
    interest, private, public; martial
    spirit; metals, coin, money
labour, slave, limited productivity 98,
    388–9, 683–4 & n., *see also*
    slaves
labour, the real measure of exchangeable
    value 47 & n., 48–55
  the only universal and accurate measure
    of value 54, *see also* value
labour embodied (beaver and deer) 65
  equality of embodied and commanded
    65, divergence of in advanced
    societies 65–7, 82–3
  labour commanded determines real value
    of component parts of price 67, *see*
    also price
labour, productive/unproductive:
  distinguished 10–11, 330, 675

labour, productive/unproductive (*cont.*):
  free circulation of, impediments to
    135–40, 151–7
  see also apprenticeship, corporations
  productive 332, 333 & n., 334–5, 337–9,
    341, 343–5, 350–3, 355–6, 360,
    362 & n., 363–74, 600–2, 607–9,
    611–12, 629, 633, 669, 672, 676–8,
    862, 872–3, 887, 897–8, 924–5,
    927
labour, productive powers of 10, 13,
    15–16, 82, 104, 206, 264, 277,
    287, 291–2, 447–8, 669, 676,
    681
labour, wages of, distinguished from profit
    and rent 65–71
  determinants of 83–104
  see also combination(s), wages, masters
  increase in demand for a function of
    growth 86–8, 109
  the stationary state 89–90
  declining state 90–1, 266, 864
  liberal reward of in Great Britain 91–2,
    95
  encourages productivity 98–9 & n.
    a symptom of increasing wealth 87, 91
      and marriage 565
    the example of North America 87–8
    dangers of over-work 100
    encourages population 97–9
  the subsistence wage defined 85
  different employments of (net advantages)
    116–35
  see also advantages, net, wages
  property of, sacred 138
  enjoyment of the fruits of 405,
    540 & n.
  see also condition, bettering of, interest,
    private, public
labourer(s) 126–8, 133–4, 142, 144, 147,
    152–4, 177, 182 n., 194–5, 206–8,
    219, 224, 262, 266, 279, 283, 287,
    296 n., 348 n., 355, 362, 465, 509,
    515, 540 n., 557, 565, 664, 667–9,
    675–6, 679 n., 681, 693, 698, 784 n.,
    785, 795 n., 864–5, 871, 876 n.,
    882 n., 887, 893
  see also original index
labourers, statute of 147 & n., 195
lace 226, 346 n.
Lacedemon(-ians) 436, 683 n.
Lancashire 177, 218 n.
land(s) *see* carriage, rent, tax, tenure, tythes,
    corn, labour, agriculture, original
    index
  crown lands 404 n., 411 n., 423 n., 821,
    823–4 & n.
  division of 67, 82–3, 166, 178, 257, 334,

382 & n., 384–6, 392–3, 395, 399,
    405, 414 & n., 416–20, 423–4,
    556 n., 557, 573–4, 712 n., 721,
    812
  see also feudal
  cultivation of 75 & n., 83, 142, 145,
    165–9, 171–2, 175–7, 179–82,
    192–3, 206–7, 228, 234, 237–45,
    251, 258–60, 279–85, 307, 313,
    360, 365, 374, 377–9, 385–6,
    389–90, 395–6, 409, 423, 425, 460,
    529, 531–2, 566, 572 & n., 573,
    611, 627, 669–72, 678, 682–3,
    686–8
  see also labour, annual, produce of land
    and, Rent
  cultivation of, in the colonies 565–7 & n.,
    570, 572–4, 580–2, *see also*
    colonies
landlord(s):
  capital of, secure 378
  causes of increase in wealth of 264–5
  encouraged to cultivate 666, 832
  ignorance of 160, 265, 831
  income costs neither labour nor care 265
  acts as monopolist 134, 160–1
  as petty princes 383–6
  decline of 420–1
  reap where they never sowed 67, 83
  responsibilities of 927
  see also economists; land tax, tax,
    original index; Rent; tenants,
    leases
land-tax:
  solicited from country-gentlemen by the
    government of King William 215
  additional 442
  supplies a great part of the Revenues of
    China, Egypt and Indostan 683,
    730
  the tythe as 812
  amount of British 822
  proportioned to rent 828–36
  proportioned to produce 836–40
  the British on houses 845
  cannot raise rents 848
  the British, intended to tax stock as well
    as land 849
  the British, not intended to fall on capital
    852
  that of the king of Sardinia a tax on land
    held by ignoble tenure 854
  the British, resembles the vingtième 858,
    904
  the British, higher on offices 866–7
  additional is for three years 923
  may make landlord unable to maintain
    improvements 927

a more equal, in Great Britain might greatly augment the revenue 933
more could be paid in Great Britain if there were no tithe 934
language, German 414 n.
  Latin 764–6, 785
  Greek 766
  Hebrew 766
Languedoc 171 & n., 726, 854, canal 726
lastage 398
Latium, cultivation of corn discouraged in 785
lawyers, fees of 122–3, 148–9, 718, 760
  unproductive labour of 331
  see also original index
law, lottery of 123
  natural progress of 564 n.
  corruption of language of 721
  see also government, original index
laws, continue in force, after circumstances change 383 & n.
lead 656
lead mines 186, 205
Lead Smelting Company 758
leases:
  long, and the distinction between real and nominal values 55
  for life 392
  heirs of entail prevented from letting long leases 393, cf. 421, 854
  usual conditions of 831
  see also Rent
leather:
  used as currency 38
  taxes increase the price of 96, 240, 466, 873
  restrictions on the exportation of 654–5
  shoes, a necessary of life in England 870, 874
  duty on 879
lecture, a sham 763–4
Leeds 409
legacy, legacies 77, 660, 859
Leghorn 479
legislator(s) ancient landlords as 383, 393, 415 n.
  political economy as a branch of 428
  contrasted with the politician 468
  and the regulation of private interests 456, 531, 540, 687
  and the system of perfect liberty 606
  American colonists as 623
  should discourage the interested diligence of the clergy 791
  see also statesman, Solon
legislature(s):
  counselled by the masters 157
  negligence of 198, 201–2, 874

country-gentlemen as a proportion of 215
  good intention to favour agriculture 425
  special interests intimidate 267, 452, 471, 518, 643–4, 647, 733
  seeks to improve naval power of Great Britain 577–8
  see also navigation, acts of
  colonial, do not include hereditary nobility 585
Leith 33 & n., 127, 134
letters, men of 148–9, 249, 331, 760 n., 778 n., 780, 810–12, 830
Lerwick 134
Levant 408 & n.
levity, vice of 794, 810
liberty:
  boasted liberty of the subject 660
  perfect 73, 79, 116, 131, 135, 467 n., 606, 673–4, 678
  natural 157, 324, 470, 530, 606, 687, 707, 747
  and justice, security 145, 345, 395, 405, 412, 541 n., 664, 722, 910
  and independency, effect of commerce 399, 412 & n., 803, 910
  standing armies dangerous to 766–7 & n., 787 & n.
  violation of, when justified 324
  see also original index
licentious, licentiousness 707, 795 n.
light come, light go 613
Ligue 623
Lima 222 & n., 568
linen:
  different trades employed in the manufacture of 16, 23
  stamps on 40, 139
  variations in price of, less than that of corn 76
  improvements in the manufacture of, benefit the poor 96
  earnings of journeymen little more than day-labourers 119
  demand for, uniform 132
  spinning of in Scotland 134, 138
  in England, the manufacture open 152
  manufacturers seek prohibition of imports 452
  might suffer from freedom of trade 469
  development of, retarded by drawbacks 584
  used to purchase tobacco 604, 628
  exportation of, in ancient Egypt 683
  price of, in ancient times 685
  linen shirt, not a necessary of life 870
  decency requires 876

linen (*cont.*):
  use of, renders soap a necessary 874
  duties on Scottish 913
Linmois 185
liquor(s):
  become dear, as a result of taxation 96
  private individuals, ruin fortunes of in
      purchase 492
  differential taxes to discourage
      consumption of 852, 863, 887,
      891
  a luxury 870, 871 n.
  tax on does not raise price of common
      labour 872
  taxes on 877, 887–8, 890–2, 897, 936,
      938–9
Lisbon:
  gold and silver imported to 226
  both residence of a court and a trading
      city 336
  gold and silver easily brought from 435,
      547
  carrying trade of 454
  bills paid in common currency 479
  exhorbitant profits of 612
  merchants, magnificent 613, 627
literature, rewards of 148–50
Liverpool, and the Africa Company 738
Loango 558 & n.
Lochabar 416
Locri 566
lodging:
  cheapness of in London 134, 135
  one of the two great wants of mankind
      178–81
logick 766, 770, 772, 777 n.
Lombard 408 n., 820
Lombardy 408 n., 426
London 32 & n., 756–8, 872
  road and sea traffic to Edinburgh and
      Calcutta 32–3
  price of silver 55
  gold circulating in, less degraded than
      silver 58
  wages of master tailors set by statute 76 n.
  wages lower than in New York 87
  wages 92
  early decay of carpenters 100
  bankers pay no interest 107
  great companies borrowed at 5 per cent
      after the late war 110
  wages of labourers and bricklayers and
      masons 120
  chairmen employed as bricklayers, ibid.
  employment from day to day, ibid.
  tailors often out of employment 121
  coalheavers, ibid.
  wages of common labour, ibid.

  wages of seamen and other labourers
      compared with those paid at
      Edinburgh 127
  lodging cheap 134
  silkweavers' byelaw 136
  earnings of journeymen shoe-makers in
      147
  counties near, petitioned against turnpikes
      164
  meat fallen in price compared with bread
      167
  societies of merchants buy land in sugar
      colonies 174
  chairmen, porters, coalheavers and
      prostitutes, Irish 177
  stone quarry near, affords considerable
      rent 179
  paving stones from Scotland, ibid.
  civil war raised the price of corn 212
  price of meat 238, 243
  merchants have not the advantage of
      Scotch cash accounts 300
  transactions of Scotch banks 303
  drawing and redrawing 309
  bills of exchange in 311–12, 314–15
  no bank notes under £10 322, 323
  exchange with Carlisle and Dumfries 326
  residence of a court, but a trading city
      336
  fire and plague 344
  trade with Scotland 368
  coal trade with Newcastle 371
  French cambrics may be imported 473
  exchange with Paris 476
  and other foreign towns 479
  Herring fishery company 522
  advantages of linen-merchants in 32 n.,
      530
  fifth of gold and silver found in colonies
      reserved to the king in the patent of
      the London Company 564
  tobacco normally sold for ready money
      603
  merchants not so magnificent as those of
      Cadiz and Lisbon, nor so
      parsimonious as those of
      Amsterdam 613
  entrepôt for German and American trade
      628
  streets better cared for by local
      administration 730–1
  expensive port 735
  represented on the committee of the
      African Company 738
  land tax 822, 850
  windows and rent 846
  tax on beer has not raised the value of
      common labourer in 872

porter brewery 889

London Assurance Company 756–7

lord(s), feudal, allodial 416–18 & n., 693 n., 694–5, 716, 801, 821, 854, 908

Lords, House of 585, 779 n.

Lorraine 905

lottery, lotteries 122–3, 124 n., 125–6, 918
of the army 126–7
of the church 148
of the law 123
mining as 187 & n., 562
of politics 623
of the sea 126–7

Lucayan islands 559

Lucca 407–8

Lucerne 860

luck 124 n., 126

Luctuosa Hereditas 859

Lutheran, faith 807

luxury:
complaint that it is extended to the lowest ranks 96
in the fair sex: weakens the power of generation 97

luxuries, of the rich 842
taxes on 826, 869–73, 876, 878–9, 886–7, 894, 896, 903

Lyceum 778

Lyons 364, 408

M

machine:
invention of attributable to the division of labour among free men 14, 19–21, 104, 277, 684
philosophers and the invention of 21–2
as a source of increased productivity 17, 19, 260, 263, 676
human capital akin to 118
clocks and watches, beautiful examples of 139–40
improvements in, involved in the woollen manufacture 263
part of the fixed capital of society 282, 291
originally derived from a circulating capital 283
improved, requires additional capital 343
monopoly of new, properly granted to the inventor 754
see also original index, capital, invention, labour, division of

madder, *see* original index

Madeira wine 502 & n.

Madras 641, 749, 751

Madrid 219 n., 336

Maese, River 35

magistrate(s) 85, 158 n., 400–3, 556, 587–8, 616, 696, 707, 709 & n., 710, 711 n., 722 n., 729, 774 & n., 775 n., 789–92, 793 & n., 806, 809, 812, 814, 816–17, 850
see also legislators

Mahometan, nations, high interest in 112
government of Bengal 838

majorazzo 572

Malacca 635

malt-house 889, 981

malt tax 196, 201 n., 212 n., 260, 320, 466 n., 492, 536 n., 878, 887–93, 897, 912, 936, 938–9

Malta, the order of, land tax paid in Silisia 834

maltster 891 & n., 892

Mammeluks 558

man, of all sorts of luggage the most difficult to be transported 93, an anxious animal 872 n.

Manchester 20 n., 137

mandarins 680 & n., 839

Manilla 225, 227

mansion-house 814

manufactory, manufactories 15, 66, 101, 252 n., 287, 332, 379, 461, 795 n.

manufactures, permit more subdivisions of labour than agriculture 16 & n., 20
see also labour, division of manufactures, affected by the statute of apprenticeship 137, *see also* apprenticeship, statute of
effect of the progress of improvement upon the prices of 260–4
see also original index

manufacturer(s):
sophistry of 144, 467, 494
jealousy of 267, 471, 493, 500, 517, 582, 643, 660, 662
compared to country gentlemen 266–7, 462, 515
secrets of 77, *see also* secrets
see also monopoly, combination, corporations, masters, original index

Marannon 575–6

Maritime countries, *see* original index

markets, *see* carriage; fairs; labour; division of; price, market and natural, Windsor

marriage:
value of children, the greatest encouragement to 88
poverty discourages, but does not prevent 96

marriage (*cont.*):
  liberal reward of labour encourages 565
  number of rich people averse to, higher in
    France than in England 919
marriage-bed, of James I 347
Marseilles 901
martial, spirit 696 n., 697, 698 n., 782,
    786–7
  see also original index
Martinico 679
marvelous, the 317, 559, 730, 767 n.
Maryland, retail stores often belong to
    residents in England 367
  tobacco exports 500, 595, 602
  expence of civil establishment 574
  established by catholics 589
  revenue 537
  cultivation of tobacco preferred to that of
    corn 174, 175 n.
  annual purchase of tobacco in Virginia
    and Maryland 372
  planted as a colony 597
masons 29 n., 31, 120, 147, 348, 378
Massachusetts, expence of civil
    establishment 573
  tax on importation of molasses 936
  paper money 940
master(s):
  prudent master of a family 456
  vile maxim of the masters of mankind
    418
  see also manufacturers, slaves,
    school-master
mastiff 30
masts 579, 644, 645 & n.
mathematicks 125, 769 n.
Mazepa 446
meat, *see* butcher's meat
mechanical arts 419 n., 697, 782 n.
mechanics 119, 144, 348, 395, 398 n., 785
mechanics, as a discipline 769 n., 785–6
mechanic, trades 122, 140, 143, 296
Mediterranean Sea, favourable to first
    attempts in navigation 34
  carries commerce of Europe and Asia 36
  British carrying trade between ports of
    373
  expence of last war partly laid out in 442
  Venetian fleets scarcely went beyond 569
  American fish sent to 578
  British trade to, partly superseded by the
    American trade 596–8, 608
  tobacco from America exported to 602
  Gibraltar and Minorca intended to
    protect British trade with 739–40
  commercial towns of Europe, now trade
    beyond 627
mendicant orders 574, 790

mercantile jealousy 495–6, 640, *see also*
    jealousy, manufactures
mercantile system:
  confusion of wealth and money 255
  principles and practices of 429–662
  bounties supported by 505–6, 516–17
  see also bounties
  vulgar prejudices of 555
  mean and malignant 610
  splendour of, related to the discovery of
    N America 626–7
  the engines of 630, 642, 881–2
  principally encourages industry carried on
    for the benefit of the rich 644
  sacrifices the interests of the consumer to
    those of the producer 660
  agreeable to a plodding man of business
    (Colbert) 663
  encourages manufactures and foreign
    trade 686–7
  not favourable to the revenue of the great
    body of the people 881
  sophistry of 927
  see also colonies, commercial system
mercenary, troops, *see* original index
mercers 283
merchant(s):
  every man in some measure a merchant
    37
  silent with regard to their own gains 115
  sophistry of 144, 467, 494
  and the public interest 266–7
  circulating capital of 280, 283, 439
  customs of 309 & n.
  capitals dispersed 364, 426
  speculative 130–1, 133, 736
  bankers notes and 298–300, 304–5
  capitals contribute to the process of
    exchange 361–5, 368–75
  the best of improvers 411–12, 423 n.
  wholesale 129, 360, 362, 365, 454
  speculative 130, 133, 736
  and spirit of monopoly 462, 493, 504
  character of 313 n., 612–13
  government in India by 638–41
  role in colonial policy 584
  as unproductive 664, 666–9, 675
  clamorous complaints of 465, 599, 648
  exclusive company of, the worst form of
    government 570 & n., 637 & n.,
    638
  jealousy of 382, 493
  see also original index, country gentleman
Merovingian, Kings, treasures of 446
metal(s), *see* original index
metaphysics 770–1
metayer(s) 389 & n., 390, 391 n.
meteors 767

methodists 789
Metz 335 n., 901
Mexico 231, 482, 483 n.
  less civilized than Peru 221
  inferior to China, Japan and Indostan
    448
  Cortez attracted to, by quest of gold 562
  something like an Eldorado 564
  present populousness of capital city 568
  low state of the arts 568
  conquest projected by Governor of Cuba
    589
  natives beyond hunting stage 634
Michaelmas 272, 749
Milan 835 & n., 836 & n., 876, 901, 934
Miletus 566 & n.
military, discipline, education, exercise
    696–8, 701 & n., 702, 705, 776,
    786 & n.
militia(s), *see* original index
minae 149–50
mill(s), *see* original index
minerals 182, 193, 234, 253, 284, 561
mines 182, 185, 187, 188–9, 191, 219, 254,
    284
  see also original index
mining 50 n., 121 n., 123 n., 187 & n., 219,
    232 & n., 562, 656
  see also original index
Minorca 740 & n.
mint(s) 40 & n., 42 & n., 57 n., 59–60,
    62 & n., 228–330, 477–84, 488,
    501 n., 550–2, 554–5, 932
mint price 59 & n., 60–3, 213, 482–4, 550–1
Mississippi, scheme 317, 429 n., 571, 576
Modena, taxes on necessaries 876
modus 839, 840 & n., 934
molasses 579, 936, 939
Moluccas 223, 525, 636, 638
  see also spices
monarchy(-ies):
  power of, and the law of primogeniture
    383
  abolition of purveyance in Great Britain
    394
  representation of burghs in 404
  allodial lords in 694
  European, divested themselves of the
    administration of justice 722
  the rent of land supplied the exigencies of
    the state 812, 824
  moderate expences of historically 821–2
monasteries:
  destruction of, deprived the poor of
    charity 152
  suppression of 807
  see also clergy
money, makes money 110

the great wheel of circulation 289, 291,
    296
wealth does not consist in 438, 449 & n.,
    450
  see also wealth
value in proportion to the necessaries it
    will purchase 886
  see also original index, coin, coinage,
    metals, paper money; gold, silver,
    interest, water-level, analogy of
monied interest 86, 351, 910, 918 n.
monks 771 & n., 790, 799, 804
monopolist(s) 78, 134, 140, 144, 471, 489,
    638, 734, 843, 853, 893, 903
monopoly, price of 78 & n., 161, 423–5,
    575 & n., 892 & n.
as an enemy to good management 78 n.,
    163
and the colony trade 174, 362 n., 500,
    502–5, 582 n., 590, 595–615,
    616–18, 630–2, 638–41, 647, 661,
    947
wretched spirit of 461–2, 471, 474, 493,
    499–500
and the distribution of stock 630–1
monopoly powers, tantamount to the
    direction of industry 656
contrary to justice 654
and restraints on trade 451–3, 456–7,
    459, 474, 515–16, 525, 545, 657,
    660
and the colony trade 174, 362 n., 500,
    502–5, 582 n., 590, 595–616,
    616–18, 628, 630–2, 638–41, 647,
    661, 947
defended 463–9
the chief engine of the mercantile system
    630
temporary, justified 754–5
commercial, mercantile system
  see also original index, *Correspondence*
Montauban 836, 854
Moors 38 n., 163, 165, 406, 558
moralists 124
morality, rules, systems of 768 & n., 771–2,
    794–6
  see also original index
Moravia 387
moral philosophy 766, 769 & n., 770 n.,
    771 & n.
  see also systems, philosophy
mortality 85, 91, 97 & n., 101
mortgage(s) 12, 307–8, 350, 688, 824, 861,
    863, 911–13
mourning, public, raises the price of black
    cloth 76, 132
Mulattoes 222 n., 569
mulberry trees 408 & n.

mules 729
mum, liquor, tax on 890
muscovado sugar 173 n., 523, 581–2
Muscovia, trade with China by caravan 223
    yarn 643
Muscovites 223
musician(s) 331 & n.
music, to be encouraged as a public
        diversion 796
    in ancient Greece 774
    had little effect on their morals 776, 779
    popular among barbarous nations 776
    see also original index
muslins 503, 560, 583
mutilation (mental) 787–8

N

Nailer 18, 32
nails, manufacture of 18 & n., 32, 38
    use of as money 38
Naples 425, 900
nation:
    civilized 10, 22 & n., 23, 26, 44, 71, 564,
        705
    first civilized 34
    never impoverished by private expence
        342
    great commerce of 141, 284, 376, 677,
        686
    invideous eye of 493–7
    see also commercial, mercantile system
nations, *see* barbarous, savage, hunters,
        husbandmen, shepherds, original
        index
national prosperity and the balance of trade
        883
    see balance of payments, trade
    animosity 464, 473, 495
    see also commercial, mercantile system,
        jealousy
natural, *see* industry, balance of:
    liberty, violations of, unjust 157, 324,
        530
    obvious and simple system of 687
natural philosophy 766–71
Navy, unproductive labour of 331
    not supported by the bounty 518
navy-bills 911
naval powers 569, 597–8
naval stores 579, 580, 583
    see also navigation, acts of
navigable, *see* canals, carriage, water, rivers
navigation acts 463–4, 577, 579–80, 583,
        595–99, 614, 657
    see also original index
Neapolitan 900

necessaries and conveniences 10, 47, 51, 55,
        74, 87, 95, 103, 176, 207, 210, 219,
        224, 289–90, 927
necessaries of life, defined 869–70
    occasion the great expence of the poor
        842
    taxes on 465–6, 871–6, 879, 885–6, 888,
        905–7, 927, 936
    see also original index
negroes:
    and the cultivation of tobacco 174–5
    drunken 492
    slaves, sent to America in exchange
        forum 578
    cultivation of sugar-cane by 586–7
    export of to the West Indies, unprofitable
        743, 745
    addicted to music and dancing 776
    taxes on 857
    not worse fed than the lower ranks in
        England 939
    see also original index, slaves, tobacco
Nemaean, games 786
Netherlands, United Provinces of, in debt
        909
Newcastle, colliers wages 121 & n.
    price of coal at 185
    coal trade to hand on 371
Newcastle measure 658
New England, some provinces richer than
        Virginia 388 n.
    in three provinces, the eldest son has a
        double share 572
    fishery, the most important in the world
        578
    councils chosen by representatives 585
    more republican than England 585
    established by the Puritans 589
    progress not foreseen in 1660 597–8
    exports to England, not equal to imports
        942
New Granada 221
New Hampshire, cost of civil establishment
        in 573
New Jersey, established by Swedes 570
    progress obstructed by Dutch exclusive
        company 570
    cost of civil establishment 573
    possessed by Dutch in 1660 597
    exports to Great Britain less than
        imports 942
New York, province, high wages in 87
    free labour cheaper than slaves 99
    acquired by England 570
    progress obstructed by Dutch exclusive
        company 570
    expence of civil establishment 573
    possessed by Dutch in 1660 597

exports to Great Britain, less than imports 942

New York City, second great town of the English colonies 568

Newfoundland, use of dried cod as currency 38

Nicuessa 562

nightingale, extravagant price of 236

Nile, navigation of as a cause of improvement in Egypt 35 & n.

importance in trade prior to the discovery of the Cape of Good Hope 406 n., 558 n.

irrigation works 681

Nimeguen, Peace of 467

Norfolk, master-weavers restricted to two apprentices 136

Norman Conquest, *see* Conquest, Norman

Normandy 391 n., 402 n., 901

North America:

natural grasses in 241

paper currency in 322–3, 326

first English settlers offered one-fifth of gold discovered to the king 564

poll taxes in 857

revenue of the principal colonies in 937

see also America, colonies

North Carolina, expence of civil establishment 574

revenue of 937

Northumberland, mountains of infertile, destined to be breeding ground for cattle 460

North West passage 564

Norway, desert moors in produce pasture for cattle 163

woods of, find a market in Britain 180

exempted from Eastland Company's monopoly 735

Norwich, master-weavers restricted to two apprentices 136

banks of, stopped 312 n.

notes, promissory 58, 107, 292, 298, 299–300, 325–6, *see also* bank notes

Nova Belgia, divided into New York and New Jersey 570

Nova Scotia, expence of civil establishment 573

colony not planted 597

Nuremberg, Bank of 480

in Scotland, cheaper than meat a hundred years ago 165

common people, fed on oatmeal less handsome than the English 177

bounty on the exportation of 542

Oceana, as likely as free trade 471

œconomy, *see* economy, economists

offices, salaries of public, taxable 866–7

Oieda 562

Oil 75, 463, 831, 876

Olympic games 786

ontology 771–2

opera-dancers 124

opera-singers 331

opium 636

optional, clause 325 & n., 326

opulence:

does not consist in money 37 n., 44 n., 339 n., 429 n.

progress of 42 n., 276 n., 376–80, 381 n., 399 n., 428, 616 n., 821 n.

decisive marks of 190

see also wealth

oranges 74

orator(s) 331, 779 n., 811 & n.

ornament(s), conveniency of, and desire 181, 190–3, 220–1, 349

ortolans 241

outports 522

out-servants 95, 133

over-stocking 748

overtraded, overtrading 308, 437–8, 442

ox, oxen 38 & n., 39, 143, 164, 167, 205, 229–30, 243 n., 249–50, 361, 429, 856

Oxford:

university of, public professors have given up even the pretence of teaching 761 & n.

see also original index

Oxfordshire, coal and wood mixed 184

O

oaths 94, 486, 775 n., 779, 827 n., 850–1, 883

oatmeal, staple of the common people of ·Scotland 93

cotters receive two pecks 133

P

painters, painting 119, 208, 331 n., 796

Palos 559

Pannonian, frontier 704

Papal, authority 801

bulls 803 n.

court 806

paper-money, issued by banking companies in Scotland 306–8, 315–17

issued upon circulating bills of exchange 311

great multiplication of in Scotland 325

issued in the colonies 328

advantages of well-regulated 437 & n.

see also original index

paradox, love of 678 & n., *see also* value,
    paradox of
Paraguay 221
Paris, lodging cheaper than in London
    134
    apprenticeship in 138
    Rouen the entrepôt for 335
    exchange with London 476
    custom regarding inheritance 572
    defended itself against Henry IV 624
parliament, no acts of, against combining to
        lower the price of work 84
    particular acts of attempt to regulate
        wages 157
    of Scotland, did not adopt Law's scheme
        317
    intimidated by private interests 471 & n.
    managed by the sovereign 619, 799
    of England, originally illiberal in
        supporting the civil and military
        establishments 619
    and taxation of the colonies 619–22
    representation of the colonies in 624–5,
        933
    wisdom of, and the administration of
        roads 726
    Smith-Sea company petitions 745
    see also legislature
Parliaments, French 335, 720, 799, 918
Parma, taxes on bread 876, separate excises
    in 902
parsimony, destroyed by high profits 612
    see also original index, frugality
Parthia 703
Partiarii 389
passage duties 397–8, 894
pasture(s) 28 n., 163–5, 167–9, 170 n.,
        171–2, 176, 183, 188 n., 237–8, 241,
        321, 653, 791
patents, justification of 754
pawn-shop, public at Hamburgh 820
peages 815 & n., 894 n.
pedlars, tax on 397 & n., 852 & n.
Pekin, caravans from Muscovy 223
    mandarins of 680
Peloponesians 693, 694 n.
peltry 178, 579
Pennsylvania, paper currency in 326, 820,
        940
    Quakers liberated their slaves 388,
        389 & n.
    no right of primogeniture in 572
    expence of civil establishment 573
    established by Quakers 589
    not planted in 1660 597
    no religious establishment 793
    imports from Great Britain, exceed
        exports 942

see also original index
pensions, a derivative revenue 70
    value of equal to their power of
        purchasing 291
people, *see* original index
perpetuities:
    abhorred by English common law 385
    prevent division of estates in Europe 423
Persia, gulf of 36
    servants, rather than soldiers at the court
        of 446
    militia effeminate 702
    defeated by the Greeks 704–5
Peru, tax paid to the King of Spain from the
        mines of 186–7, 188, 219
    richest mines afford a rent 191
    visited by Frezier 222
    importation of gold by Spain 436
    colonized by Spanish adventurers in
        search of gold 562–4, 589–90
    funds spent on reception of new vice-roy
        574
    natives of, not hunters 634
    see also original index
Phenicians 34
phenomena, natural 767, 769
    see also wonder
Philadelphia, high wages in 99
    third great city of the English colonies
        568
    see also Boston, New York
philosophers, men of speculation 21
    division of 21–2
    and the porter 28–30
    see also porter
    prone to assert the absurd 876
    see also letters, men of
philosophers stone 563
philosophy, a distinct trade 21–2
    honour the reward of 123
    natural, origins and objects of 767–8
    the first recorded by history 767–8
    moral 768–9
    logic 769–70
    moral and natural, taught as subservient
        to theology 771–2
    debased system of, taught in the greater
        part of European universities 772
    Ancient Greek, divided into three
        branches 766–7
    fashionable in Greece and Rome 778–80
    beauty of systematical arrangement in
        768–9
    study of, should be universal among the
        upper ranks 796
    see also original index
physician(s) 32 n., 119, 122, 128–9, 148–9,
        331 & n., 673, 759 n., 791

physick 123, 148–9, 762, 811
physics 766, 770–2
Physiocrats, *see* economists, French
Picardy 391 n., 462 n., 901
piece-goods 883
piece-work 100, 759 n.
Piedmont 835
pig, iron 579, 580 & n., 582, 643
pigs 243
Pillars of Hercules 34
pin(s), pin-maker 14–15 & n., 17 n., 18 & n.
Pisa, encouraged by Crusades 406
Pizzarro 562
Placentia, bread taxes 876
plantation(s) 34, 70, 128 n., 136, 170–1,
    173 n., 174–5, 247, 250–1, 389,
    402 n., 423, 463, 499, 558, 577–9,
    581–4, 595, 634, 636, 644–6, 875,
    900, 943–5, 937–8, 940, 942–3
planter(s) 70, 109, 173–4, 176, 379, 388 n.,
    390 n., 587, 602, 857, 893, 941, 943
plate-tax 876
Plate, River 164
plate, sterling mark on 41, 139
    fashion increases the value of 62
    service of, as a frivolous ornament 192,
        199
    enhanced demand for 208, 220–1
    annual consumption of 225
    melting down of 441
    current price of service of, lower than in
        the fifteenth century 447
    plate dearer in Europe than it might have
        been 449
    degradation in the value of silver, and the
        cost of plate 510
    profusion of, in Spanish and Portuguese
        houses 512
    new plate chiefly made from old 550
players, rewards of 124, 331
plough(s) 19 n., 21 n., 96, 143, 166, 259,
    568, 586, 636, 669
plough-wrights 378
ploughman (men) 16, 70, 143, 180 n.
    see also original index
Plymouth Company 564, 576
pneumaticks 770–1
pneumatology 772
Po, River 894
poacher 118
Poland:
    price of corn in 16, 217
    feudal government of 256, 387, 390 n.
    declining state of 258
    trade of 371, 407
    industry encouraged by colonization of
        America 591
    pacification and partition of 607

Russian invasion 705
police, regulations of keep market above
        natural price 77, 79
    violent, of Indostan and Egypt 80
    rules of, the statute of apprenticeship 137
    rules of, the laws of settlement 152
    proprietors unlikely to mislead the public
        with respect to 265
    the best, to leave things to their natural
        course 453, 506 n.
    of Europe, nowhere leaves things at
        perfect liberty 16, 135
    vigilant police of Portugal and Spain with
        respect to the exportation of the
        metals 512, 541
officers of 573
    vigorous, and military exercises 698
    maintenance of roads as a branch of
        729–30
    expences of, which benefit a local
        community should be paid for
        locally 815
    see also defence, justice, public works
political, arithmetic, and Smith's lack of
        faith in 95 & n., 205 n., 534, 535 & n.
    writers, prejudices of 361
political economy, *see* economy, political
politician:
    insidious and crafty animal 468 & n.
    comfort of those who measure national
        prosperity 883, 942
politics:
    the lottery of British 623
    what is vulgarly called 722
    and religion 792
poll-tax(es) 398–9, 857, 868
Pondichery 749
pondo 42
pontage 398
poor, countries 10, 16, 17 & n., 134, 207–8,
    220, 255, 262, 266, 334–5, 407, 541,
    632, 706, 708–9
Poor Law 95 n., 152–7, 470
    see also Settlement, Laws of
poor, oppression by the rich 709–10, 715 & n.
    luxury of 871 & n., 872–3, 887
    see also taxes
Pope, the, universities founded by the
        authority of 765
    great power of 800
    how reduced 804–6
population, limited by subsistence 35 n.,
        97, 180
    adverse effect on, of poverty 97
    encouraged by the liberal reward of
        labour 98–9
    the demand for men regulates the
        production of men 98

population, limited by subsistence (*cont.*):
  encouraged in the colonies 109, 566
  taxation, enforced frugality increases
    ability to bring up families 872
  growth, of, sources, *see* capital
  growth of, consequences, *see* under Rent
  the analysis of the 'Different Effects of
    the Progress of Improvement'
    234–60
  see also original index
populous, populousness 31, 34, 89, 166,
  179–80, 221–3, 388 n., 427, 568, 580,
  589 n., 609, 634, 682, 940, 945
porter (liquor), tax on 872
  price of 878
  malt used in brewing 889
porter(s), can only find employment in a
  town 31
  Irish, in London 177
  in Scotland, able to read and write 785 n.
  compared with philosophers 28–31
Portugal, small part of Europe 220
  carried on a regular trade to the East
    Indies in the sixteenth century
    222, 449
  lost that trade to the Dutch 222
  annual importation of gold 226–7 & n.
  tax upon the gold of Brazil 231 & n.
  annual produce declining 258
  government of, not much improved,
    following the abolition of the
    feudal system 256 & n., 404 n.,
    412 n.
  foreign commerce of, considerable 425
  prohibition on the export of gold 431
  importation of, its consequences 436,
    444, 510–12, 513–14
  expence of last war laid out in 442
  examination of the advantages of trade
    with Great Britain 547–9
  British duties on wine of 473, 493
  wines of France better and cheaper 475
  among the most beggarly countries 541
  explorations conducted by 558–9
  colonies of 558–62
  settlement of Brazil 569
  exclusive companies recently established
    575–6
  prohibition of the import of tobacco,
    except from the colonies 583
  banished Jews to Brazil 589
  absolute government in colonies 586
  trade with America, has enhanced
    industry 591
  colonies of alone in contributing revenue
    to the mother country 593
  exorbitant profits of merchants have not
    augmented capital 612–13
  colonies of, give more encouragement to
    the trade of other countries 627
  fall of, contributed to open trade with the
    East Indies 631
  trade with, without an exclusive company
    633, 635
  summary of the effect of the Methuen
    Treaty 661
  slave trade unprofitable 745
  see also original index
post-office, affords a revenue to the state
  724
  can be managed by government 818
post-chaises, taxes on 725
potatoes, price of, half that of forty years ago
  95
  quality of as a food and cultivation of
    176–7
  difficulty of storing 177
  improvements in agriculture bring
    cheaper to market 259
  see also original index
Potosi, mines of 164, 185, 191, 211, 220
pots and pans, augmentation of 439–40
poultry 200, 201 n., 205–7, 230, 234, 242–4,
  256, 259, 801, 831
  see also original index
poundage, duties, subsidy of 263, 537, 657,
  879–80, 883, 913
poverty:
  and inhuman customs 10
  and the production of children 96–7
  in China 89
  in France 496
  in Spain and Portugal 541
  in Mohametan nations 112–13
  disgraceful degree of 870
  and barbarism 205, 255, 256, 382, 712,
    902
power, and riches 48 & n., 372, 415, 419,
  496
  see also barons, clergy, executive, riches
pragmatic, sanction, in France 804–5
precious:
  metals 39, 123 n., 182, 185–9, 191–3, 199,
    207, 210, 223–4, 225–30, 234–56,
    340, 354 n., 482, 507 n., 511–13,
    541, 562, 564, 728, 839
  stones 45 n., 189–90 & n., 191–3, 224,
    231, 419, 564
  see also diamonds; stones, precious
preference or restraint, systems of 687
  see also commercial, mercantile systems
preferments, ecclesiastical 798–800, 804
prejudice(s):
  prejudice, mercantile, national 145,
    340, 429, 471, 474–5, 503, 517,
    555 & n., 581 n., 640, 663

of some political writers against
shopkeepers 361
prejudices, popular 533, 543, 616 n., 810,
934
prejudices, obsolete and exploded systems
772
political and religious, odious 944
vulgar 340 & n., 555
press-gang 132
premiums 474 n., 523 & n., 581 n.
see also bounties
and education 786 & n.
presbyterian:
church 809
clergy 810, 813
countries 810, 838
price(s):
market and natural 73, 74–5, 77, 79
real and nominal 46–64
component parts of 65–71
more affected by high profits than high
wages 114–15
of free competition 78–9
of commodities, real and nominal 51, 55,
250, 254–7, 555
tendency to fall 260–5
of monopoly, the highest that can be got
78, 161
see also monopoly
and taxes on consumable commodities
869–906
see also e.g., diamonds, labour, mint,
monopoly, necessaries, rent and
taxes; metals, provisions, original
index
pride:
pride of man, makes him domineer 388
of nations, mortification of 617
primogeniture:
origin and laws of 381 n., 382–3, 384–5,
423, 425
does not apply in Pensylvania 572 & n.
prince, accommodation of 24
printing, art of 148–9
privileges, exclusive 79, 122, 135, 146,
151–2, 158, 449, 451, 462, 470, 551,
571, 575, 584, 741–3, 745, 747,
754 n., 755–7
prize(s), lottery 122, 125–7, 187, 562, 623
see also lottery
in Olympic Games 786
prodigal(s) 315 n., 339–40, 350, 357, 438
prodigality 294, 337 & n., 339–40, 341 & n.,
342–3, 346, 599 n.
production, consumption the sole object of
660
productive labour, *see* labour, productive
professions, exertion in proportion to

necessity 759 & n., 760–1, 785, 788,
790
professor(s), in universities 760 n., 761,
810–11, *see also* universities
profit, unrelated to the labour of inspection
66
distinct from wages 67, 83, 107, 129
and rent 70, 160
as a component of price 68–9
one of the original sources of revenue 69,
825
average rate of 72, 310
affected by riches or poverty 80, 159,
266
fall of, the consequence of prosperity 105,
108, 352
raised by the acquisition of new outlets
110
clear and gross 113
relationship of to the rate of interest
105–15, 310, 352–3
ordinary rate of, varies with certainty of
returns 127–8
affected by the nature of employments
116, 118, 120, 122, 127–8, 132–5
and speculation 131
affected by fluctuations in price 76, 105,
132–3
and by the policy of Europe 135–47,
152
in the colonies of N America 109, 174,
596, 598, 599 & n., 600–2, 604,
606, 608, 611 & n., 612–13,
616–17, 629–30
high rate of destroys parsimony 612
in the physiocratic system 665–8, 670–1,
672 & n.
in the Hungarian mines 684
of Regulated Companies 733, 736–7, 745,
748–50, 755
taxes on 847–52
in the stationary state 111
see also capital, colonies, interest, saving,
taxes, original index; risk
profusion, economic effects of 341, 344–5,
347
see also prodigality
progressive state, favourable condition of
labour in 87–8, 99
projects, unsuccessful 131 n., 187, 341,
562 & n., 851
direct the operation of labour 266
projectors 304, 307, 310–12, 315–16, 357,
374
property, sacred 138, 188
security of, and economic activity 199,
284–5, 345 n., 395, 401–2, 405 & n.,
412, 540 & n., 566–7 n., 586

property, sacred (*cont.*):
  and manners 416–17
  small, inspires affection 423
  and injury 709–10
  and the origin of government 715 & n.
  see also justice
proprietors:
  seldom great improvers 385–6
  sources of power in the feudal period
    383, 414–18
  impact on of manufactures and commerce
    418–21
  see also allodial, barons, feudal system,
    church, primogeniture
proselytes 789, 794, 806
prosperity, human, the course of 367, 425
  see also progressive state
prostitutes, Irish the most beautiful women
  177
prostitution, public 124
  see also advantages, net
Protestant Churches 148, 790, 813
  countries 811–13
  persecution of 789
  of Ireland 944
Provence, taille in 854
proverbs 110, 181 n., 335, 370 n., 531, 613,
  616 n., 664, 768
provisions, price of varies from year to year
  92
  variations in the price of labour do not
    correspond to 93
  influence of price on wages 103–4, 864
  cheap, influence on employment 101,
    409
  historical prices of 167–8, 257–8, 325
  see also corn, original index
Provisors, statute of 804
prudence:
  in the conduct of a private family, cannot
    be folly in that of a great kingdom
    457
  see also frugality, parsimony
Prussia 441, 834–5 n., 836 & n., 909, 934
Prussian army 700, 705
  majesty 835
  dominions 904
public mourning 76, 132
  interest, ignored by employers 266–7
  see also black cloth; frugal(ity),
    prodigality, merchants
public schools, in England, less corrupt than
  universities 764
public workhouse 338
public good, ill served by those who affect it
  456
public works, in colonies, expence of
  moderate 573

the duty of government to erect and
  maintain 687–8
and services, induced efficiency 719, 759
deficiencies in the receipts of, to be made
  good by taxes 815–16
six days labour originally sufficient for
  821
see also original index, defence, justice,
  education, roads, canals, harbours
Punic war, *see* wars
pupils, payment of fees by, encourages
  competence of the teacher 760–1
advocates freedom of choice for 763
teachers had no jurisdiction over, in
  classical times 778
parochial clergy, similar to those teachers
  who derive their income from fees
see also public works, students, teachers,
  universities
Puritans, founded New England 589
purveyance, a service skill exacted in most
  parts of Europe 394

Q

Quakers, emancipation of slaves 388 & n.
  established the colony of Pennsylvania
    589
  in a majority there 793
  see also original index
quit-rent 334, 414, 572
Quito, populousness of that city 568

R

racked rent 665
Rates, book of 537, 658, 880, 883
recoinage of gold, silver 58–9, 213, 912
Reformation, *see* original index
Reformers and the Bible 766
registration, duties on 858, 861, 863
relief, a feudal casuality 860
religion 788–814
  in ancient Egypt 80, 367 n.
  Gentoo 682
  corn laws, resemble attitudes respecting
    539
  instruction in, may be paid for from taxes
    815
Rent, defined 67, 70
  corn 53 & n., *see also* corn
  varies with fertility and situation 163
  circumstances where not paid 113
  in the feudal period, contrasted with
    modern times 334, 391, 393, 395,
    414, 417–18, 420–1, 803

affords twenty millions in Great Britain
823
gross and neat 286, 288
house rent 134–5, 281
taxes upon 840–7
and the rate of interest 358–9
as a deduction from the produce of labour
83, 163
of cultivated land of which the produce is
human food, regulates the rent of
others 168–77, 238, 245, 259
and minerals/metals:
of coal mines 182–5
of silver mines 185–92, 219, 231
of tin mines 186
perpetual, should not be stated in money
51–2, 55, 200
as a monopoly price 160–1
in the Physiocratic system 665–8, 672 & n.
as a component part of price 67–71,
72 & n., 73–6, 80, 113, 162, 286
and the price of land 610–12
and the price of provisions 101
of the produce of land which always
affords rent 162–77
of the produce of land which may afford
rent 178–93
demanded for the natural produce of land
67
causes of variation in 78, 364
and towns, rent certain 399, 400–2, 903
tendency to rise over time 264–66
taxes upon 823–36, 836–40
the fund from which the exigencies of the
state may be supplied 812–13
see also original index
representation, unknown in ancient times 624
representatives, and American colonial
government 585, 620, 622, 624–5,
see also America
republics, of letters 811
mercantile 443–4
see also Berne, Greece, Italy, Hamburg,
Holland, Switzerland
retail trade 129–30, 322, 364, 367, 374,
529–31, 557, 852–3, 863, 885
retailers 129, 360–4, 378, 492, 529, 531,
735, 853, 863, 887, 891, 937
retainers, feudal 334, 413, 414–15 & n.,
418 & n., 419 n., 420–1, 446, 693 n.,
790–1, 800–1, 803, 908
see also feudal (system)
returns, *see* Rent, wages, profit
forms of easily confused 70–1, 83
revenue, original sources of 69–70, 611–12,
825, 927
may maintain productive or unproductive
labour 332–49

public, sources of 817–906
of society 11–12, 106, 188, 265, 287–8,
332, 364, 366, 376, 447–8, 451,
455–6, 458, 489–90, 497
gross and neat 286–95
see also original index; taxes
Revolution, English 211 n., 318, 344,
381 & n., 540, 742, 829, 846, 912,
913 n., 944
Revolution, a, of the greatest importance to
the public happiness 422
rhetorick 150, 777 & n., 811
Rhine, river 35
Rhode Island 573, 585
rice 54 n., 89, 173, 176, 208, 223, 527–8,
579 & n., 626, 683
rich, country 16–17, 39, 87, 107, 208–9,
234, 257, 263, 266, 334–5, 347, 429,
494, 496, 560, 632
see also poor country
rich man/men, economy of 93, 98, 112, 129,
146, 149, 169, 180–1, 182, 190 & n.,
333, 338, 413, 422, 429, 494, 562,
644, 709–11, 715, 725, 842–3, 873,
888, 931
riches, parade of 190 & n.
Riding School 764
Riga 369, 477, 488 n.
rights, personal 154, 188 & n., 285, 351,
382 n., 383 & n., 384, 385 n., 392
& n., 397 n., 416–17, 425, 543 n.,
582, 610, 626, 722–3, 742 n., 762,
799, 800 n.
rights, sacred 138, 188, 582
risk, the borrower of capital runs a risk in
employing it 69
and the rate of interest 114
undervalued 125–6
perception of, affects profits 128
affects interest 356–7, *see also* interest
and exchange 432–3, 476
risks involved in establishing a new trade
131, 754
see also joint stock companies
risk, and the employment of stock 847–8,
902
see also profits
risk, value of 756
see also insurance
rivers, navigable, effect on commerce
32 & n., 33 n., 34, 35–6 & n., 109,
163–4, 336, 372 & n., 405 & n., 424,
682, 690, 725, 894
see also carriage, sea coast
roads, administration and advantages of
163–4, 179, 182, 307, 321 n., 365,
393 & n., 724–6, 727 & n., 729–30,
815, 821, 838, 894

Roman, armies:
    Constitution 624, 775 n.
    in receipt of pay 695
    the trade of a soldier not distinct 696
    militia of 698, 702–3, 821
    education and martial spirit 786–7
    a standing army from the end of the
        Carthaginian War 703
    standing army destroyed the republic 706
    relaxation of discipline of 704
    declension of powers; allies of Rome bear
        the burden of defence 622
    Empire, downfall of 11, 56, 111–12,
        211 n., 381–2, 397, 407, 427, 694,
        703, 716
Roman Catholic:
    countries, the lottery of the church
        advantageous 148
    clergy, industry and seal of, kept alive by
        self-interest 789–90
        turbulence of 798, 803 n.
        of the different countries of Europe,
            formed a spiritual army 800
        wealth of, generated a power that
            matched that of the barons
            802
        decline in the power of the church,
            spiritual and secular 805–7
    clergy and the vulgate 766
    of France show less respect to the decrees
        of the Papal court 805
    benefices of, draw men of letters from the
        universities 811
    church, claiming credit for the abolition
        of slavery 390
    ancient constitution of 799
Roman, colonies:
    origins of 556–7
    as plantations, differ from Greek 558
    history of, less brilliant than Greek 567
    advantages derived from 593
    admission of the greater part of the
        inhabitants of Italy to citizenship,
        ruined the republic 622, 624
Roman empire 11, 56, 112, 381–2, 397, 407,
    427, 683, 694, 716, 722, 725
Romans:
    use of copper as money 39, 42, 56
    exposure of children 90 n.
    Athenian ambassadors to 150
    prosperity of 166
    laws silent with regard to apprenticeship
        139
    high prices paid for rare birds and fishes
        235, 241
    and for woollen goods 685
    inferior ranks, dissolute 335
    entails unknown to 384

slavery in feudal period milder 386
    condition of slaves among 587
    ancient Egypt, the granary of 116, 683
    administration of justice 722, 779
    education of 774–9
    morals superior to Greeks 774–5
    laws against corruption 931
    lacked linen 870
    see also original index, *Correspondence*
Rouen, silk and linen manufacture in 102
    a Parliament town, but with great trade
        335–6
Rouge, Cape 737–9
Royal African Company 737 n., 741,
    742–3 & n.
Royal Bank 297, 756 n.
Royal Caroline 745
Royal Exchange Assurance Company 756
rum, pint of, supplement wages in New
    York 87
    defrays the cost of sugar cultivation 173
    a non-enumerated commodity 577–8
    in common use 883
    excise duties on 885
    a proper subject of taxation 936, 939
    trade in 942
Russia, improvement since the discovery of
    America 220
    serfs still exist in 387, 390 n.
    peace with Turkey 607
    fleet in Archipelago 607
    first embassies to/from England,
        prompted by commercial interests
        732
    soldiers not inferior to Prussian 705
    civilized under Peter I 706
    poll taxes on bondsmen employed in
        cultivation 857
Russian company 734

S

sailors, payment regulated by rates in the
    Port of London 127
    risks faced by 127
    wages rise in the event of war 132
    defence of Britain depends on 463
    no sensible inconvenience felt by those
        disbanded at the end of a war
        469–70
Saint Christopher island 597, 943
Saint Domingo, mines abandoned 185
    poor inhabitants of 192
    Columbus in 559–61
    established by pirates 571
    completely cultivated 588
Saint Etienne, election of 102

Saint James' Palace, land-tax on 822
Saint Thomas island 570
Saint Vincents, new field for speculation 943
Salle 738
salmon fishery pays a rent 69
salt:
    instrument of commerce in Abyssinia
        38 & n.
    excise duty on Scotch 519–20
    price of, increased by taxes 96, 260, 466
    taxation of 873–6, 896, 901, 903–4
    provisions 244, 246, 425 n., 452, 459–60,
        463, 519, 577–8, 875
salters, an example of slave labour 387
saltpetre 523
Santa Cruz 570
Saracens 406 & n.
Sardinia, the land tax there 835–6 & n.,
        854, 934
Savage nations 10, 24 & n., 27 n., 90 n.,
        180 & n., 221, 344 & n., 381 n., 448,
        495, 559, 564–5, 567, 691–2 n.,
        696 n., 783 n.
saving, motive to 337–8, 341–2, 366, 385,
        411, 446 n., 908
    see also frugality
Savoy 835
Saxon(s) 41, 43, 57, 247 & n., 344, 382 n.,
        414 n., 416 & n., 417 n., 446, 704 n.,
        716 n., 894
Scandinavians, ancient 776
scarcity, effect of years of, on industry and
        wages 100–1, 103–4
    effect on prices 45 n., 50 n., 132, 183,
        189, 190–2, 216–17, 242–3, 401,
        466, 525
scherif, Arabian, authority of 713
scholarships, effect on wages of labour 146
    attach students to particular colleges 762
schools, endowments of 759–60
    in England, public schools less corrupted
        than the universities 764
    damage morals 773
    should be established in every district
        785–6 & n.
school-master, should be partly paid by the
        public 785
science, the antidote to superstition 796
Scotland:
    in the Highlands every farmer a butcher,
        etc. 31
    village in, where nails are currency 38
    reduction of value of the coin 42–3, 53
    wages in low country vary less than in
        England 92
    grain dearer in seventeenth century, ibid.
    wages in seventeenth century 5d to 6d
        94

    wages in different parts, ibid.
    workmen less diligent than in England 99
    linen manufacture 102
    wages lower than in England 107
    much poorer and advancing less rapidly
        than England, ibid. 108
    wages of colliers and common labourers
        compared 121
    knitted stockings in many places cheaper
        than woven 134
    no country in Europe in which
        corporation laws are so little
        oppressive 138
    no law regulating apprenticeship 138
    wages of spinners, ibid.
    church, respectable though poorly paid
        148
    easy migration of labour 156
    assize of bread could not be fixed there
        158
    incorporation of bakers in, ibid.
    rent for kelp shores 161
    desert moors yield rent 163
    union with, opened English market to
        cattle of 165, 237
    high rent of enclosed land 167
    land could not be cultivated by factors
        174
    oatmeal said to be better food than wheat
        flour 177
    stone quarry affords no rent in some parts
        179
    bark the only part of wood sent to market
        in parts of the Highlands, ibid.
    rent for quarries of London paving stones
        179–80
    many coal mines yield no rent 182
    sixth part a common rent of fertile lead
        mines 186
    conversion prices 200
    wages higher than in France 207
    price of corn in England and Scotland
        compared 208–9
    proportion of gold and silver in the
        coinage 230
    price of cattle affected by the union
        237–40
    dairy farming 244
    calves formerly killed young 250
    price of wool fell as a consequence of the
        Union 252
    commerce of, not very great 299
    cash accounts do not exclude bill
        discounting 300
    twenty-shilling notes lowest paper money
        current, ibid.
    limit of paper money reached twenty-five
        years ago 308

Scotland (*cont.*):
    issue of small notes extends the paper circulation to retail trade 322
    and banishes gold and silver 323
    union caused nobility to cease residing in Edinburgh 336
    wool manufactured in Yorkshire 365
    trade with London 368
    one fifth or one third of the land entailed 385
    steel bow tenants 391
    long leases 393
    no leasehold carries a parliamentary vote, ibid.
    hospitality in the Highlands 413
    small rent for Highland farms 414
    territorial jurisdictions in the Highlands 416
    prohibition of export of gold and silver 431
    manufacturing wine in 458
    mountains destined for breeding grounds 460
    herring fishery 519–22, and Appendix
    salt duty 519
    herrings an important part of food of common people 521
    English bounty on hemp imported from 645
    judges' salary from interest of money 721–2
    parish schools 785
    respectable clergy 810
    eminent men of letters professors 811
    excellent character of church, ibid.
    foris-familiated children 859
    shoes not a necessary of life to women in 870
    linen subject to duty on importation into England 913
    little malt liquor consumed 938
    more smuggling than in England, ibid.
    redundant paper money the consequence of enterprising spirit 941
    has banished gold and silver in, ibid.
    less spirit of party than in England 945
    variegated stones gathered in 69
    conversion price in 201 & n.
    highlands of, old families in 421
    see also original index, *Correspondence*
Scythia, barbarous because inland 36
    overran Western Empire 381
    if united could conquer Europe and Asia 692
    militia of Mithridates 703
    military organization preserved after fall of Western Empire 705

    administration of justice a source of revenue 716
    not much beyond shepherd stage at fall of Western Empire 717
sea coast, proximity to encourages industry 32–4, 183, 405–6, 408, 650
    extent of in England 424
    see also rivers, Egypt, Italy, Mediterranean, Venice, Genoa, Pisa, carriage, water
sea-risk 125–6, 756 & n.
seas, *see* Aegean; Adriatic, Baltic, Black; Caspian, Euxine; Indian, Mediterranean
sea-sticks 519–20
secret(s), in manufactures, trade 77–8
sect(s), religious 789, 792–3, 795–6
seignorage 59, 62 & n., 302, 478 n., 551 & n., 552–5, 724
self-love 26, 27 & n.
    see also original index
Senegal 657, 738, 743 n., 881
servants, *see* original index
Sestertii 56, 235–6
Settlement, Laws of 92 n., 136 n., 152–7, 470
    see also original index
sexes, breach of chastity by 794
Seymour, family of 347
sheep, *see* original index
Sheffield 20 n., 131 & n., 136, 260, 409 & n.
shells, use as currency 38 & n.
shepherds, state of 178, 413–14, 422 & n., 430, 634 & n., 637 n., 689 n., 691–4, 697, 701, 704–5, 717, 817, 821
    see also original index
Shetland, wages in 134
    rents 161
    herring-fishery 520
shilling, originally a denomination of weight 42–3
ship-building, limitation of affected ancient commerce 34
shirt, linen 23, decency requires 348 n., 870, 876
shoe-makers 32 n., 122–3, 147, 280, 378, 457, 655, 682, 873
shoes, as necessary of life 96 n., 870, 873, 876
shop-keepers, prejudice against, unfounded 361
    nation of 613, navigation act, inspired by 614
    proposed tax on 852
Shropshire 185
Siam, gulf of 36
Siberia, limited possibilities of growth in 36
    caravans through 223

Sicily, price of wheat in ancient 235–6
  silk manufactures imported 364
  exported to Venice 408
  colonization of 556 & n., 566 & n.
Silesia, lawns of 473, land tax in 834
silk, manufacture 102, 136, 151, 364 n.,
    406 n., 501 n., 646, 659
  limited to two apprentices 136, 151
  transferred from Lucca to Venice 407
  could suffer from freedom of trade 469
  effect of import prohibition 452
  high duties on importation of 17, 523,
    886, 906
  bounty upon new silk exported 523
  an enumerated commodity 579, 583
  bounty upon raw silk imported from the
    colonies 646
silk-worm(s) 408 & n.
silver:
  degradation in the value of 52
  variation in the value of 49, 52–5, 62–3
  variation in the value of, historically
    195–225
silver, seldom found virgin 189
  consumption of 225–6
  a proper subject for taxation 232
  determination of value of 328–32
  durability of 439
  see also original index, gold and silver
silver mines, in America 210–11, 220–29
  of Peru 185–8, 219–20
  of Spanish America 232
sinking fund(s) 442, 615, 750, 915–16,
    920–2, 938
  see also *Correspondence*
slaves/slavery:
  and man's love of domination 388 & n.
  high cost of work done by 98–9, 387–8, 684
  lacks incentive to invention 684 & n.
  economic use of in Rome and Greece
    388, 557, 683
  domestic pedagogues usually slaves in
    Rome and Greece 777
  and dependence, illustrated by reference
    to the early stages of society
    711–18
  in feudal times 401–2, 416–17
  see also hunters, shepherds, feudal
    government
  feudal as compared to ancient 386
  more secure under arbitrary government
    587–8
  emancipation of: by Augustus 587–8 & n.
  confined to the western and southern
    parts of Europe 387 & n.
  in feudal times 389–91, 400
  claims of the Church of Rome 390 & n.,
    803 n.

slavery, and the colonies:
  negroes, trade in 578, in a state of 939
  use of in sugar and tobacco 388–9
  management of in French and English
    colonies 565, 586 & n., 587–8
  condition of better under abitrary
    government 587 & n.
  emancipation by Quakers 388 & n.
  restrictions on American trade, a badge of
    582, 615
  poll tax on 857 & n.
  see also original index
Slitt mills 280, 582
smelting-house 23, 307
smith(s) 16 & n., 18 & n., 23, 28, 31–2 & n.,
    283, 695, 965 n.
smugglers 128, 474
smuggling, of gold 189, 226–7, 432
  of silver 187, 226–7, 432
  of tea 223
  of spirits 891
  generally ruinous 128
  moderate tax does not encourage 553
  encouraged by high duties 826, 881–2,
    884, 903
  and excise laws 884, 886
  as a crime 898
  opportunities in sparsely populated
    countries 939
  scruples concerning the purchase of
    smuggled goods 898
snuff-boxes 230
soap, dear in consequence of taxes 96, 260,
    466, 873, 878
  rendered necessary by the use of linen
    874
  use of kelp in the manufacture of 161
sober, undertakings 317
  people, as opposed to prodigals and
    projectors 357 & n., 437–8, 851
  virtue superfluous when profits are high
    612
  the industrious poor 872
  see also parsimony, frugality, population
sobriety 492, 877, 896 n.
society, first principles of 26–7, 28 n.
  rude state of 15, 36, 38, 65, 90 n., 117,
    247, 276, 344, 415 & n., 566 n.,
    689, 695, 711–13, 715, 782–3, 817,
    907–8
  see also hunters, shepherds
society, improved 15, 26, 37, 65, 68, 97,
    118, 180, 234, 257, 265, 376, 712–13,
    782–5, 788, 794–5, 814–17, 824, 910
  general stock of 278, 281–2, 284, 286,
    288, 295, 362, 380, 447, 453,
    631, 675–8, 686–7, 758, 898,
    925, 929

society, improved (*cont.*):
  see also advancing (stationary or
    declining), state of; feudal,
    commercial; stock, capital
  progressive, stationary or declining 80,
    90–1, 99, 105, 151–2, 159, 209, 258
soldier(s):
  pay of 94 & n., 126
  numerous children of 97
  industry of, when paid by the piece 100
  recruitment, motivated by risk 126 & n.,
    782
  must obey the prince who pays them 413
  redundant at the end of a war 469–71
  drunkenness and sobriety of 492
  emergence of, as a separate trade 695–700
  efficiency of, in a standing army 698–701,
    705, *see also* armies
  and the invention of fire-arms 707
  employment on roads 727
  martial spirit of a people, reduces the
    required number of 787
  see also original index; sailors
sophisms 769, 771
sophists 149 & n.
sound, analogy of 768 n.
South Sea Stocks 108 n., 921
South Sea Company 319, 741–6, 756 n.,
  914–15
  see also original index
South Carolina, expence of civil
  establishment 573
  duty on molasses 936
sovereign, avarice and injustice of 43–4, 51
  as an unproductive labourer 330–1
  feudal: lords make war against 383
    permit tallage 394
    taxation in 854
  let taxes in farm 399
  grant powers of self-government to cities
    401
  loss of authority 403
  but not entirely in France or England 404
  political economy proposes to enrich 428
  in absolute governments 586
  a company of merchants, incapable of
    considering themselves as 637–8
  citizens bound to contribute to support of
    654
  of ancient Egypt 681, 683, 838
  expence of preparing an army devolves
    upon 696
  and standing armies 706, 718
  judicial authority of 715–19, 722
  and the protection of trade 733
  opposed by religious interests 797–800,
    802, 804–7
  expence of supporting the dignity of 814

inconsistent with being a trader 818–19
parsimony, lack of 909
see also original index, feudal, King,
  legislator, parliament
Spain:
  avidity for gold 192–3, 429–30, 561–4
  colonies of 221–2, 562–4, 567–9, 572,
    586, 590–1, 609, 627
  power of, supported by taxes on colonies
    567, 574 & n., 593
  tax on Peruvian mines 185–7, 219–20,
    231, 232 & n., 233
  quantity of gold imported 226–7, 436,
    444, 512
  prohibition on export of metals 431,
    436 & n., 510, 511 & n., 514, 541
  beggarly state of 220, 256, 541
  agriculture, discouraged by the cheapness
    of gold and silver 512
  exorbitant profits of merchants have not
    augmented the capital of 576,
    612–13
  no manufactures for distant sale
    developed in 425–6
  required Portugal to exclude English
    ships 549
  prohibition of English woollens in
    Flanders 468
  wool of 248, 261, 365, 408, 410, 642 n.,
    651, 881
  Alcavala of 899
  Ambassador gave Queen Elizabeth
    stockings 262
  debts, of old standing 928
  Flota, drained Germany of many
    commodities 607
  government, arbitrary 256, 427, 567,
    586
  Majorazzo in 572
  mark, affixed to gold 41
  opulence under Moors 406
  sheep and cattle killed for tallow 247
  sobriety of 492
  taxes upon contracts 900
  universities of 766
  war of 1739 615–16, 705, 922, 946
  see also original index, Columbus,
    Portugal, *Correspondence*
Spartans, use of metals by 39, 436
spectator(s), view of, in a work-house 14
  impartial, in the sphere of politics 945
speculation, trade of 130–1
  see also philosophers, philosophy
spendthrift(s) 70, 236 n., 346, 437, 912
spices, destruction by Dutch to support
  prices 175, 525, 636
  imported to Britain 883
spindle 263

spinner(s) 16, 22, 68, 75, 114–15, 134, 143, 276 n., 644, 870 n.
spinning-wheel 263
spirits, licence to retail 852
   wages not affected by taxes on 872, 877
   policy to discourage consumption 891
Spitalfields 408
stage, *see* original index
stallage 398
stamp(s) 39–41 & n., 139, 221 n.
stamp-duty(-ies) 605, 721, 858, 860–3, 935
stampmaster(s) 40, 139 n.
Stamp Act 102 & n., 605 & n.
stamps on linen 40, 139
standard money 57, 480–1, 829
   see also debasement
statesman/men:
   political economy considered as a branch of the science of 428, 523
   should not direct the interest of private people 456 & n.
   insidious and crafty animal in a government influenced by shop-keepers 613, cf. 623
   in barbarous societies 783
   see also Solon, legislators
statuaries 208
statues 150 & n., 208, 346–7, 686
statute of apprenticeship 32 n., 79 & n., 136 n., 137, 139, 151 & n., 152, 470, 762 & n.
statute of assize 196–7, 201–3
statute of labourers 195
statute of provisors 804
statute of tumbrel and pillory 202
   see also Poor Laws, Settlement
steel furnaces, prohibited in the colonies 582
steel-bow tenants 389 n., 391 & n.
sterling mark 41, 138–9
stock:
   capital and the employment of productive labour 11
   see also capital, labour
   early state of society preceding accumulation of 65
   see also accumulation
   circulation of, obstructed 135, 152, 453, 602, 632–3
   see also industry, natural balance of
   society, division of 281–9
   lent at interest 350–9
   see also interest
   easily removed 848–9
   see also companies, taxes, original index, industry
stock-jobbing 317, 486, 745
stockings, cheap in many parts of Scotland 134

art of knitting unknown at the time of Edward IV 262
   prohibition of the export of machines used in the manufacture of 659
   first worn by Queen Elizabeth 262
Stoics 150, 778 & n.
   see also Diogenes, Epicurus, Zeno
stomach, narrow capacity of 180 n., 181
stones, precious 45 n., 182, 190 n., 191–3, 224, 231
   see also original index
stone-quarries, value depends on situation 179, 193
Stowe 347
students, effect of on the organization of colleges 762–6
   see also pupils, universities
Suabia, House of 401 n., 403
subject and subordinate provinces 572, 593, 615, 621, 638, 901
subordination, under feudal government 414 & n., 417–18
   and inequality of fortune 715
   habit of in new colonies 564–5
   see also original index, authority, feudal, hunters, shepherds, commerce
subsidy(-ies) 185 n., 249, 394 n., 402 n., 473–4, 499–500, 501 & n., 503, 536 n., 583, 656, 658, 704 n., 853, 877 n., 880, 883, 911, 913
   see also original index
succession, laws of 382 & n., 383 & n., 384, 446, 556, 572–3, 711, 742 n., 859, 861
sugar:
   used as an instrument of commerce in West Indian colonies 38 & n.
   variation in price of 133, 173
   colonies 173–4, 500, 570–1, 577–8, 588, 594, 942
   can afford the expence of slave cultivation 388–9, 586–7
   of profitable article of cultivation 173, 389
   bounty on 523
   drawbacks on 500
   a non-enumerated commodity 577, 578
   duties upon 581
   preferential treatment of 583
   a luxury 871, 886, 936
   of general use 883
sugar-cane 586, 589
sugar-plantation 389
sumptuary laws 261–2, 346, 871–2, 878
superstition 367, 566 n., 635, 767 & n., 770 n.
   and enthusiasm 539 n., 793, 796
   popular 539 n., 793, 796
   delusions of 803
   among the ancient Egyptians 367, 682

Surinam, colony of 570
surmullet 236
surplus, produce 28, 31, 37, 86, 113, 161,
    163–4, 172, 175–8, 181, 212, 236,
    251, 337 n., 361, 363 n., 365, 367–8,
    371–4, 376–7, 379–80, 408–9,
    413–14, 418, 420, 439, 444–6, 461 n.,
    489, 517, 537, 570, 574–5, 577–8,
    584, 591 & n., 592–4, 596, 635,
    637–9, 666 n., 669–72, 682, 744, 897,
    940, 943–4
Sussex, restrictions on transport of wool
    650
Sweden, improved since the discovery of
    America 220
  tea smuggled from 223
  exclusive company for the East India
    trade 449
  settlements in New World 570
  pitch and tar company of 580
  without an exclusive company would
    never have sent a ship to East
    Indies 632
  and would have suffered no loss 633
  exempted from Eastland Company's
    exclusive privilege 735
  Reformation in 806
  eminent men of letters professors 811
Switzerland:
  farmers not inferior to the British 395
  cities became independent 403
  sometimes may be necessary to restrain
    export of corn 539
  militia regimented 699
  militia defeated Austrian and Burgundian
    militia 705
  whole people exercised in use of arms 787
  establishment of the reformation in Bern
    and Zurich 806
  many cities capitals of little republics 88
  respectable clergy 810
  eminent men of letter professors in
    Protestant cantons 811
  the clergy there zealous and industrious
    812–13
  both religions established in some cantons
    813
  taxes how paid there 850–1, 860
Syracuse a great colony 566
Syria 703
system, theoretical 768–9 & n.
  see also beauty

T

Taille, the nature of the tax 394–5, 854 & n.
  real or predial 835–6

real and personal 854–6
  a tax on wages 865–6
  exemption from 869
  not farmed 904
  should be abolished 904
tailors, wages in London 120–1
  regulated by Statute 84 n., 157–8 & n.
talents, differences of 29–30
  acquired by long application 65 & n.
  superior, and rewards 123–4, 148–9
  as a part of fixed capital 282
tallage(s) 394, 879
tallow 247, 874 n.
tanner(s) 28, 250, 378, 655, 873 & n.
tar 24 n., 579–80, 644–5
Tarentum 566
Tartars:
  primitive, due to limited opportunity for
    growth 32 n., 36 & n.
  ignorant 221
  but more advanced than the inhabitants of
    Mexico and Peru 221
  caravans through 223
  taxes levied upon the goods of travellers
    397
  authority of chiefs 416 n., 712–13
  their treasures 446, 908
  sources of revenue 817
  regard to kindred in 421 n., 422
  sheep and cattle regarded as wealth
    429–30
  as a nation of shepherds 422, 690 & n.,
    704
  prepared for war 690, 691 & n.
  dreadful invasions of 692 & n., 705, 789
  militia of 700–1, 703
  administration of justice 716 & n.
tavern, a disagreeable trade, profits of 118
taxes:
  origin of, under the feudal government
    397–8, 404
  a derivative revenue 70
  maintains unproductive labour 333, *see
    also* labour, productive/
    unproductive
  on tin 187
  on tobacco 174
  on gold and silver 186–9, 219, 231–3,
    513, 541
  of the colonies 620–2, 625, 933 ff.,
    946–7
  moderation of, in American colonies 573
  insufficient to defray their cost 593–4
  British system of, could be extended to
    the colonies 933 ff.
  upon foreign commodities, advantageous
    465–9, 472
  upon the necessaries of life 466, 508

upon consumable commodities 826,
      869 ff., 906, *see also* consumable
      commodities
upon private luxury and extravagance
      574
on carriages, equitable 725, 728
discourage industry 897
maxims, canons of 825–7 & n.
on rent 828–36, 836–40
on the rent of houses 840–7
on profit 847–52
on the profits of particular employments
      852–8
on wages 864–7
fall light upon the people of Great Britain
      899
uniform system of in Great Britain 900
subjects of, when proper means exhausted
      906
see also original index, necessaries of life,
      luxury, customs, duties, excise,
      smuggling, Taille, tithes, land-tax,
      physiocrats, *Correspondence*
tea:
   importation of in Great Britain 223
   quantities smuggled 436
   tax on 871
   Dutch licences to drink 878
   and customs revenue 883
   duty falls on middle of upper ranks 886
teacher(s):
   term, anciently synonymous with doctor
      137
   in classical times 149–50, 772, 778
   private and public 149, 762 & n., 778 n.,
      780, 811
   emoluments of 148–50, 760 & n.,
      778 & n., 790, 796, 881 n.
   repetition of subject matter renders
      competent 812
   see also original index, universities
tenant(s):
   pay the highest rent in the circumstances
      of the land 160
   payments in kind 200
   writ of ejectment 392
   at will 334, 383, 386, 389, 414–15, 418,
      420, 801
   steel bow 389–91
   tallages on 394
   rights, affected by length of lease
      393 & n.
   advances tax upon rent 828
   leases which prescribe a mode of
      cultivation 831
   see also farmers, landlords, leases,
      metayers, rent, taxes
tenths and fifteenths 394

tenures, feudal 334, 383, 389, 572, 821,
      834–5, 854, 860
terra firma 560
theology 765–6, 770–2
Thessalians 702
Thracians 702
Thrasymenus 702
thunder and lightning, superstitious and
      scientific reaction to 767 & n.
tillage 165–6, 176, 183, 212 & n., 214, 216,
      237–8, 282, 363, 461, 507 & n., 508,
      514, 534, 875 & n.
timber 23, 24 n., 179 & n., 183 & n., 223 n.,
      260, 283, 577, 580, 644, 645 & n.,
      646
tin 40 n., 186, 187 & n., 188 & n., 190, 285,
      563, 656
   see also original index
tithe(s) 235, 236 & n., 390, 425, 574 & n.,
      666, 683, 801 n., 812 n., 837 n.,
      856 n., 934
tobacco:
   used as currency in Virginia 38
   colonists pay for British goods in 941–2
   can afford the use of slave cultivation
      388–9
   profits of 173, 389
   an enumerated commodity 579, 602–4
   export of 591, 602–4, 606
   use of in trade 369–70, 490, 628
   drawbacks upon 500, 504
   bounties on 583
   in general use and consumption 883
   not a necessary of life 936
   excise scheme of Sir Robert Walpole 886
   tax on, farmed in France 903–4
   see also original index
Tobago 943
tolls:
   abuse of tolls 726
   on carriages, an unequal tax 728
   lay expence of maintaining roads on the
      users of them 815
   see also original index
tonnage and poundage:
   duty of 263, 879–80
   subsidy of 880, 913
tonnage bounties 518–22
Tonquin, vessels of Batavia 635
Tontines, in the French finances 917–18
tools 18–19, 22 n., 23, 89, 276–7, 294–6,
      320, 351, 513, 666
Toul, bishopric of 901
Toulouse, Parliament of 720
tower-weight 42 & n., 195, 197
towns:
   commerce of, disrupted by the fall of
      the Roman Empire 381 & n., 397

towns (*cont.*):
  feudal taxes on 398
  arrived at a state of liberty before the
    occupiers of land 399 & n., 405
  rise and progress of 397–410
  privileges of self-government granted to
    400–1
  royal alliances with 402–3
  not entirely independent in France and
    England 404
  may grow up to great wealth and
    splendour, independent of the
    country 405, 406 n.
  effect of development of manufactures
    and trade on the country 408–27
  policy of Europe favourable to 11,
    679
  some sorts of industry can only be
    performed in 31
  wages of labour higher than in the
    country 92, 99
  reciprocal relations with the country 376,
    677, 686
  see also cities
trade(s):
  wholesale and retail, distinguished 361
  put into nation different quantities of
    productive labour 362–3
  the capital of the wholesale trade has no
    fixed location 364–5
  wholesale, may be reduced to three
    different sorts 368–9
  carrying trade contrasted with home-trade
    370–1
  carrying trade as a sympton of national
    wealth 373–4
  little good done by those who affect to
    trade for the public good 456
  home-trade normally preferred to foreign
    trade by wholesale manufacturers
    454–5
  see also original index, carrying-trade,
    corn, balance of trade
Trade, Board of 736
traites, in France 901, 904
transfer of property, taxes on 858–9, 861–4,
  895
transit duties 894
transport, *see* carriage, land, water, public
  works
travel, for education, pernicious effects of
  773
travellers, weak and wondering 89, 559,
  681, 729
treasures, a resource in war 441, 445
treasure-trove 285, 908
treasures 226, 441, 446, 908
Trebia, battle of 702

Triclinaria, high price of 685 & n.
trinkets 230, 346, 349, 421, 712, 908
Trojan War 38 n., 383 n., 717, 776
Troyes, weight 42
truck, barter and exchange, propensity to
  25 & n., 27 & n., 29, 30
Tumbrel and Pillory, statute of 202
Turdi, fed by the Romans 241
Turkey 54 & n., 285, 406, 558, 607, 736
Turkey Company 732, 734–5, 740
Turks 406, 558, 684
turnpikes, acts, roads, tolls 33 n., 164,
  394 n., 726, 727 & n., 728–9, 815,
  894
  see also tolls
turpentine 579, 644–5
Tuscany 38 n., 426
Twelve Tables 778
tythes 390, 574, 788, 801, 812, 837–9

U

Ukraine 221, 446
undertakers 66 & n., 100, 106 n., 112 n.,
  125, 182, 184 & n., 187, 219, 231,
  232 n., 281, 287, 292, 296, 304,
  307–8, 332, 343, 407, 461, 471, 517,
  522, 564–5, 757–8
Union, of Scotland and England 165, 230,
  237, 239–40 & n., 252, 298, 336,
  625 n., 944
Union, of Great Britain with America 617 n.,
  622 n., 624–5, 936–7, 944–5 & n.
universe, great system of 770
university(-ies):
  degrees no assurance of competence
    122 n.
  incorporations, anciently called 136
  period of study, designed for commercial
    reasons 137 n.
  grant licenses to their scholars to beg
    149
  originally, ecclesiastical corporations
    765
  constitution of 151, 760–4, 772, 790
  see also original index, *Correspondence*
upstart(s) 585, 713 & n., 902, 919 n.
usurers 357
usury 106, 107 n., 111, 113 n., 350, 356,
  357 n., 908
  see also interest
utensils 23 & n., 28 n., 39 n., 86 n., 190 & n.,
  439–40, 659, 745
utility:
  and value 44, 189, 190 n., 191
  see also value, paradox of
Utopia 471, 934

Utrecht 486
Utrecht, Treaty of 745, 921 & n.

V

vacations, French fees of court 720
value:
two different meanings of the term 44
in exchange, determined by the quantity
of labour embodied 65, *see also*
exchangeable value; labour,
embodied and commanded; labour
as the real measure of exchangeable
value
paradox of 45 & n.
affected by scarcity 45 & n., 189–92,
563
and the perception of beauty 189,
190 & n., 191
see also diamonds, utility, silver, gold,
money, price
vegetable food 167, 176–7, 206–7, 259,
560–1, 876
velvet(s) 346 n., 407, 501 n., 881, 886
Venice:
history of 403–4
shipping encouraged by Crusades 406
exchange with London 479
bank of 480, 818
envied by the Portuguese 558
fleets of, in Mediterranean 569
public debt of 928
see also original index
venison 27–8, 241–2, 259
see also original index
Vera Cruz 746
Verde, Cape of 558
Verdun 901
Versailles, idle because residence of a court
335
an ornament to France 347
vice, of levity 794, 810
Vicesma Hereditatum 859
village(s):
limited scope in for the division of labour
31
in Scotland, use of nails in 38
erection of banking companies in 297
requirements of stock in 106
wages of labour in, as compared to towns
107
profits in 129–30
statute of apprenticeship does not apply in
137
idleness in 336
formation of 378
moral conduct in 795

villains, feudal 386 n., 389, 390 & n., 399 n.,
803 n.
villanage 389, 397, 400, 405, 414
vinegar 473 & n., 501–2 n., 890
vineyard(s):
profitability of, in ancient agriculture
170–1
affected by fertility of the soil 172
rent of 78
taxes on 893
favours shown to in France 901
Vingtieme 858 & n., 859 n., 904
Virginia:
tobacco as currency in 38
tobacco more profitable than corn 174
with Maryland, a chief source of 174
tobacco trade with 372, 500, 595, 602
see also tobacco
trade with 370, 490
expence of civil establishment 573
progress of unforeseen in 1660 597–8
no necessity for gold and silver money
942
stores and warehouses belong to residents
of England 367
Visiapour, diamond mines 191
Vulgate 766

W

wages, defined 65–6, 69
allowance for hardship 48–9
of inspection and direction 66
one of three sources of revenue 69, 825
confused with profit and rent 70
natural rate of 72, subsistence defined
85–6, 98
and the cost of subsistence 93–6, 101–4
determined by a bargain between
opposing interests 83–5
difficulty in determining the usual rate of
105
constantly rising since the time of Henry
VIII 106
real value has risen in the eighteenth
century 94–5, 219
in Great Britain, wages exceed
subsistence levels 91–3
higher in the Colonies than in England
87, 109
high wages have less effect on prices than
high profits 114
masters silent on this topic 115, 599
high levels of to be approved of on
grounds of equity 96
liberal reward as a natural symptom of
increasing wealth 91

wages, defined (*cont.*):
  liberal reward and the survival of children 98–9, 565
  and the capital stock 106–7, 110–11, 353
  level of, affected by the state of the economy 80
    in the progressive state 86–8, 266
    in the stationary state 89–90, 111, 224
    in the declining state 90–1
  and productivity 99–100, 104
  dangers of piece-work 100
  affected by the nature of employments 116 ff.
  inequalities of, as affected by the policy of Europe 135–59
  taxes on subsistence raise pecuniary wages 508, 871
  on wages 864–7, 869, 872–5, 887–8
  see also original index
  advantages net, doctrine of, capital, labour
Wales, stone quarries afford no rent 179
  old families common in 421
  breeding of cattle in 460
wants of mankind 37, 178, 276
war(s), civil 212, 214, 344, 427, 515, 793
  the late 106 & n., 108, 110, 223, 308, 310 n., 345 & n., 441, 443–5, 469, 502–3, 546 n., 549, 572, 615, 657, 661, 701 n., 743, 749, 852, 917, 923 & n., 929, 944, 946
  the present 474, 521, 601 n., 616 n., 701, 920 & n.
  Dutch 597
  Peloponesian 693, 694 n.
  Persian 693
  Punic 56 & n., 702–3, 930–1
  Spanish 615 & n., 705, 946
  Trojan 38 n., 383 n., 717, 776
war, sources of payment for 431, 440–6
  officers of, unproductive labourers 331, 342
  confused scramble of 628
  art and cost of, and the role of government in modern times 697
  advantage of developed nations in 708 & n.
  popularity of, how it might be removed 926
  see also original index
watches (time-pieces) 13 n., 17 n., 139, 260
watch-cases 230, 655
watch-makers 656
water, value of 44–5 & n.
  see also carriage, water, and value, paradox of
water-level, analogy of, as applied to banking 304 & n., 311, 316

analogy of, as applied to the prohibition of the export of gold and silver 511–13
water-works, a business suitable for a joint stock company 756–8
wealth, real 12, 255, 258, 337, 340, 344–7, 451, 565
  national 87, 89, 255, 258, 265
  represented as consisting in gold and silver 193 n., 255, 340, 429, 432 n., 438–40, 449, 555, 559, 561
  that of England increased since 1660 344
  of a neighbouring nation, advantageous in trade 494
  land, the most durable part of 258
  represented by the Physiocrats as the sole source of 663–4
  as power (Hobbes) 48
  see also original index
weavers 16, 18, 22–3, 31 n., 68, 75–6, 86, 99 n., 114–15, 117, 123, 136, 138, 140 n., 143, 151, 276, 280, 379, 419 n., 644, 681, 695 & n.
welfare, of civil society 11, 159, 629, 807
West Indies:
  sugar currency 38
  planters farm their own estates 70
  wages higher than in England 109
  British acquisitions in, raised profit 110
  sugar colonies resemble esteemed vineyards 173
  interest fallen since the discovery of 354
  carrying trade between, and Europe 373
  would have progressed less rapidly if no capital but their own had been employed in the export trade 380
  slavery harsher than in mediaeval Europe 386
  high profits of sugar and consequent greater number of slaves in sugar colonies 389
  importation of gold and silver from the Spanish 437
  expense of last war largely laid out in 442
  British monopoly in sugar of 500
  Madeira wine imported direct 502
  interest which caused settlements in 556
  no necessity for settlements 558
  plenty of good land 567, 572
  Dutch originally under an exclusive company 570
  St Domingo the most important of the sugar colonies 571
  price of European goods enormous in Spanish 576
  some most important productions non-enumerated 577

freedom of trade with British American colonies 580
effects of colonial monopoly 601
returns of trade with, more irregular and uncertain than with any part of Europe 602
expense of preventing smuggling 615
proposal for obtaining war contributions from 621
natives not benefited by the European discovery of 626
gum senega treated like an enumerated commodity from 657
colonial system sacrifices consumer to producer 660
slave trade a loss to the African Company 743
French and Portuguese companies ruined by slave trade 745
South Sea Company's trade to the Spanish, ibid.
some productions of, yield large portion of British customs revenue 883
more able to pay land-tax than Great Britain 934
see also original index
Westminster, land tax 822, 850
Westminster Hall (Rufus) 413 & n.
Westmoreland, price of coal in 185
whale-fisheries 518, 745
wheat, *see* corn
wheel-wrights 138, 378
wholesale trade 129–30, 322, 360, 362–5, 368, 374, 454, 529–31, 885
widows, young, courted in the American colonies 88
wild-fowl 235, 259
Wilton, an honour to England 347
window-tax 846
Windsor market 168, 211–12, 214, 217, 257, 272
wine-countries, regard the vineyard as the most valuable part of the farm 170
see also vineyards
wine, restrictions on output to sustain prices 171
see also France
may be made in Scotland, but at great expence 458
taxes on 473, 501 & n., 502, 877, 879, 886, 893
French, clandestinely imported 475
cheap, a cause of sobriety 492
restrictions on trade in Britain favour Portugal 493
encouragement to the carrying-trade in wine 501–2
consumption of Madeira 502–3

public cellar a source of revenue in Hamburg 817–18
licences to sell 853, 863
a luxury 870
witchcraft, fear of, compared to that of engrossing and forestalling 528 n., 534
Wolverhampton 137, 409
woman, women, barrenness of, uncommon among the lower ranks 96–7
employment of 103, 366
Irish prostitutes, the most beautiful women in the British dominions 177
in Tartar Societies 690–1
in the agrarian state 693
purpose and content of their education 781
dress of, affected by custom 870
of quality in France, disdain to marry bankers 919
wonder, sense of, and the great phenomena of nature 767 & n.
wood, value of varies with economic circumstances 179, 183
policies to encourage consumption in the Colonies 577, 580, 646
a more wholesome fuel than coal 182–3
price of relative to coal 183–4, 189
see also original index
woodcocks, cannot be much increased 235
wool, from Spain 261, 365, 408, 410, 651, 881
restrictions on trade in the American colonies 582 & n., 610 n.
prohibitions on importation of 452 n., 642, 647, 933 n.
prohibitions on exportation 248–9, 647–8 & n., 649, 650–3, 654–5, 881
taxes on 879
woollen, cloth, division of labour in production of 16, 22–3
stable price of 75–6, 132
stamps on, as security for quality 139
price of English, fallen since the time of Edward III 248
price of in ancient Rome 685
prohibitions on importation 452
and the Methuen Treaty 546
see also original index
woollen manufacture, wages in, little more than common trades 119, 151
as a major employer of labour 469
woollen manufacturers, among the most successful in persuading the legislature to protect their interests 647, 651 & n.

workhouse(s) 14, 19, 20 n., 104, 189, 282, 307, 471, 529
  public 338

Y

yeomanry, position of English 392–5, 425
Yorkshire, woollen manufacture in 102
  cloth fallen in price 261–2
  paper currency in 322, 326
  Scotch wool manufactured there 365
young, the, generosity to their teachers 764, 778

  see also colleges, teachers, universities
Yucatan 221

Z

Zama, battle of 703
Zealand, French wine smuggled from 475
  expense of protecting from the sea 906
Zemidaries 839
Zurich, magistrates of 806
  taxation in 850–2

Index of Persons

A

Abassides 406 & n.
Abraham 41 & n.
Achilles 718
Adam, C. E. 393 n.
Adams, John 164 n., 187–8 n., 220 n.,
    222 n., 247 n., 568 n., 574 n.,
    576 n.
Addison, W. I. 148 n.
Æsop's Fables 768
Agamemnon 717
Agrippina 236 & n.
Alexander I (of Scotland) 42
Alexander the Great 42, 150 & n., 560,
    702 n.
Alexander III 390 & n.
Almagro, Diego de, conquistador 562
Anderson, Adam 322 n., 444 n., 475 n.,
    487 n., 580 n., 585 n., 651 n., 732 n.,
    734 n., 740–3 n., 744 & n., 745–7 n.,
    749 n., 753 n., 758 n., 915 n., 917 n.,
    920 n.
Anderson, James, (*Selectus diplomatum* . . .)
    203 n., 230 n., 298 n.
Anderson James, (*Observations on . . .
    Industry*) 515–16 n.
Anderson, John, (*Commonplace Book*)
    90 n., 97 n., 121 n., 689 n., 711 n.,
    722 n.
Anon 690 n., 700
Antoine, M. 171 n.
Antoninus, Marcus 778
Arbuthnot, Dr, John 149–50 n., 685 & n.
Argyle, Duke of 416
Aristotle 40 n., 90 n., 150 & n., 388 & n.,
    406 n., 775 & n., 778, 811
Asinius Celer 236
Asdrubal, *see* Hasdrubal
Ashton, T. S. 167 n.
Augustus 587 & n., 588 n., 685 n., 859

B

Ball, V. 191 n.
Baretti, J. 436 n., 547–8 & n.
Barker, T. C., McKenzie, J. C., and
    Yudkin, J. 93 n.
Bazinghen, M. Abot de 551 n.
Beaumont, J., *see* Moreau de

Becket, Thomas, Archbishop of Canterbury
    413 & n.
Bell, John 680 n.
Bentham, J. 351 n., 357–8 n.
Beresford, M. W. 402 n.
Bergeron, N. 429 n.
Bernier, François 730 & n.
Bible 41, 765–6, 838
Bindon, D. 924 n., 926 n., 932 n.
Birch, Thomas 167 & n.
Blackstone, Sir William 52 & n., 391 & n.
Bolts, W. 637 n., 639–40 n.
Bonar, J. 170 n.
Borlase, William 186 n., 188 n.
Born, Ralph de 196
Boswell, James 134 n.
Bouchaud, M. A. 859 n.
Brady, Robert 394 n., 398 & n., 400 n.,
    403 n.
Brock, I. 730 n.
Bruce, Robert 42
Brutus, Marcus 111 & n.
Buffon, G. L. L. 243 & n., 560 & n.
Burman (Burmannus, P.) 859 n.
Burn, Richard 95 & n., 147 n., 153–7 & n.
Byron, John 205 & n.

C

Caesar, Julius 199, 344, 588 n., 690 n.,
    706 & n., 859 n.
Calcraft, John 923
Calvin 808
Cameron, Mr, of Lochiel 416, 417 n.
Campbell, R. H. 93 n., 102 n., 313 n., 741 n.
Cantillon, Richard 32 n., 38–40 n., 45 n.,
    47 n., 50–1 n., 66 n., 75 n., 85 & n.,
    86 n., 90 n., 97 n., 106 n., 112 n.,
    117 n., 119 n., 139 n., 160 n., 180 n.,
    184 n., 189 n., 210 n., 225 n., 229 n.,
    291 n., 320 n., 331 n., 354 n., 358 n.,
    405 n., 425 n., 432 n., 436 n., 442 n.,
    505 n., 512 n., 535 n., 581 n., 691 n.
Capet, Hugh 417 n.
Capet, Robert 805
Carneades 150 & n.
Carreri, Gemelli 568 & n.
Carr, C. T. 742 n.
Castracani, Castruccio 407
Cato 166 & n., 462 & n.

Chalmers, G. 88 & n., 95 n., 215 n., 296 n.,
    535 n.
Chambers, E. 15 n.
Charles II, 649 n., 655 n., 881 n.
Charles V, of Spain 220, 806
Charles VI, Emperor of Germany 835 & n.
Charles VIII, of France 425–6
Charles XII, of Sweden 422 n., 446
Charlemagne 42
Charlevoix, François 559–60 n., 571 & n.,
    690 n.
Chatham, Lord (William Pitt) 923
Child, Josiah 432 n., 735 & n., 737 & n.
Choiseul (Etienne, François), Duke of 799
Christiern II, of Denmark 806
Churchill, A. and J. 568 n.
Cicero, Marcus Tullius 111 & n., 166 & n.,
    236 n., 683 n., 769 n., 812 n., 876 & n.
Clapham, J. H. 137 n., 151 n., 318–20 n.,
    322 n., 916 n.
Cobbett, W. 218
Colbert, Jean-Baptiste 467 & n., 663 & n.,
    664
Columbus 225 n., 559, 560–2, 564, 589 n.
Columella 169–70 & n., 241, 388 & n.
Conrad, A. H. and Meyer, J. R. 387 n.
Constantine, Emperor of Rome 704
Cooper, Sir Grey 518 n., 861 n.
Cooper, Thomas (*Regiam Majestatem*) 202–3
Cortez 562, 589 n.
Cregeen, E. R. 161 n.
Cromwell, Oliver 597, 706 & n.

D

Daniel, Gabriel 403 & n.
D'avenant, Charles 88 n., 95 & n., 215 n.,
    891 & n.
Davies, K. G. 742 n., 743 n., 745 n.
Davis, H. 882 n.
Deane, P., and Cole, W. A. 598 n.
Decker, Sir Matthew 514 & n., 597 & n.,
    873 & n., 877 & n., 936 & n.
Democritus 169
Denisart, Jean-Baptiste 107 & n.
Dercyllidas 446 & n.
Derry, T. K. and Williams, T. I. 20 n.
De Lange 680 & n.
Devine, T. M. 412 n.
Dickson, P. G. M. 746 n.
Dioclesian 704
Diogenes of Babylon 150 & n.
Diomedes 38 & n.
Dion Cassius 859
Dionysius of Halicarnassus 706 n.,
    774–5 & n., 779, 812 n.
Dobbs, Arthur 744 & n.

Douglass, William 175 & n., 317 n., 326–7 n.,
    744 n., 941 n.
Draco 648
Drummond, Mr 58
Du Fresne, C., Sieur du Cange 403 n.,
    932 n.
Du Halde, J. B. 90 n., 680 n.
Dupleix, Joseph François 749
Dupont de Nemours, P. S. 673 n., 679 n.
Dupré de St Maur, F. 199 & n., 204,
    205 n., 216, 258
Du Tot 317 & n.
Duverney, J. 317 & n., 912 & n.

E

Eden, W. 267 n., 452–3 n., 520 n., 523 n.,
    605 n., 651 n., 933 n.
Edward I 42, 64, 402 n., 801 n.
Edward III 57, 248, 252, 394 n., 651 n., 879
Edward IV 262
Edward VI, 106, 803 n., 932
Elizabeth, Queen 197, 262, 344, 404 n.,
    408, 414 n., 424–5, 746, 803 n.
Ephron 41 & n.
Epictetus 811
Epicurus 778
Esau 421
Expilly, Abbé, Jean Joseph d' 496 n., 905 & n.

F

Feaveryear, A. 57 n.
Ferdinand and Isabella 559, 589 n.
Feguson, Adam 412 n., 689–90 n., 782 n.,
    795 n., 870 n.
Firth, C. H. and Rait, R. S. 464 n.
Fleetwood, William 43 n., 51 n., 196 n.,
    199 n., 201 & n., 203 & n., 204, 205 n.,
    249 & n., 267 n., 268–71 n., 273
Folkes, M. 42 n., 195–6 n.
Forster, E. S., and Heffner, E. H. 169 n.,
    241 n.
Forster, J. R. 240 n.
Frederick of Holstein 806
Frézier, A. F. 186, 188, 222

G

Gama, Vasco de 559
Gassendi, Abbé Pierre 811
Gee, Josiah 432 n., 434 n., 476 n., 496 n.
Gemelli, *see* Carreri
Gengis Khan 429
Gesnerus (Gesner), J. M. 170 n.

Gilbert, Sir Geoffrey 391 & n.
Gilboy, E. W. 218 n.
Glaucus 38 & n.
Gorgias of Leontini 150 & n.
Gorgias of Mitylene 566 n., 777
Grant, I. F. 138
Gras, N. S. B. 204 n.
Gray, M. 133 n.
Green, T. H. and Grose, T. H. 47 n., 50 n.,
    90 n., 151 n., 171 n., 180 n., 291 n.,
    297 n., 299 n., 313 n., 325 n., 331 n.,
    354 n., 410 n., 412 n., 413 n., 419 n.,
    430 n., 435–6 n., 474 n., 511 n., 540 n.,
    567 n., 692 n., 795 n., 813 n., 896 n.,
    926 n.
Greig, J. Y. T. 425 n.
Grenville, George 618 n., 922 n.
Grotius 40 n., 45 n.
Guicciardini, Francesco 426 & n.
Gulvin, C. 252 n.
Gumilla, Joseph 563 n.
Gustavus, Vasa 806
Guttridge, G. H. 605 n., 615–17, 622–4,
    707

H

Habakkuk, H. J. 87 n.
Hailes, Lord 199–203 n., 205 n., 216 n.,
    399 n., 414 n., 551 n., 723 n.
Hale, Sir Matthew 95 n.
Halkett, S., and Laing, J. 690 n.
Hamilcar 702
Hamilton, H. 304 n., 313 n.
Hamilton, Sir William 67 n.
Hannibal 702–3, 706 n.
Hanway, J. 346 n.
Harris, J. 13–14 n., 28 n., 38 n., 40 n.,
    42–5 n., 47 n., 54 n., 57–8 n., 86 n.,
    117 n., 207 n., 234 n., 430 n., 477 n.,
    480 n., 512 n., 581 n.
Harte, W. 395 n.
Hasdrubal 702–3
Hawkins, Serjeant W. 648 & n.
Heaton, H. 102 n.
Henault, Charles, Jean, François 623
Herbert, Claude-Jacques 199 n., 216
Henry VII 353 n.
Henry VIII 806–7, 932
Henry IV of France 624, 909
Henry, Prince 167 & n., 168
Hesiod 768
Higgs, Henry 32 n., 38–40 n., 45 n., 47 n.,
    50–1 n., 85–6 n., 90 n., 97 n., 106 n.,
    112 n., 117 n., 119 n., 139 n., 160 n.,
    180 n., 184 n., 189 n., 210 n., 225 n.,
    229 n., 291 n., 320 n., 331 n., 354 n.,

358 n., 405 n., 425 n., 432 n., 436 n.,
    505 n., 512 n., 535 n., 581 n.,
    691 n.
Hippias 150, 777
Hobbes, Thomas 48 & n.
Homer 29 n., 38 & n., 692 n., 718 & n.,
    776 & n., 778
Hope, Henry, of Amsterdam 9
Horsefield, J. K. 213 n.
Horsely, W. 442 n.
Hull, C. H. 13 n., 88 n., 296 n.
Hume, D. 24 n., 28 n., 41 n., 43 n., 47 n.,
    50 n., 62 n., 72 n., 90 n., 94 n., 122 n.,
    151 n., 171 n., 180 n., 247 & n., 291 n.,
    293 n., 297 n., 299 n., 312–15 n.,
    325 & n., 331 n., 351–2 n., 354 & n.,
    385 n., 394 n., 398 n., 401 n., 403 n.,
    410 n., 412 & n., 413–16 n., 418–19 n.,
    425 n., 429–30 n., 432 n., 435–6 n.,
    445 & n., 474 n., 511 n., 540 n., 551 n.,
    566 n., 589 n., 605 n., 618 n., 654 n.,
    673 n., 692 n., 708 n., 740 n., 790–1 & n.,
    793 n., 795 n., 805–6 n., 813 n., 896 n.,
    911 n., 926 n.
Hutcheson, Francis 24 n., 28 n., 40 n.,
    44–5 n., 50 n., 52–3 n., 117 n., 124 n.,
    353 n., 358 n., 425 n., 581 n., 769 n.,
    827 n.
Hutchinson, Thomas 941 n.
Hyder, Ali 753

I

Isabella of Castile 559
Isocrates 149–50, 811

J

James I 34 n., 43 n., 57, 203 n., 347,
    706 n., 880, 932
James II 747
James V 201 n.
John, King of England 398 n., 402 & n.
John, King of France 932
Johnson, E. A. G. 581 n.
Johnson, Samuel 179 n.
Jones, E. L. 217 n.
Juan, G., and De Ulloa, A. 164 n., 187–8 n.,
    200 n., 222 n., 247 n.
Justamond, J. 225 n., 227 n., 511 n., 568 n.
    575–6 n., 589 n., 626 n.

K

Kalm, Peter 240 & n., 241 n.

Kames, Henry Home, Lord 412 n., 418 n.,
    425 n., 625 n., 689 n., 696 n., 782 n.,
    795 n., 827 n.
Kaye, F. B. 13 n., 20–2 n., 24 n., 26–7 n.,
    38 n., 45 n., 48 n., 73 n., 99 n., 118 n.,
    124 n., 126 n., 256 n., 257, 337 n.,
    341–2 n., 388 n., 432 n., 454 n., 465 n.,
    512 n., 759–60 n., 777 n., 870–1 n., 906 n.
King, Charles 462, 546
King, Gregory 88 n., 95 n., 215 & n.,
    296 n., 462 n.
Kippax, J. 222 n., 511 n., 900 n.
Kitchen, A. H., and Passmore, R. 93 n.
Knox, J. 950
Knox, W. 108, 442 n., 443 n.
Koebner, R. 625 n.
Kuczynski, M., and Meek, R. L. 672 n.
Kyd, J. G. 535 n.

L

Lange, Laurent, de 680 n.
Laverdy, Clement Charles François de 107
Law, John 37 n., 39 n., 45 n., 194 n.,
    317 & n., 353 & n., 429 n.
Lehmann, W. C. 389 n., 710 n.
Lester, R. A. 326 n.
Lewis the Fat 403
Lindsay, A. D. 775 n.
Livy 694 n., 775 n.
Lochiel, Cameron of 416, 417 n.
Locke, John 24 n., 54 n., 60 & n., 189 n.,
    353 & n., 357–8 n., 430 & n.,
    434 n., 496 n., 547, 710 n., 933 n.
Lorenzo de Medici 819
Lowndes, William 41 n., 213 & n., 478
Loyn, H. R. 41, 213 n.
Lucian 778 & n.
Luther, Martin 807
Lycurgus 436 & n.
Lysias 694 n., 811 & n.

M

Macedon, *see* Philip of
Machiavelli, N. 407, 426 n., 790 & n., 819 & n.
MacKay, D. 743–4 n.
MacKenzie, W. M. 140 n.
Madox, Thomas 136 n., 141 & n., 199 n.,
    399 & n., 401–2 & n.
Magens, Nicholas 60 n., 108 n., 226 & n.,
    229 & n., 320 n., 442 n., 444 n., 487 n.
Mahomet 113 n., 692 & n.
Mandeville, B. 13 n., 20–2 n., 24 n.,
    26–7 n., 38 n., 45 n., 48 n., 73 n., 99 n.,
    118 n., 124 n., 126 n., 256 n., 337–9 n.,

    341–2 n., 388 n., 432 n., 454 n., 465 n.,
    496 n., 512 n., 760 n., 777 n., 870 n.,
    906 n.
Marco Polo 89 & n., 559 & n., 560
Marcus, Antoninus 778
Maria Theresa 835
Marion, M. 358 n., 496 n.
Marshall, D. 152 n.
Medici, Lorenzo de 819
Meek, R. L. 14 n., 663 n., 672–3 n., 679 n.,
    689 n.
Melon, Jean François 924 n., 926 n., 932 n.
Mercier de la Riviere, Pierre Paul 679 & n.
Messance 102 & n., 199 n., 216 & n., 257 & n.
Methuen, John 546 & n.
Millar, John 388 n., 412 n., 689 n., 710 n.
Mingay, G. E. 392 n.
Mirabeau, Victor Riquetti, Marquis de
    663 n., 679 & n., 689 n.
Mitchell, B. R. 102 n., 302 n., 496 n.
Mitchison, R. 94 n.
Mithridates 568
Monteath, H. H. 385 n.
Montesquieu, Charles Louis de Secondat,
    Baron 19 n., 38–9 n., 43–4 n., 80–90 n.,
    112 n., 113 & n., 124 n., 341 n.,
    353 & n., 367 n., 382–3 n., 387 n.,
    399 n., 416–18 n., 474 n., 513 n., 556 n.,
    563 n., 565 n., 590 n., 624 n., 683 n.,
    684 & n., 689 n., 691–2 n., 696 n., 706 n.,
    711 n., 716 n., 722 n., 775 n., 776–7 n.,
    826–7 n., 849 n., 857 n., 931 n.
Montezuma 568
Moreau de Beaumont, J. L. 817 & n.,
    819–20, 830, 834–6, 845, 850–1, 855,
    859–61, 866, 869, 876, 899
Morellet, Abbé, André 663 n., 673 n.,
    679 n., 755 & n.
Morgan, E. V. 56–7 n.
Mun, Thomas 24 n., 431, 432 n., 434 n.,
    496 n., 555 n.
Mure, W. 134 n.

N

Necker, Jacques 62 n., 496 n., 507 n.,
    551 n., 905 & n.
Neumann, F. 19 n.
    see also Montesquieu
Newton, Isaac 123 n., 207, 229 n., 769 n.
Nicuessa, Diego de 562
Nugnes de Balboa, Vasco 562

O

Oieda, Don Alonzo de 562

Oldfather, C. H., and W. A. 175 n.
Oncken, A. 89 n., 391 n., 681 n.
  see also Quesnay
Orleans, Philippe, Duc de 317

P

Palladius 169, 170 n.
Paton, G. C. H. 385 n.
Paton, W. R. 775 n.
Payne, P. L. 186 n., 741 n.
Pelham, Henry 217, 915 n., 922 & n.,
  923
Penelope 551 & n.
Percy, Henry Algernon (Northumberland)
  197
Peter the Great 390 n., 706
Petty, Sir William 13 n., 88 n., 296 n.,
  535 n.
Pfeffel von Kriegelstein, C. F. 401 n.,
  403 n.
Philip of Macedon 150, 402, 702 & n.
Philip I of France 402
Phocyllides 758
Pitt, William, *see* Chatham
Pizarre, Francesco 562
Plano Carpino 429
Plato 45 n., 90 n., 150, 388, 775 & n., 778,
  811 & n.
Pliny 39 & n., 43 n., 56 n., 150 n., 236 & n.,
  388 & n., 685 & n., 931 n.
Plutarch 150 & n., 436 n., 777 n., 811
Pococke, Richard 413 & n.
Poivre, Pierre 173 & n., 679–80 n.
Polybius 774, 775 & n., 779, 812 n.
Porrée, Father, Charles 811
Postlethwayt, James 318 n., 912–13 n.,
  921–2 n.
Postlethwayt, Malachy 108 n.
Pownall, Thomas 25 n., 47–8 n.,
  50 n., 72 n., 87 n., 293–4 n., 321 n.,
  327 n., 362 n., 370 n., 452 n., 457 n.,
  461 n., 507 n., 515 n., 594 n., 599 n.,
  601–2 n., 605 n., 613–14 n., 616 n.,
  768–9 n.
Price, R. 88 n.
Protagoras 150, 777
Pufendorf 40 n., 45 n., 54 n., 175 n., 180 n.,
  754 n.
Pythagoras 566 n., 567, 678 n.

Q

Quesnay, François 89 n., 391 n., 467 n.,
  663 n., 672–3 & n., 674 n., 679 & n.,
  681 n.

Quintilian 812

R

Rae, J. 171 n., 358 n., 663 n., 811 n.
Raleigh, Sir Walter 563 & n., 564
Ramazzini, Bernadino 100 & n.
Raynal, Abbé Guillaume, Thomas François
  225 n., 226–7 & n., 444 n., 511 n.,
  575 n., 589 n., 626 n.
Riquet, Pierre Paul de (the engineer) 726
Robert II, of France 805
Robertson, William 412 n., 626 n., 768 n.
Rousseau, J. J. 689 n.
Ruddiman, Thomas 203 & n., 230 & n.,
  298 n.
Ruffhead, Owen 40 n., 42–3 n., 60 n.,
  106 n., 136–7 n., 139 n., 147 n., 153 n.,
  155 n., 195 n., 202 & n., 248 n., 251 n.,
  318 n., 424 n., 452 n., 459 n., 468 n.,
  470 n., 501 n., 523 n., 538, 552 n., 580 n.,
  582 n., 642 n., 644–5 n., 648–51 n.,
  654–6 n., 734 n., 742 n., 748–9 n.,
  809 n., 846 n., 849 n., 852 n., 875 n.,
  880–1 n., 915 n.

S

Sandi, Victor 407 n.
Saxby, H. 248 n., 501 n., 536 n., 642–3 n.,
  874–5 n., 881 n., 883 n.
Scipio 685 n., 703, 812 n.
Schumpeter, E. B. 373 n., 476 n.
Scott, Lady Frances 674 n.
Scott, Sir Walter 315 n.
Scott, W. R. 21 n., 252 n., 298 n., 318 n.,
  403 n., 412 n., 742 n., 744 n., 747–8 n.,
  756 n.
Seius, Marcus 236
Sen, S. R. 751
Seneca 588 n.
Servius Tullius 39 & n., 42
Sesostris 25 n., 80 n., 681 n.
Seymour, family of 347
Sforza, Ludovic, Duke of Milan 408 n.
Shannon, H. A. 741 n.
Sinclair, Sir John 173 n., 442 n., 518 n.,
  614–16 n., 740 n., 817 n., 871 n.
Skene, Sir J. 203 n.
Skinner, A. S., *see* Steuart
Smith, Adam:
  America, Thoughts on 605, 615–17,
    622–3, 625, 707
  Ancient Physics 770
  Astronomy 20, 21, 35, 381, 406, 566, 678,
    767, 777

Smith, Charles 199, 211, 217–18, 272, 461, 506, 508, 534, 536, 538
Smith, John 248, 252, 652
Smout, T. C. 182 n., 186 n.
Solomon 768
Solon 112 n., 543 & n., 777 & n.
Solorzano, Pereira, Juan de 219 n.
Stair, Lord (James Dalrymple) 383 n.
Stark, W. 351 n.
Stephens, Walker 689 n.
Steuart, Sir James 9 n., 19 n., 44 n., 46 n., 62 n., 73–4 n., 94 n., 97 n., 133–4 n., 139 n., 181 n., 235 n., 317 n., 325 n., 331 n., 357 n., 409 n., 412 n., 414 n., 425 n., 436 n., 479 n., 581 n., 612 n., 689 n., 691 n., 733, 751 n., 795 n., 827 n., 870 n., 876
Stewart, Dugald 67 n., 674 n., 687 n., 768 n.
Suetonius 812
Sutherland, L. S. 751 n.
Swift, Jonathan 496 n., 882 & n.

T

Tavernier, Jean Baptiste 191 & n.
Tartar, Khan 422
Terray, Abbé, Joseph Marie 107
Thales 567
Theocritus 118 & n.
Theognis 768
Thom, William 761 n.
Thorn, William 196
Thucydides 692 & n., 693, 694 n.
Timaeus 39 & n.
Troll, Gustav, Archbishop of Upsala 806
Turgot, A. J. 14 n., 73 n., 276 n., 337–8 n., 358 n., 360 n., 391 n., 663 n., 672–3 n., 689 n., 817
Tyrell, James 716 & n.

U

Ulloa, Antonio 164 & n., 186–8 & n., 205,

220 n., 222 & n., 247 n., 568 & n., 574 n., 576 & n.
Uztariz, G. 222 n., 511 n., 899, 900 n.

V

Varro 170 & n., 241 & n.
Vasa, Gustav 806
Vedius Pollio 587 & n., 588 n.
Virgil 590 n.
Voltaire 487 n., 811 & n.

W

Walpole, Sir Robert 886 & n., 926
Ward, J. T. and Wilson, R. G. 412 n.
Warwick, Richard Neville, the Earl of 413 & n., 415 n.
Webster, A. 495 n., 535 n.
Wedderburn, Alexander 605 n.
Whateley, Thomas 618 n., 922
William the Conqueror 43
Whitworth, C. 88 n., 95 n., 215 n., 599 n., 891 n.
William Rufus 413
William III (of Orange) 60, 215, 868, 879

X

Xenophon 446 n., 593 n.

Y

Youngson, A. J. 183 n., 518 n.

Z

Zeno of Citta 778
Zeno of Elea 777
Zwinglius, Huldrich 808

Index of Statutes

51 Henry III (Bread and Ale) 42, 196, 202

51 Henry III (Tumbrel and Pillory) 202

28 Edward I, c. 20 (1300) 139 & n., 296 n.

25 Edward III, st. 2 (1350) 147 & n., 195 & n.

28 Edward III, c. 5 (1354) 656 n.

15 Henry VI, c. 2 (1436) 198 & n.

3 Edward IV, c. 2 (1463) 198 & n.

3 Edward IV, c. 4 (1463) 642 & n.

3 Edward IV, c. 5 (1463) 262 & n.

4 Edward IV, c. 1 (1464) 452 & n.

4 Edward IV, c. 8 (1464) 655 & n.

4 Henry VII, c. 8 (1488) 261 n.

33 Henry VIII, c. 7 (1541) 656 & n.

37 Henry VIII, c. 9 (1545) 106 & n., 354 & n.

2 & 3 Edward VI, c. 37 (1548) 656 & n.

5 & 6 Edward VI, c. 14 (1551) 528 & n. (2), 532 & n. (2)

5 & 6 Edward VI, c. 20 (1551) 106 & n.

5 & 6 Edward VI, c. 25 (1551) 852, 856 n.

1 & 2 Philip and Mary, c. 5 (1554) 198 & n. (2)

1 Elizabeth I, c. 11 (1558) 198 & n. (2)

5 Elizabeth I, c. 4 (1562) 137 & n.

5 Elizabeth I, c. 5 (1562) 198 & n.

5 Elizabeth I, c. 12 (1562) 528 & n., 532 & n.

5 Elizabeth I, c. 22 (1562) 251 & n.

8 Elizabeth I, c. 11 (1566) 136

8 Elizabeth I, c. 14 (1566) 251 & n.

13 Elizabeth I, c. 8 (1571) 106

18 Elizabeth I, c. 6 (1575) 52 & n.

18 Elizabeth I, c. 9 (1575) 251 & n.

39 Elizabeth I, c. 14 (1597) 642 & n.

39 Elizabeth I, c. 20 (1597) 139 & n.

43 Elizabeth I, c. 2 (1601) 152 & n., 153

43 Elizabeth I, c. 10 (1601) 139 & n.

1 James I, c. 17 (1603) 136 & n.

1 James I, c. 25 (1603) 655 & n.

7 James I, c. 14 (1609) 655 & n.

21 James I, c. 17 (1623) 106 & n., 354 & n.

3 Charles I, c. 5 (1627) 642 & n.

12 Charles II, c. 4 (1660) 499, 500, 501 n., 537, 643 & n., 655 & n., 656 & n., 658 & n., 880 & n. (2)

12 Charles II, c. 13 (1660) 106 & n., 354 & n., 849 & n.

12 Charles II, c. 16 (1660) 137 & n., 470 & n.

12 Charles II, c. 18 (1660) 463 & n., 577 & n., 595 & n.

12 Charles II, c. 32 (1660) 648 & n., 649 & n., 654 & n.

12 Charles II, c. 34 (1660) 174 & n.

14 Charles II, c. 2 (1662) 852 & n.

14 Charles II, c. 5 (1662) 136 & n.

14 Charles II, c. 7 (1662) 251 & n., 654 & n.

14 Charles II, c. 10 (1662) 845 & n.

14 Charles II, c. 11 (1662) 655 & n., 656 & n.

14 Charles II, c. 12 (1662) 153 & n., 155 & n.

14 Charles II, c. 13 (1662) 468 & n.

14 Charles II, c. 18 (1662) 248 & n., 648 & n., 649 & n., 654 & n., 655 & n., 881 & n.

14 Charles II, c. 19 (1662) 642 & n.

15 Charles II, c. 7 (1663) 424 & n., 425, 502 & n. (2), 532 & n., 533, 534, 537 & n., 538

15 Charles II, c. 13 (1663) 845 & n.

15 Charles II, c. 15 (1663) 152 & n.

16 Charles II, c. 3 (1664) 845 & n.

18 & 19 Charles II, c. 2 (1666) 424 & n., 452 & n., 459 & n., 875 & n.

18 & 19 Charles II, c. 5 (1666) 552 & n.

19 & 20 Charles II, c. 10 (1667) 655 & n.

19 & 20 Charles II, c. 11 (1670) 136 & n.

22 Charles II, c. 13 (1670) 424 & n., 452, 459 & n., 515 & n., 536, 537 & n., 875 & n.

25 Charles II, c. 6 (1672) 464 & n., 879 & n.

25 Charles II, c. 7 (1672) 735 & n.

32 Charles II, c. 2 (1680) 425 & n.

1 James II, c. 3 (1685) 501 & n.

1 James II, c. 17 (1685) 153 & n.

1 William and Mary c. 10 (1688) 846 & n.

1 William and Mary c. 12 (1688) 212 & n., 215 & n., 506 & n., 537 & n., 875 & n.

1 William and Mary, sess. 1, c. 13 (1688) 868 & n.

1 William and Mary, c. 32 (1688) 650, 651 & n.

1 William and Mary, sess. 2. c. 7 (1688) 868 & n.

2 William and Mary, c. 2 (1689) 742 & n.

3 William and Mary, c. 6 (1691) 868 & n.

3 William and Mary, c. 11 (1691) 153 & n., 154 & n.

4 William and Mary, c. 1 (1692) 828 & n.

4 William and Mary, c. 3 (1692) 916 & n.

4 William and Mary, c. 5 (1692) 473 & n., 500 & n., 501 & n.

4 William and Mary, c. 15 (1692) 742 & n.

5 William and Mary, c. 5 (1693) 916 & n.

5 & 6 William and Mary, c. 17 (1694) 656

5 & 6 William and Mary, c. 20 (1694) 318 & n., 916 & n.

6 & 7 William and Mary, c. 5 (1694) 916 & n.

7 & 8 William III, c. 1 (1695) 60 & n.

7 & 8 William III, c. 2 (1695) 916 & n.

7 & 8 William III, c. 18 (1695) 846 & n.

7 & 8 William III, c. 19 (1695) 655 & n.

7 & 8 William III, c. 20 (1695) 473 & n., 501 & n., 659 & n.

7 & 8 William III, c. 28 (1695) 648 & n., 650 & n., 655 & n.

8 & 9 William III, c. 20 (1696) 318, 913 & n.

8 & 9 William III, c. 25 (1696) 852 & n.

8 & 9 William III, c. 30 (1696) 155 & n.

9 William III, c. 9 (1697) 468 & n.

9 William III, c. 11 (1697) 155 & n. (2)

9 William III, c. 23 (1697) 501 & n., 880 & n.

9 William III, c. 26 (1697) 656 & n., 742 & n.

9 William III, c. 27 (1697) 852 & n.

9 William III, c. 28 (1697) 507, 655 n.

9 William III, c. 40 (1697) 650 & n.

9 William III, c. 44 (1697) 747 & n.

10 William III, c. 3 (1698) 213 & n.

10 William III, c. 6 (1698) 734 & n.

10 William III, c. 16 (1698) 248 & n., 582 & n., 649 & n.

11 William III, c. 11 (1698) 468 & n.

11 William III, c. 20 (1698) 538

12 & 13 William III, c. 11 (1700) 852 & n.

1 Anne, st. 2, c. 22 (1702) 158 & n.

2 & 3 Anne, c. 18 (1703) 501 & n., 880 & n.

3 & 4 Anne, c. 3 (1704) 501 & n., 880 & n.

3 & 4 Anne, c. 9 (1704) 508 & n., 644 & n., 645 & n.

3 & 4 Anne, c. 18 (1704) 852 & n.

6 Anne, c. 50 (1707) 756

6 Anne, c. 71 (1707) 742 & n., 748 & n., 749 & n.

7 Anne, c. 30 (1708) 318 & n.

8 Anne, c. 10 (1709) 846 & n., 875 & n.

9 Anne, c. 6 (1710) 655 & n., 875 & n.

9 Anne, c. 12 (1710) 251 & n., 655 & n.

9 Anne, c. 15 (1710) 742 & n.

9 Anne, c. 16 (1710) 852 & n.

10 Anne, c. 21 (1711) 809 & n.

10 Anne, c. 23 (1711) 40 & n., 139 & n.

10 Anne, c. 34 (1711) 742 & n.

12 Anne, c. 9 (1712) 645 & n.

12 Anne, c. 12 (1712) 523 & n.

12 Anne, c. 14 (1712) 137 & n., 470 & n.

12 Anne, c. 18 (1712) 155 & n.

13 Anne, c. 11 (1713) 147 & n.

13 Anne, c. 15 (1713) 106 & n., 354 & n., 849 & n., 915 & n.

13 Anne, c. 18 (1713) 655 & n.

1 George I, c. 12 (1714) 501 & n., 914 & n.

3 George I, c. 7 (1716) 914 & n.

3 George I, c. 8 (1716) 319 & n., 914 & n.

4 George I, c. 11 (1717) 649 & n.

5 George I, c. 3 (1718) 914 & n.

5 George I, c. 19 (1718) 917 & n.

5 George I, c. 27 (1718) 659 & n.

5 George I, c. 30 (1718) 394 & n.

6 George I, c. 4 (1719) 917 & n.

6 George I, c. 18 (1719) 756 & n.

7 George I, st. 1, c. 13 (1720) 84 & n., 158 & n.

7 George I, st. 1, c. 21 (1720) 500 & n., 881 & n.

8 George I, c. 12 (1721) 645 & n. (2)

8 George I, c. 15 (1721) 523 & n., 643 & n., 656 & n. (2), 658 & n.

8 George I, c. 21 (1721) 319 & n.

9 George I, c. 6 (1722) 746 & n.

9 George I, c. 7 (1722) 155 & n.

12 George I, c. 34 (1725) 84 & n.

12 George I, c. 35 (1725) 84 & n.

13 George I, c. 26 (1726) 40 & n.,
  139 & n.

2 George II, c. 35 (1728) 645 & n.

3 George II, c. 28 (1729) 579 & n.

4 George II, c. 27 (1730) 643 & n.,
  881 & n.

4 George II, c. 29 (1730) 523 & n.

5 George II, c. 22 (1731) 136 & n.,
  582 & n.

6 George II, c. 28 (1732) 746 & n.

12 George II, c. 21 (1738) 642 & n.,
  649 & n.

12 George II, c. 30 (1738) 578 & n.

13 George II, c. 8 (1739) 158 & n.

17 George II, c. 17 (1743) 749 & n.

18 George II, c. 9 (1744) 502 & n.

18 George II, c. 36 (1744) 473 & n.,
  501 & n., 644 & n.

20 George II, c. 3 (1746) 846 & n.

20 George II, c. 50 (1746) 393 & n.

21 George II, c. 2 (1747) 523 & n.,
  880 & n.

21 George II, c. 26 (1747) 473 & n.,
  501 & n., 644 & n.

21 George II, c. 30 (1747) 645 & n.
  (2)

22 George II, c. 27 (1748) 84 & n.

23 George II, c. 13 (1749) 659 & n.

23 George II, c. 24 (1749) 518 & n.,
  522

23 George II, c. 29 (1749) 580 & n.,
  582 & n., 643 & n.

23 George II, c. 31 (1749) 737 & n.,
  743 & n.

24 George II, c. 46 (1750) 643 & n.

25 George II, c. 32 (1751) 657 & n.

25 George II, c. 40 (1751) 743 & n.

26 George II, c. 1 (1753) 915 & n.

26 George II, c. 8 (1753) 643 & n.

26 George II, c. 18 (1753) 735 & n.

26 George II, c. 21 (1753) 501 & n.

28 George II, c. 25 (1755) 645 & n.

29 George II, c. 15 (1756) 643 & n.,
  881 & n.

30 George II, c. 4 (1757) 915 & n.

30 George II, c. 7 (1757) 538

31 George II, c.12 (1757) 838 & n.

31 George II, c. 22 (1757) 846 & n.,
  867 & n.

31 George II, c. 29 (1757) 158 & n.

32 George II, c. 10 (1758) 853 & n.,
  880 & n.

32 George II, c. 11 (1758) 425 & n.,
  452 & n., 459 & n., 875 & n.

32 George II, c. 32 (1758) 473 & n.,
  501 & n., 644 & n.

1 George II, c. 7 (1760) 872 & n.

3 George III, c. 6 (1762) 158 & n.

3 George III, c. 8 (1762) 137 & n.,
  470 & n.

3 George III, c. 12 (1762) 502 & n.

3 George III, c. 25 (1763) 645 & n.

4 George III, c. 1 (1763) 425 & n.

4 George III, c. 9 (1763) 658 & n.

4 George III, c. 15 (1764) 503 & n.,
  577, 583 & n.

4 George III, c. 20 (1764) 738 & n.

4 George III, c. 25 (1764) 319 & n.

4 George III, c. 26 (1764) 645 & n.

4 George III, c. 34 (1764) 327 & n.

5 George III, c. 10 (1765) 425 & n.,
  459 & n., 875 n.

5 George III, c. 18 (1765) 838 & n.

5 George III, c. 37 (1765) 657 & n.,
  881 & n.

5 George III, c. 44 (1765) 738 & n.

5 George III, c. 45 (1765) 579 & n.,
  646 & n.

5 George III, c. 49 (1765) 297 & n.,
  322 & n., 326 & n.

6 George III, c. 28 (1766) 452 & n.,
  501 & n.

6 George III, c. 52 (1766) 579 & n.,
  643 & n.

7 George III, c. 28 (1766) 452 & n.

7 George III, c. 43 (1766) 473 & n.,
  501 & n., 644 & n.

7 George III, c. 49 (1767) 750 & n.

8 George III, c. 9 (1768) 425 & n.

8 George III, c. 11 (1768) 750 & n.

8 George III, c. 17 (1768) 157 & n.,
  158 & n.

9 George III, c. 24 (1769) 750 & n.

9 George III, c. 25 (1769) 552 & n.

9 George III, c. 38 (1769) 646 & n.

9 George III, c. 39 (1769) 250 & n.,
  643 & n.

10 George III, c. 38 (1770) 643 & n.,
  644 & n., 881 & n.

10 George III, c. 51 (1770) 393 & n.

11 George III, c. 31 (1771) 518 & n.

11 George III, c. 38 (1771) 518 & n.,
  578 & n.

11 George III, c. 49 (1771) 452 & n.,
  501 & n.

11 George III, c. 50 (1771) 646 & n.

12 George III, c. 2 (1772) 425 & n.
  (2), 459 & n., 875 n.

12 George III, c. 54 (1772) 223 & n.

12 George III, c. 71 (1772) 533 & n.
  (2)

13 George III, c. 43 (1772) 541 & n.

13 George III, c. 63 (1772) 751 & n.

14 George III, c. 10 (1774) 658 & n.,
  881 & n.

14   George III, c. 70 (1774) 58 & n.
14   George III, c. 71 (1774) 659 & n.
14   George III, c. 86 (1774) 250 & n.,
         643 & n.
15   George III, c. 31 (1775) 643 & n.
15   George III, c. 51 (1775) 326 & n.
17   George III, c. 39 (1776) 857 & n.
17   George III, c. 44 (1776) 645 & n.
18   George III, c. 26 (1778) 843 & n.
18   George III, c. 27 (1778) 502 & n.
18   George III, c. 30 (1778) 857 & n.
19   George III, c. 25 (1779) 502 & n.
19   George III, c. 27 (1779) 643 & n.,
         644 & n., 881 & n.

19   George III, c. 37 (1779) 646 & n.
19   George III, c. 59 (1779) 843 & n.
20   George III, c. 30 (1780) 502 & n.
21   George III, c. 29 (1781) 250 n.,
         251, 643
22   George III, c. 51 (1782) 753 & n.
22   George III, c. 66 (1782) 502 & n.
22   George III, c. 73 (1782) 174 & n.
23   George III, c. 36 (1783) 753
23   George III, c. 83 (1783) 753 & n.
3   George IV, c. 41 (1822) 648 & n.
19 & 20   Victoria, c. 64 (1856) 649 & n.
10   Edward VII, 1 George V, c. 8
         (1910) 533 & n.

Index of the Acts of the Parliaments of Scotland

Act of takis of landis for termes and takis of wadset landis eftir the oute quyting of the lande, 1449 (APS, ii. 35) 393 & n.

Act anent the having of the money furth of the Realme, 1487 (APS, ii. 183) 431 & n.

Act anent the punisement of strang and ydle beggaris and provisioun for the sustentatioun of the puyr and impotent, 1574 (APS, iii. 86–9) 149 & n.

Act for Erecting a Publick Bank, 1695 (APS, ix. 494–5) 297 & n., 756

Act allowing the Exportation of Wool, etc., 1704 (APS, xi. 190) 252 & n.

Original Index

A

Absentee tax, the propriety of, considered, with reference to Ireland, 895.

Accounts of money, in modern Europe, all kept, and the value of goods computed, in silver, 57.

Actors, public, paid for the contempt attending their profession, 124.

Africa, cause assigned for the barbarous state of the interior parts of that continent, 35–6.

African company, establishment and constitution of, 737. Receive an annual allowance from parliament for forts and garrisons, 739. The company not under sufficient controul, ib. History of the Royal African company, 741–3. Decline of, ib. Rise of the present company, 743.

Age, the foundation of rank and precedency in rude as well as civilized societies, 711.

Aggregate fund, in the British finances, explained, 914.

Agio of the bank of Amsterdam explained, 479. Of the bank of Hamburgh, 480. The agio at Amsterdam, how kept at a medium rate, 486.

Agriculture, the labour of does not admit of such subdivisions as manufactures, 16. This impossibility of separation, prevents agriculture from improving equally with manufactures, ib. Natural state of, in a new colony, 109. Requires more knowledge and experience than most mechanical professions, and yet is carried on without any restrictions, 143. The terms of rent, how adjusted between landlord and tenant, 160. Is extended by good roads and navigable canals, 163. Under what circumstances pasture land is more valuable than arable, 165. Gardening not a very gainful employment, 169–70. Vines the most profitable article of culture, 170. Estimates of profit from projects, very fallacious, ib. Cattle and tillage mutually improve each other, 237. Remarks on that of Scotland, 239. Remarks on that of North America, 240–1. Poultry a profitable article in husbandry, 242. Hogs, 243. Dairy, 244–5. Evidences of land being completely improved, 245. The extension of cultivation as it raises the price of animal food, reduces that of vegetables, 259.

Agriculture, by whom and how practised under feudal government, 334. Its operations not so much intended to increase, as to direct, the fertility of nature, 363–4. Has been the cause of the prosperity of the British colonies in America, 366. The profits of, exaggerated by projectors, 374. On equal terms, is naturally preferred to trade, 377. Artificers necessary to the carrying it on, 378. Was not attended to by the Northern destroyers of the Roman Empire, 381–2. The ancient policy of Europe unfavourable to, 396. Was promoted by the commerce and manufactures of towns, 422. The wealth arising from, more solid and durable, than that which proceeds from commerce, 427. Is not encouraged by the bounty on the exportation of corn, 509. Why the proper business of new companies (colonies), 609.

The present agricultural system of political oeconomy adopted in France, described, 663. Is discouraged by restrictions and prohibitions in trade, 671–2. Is favoured beyond manufactures, in China, 679. And in Indostan, 681. Does not require so extensive a market as manufactures, 682. To check manufactures, in order to promote agriculture, false policy, 686. Landlords ought to be encouraged to cultivate part of their own land, 832.

Alcavala, the tax in Spain so called, explained and considered, 899. The ruin of the Spanish manufactures attributed to this tax, ib.

Alehouses, the number of, not the efficient cause of drunkenness, 362, 492.

Allodial rights, mistaken for feudal rights, 415–16. The introduction of the feudal law tended to moderate the authority of the allodial lords, 417–18.

Ambassadors, the first motive of their appointment, 732.

America, why labour is dearer in North America than in England, 87–8. Great increase of population there, 88. Common rate of interest there, 109. Is a new market for the produce of its own silver mines, 220. The first accounts of the two empires of Peru and Mexico, greatly exaggerated, 221, 448. Improving state of the Spanish colonies, ib. Account of the paper currency of the British colonies, 326–8.

Cause of the rapid prosperity of the British colonies there, 366. Why manufactures for distant sale have never been established there, 378–9. Its speedy improvements owing to assistance from foreign capitals, 380. The purchase and improvement of uncultivated land, the most profitable employment of capitals, 423–4. Commercial alterations produced by the discovery of, 447–8. But two civilized nations found on the whole continent, 448. The wealth of the North American colonies increased, though the balance of trade continued against them, 497–8.

Madeira wine, how introduced there, 502. Historical review of the European settlements in 559. Of Spain, 567–8. Of Holland, 571. Of France, 571. Of Britain ib. Ecclesiastical government in the several European colonies, 574. Fish a principal article of trade from North America to Spain, Portugal, and the Mediterranean, 578. Naval stores to Britain, 579. Little credit due to the policy of Europe from the success of the colonies, 588. The discovery and colonization of, how far advantageous to Europe, 591. And to America, 626. The colonies in, governed by a spirit of monopoly 630–1. The interest of the consumer in Britain sacrificed to that of the producer, by the system of colonization, 661–2. Plan for extending the British system of taxation over all the provinces of, 934–5. The question how the Americans could pay taxes without specie considered, 940. Ought in justice to contribute to discharge the public debt of Great Britain, 944. Expediency of their union with Great Britain, 944–5. The British empire there, a mere project, 947.

Amsterdam, agio of the bank of, explained, 479. Occasion of its establishment, 480. Advantages attending payments there, 481. Rate demanded for keeping money there, 482. Prices at which bullion and coin are received, 482–3. *Note*. This bank, the great warehouse of Europe for bullion, 484. Demands upon, how made and answered, 485. The agio of, how kept at a medium rate, 486. The treasure of, whether all preserved in its repositories, ib. The amount of its treasure only to be conjectured, 487. Fees paid to the bank for transacting business, ib.

Annuities for terms of years, and for lives, in the British finances, historical account of, 915–17.

Apothecaries, the profit on their drugs unjustly stigmatized as exorbitant, 28–9.

Apprenticeship, the nature and intention of this bond servitude explained, 119. The limitations imposed on various trades, as to the number of apprentices, 135–6. The statute of apprenticeship in England, 137. Apprenticeships in France and Scotland, 137–8. General remarks on the tendency and operation of long apprenticeships, 138–40.

The statute of, ought to be repealed, 470.

Arabs, their manner of supporting war, 690–1.

Army, three different ways by which a nation may maintain one in a distant country, 441.

Standing, distinction between and a militia, 698. Historical review of, 701. The Macedonian army, 702. Carthaginian army, 702–3. Roman army, 703–4. Is alone able to perpetuate the civilization of a country, 705–6. Is the speediest engine for civilizing a barbarous country, 706. Under what circumstances dangerous to, and under what, favourable to liberty, 706–7.

Artificers, prohibited by law from going to foreign countries, 659. Residing abroad, and not returning on notice, exposed to outlawry, 660. See *Manufactures*.

Asdrubal, his army greatly improved by discipline, 702. How defeated, 703.

Assembly, houses of, in the British colonies, the constitutional freedom of, shewn, 585.

Assiento contract, 745.

Assize of bread and ale, remarks on that statute, 196, 201–2.

Augustus, emperor, emancipates the slaves of Vedius Pollio, for his cruelty, 587.

B

Balance of annual produce and consumption explained, 497. May be in favour of a nation, when the balance of trade is against it, 497–8.

Balance of trade, no certain criterion to determine on which side it turns between two countries, 412. The current doctrine of, on which most regulations of trade are founded, absurd, 488. If even, by the exchange of their native commodities, both sides may be gainers, 489. How the balance would stand if native commodities on one side, were paid with foreign commodities on the other, ib. How the balance stands when commodities are purchased

with gold and silver, 490–1. The ruin of countries often predicted from the doctrine of an unfavourable balance of trade, 496.

Banks great increase of trade in Scotland, since the establishment of them in the principal towns, 297. Their usual course of business, 298–9. Consequences of their issuing too much paper, 301–2. Necessary caution for some time observed by them with regard to giving credit to their customers, 305. Limits of the advances they may prudently make to traders, 306–7. How injured by the practice of drawing and redrawing bills, 311. History of the Ayr bank, 313. History of the bank of England, 318. The nature and public advantage of banks considered, 320–1. Bankers might carry on their business with less paper, 323–4. Effects of the optional clauses in the Scots notes, 325–6.

    Origin of their establishment, 480. Bank money explained, 481. Of England, the conduct of, in regard to the coinage, 552.

    Joint stock companies why well adapted to the trade of banking, 756–7. A doubtful question whether the government of Great Britain is equal to the management of the Bank to profit, 818.

Bankers, the credit of their notes, how established, 292. The nature of the banking business explained, 292, 298.

    The multiplication and competition of bankers under proper regulation, of service to public credit, 329.

Baretti, Mr. his account of the quantity of Portugal gold sent weekly to England, 547.

Barons, feudal, their power contracted, by the grant of municipal privileges, 401. Their extensive authority, 415. How they lost their authority over their vassals, 418–19. And the power to disturb their country, 421.

Barter, the exchange of one commodity for another, the propensity to of extensive operation, and peculiar to man, 25. Is not sufficient to carry on the mutual intercourse of mankind, 37. See *Commerce*.

Batavia, causes of the prosperity of the Dutch settlement there, 635.

Beaver skins, review of the policy used in the trade for, 658.

Beef, cheaper now in London, than in the reign of James I, 167. Compared with the prices of wheat at the corresponding times, 167–8.

Benefices, ecclesiastical, the tenure of, why rendered secure, 798. The power of collating to, how taken from the Pope, in England and France, 804. General equality of, among the Presbyterians, 809. Good effects of this equality, 810.

Bengal, to what circumstance its early improvement in agriculture and manufactures was owing, 35. Present miserable state of the country, 91. Remarks on the high rates of interest there, 111.

    Oppressive conduct of the English there to suit their trade in opium, 636. Why more remarkable for the exportation of manufactures than of grain, 683.

Berne, brief history of the republic, 403. Establishment of the reformation there, 806. Application of the revenue of the Catholic clergy, 812–13. Derives a revenue from the interest of its treasure, 819.

Bills of exchange, punctuality in the payment of, how secured, 309. The pernicious practice of drawing and redrawing explained, 309–10. The arts made use of to disguise this mutual traffic in bills, 311–12.

Birth, superiority of, how it confers respect and authority, 713.

Bishops, the ancient mode of electing them, and how altered, 800, 804–5.

Body, natural and political, analogy between, 674.

Bohemia, account of the tax there on the industry of artificers, 866.

Bounties, why given in commerce, 450. On exportation, the policy of granting them considered, 505. On the exportation of corn, 506. This bounty imposes two taxes on the people, 508. Evil tendency of this bounty, 513–14. The bounty only beneficial to the exporter and importer, 514. Motives of the country gentlemen in granting the bounty, 515. A trade which requires a bounty, necessarily a losing trade, 516. Tonnage bounties to the fisheries considered, 518. Account of the white herring fishery, 522. Remarks on other bounties, 522–3. A review of the principles on which they are generally granted, 644. Those granted on American produce founded on mistaken policy, 647. How they affect the consumer, 661.

Bounty on the exportation of corn, the tendency of this measure examined, 212–13.

Bourdeaux, why a town of great trade, 335–6.

Brazil, grew to be a powerful colony under neglect, 569. The Dutch invaders expelled by the

Portugueze colonists, 569. Computed number of inhabitants there, 569. The trade of the principal provinces oppressed by the Portuguese, 575.

Bread, its relative value with butcher's meat compared, 164, 167.

Brewery, reasons for transferring the taxes on, to the malt, 889.

Bridges, how to be erected and maintained, 724.

Britain, Great, evidences that labour is sufficiently paid for there, 91. The price of provisions nearly the same in most places, 92. Great variations in the price of labour, 92. Vegetables imported from Flanders in the last century, 96. Historical account of the alterations interest of money has undergone, 106. Double interest deemed a reasonable mercantile profit, 114.

In what respects the carrying trade is advantageous to, 371. Appears to enjoy more of the carrying trade of Europe, than it really has, 373. Is the only country of Europe in which the obligation of purveyance is abolished, 394. Its funds for the support of foreign wars inquired into, 442. Why never likely to be much affected by the free importation of Irish cattle, 459–60. Nor salt provisions, 460. Could be little affected by the importation of foreign corn, 461. The policy of the commercial restraints on the trade with France examined, 473–4. The trade with France might be more advantageous to each country than that with any other, 495. Why one of the richest countries in Europe, while Spain and Portugal are among the poorest, 541. Review of her American colonies, 572–5. The trade of her colonies, how regulated, 576–7. Distinction between enumerated and non-enumerated commodities, explained 577. Restrains manufactures in America, 581. Indulgences granted to the colonies, 583. Constitutional freedom of her colony government, 584. The sugar colonies of, worse governed than those of France, 586. Disadvantages resulting from retaining the exclusive trade of tobacco with Maryland and Virginia, 595. The navigation act has increased the colony trade, at the expence of many other branches of foreign trade, 596. The advantage of the colony trade estimated, 600. A gradual relaxation of the exclusive trade, recommended, 606. Events which have concurred to prevent the ill effects of the loss of the colony trade, 606–7. The natural good effects of the colony trade, more than counterbalance the bad effects of the monopoly, 608–9. To maintain a monopoly, the principal end of the dominion assumed over the colonies, 615. Has derived nothing but loss from this dominion, 616. Is perhaps the only state which has only increased its expences by extending its empire, 621. The constitution of, would have been completed by admitting of American representation, 624. Review of the administration of the East India Company, 638. The interest of the consumer sacrificed to that of the producer in raising an empire in America, 661–2.

The annual revenue of, compared with its annual rents and interest of capital stock, 822. The land-tax of, considered, 828. Tythes, 837. Window tax, 846. Stamp duties, 860–1, 863–4. Poll taxes in the reign of William III, 868. The uniformity of taxation in, favourable to internal trade, 900. The system of taxation in, compared with that in France, 905. Account of the unfunded debt of, 911. Funded debt, 912. Aggregate, and general funds, 914. Sinking fund, 915. Annuities for terms of years and for lives, 916. Perpetual annuities the best transferable stock, 919. The reduction of the public debts during peace, bears no proportion to their accumulation during war, 921. The trade with the tobacco colonies, how carried on, without the intervention of specie, 941–2. The trade with the sugar colonies explained, 942. Ireland and America ought in justice to contribute toward the discharge of her public debts, 944. How the territorial acquisitions of the East India company might be rendered a source of revenue, 945. If no such assistance can be obtained, her only resource pointed out, 946.

Bullion, the money of the great mercantile republic, 443. See *Gold* and *Silver*.

Burghs, free, the origin of, 400. To what circumstances they owed their corporate jurisdictions, 400–1. Why admitted to send representatives to parliament, 404. Are allowed to protect refugees from the country, 405.

Burn, Dr., his observations on the laws relating to the settlements of the poor, 153–6.

Butcher's meat, no where a necessary of life, 876.

C

Calvinists, origin of that sect, 807. Their principles of church government, 808.

Cameron, Mr., of Lochiel, exercised within thirty years since, a criminal jurisdiction over his own tenants, 416.

Canada, the French colony there, long under the government of an exclusive company, 571. But improved speedily after the dissolution of the company, ib.

Canals, navigable, the advantages of, 163. How to be made and maintained, 724. That of Languedoc, the support of, how secured, 726. May be successfully managed by joint stock companies, 756–7.

Cantillon, Mr. Remarks on his account of the earnings of the labouring poor, 85.

Cape, of Good Hope, causes of the prosperity of the Dutch settlement there, 635.

Capital, in trade, explained, and how employed, 279. Distinguished into circulating and fixed capitals, ib. Characteristic of fixed capitals, 282. The several kinds of fixed capitals specified, ib. Characteristic of circulating capitals, and the several kinds of, 282–3. Fixed capitals supported by those which are circulating, 283. Circulating capitals how supported, 284. Intention of a fixed capital, 287. The expence of maintaining the fixed and circulating capitals, illustrated, 288. Money as an article of circulating capital, considered, 288. Money, no measure of capital, 291. What quantity of industry any capital can employ, 295. Capitals, how far they may be extended by paper credit, 306.

Must always be replaced with profit by the annual produce of land, and labour, 332. The proportion between capital and revenue, regulates the proportion between industry and idleness, 337. How it is increased or diminished, ib. National evidences of the increase of, 343. In what instances private expences contribute to enlarge the national capital, 346–7. The increase of, reduces profits by competition, 352. The different ways of employing a capital, 360. How replaced to the different classes of traders, 362. That employed in agriculture puts into motion a greater quantity of productive labour, than any equal capital employed in manufactures, 364. That of a manufacturer should reside within the country, ib. The operation of capitals employed in agriculture, manufactures, and foreign trade, compared, 365–6. The prosperity of a country depends on the due proportion of its capital applied to these three grand objects, 367–8. Different returns of capitals employed in foreign trade, 369. Is rather employed on agriculture than in trade and manufactures, on equal terms, 377. Is rather employed in manufactures than in foreign trade, 379. The natural progress of the employment of, 380. Acquired by trade, is very precarious until realized by the cultivation and improvement of land, 426. The employment of, in the different species of trade, how determined, 453–4.

Capitation taxes, the nature of, considered, 867. In England, 868. In France, 868–9.

Carriage, land and water, compared, 32–3. Water carriage contributes to improve arts and industry, in all countries where it can be used, 34, 163, 224.

Land, how facilitated and reduced in price, by public works, 724–5.

Carrying trade, the nature and operation of, examined, 370–1. Is the symptom, but not the cause, of national wealth, and hence points out the two richest countries in Europe, 373. Trades may appear to be carrying trades, which are not so, ib. The disadvantages of, to individuals, 454. The Dutch, how excluded from being the carriers to Great Britain, 463. Drawbacks of duties originally granted for the encouragement of, 503.

Carthaginian army, its superiority over the Roman army, accounted for, 702.

Cattle, and corn, their value compared, in the different stages of agriculture, 164. The price of, reduced by artificial grasses, 167. To what height the price of cattle may rise in an improving country, 237. The raising a stock of, necessary for the supply of manure to farms, 238. Cattle must bear a good price to be well fed, ib. The price of, rises in Scotland in consequence of the union with England, 239–40. Great multiplication of European cattle in America, 240. Are killed in some countries, merely for the sake of the hides and tallow, 247. The market for these articles more extensive than for the carcase, ib. This market sometimes brought nearer home by the establishment of manufactures, ib. How the extension of cultivation raises the price of animal food, 259.

Is perhaps the only commodity more expensive to transport by sea than by land, 459. Great Britain never likely to be much affected by the free importation of Irish cattle, ib.

Certificates, parish, the laws relating to, with observations on them, 155.

Child, Sir Josiah, his observation on trading companies, 737.

Children, riches unfavourable to the production, and extreme poverty to the raising, of them, 96–7. The mortality still greater among those maintained by charity, 97.

China, to what the early improvement in arts and industry there was owing, 35. Concurrent testimonies of the misery of the lower ranks of the Chinese, 89–90. Is not however a

declining country, 90. High rate of interest of money there, 112. The price of labour there, lower than in the greater part of Europe, 224. Great state assumed by the grandees, 223. Silver the most profitable article to send thither, 224–5. The proportional value of gold to silver, how rated there, 229. The value of gold and silver much higher there than in any part of Europe, 255. Agriculture favoured there, beyond manufactures, 679. Foreign trade not favoured there, 680. Extension of the home-market, 681. Great attention to the roads there, 729. In what the principal revenue of the sovereign consists, 838. The revenue of, partly raised in kind, 839.

Church, the richer the church, the poorer the state, 812. Amount of the revenue of the church of Scotland, 813. The revenue of the church heavier taxed in Prussia, than lay proprietors, 835. The nature and effect of tythes considered, 837.

Circulation, the dangerous practice of raising money by, explained, 309–10. In traffic the two different branches of, considered, 322.

Cities, circumstances which contributed to their opulence, 405. Those of Italy the first that rose to consequence, 406. The commerce and manufactures of, have occasioned the improvement and cultivation of the country, 422.

Clergy, a supply of, provided for, by public and private foundations for their education, 146. Curates worse paid than many mechanics, ib.

Of an established religion, why unsuccessful against the teachers of a new religion, 789. Why they persecute their adversaries, ib. The zeal of the inferior clergy of the church of Rome, how kept alive, 789–90. Utility of ecclesiastical establishments, 791. How connected with the civil magistrate, 792. Unsafe for the civil magistrate to differ with them, 797. Must be managed without violence, 798–9. Of the church of Rome, one great army cantoned over Europe, 800. Their power similar to that of the temporal barons, during the feudal monkish ages, 800–1. How the power of the Romish clergy declined, 803. Evils attending allowing parishes to elect their own ministers, 808–9.

Cloathing, more plentiful than food, in uncultivated countries, 178. The materials for, the first articles rude nations have to offer, ib.

Coal, must generally be cheaper than wood to gain the preference for fuel, 182–3. The price of, how reduced, 184.

The exportation of, subjected to a duty higher than the prime cost of, at the pit, 658–9. The cheapest of all fuel, 874. The tax on, absurdly regulated, 874–5.

Coal mines, their different degrees of fertility, 182. When fertile, are sometimes unprofitable by situation, 182, 185. The proportion of rent generally paid for, 184–5. The machinery necessary to, expensive, 280.

Coal trade from Newcastle to London, employs more shipping than all the other carrying trade of England, 371.

Cochin China, remarks on the principal articles of cultivation there, 173.

Coin, stamped, the origin, and peculiar advantages of, in commerce, 40. The different species of, in different ages and countries, 42. Causes of the alterations in the value of, 43, 49, 52. How the standard coin of different nations came to be of different metals, 56. A reform in the English coinage suggested, 62. Silver, consequences attending the debasement of, 213. Coinage of France and Britain, examined, 477. Why coin is privately melted down, 550–1. The mint chiefly employed to keep up the quantity thus diminished, 551. A duty to pay the coinage would preserve money from being melted or counterfeited, ib. Standard of the gold coin in France, 551–2. How a seignorage on coin would operate, 552. A tax upon coinage is advanced by every body, and finally paid by nobody, 554. A revenue lost, by government defraying the expence of coinage, ib. Amount of the annual coinage before the late reformation of the gold coin, 555. The law for the encouragement of, founded on prejudice, ib.

Consequences of raising the denomination of, as an expedient to facilitate payment of public debts, 929. Adulteration of, 932.

Colbert, M., the policy of his commercial regulations disputed, 467, 664. His character, 663.

Colleges, cause of the depreciation of their money rents inquired into, 52. The endowments of, from whence they generally arise, 759. Whether they have in general answered the purposes of their institution, ib. These endowments have diminished the necessity of application in the teachers, 760. The privileges of graduates by residence, and charitable foundation of scholarships, injurious to collegiate education, 762. Discipline of, 764.

Colliers and coal-heavers, their high earnings accounted for, 121.

Colonies, new, the natural progress of, 109.

Modern, the commercial advantages derived from them, 451. Ancient, on what principles founded, 556. Ancient Grecian colonies not retained under subjection to the parent states, ib. Distinction between the Roman and Greek colonies, ib. Circumstances that led to the establishment of European colonies in the East Indies and America, 558. The East Indies discovered by Vasco de Gama, 559. The West Indies discovered by Columbus, ib. Gold the object of the first Spanish enterprises there, 562. And of those of all other European nations, 564. Causes of the prosperity of new colonies, 564. Rapid progress of the ancient Greek colonies, 566. The Roman colonies slow in improvement, 567. The remoteness of America and the West Indies, greatly in favour of the European colonies there, ib. Review of the British American colonies, 572. Expence of the civil establishments in British America, ib. Ecclesiastical government, 574. General view of the restraints laid upon the trade of the European colonies, 575. The trade of the British colonies, how regulated, 576. The different kinds of non-enumerated commodities specified, 577. Enumerated commodities, 579. Restraints upon their manufactures, 581. Indulgences granted them by Britain, 583. Were free in every other respect except as to their foreign trade, 584. Little credit due to the policy of Europe from the success of the colonies, 588. Throve by the disorder and injustice of the European governments, 589. Have contributed to augment the industry of all the countries of Europe, 591. Exclusive privileges of trade, a dead weight upon all these exertions both in Europe and America, 592. Have in general been a source of expence instead of revenue to their mother countries, 594. Have only benefited their mother countries by the exclusive trade carried on with them, ib. Consequences of the navigation act, 595. The advantage of the colony trade to Britain estimated, 600. A gradual relaxation of the exclusive commerce recommended, 606. Events which have prevented Britain from sensibly feeling the loss of the colony trade, ib. The effects of the colony trade, and the monopoly of that trade, distinguished, 607. To maintain a monopoly, the principal end of the dominion Great Britain assumes over the colonies, 614. Amount of the ordinary peace establishment of, 615. The two late wars Britain sustained colony wars, to support a monopoly, 615–16. Two modes by which they might be taxed, 619. Their assemblies not likely to tax them, ib. Taxes by parliamentary requisition, as little likely to be raised, 620. Representatives of, might be admitted into the British parliament with good effect, 622–3. Answer to objections against American representation, 624. The interest of the consumer in Britain, sacrificed to that of the producer, in raising an empire in America, 661.

Columbus, the motive that led to his discovery of America, 559. Why he gave the names of Indies to the islands he discovered, 559–60. His triumphal exhibition of their productions, 561.

Columella, his instruction for fencing a kitchen-garden, 169–70. Advises the planting of vineyards, 170.

Commerce, the different common standards or mediums made use of to facilitate the exchange of commodities, in the early stages of, 38. Origin of money, 38–9. Definition of the term *value*, 44.

Treaties of, though advantageous to the merchants and manufacturers of the favoured country, necessarily disadvantageous to those of the favouring country, 545. Translation of the commercial treaty between England and Portugal concluded in 1703 by Mr. Methuen, 546. Restraints laid upon the European colonies in America, 575. The present splendor of the mercantile system, owing to the discovery and colonization of America, 627. Review of the plan by which it proposes to enrich a country, 642. The interest of the consumer constantly sacrificed to that of the producer, 660. See *Agriculture, Banks, Capital, Manufactures, Merchants, Money, Stock, Trade,* &c.

Commodities, the barter of, insufficient for the mutual supply of the wants of mankind, 37. Metals found to be the best medium to facilitate the exchange of, 38. Labour an invariable standard for the value of, 50. Real and nominal prices of, distinguished, 51. The component parts of the prices of, explained and illustrated, 67. The natural, and market prices of, distinguished, and how regulated, 72. The ordinary proportion between the value of any two commodities, not necessarily the same as between the quantities of them commonly in the market, 229. The price of rude produce, how affected by the advance of wealth and improvement, 235.

Foreign, are primarily purchased with the produce of domestic industry, 368. When advantageously exported in a rude state, even by a foreign capital, 379. The quantity of, in

every country, naturally regulated by the demand, 435. Wealth in goods, and in money, compared, 438. Exportation of, to a proper market, always attended with more profit, than that of gold and silver, ib. The natural advantages of countries in particular productions, sometimes not possible to struggle against, 458.

Company, mercantile, incapable of consulting their true interests when they become sovereigns, 637. An exclusive company, a public nuisance, 641.

Trading, how first formed, 733. Regulated, and joint stock companies, distinguished, ib. Regulated companies in Great Britain, specified, 734. Are useless, 735. The constant view of such companies, 736. Forts and garrisons, why never maintained by regulated companies, 737. The nature of joint stock companies explained, 740–55. A monopoly necessary to enable a joint stock company to carry on a foreign trade, 754. What kind of joint stock companies need no exclusive privileges, 756. Joint stock companies, why well adapted to the trade of banking, ib. The trade of insurance may be carried on successfully by a stock company, ib. Also inland navigations, and the supply of water to a great city, 756–7. Ill success of joint stock companies in other undertakings, 758.

Competition, the effect of, in the purchase of commodities, 73–4. Among the venders 74, 105.

Concordat, in France, its object, 804–5.

Congress, American, its strength owing to the important characters it confers on the members of it, 623.

Conversion price, in the payment of rents in Scotland, explained, 200–1.

Copper, the standard measure of value among the ancient Romans, 56. Is no legal tender in England, 57.

Cori, the largest quadruped on the island of St. Domingo, described, 560.

Corn, the raising of, in different countries, not subject to the same degree of rivalship as manufactures, 16–17. Is the best standard for reserved rents, 52. The price of, how regulated, 53. The price of, the best standard for comparing the different values of particular commodities at different times and places, 55–6. The three component parts in the price of, 68. Is dearer in Scotland than in England, 93. Its value compared with that of butchers meat, in the different periods of agriculture, 164, 168. Compared with silver, 195. Circumstances in a historical view of the prices of corn, that have misled writers in treating of the value of silver at different periods, 200. Is always a more accurate measure of value, than any other commodity, ib. Why dearer in great towns than in the country, 209. Why dearer in some rich commercial countries, as Holland and Genoa, ib. Rose in its nominal price on the discovery of the American mines, 210. And in consequence of the civil war under king Charles I., 212. And in consequence of the bounty on the exportation of, ib. Tendency of the bounty examined, 215–16. Chronological table of the prices of, 267–76.

The least profitable article of growth in the British West Indian colonies, 389. The restraints formerly laid upon the trade of, unfavourable to the cultivation of land, 396. The free importation of, could little affect the farmers of Great Britain, 459. The policy of the bounty on the exportation of, examined, 506. The reduction in the price of corn, not produced by the bounty, 507. Tillage not encouraged by the bounty, 507–9. The money price of, regulates that of all other home-made commodities, 509. Illustration, 511. Ill effects of the bounty, 513–4. Motives of the country gentlemen in granting the bounty, 515. The natural value of corn not to be altered by altering the money price, ib. The four several branches of the corn trade specified, 524. The inland dealer, for his own interest will not raise the price of corn higher than the scarcity of the season requires, ib. Corn a commodity the least liable to be monopolized, 525. The inland dealers in corn too numerous and dispersed to form a general combination, 526. Dearths never artificial, but when government interferes improperly to prevent them, ib. The freedom of the corn trade, the best security against a famine, 527. Old English statute to prohibit the corn trade, 528. Consequences of farmers being forced to become corn dealers, 529. The use of corn dealers to the farmers, 531. The prohibitory statute against the corn trade softened, 532. But still under the influence of popular prejudices, 533. The average quantity of all corn imported and exported, compared with the consumption and annual produce, 534. Tendency of a free importation of corn, 535. The home market the most important one for corn, 536. Duties payable on the importation of grain, before 13 Geo. III., ib., *note*. The impropriety of the statute 22 Car. II. for regulating the importation of wheat, confessed by the suspension of its execution, by temporary statutes, 536. The home-market indirectly supplied by the exportation of corn, 537.

How a liberal system of free exportation and importation, among all nations, would operate, 538. The laws concerning corn, similar to those relating to religion, 539. The home-market supplied by the carrying trade, ib. The system of laws connected with the establishment of the bounty, undeserving of praise, 540. Remarks on the statute 13 Geo. III., 541.

Corporations, tendency of the exclusive privileges of, on trade, 79, 135. By what authority erected, 140. The advantages corporations derive from the surrounding country, 141. Check the operations of competition, 144. Their internal regulations, combinations against the public, 145. Are injurious, even to the members of them, 146. The laws of, obstruct the free circulation of labour, from one employment to another, 152.

The origin of, 400. Are exempted by their privileges from the power of the feudal barons, 401. The European East India Companies disadvantageous to the eastern commerce, 449. The exclusive privileges of corporations ought to be destroyed, 470.

Cottagers, in Scotland, their situation described, 133. Are cheap manufacturers of stockings, 134. The diminution of, in England, considered, 243.

Coward, character of, 788.

Credit. See *Paper-money*.

Crusades to the Holy Land, favourable to the revival of commerce, 406.

Currency of states, remarks on, 479.

Customs, the motives and tendency of drawbacks from the duties of, 499. The revenue of the customs increased, by drawbacks, 503.

Occasion of first imposing the duties of, 732. Origin of those duties, 878. Three ancient branches of, 879. Drawbacks of, 880. Are regulated according to the mercantile system, 881. Frauds practised to obtain drawbacks and bounties, 882. The duties of, in many instances uncertain, 883. Improvement of, suggested, ib. Computation of the expence of collecting them, 896.

D

Dairy, the business of, generally carried on as a save-all, 244. Circumstances which impede or promote the attention to it, ib. English and Scotch dairies, 244–6.

Danube, the navigation of that river why of little use to the interior parts of the country from whence it flows, 36.

Davenant, Dr. his objections to the transferring the duties on beer to the malt, considered, 891.

Dearths, never caused by combinations among the dealers in corn, but by some general calamity, 526. The free exercise of the corn trade the best palliative against the inconveniences of a dearth, 532. Corn dealers the best friends to the people at such seasons, 535.

Debts, public, the origin of, traced, 909. Are accelerated by the expences attending war, ib. Account of the unfunded debt of Great Britain, 911. The funded debt, 912. Aggregate and general funds, 914. Sinking fund, 915, 921. Annuities for terms of years, and for lives, 916. The reduction of, during peace, bears no proportion to its accumulation during war, 921. The plea of the interest being no burden to the nation, considered, 926–7. Are seldom fairly paid when accumulated to a certain degree, 929. Might easily be discharged, by extending the British system of taxation over all the provinces of the empire, 933. Ireland and America ought to contribute to discharge the public debts of Britain, 944.

Decker, Sir Matthew, his observation on the accumulation of taxes, 873. His proposal for transferring all taxes to the consumer, by annual payments, considered, 877.

Demand, though the increase of, may at first raise the price of goods, it never fails to reduce it afterward, 748.

Denmark, account of the settlements of, in the West Indies, 570.

Diamonds, the mines of, not always worth working for, 191.

Discipline, the great importance of, in war, 700. Instances, 701.

Diversions, public their political use, 796.

Domingo, St. mistaken by Columbus for a part of the East Indies, 559. Its principal productions, 560. The natives soon stripped of all their gold, 561–2. Historical view of the French colony there, 571.

Doomsday book, the intention of that compilation, 834.

Dorians, ancient, where the colonies of, settled, 556.

Dramatic exhibitions, the political use of, 796.

Drawbacks, in commerce, explained, 450. The motives to, and tendency of, explained, 499. On wines, currants, and wrought silks, ib. On tobacco and sugar, 500. On wines, particularly considered, 501. Were originally granted to encourage the carrying trade, 503. The revenue of the customs increased by them, ib. Drawbacks allowed in favour of the colonies, 584.

Drugs, regulations of their importation and exportation, 656–7.

Drunkenness, the motive to this vice inquired into, 492–3.

Dutch, their settlements in America slow in improvement because under the government of an exclusive company, 570. Their East India trade checked by monopoly, 632. Measures taken by, to secure the monopoly of the spice trade, 636. See *Holland*.

E

East India. Representation of the miserable state of the provinces of, under the English settlement there, 91. Historical view of the European trade with those countries, 222–3. Rice countries more populous and rich than corn countries, 223. The real price of labour lower in China and Indostan, than in the greater part of Europe, 224. Gold and silver the most profitable commodities to carry thither, ib. The proportional value of gold to silver, how rated there, 229.

Great extension of foreign commerce by the discovery of a passage to, round the cape of Good Hope, 448. Historical review of the intercourse with, 449. Effect of the annual exportation of silver to, from Europe, ib. The trade with, chiefly carried on by exclusive companies, 631. Tendency of their monopolies, ib.

Company, a monopoly against the very nation in which it is erected, 631. The operation of such a company in a poor, and in a rich country, compared, 632. That country whose capital is not large enough to tend to such a distant trade ought not to engage in it, 634. The mercantile habits of trading companies render them incapable of consulting their true interests when they become sovereigns, 638. The genius of the administration of the English company, ib. Subordinate practices of their agents and clerks, 638–9. The bad conduct of agents in India owing to their situation, 641. Such an exclusive company a nuisance in every respect, ib.

Brief review of their history, 746. Their privileges invaded, 747. A rival company formed, ib. The two companies united, 748–9. Are infected by the spirit of war and conquest, 749. Agreements between the company and government, 749–50. Interference of government in their territorial administration, 751. And in the direction at home, 751–2. Why unfit to govern a great empire, 752. Their sovereign and commercial characters, incompatible, 819. How the territorial acquisitions of, might be rendered a source of revenue, 945.

Edinburgh, its present share of trade owing to the removal of the court and parliament, 336.

Education, the principal cause of the various talents observable in different men, 28–9.

Those parts of, for which there are no public institutions, generally the best taught, 764. In universities, a view of, 771–2. Of travelling for, 773–4. Course of, in the republics of ancient Greece, 774. In ancient Rome, 774–6. The ancient teachers superior to those in modern times, 780. Public institutions injurious to good education, 781. Inquiry how far the public ought to attend to the education of the people, ib. The different opportunities of education in the different ranks of the people, 784–5. The advantages of a proper attention in the state to the education of the people, 788.

Egypt, the first country in which agriculture and manufactures appear to have been cultivated, 34–5.

Agriculture was greatly favoured there, 681. Was long the granary of the Roman empire, 683.

Ejectment, action of, in England, when invented, and its operation, 392.

Employments, the advantages and disadvantages of the different kinds of, in the same neighbourhood, continually tend to equality, 116. The differences or inequalities among, specified, 116–17. The constancy or precariousness of, influences the rate of wages, 120.

England, the dates of its several species of coinage, silver, gold and copper, 57. Why labour is cheaper there, than in North America, 87. The rate of population in both countries compared, 88.

The produce and labour of, have gradually increased from the earliest accounts in history, while writers are representing the country as rapidly declining, 344. Enumeration of obstructions and calamities which the prosperity of the country has surmounted, 345. Circumstances that favour commerce and manufactures, 424. Laws in favour of agriculture, 424–5. Why formerly unable to carry on foreign wars of long duration, 445. Why the commerce with France has been subjected to so many discouragements, 495. Foundation of the enmity between these countries, 496. Translation of the commercial treaty concluded in 1703, with Portugal, 546. Inquiry into the value of the trade with Portugal, 547–8. Might procure gold without the Portugal trade, 548. Consequences of securing the colony trade by the navigation act, 595.

Engrossing. See *Forestalling.*

Entails, the law of, prevents the division of land by alienation, 382. Intention of, 384.

Europe, general review of the several nations of, as to their improvement since the discovery of America, 220. The two richest countries in, enjoy the greatest shares of the carrying trade, 373. Inquiry into the advantages derived by, from the discovery and colonization of America, 591. The particular advantages derived by each colonizing country, 593. And by others which have no colonies, 627.

Exchange, the operation of, in the commercial intercourse of different countries, 432–3. The course of, an uncertain criterion of the balance of trade between two countries, 475–6. Is generally in favour of those countries which pay in bank money, against those which pay in common currency, 488.

Excise, the principal objects of, 878. The duties of, more clear and distinct than the customs, 883. Affects only a few articles of the most general consumption, ib. The excise scheme of Sir Robert Walpole defended, 886. The excise upon home-made fermented and spirituous liquors, the most productive, 887. Expence of levying excise duties computed, 896. The laws of, more vexatious than those of the customs, 898.

Exercise, military, alteration in, produced by the invention of fire arms, 699.

Expences, private, how they influence the national capital, 346. The advantage of bestowing them on durable commodities, 346–9.

Export trade, the principles of, explained, 372. When rude produce may be advantageously exported, even by a foreign capital, 379–80. Why encouraged by European nations, 449. By what means promoted, 450. The motives to, and tendency of, drawbacks of duties, 499. The grant of bounties on, considered, 505. Exportation of the materials of manufactures, review of the restraints and prohibitions of, 647.

F

Faith, articles of, how regulated by the civil magistrate, 797–8.

Families, seldom remain on large estates for many generations in commercial countries, 421.

Famine. See *Dearth.*

Farmers of land, the several articles that compose their gain, distinguished, 70. Require more knowledge and experience than the generality of manufacturers, 144. In what their capitals consist, 280.

The great quantity of productive labour put into motion by their capitals, 363. Artificers necessary to them, 378. Their situation better in England than in any other part of Europe, 392. Labour under great disadvantages every where, 394–5. Origin of long leases of farms, 421. Are a class of men least subject to the wretched spirit of monopoly, 461. Were forced, by old statutes, to become the only dealers in corn, 529. Could not sell corn cheaper than any other corn merchant, 530. Could seldom sell it so cheap, 531. The culture of land obstructed by this division of their capitals, ib. The use of corn dealers to the farmers, 531–2.

How they contribute to the annual production of the land, according to the French agricultural system of political œconomy, 665. Of the public revenue, their character, 902, 919.

Feudal government, miserable state of the occupiers of land under, 334. Trade and interest under, 334–5. Feudal chiefs, their power, 383. Slaves, their situation, 386–7. Tenures of land, 389. Taxation, 394. Original poverty and servile state of the tradesmen in towns, 397. Immunities seldom granted but for valuable considerations, 398. Origin of free burghs, 400. The power of the barons reduced by municipal privileges, 401–2. The cause and effect

of ancient hospitality, 412–13. Extensive power of the ancient barons, 415. Was not established in England until the Norman conquest, 416. Was silently subverted by manufactures
and commerce, 418.

Feudal wars, how supported, 694. Military exercises not well attended to, under, 697. Standing armies gradually introduced to supply the place of the feudal militia, 705. Account of
the casualties or taxes under, 858. Revenues under, how enjoyed by the great landholders,
907.

Fiars, public, in Scotland, the nature of the institution explained, 200.

Fines, for the renewal of leases, the motive for exacting them, and their tendency, 831.

Fire arms, alteration in the art of war, effected by the invention of, 699, 708. The invention of,
favourable to the extension of civilization, 707–8.

Fish, the component parts of the price of, explained, 69. The multiplication of, at market, by
human industry, both limited and uncertain, 252, How an increase of demand raises the
price of fish, 253.

Fisheries, observations on the tonnage bounties granted to, 518. To the herring fishery, 519.
The boat fishery ruined by this bounty, 521.

Flanders, the ancient commercial prosperity of, perpetuated by the solid improvements of
agriculture, 427.

Flax, the component parts of the price of, explained, 68.

Fleetwood, bishop, remarks on his Chronicon Preciosum, 201, 204.

Flour, the component parts of the price of, explained, 68.

Food, will always purchase as much labour as it can maintain on the spot, 162. Bread and
butcher's meat compared, 164, 167. Is the original source of every other production, 182.
The abundance of, constitutes the principal part of the riches of the world, and gives the
principal value to many other kinds of riches, 192.

Forestalling and engrossing, the popular fear of, like the suspicions of witchcraft, 534.

Forts, when necessary for the protection of commerce, 731–2.

France, fluctuations in the legal rate of interest for money there, during the course of the present century, 107. Remarks on the trade and riches of, 107–8. The nature of apprenticeships
there, 137–8. The propriety of restraining the planting of vineyards, examined, 170, 174–5.
Variations in the price of grain there, 198–9. The money price of labour has sunk gradually
with the money price of corn, 219. Foundation of the Mississippi scheme, 317. Little trade
or industry to be found in the parliament towns of, 335. Description of the class of farmers
called metayers, 389. Laws relating to the tenure of land, 393. Services formerly exacted be-
side rent, ib. The taille, what, and its operation in checking the cultivation of land, 394. Origin of the magistrates and councils of cities, 403. No direct legal encouragement given to
agriculture, 425. Ill policy of M. Colbert's commercial regulations, 467. French goods
heavily taxed in Great Britain, 474. The commercial intercourse between France and
England now chiefly carried on by smugglers, 474. The policy of the commercial restraints
between France and Britain considered, 474–5. State of the coinage there, 478. Why the
commerce with England has been subjected to discouragements, 495. Foundation of the
enmity between these countries, 496.

Remarks concerning the seignorage on coin, 551–2. Standard of the gold coin there, 552.
The trade of the French colonies, how regulated, 576. The government of the colonies conducted with moderation, 586. The sugar colonies of, better governed, than those of Britain,
586. The Kingdom of, how taxed, 620–1. The members of the league, fought more in
defence of their own importance, than for any other cause, 624.

The present agricultural system of political œconomy adopted by philosophers there, described, 663. Under what direction the funds for the repair of the roads are placed, 728.
General state of the roads, 729. The universities badly governed, 762. Remarks on the management of the parliaments of, 799. Measures taken in, to reduce the power of the clergy,
804–5. Account of the mode of rectifying the inequalities of the predial taille in the generality of Montauban, 836. The personal taille explained, 854. The inequalities in, how reme-
died, 855. How the personal taille discourages cultivation, 856–7. The Vingtieme, 858.
Stamp duties and the controle, 861–3. The capitation tax, how rated, 868. Restraints upon
the interior trade of the country by the local variety of the revenue laws, 900–1. The duties
on tobacco and salt, how levied, 903. The different sources of revenue in, 904. How the
finances of, might be reformed, ib. The French system of taxation compared with that in

Britain, 905. The nature of tontines explained, 917. Estimate of the whole national debt of, 918.

Frugality, generally a predominating principle in human nature, 341.

Fuller's earth, the exportation of, why prohibited, 654.

Funds, British, brief historical view of, 911. Operation of, politically considered, 923. The practice of funding, has gradually enfeebled every state that has adopted it, 928.

Fur trade, the first principles of, 178.

G

Gama, Vasco de, the first European who discovered a naval track to the East Indies, 559.

Gardening, the gains from, distinguished into the component parts, 71. Not a profitable employment, 169.

Gems. See *Stones.*

General fund, in the British finances, explained, 914.

Genoa, why corn is dear in the territory of, 209.

Glasgow, the trade of, doubled in fifteen years, by erecting banks there, 297. Why a city of greater trade than Edinburgh, 336.

Gold, not the standard of value in England, 57. Its value measured by silver, 58. Reformation of the gold coin, 58, 59. Mint price of gold in England, 59. The working the mines of, in Peru, very uprofitable, 188. Qualities for which this metal is valued, 191. The proportional value of, to silver, how rated before and after the discovery of the American mines, 228–9. Is cheaper in the Spanish market than silver, 231. Great quantities of, remitted annually from Portugal to England, 547. Why little of it remains in England, 548. Is always to be had for its value, ib.

Gold and *silver*, the prices of, how affected by the increase of the quantity of the metals, 207. Are commodities that naturally seek the best market, 208. Are metals of the least value among the poorest nations, 209. The increase in the quantity of, by means of wealth and improvement, has no tendency to diminish their value, 210. The annual consumption of these metals very considerable, 225. Annual importation of, into Spain and Portugal, 226–7. Are not likely to multiply beyond the demand, 228. The durability of, the cause of the steadiness of their price, ib. On what circumstances the quantity of, in every particular country, depends, 253. The low value of these metals in a country, no evidence of its wealth, nor their high value of its poverty, 256.

If not employed at home, will be sent abroad notwithstanding all prohibitions, 340. The reason why European nations have studied to accumulate these metals, 430–1. Commercial arguments in favour of their exportation, 431–2. These, and all other commodities, are mutually the price of each other, 435. The quantity of, in every country, regulated by the effectual demand, ib. Why the prices of these metals do not fluctuate so much as those of other commodities, 437. To preserve a due quantity of, in a country, no proper object of attention for the government, ib. The accumulated gold and silver in a country distinguished into three parts, 441. A great quantity of bullion alternately exported and imported for the purposes of foreign trade, 443. Annual amount of these metals imported into Spain and Portugal, 444. The importation of, not the principal benefit derived from foreign trade, 446. The value of, how affected by the discovery of the American mines, 447. And by the passage round the Cape of Good Hope to the East Indies, 448. Effect of the annual exportation of silver to the East Indies, 449. The commercial means pursued to increase the quantity of these metals in a country, 450, 474. Bullion how received and paid at the bank of Amsterdam, 481. At what prices, 482–3.

Note. A trading country without mines, not likely to be exhausted by an annual exportation of these metals, 491. The value of, in Spain and Portugal, depreciated by restraining the exportation of them, 511. Are not imported for the purposes of plate or coin but for foreign trade, 549. The search after mines of, the most ruinous of all projects, 562. Are valuable, because scarce, and difficult to be procured, 563.

Gorgias, evidence of the wealth he acquired by teaching, 150.

Government, civil, indispensably necessary for the security of private property, 710. Subordination in society, by what means introduced, ib. Inequality of fortune introduces civil

government for its preservation, 715. The administration of justice, a source of revenue, in early times, ib. Why government ought not to have the management of turnpikes, 727–8. Nor of other public works, 730. Want of parsimony during peace, imposes a necessity of contracting debts to carry on a war, 909. Must support a regular administration of justice to cause manufactures and commerce to flourish, 910. Origin of a national debt, 910–11. Progression of public debts, 911. War, why generally agreeable to the people, 920.

Governors, political, the greatest spendthrifts in society, 346.

Grasses, artificial, tend to reduce the price of butcher's meat, 167.

Graziers, subject to monopolies obtained by manufacturers to their prejudice, 655.

Greece, foreign trade prohibited in several of the ancient states of, 683. Military exercises, a part of general education, 696. Soldiers not a distinct profession, in, ib. Course of education in the republics of, 774. The morals of the Greeks inferior to those of the Romans, ib. Schools of the philosophers and rhetoricians, 777. Law no science among the Greeks, 778. Courts of justice, ib. The martial spirit of the people, how supported, 787.

Greek colonies, how distinguished from Roman colonies, 558. Rapid progress of these colonies, 566.

Greek language, how introduced as part of university education, 766. Philosophy, the three great branches of, ib.

Ground rents, great variations of, according to situation, 840–1. Are a more proper subject of taxation than houses, 843.

Gum senega, review of the regulations imposed on the trade for, 657–8.

Gunpowder, great revolution effected in the art of war by the invention of, 699, 707–8. This invention favourable to the extension of civilization, 708.

Gustavus, Vasa, how enabled to establish the reformation in Sweden, 806.

H

Hamburgh, agio of the bank of, explained, 480.

Sources of the revenue of that city, 817–18, 820. The inhabitants of, how taxed to the state, 850.

Hanseatic league, causes that rendered it formidable, 403. Why no vestige remains of the wealth of the Hans towns, 426.

Hearth money, why abolished in England, 845–6.

Henry VIII, of England, prepares the way for the reformation by shutting out the authority of the Pope, 806–7.

Herring buss bounty, remarks on, 519. Fraudulent claims of the bounty, 520. The boat fishery the most natural and profitable, 521. Account of the British white-herring fishery 522. Account of the busses fitted out in Scotland, the amount of their cargoes, and the bounties on them, 948.

Hides, the produce of rude countries, commonly carried to a distant market, 246. Price of, in England three centuries ago, 249. Salted hides inferior to fresh ones, 250. The price of, how affected by circumstances, in cultivated and in uncultivated countries, 251.

Highlands of Scotland, interesting remarks on the population of, 97. Military character of the Highlanders, 701.

Hobbes, Mr. remarks on his definition of wealth, 48.

Hogs, circumstances which render their flesh cheap or dear, 243.

Holland, observations on the riches and trade of the republic of, 108. Not to follow some business, unfashionable there, 113. Cause of the dearness of corn there, 209.

Enjoys the greatest share in the carrying trade of Europe, 373. How the Dutch were excluded from being the carriers to Great Britain, 463. Is a country that prospers under the heaviest taxation, 467. Account of the Bank of Amsterdam, 480. This republic derives even its subsistence from foreign trade, 497.

Tax paid on houses there, 845. Account of the tax upon successions, 859. Stamp duties, 861. High amount of taxes in, 875, 905–6. Its prosperity depends on the republican form of government, 906.

Honoraries from pupils to teachers in colleges, tendency of, to quicken their diligence, 760.

Hose, in the time of Edward IV, how made, 262.

Hospitality, ancient, the cause and effect of, 412–13, 907.

House, different acceptations of the term in England, and some other countries, 134–5. Houses considered as part of the national stock, 281. Houses produce no revenue, 281, 282.

The rent of distinguished into two parts, 840. Operation of a tax upon house rent, payable by the tenant, 841. House rent the best test of the tenant's circumstances, 843. Proper regulation of a tax on, ib. How taxed in Holland, 845. Hearth money, 845–6. Window tax, 846.

Hudson's bay company, the nature of their establishments and trade, 743. Their profits not so high as has been reported, 744.

Hunters, war how supported by a nation of, 690. Cannot be very numerous, 691. No established administration of justice, needful among them, 709. Age the sole foundation of rank and precedency among, 711. No considerable inequality of fortune, or subordination to be found among them, 712. No hereditary honours in such a society, 713.

Husbandmen, war how supported by a nation of, 692–3.

Husbandry. See *Agriculture*.

I

Idleness, unfashionable in Holland, 113.

Importation, why restraints have been imposed on, with the two kinds of, 450. How restrained to secure a monopoly of the home market to domestic industry, 452. The true policy of these restraints doubtful, 453. The free importation of foreign manufactures more dangerous than that of raw materials, 459. How far it may be proper to continue the free importation of certain foreign goods, 466–7. How far it may be proper to restore the free importation of goods, after it has been interrupted, 468–9. Of the materials of manufacture, review of the legal encouragements given to, 642.

Independents, the principles of that sect explained, 793.

Indies. See *East* and *West*.

Indostan, the several classes of people there kept distinct, 681. The natives of, how prevented from undertaking long sea voyages, 682.

Industry, the different kinds of, seldom dealt impartially with by any nation, 11. The species of, frequently local, 31–2. Naturally suited to the demand, 75. Is increased by the liberal reward of labour, 99. How affected by seasons of plenty and scarcity, 100–1. Is more advantageously exerted in towns than in the country, 142. The average produce of, always suited to the average consumption, 206. Is promoted by the circulation of paper money, 293–5, Three requisites to putting industry in motion, 295.

How the general character of nations is estimated by, 335. And idleness, the proportion between how regulated, 336. Is employed for subsistence, before it extends to conveniences and luxury, 377. Whether the general industry of a society, is promoted by commercial restraints on importation, 453. Private interest naturally points to that employment most advantageous to the society, 454. But without intending or knowing it, 456. Legal regulations of private industry, dangerous assumptions of power, ib. Domestic industry ought not to be employed on what can be purchased cheaper from abroad, 457. Of the society, can augment only in proportion as its capital augments, 458. When it may be necessary to impose some burden upon foreign industry, to favour that at home, 463. The free exercise of industry ought to be allowed to all, 470. The natural effort of every individual to better his condition, will, if unrestrained, result in the prosperity of the society, 540.

Insurance, from fire, and sea risks, the nature and profits of, examined, 125–6. The trade of insurance may be successfully carried on by a joint stock company, 756.

Interest, landed, monied, and trading, distinguished, 351. For the use of money, the foundation of that allowance explained, 69. Historical view of the alterations of, in England, and other countries, 106. Remarks on the high rates of, in Bengal, 111. And in China, 112. May be raised by defective laws, independent on the influence of wealth or poverty, ib. The lowest ordinary rate of, must somewhat more than compensate occasional losses, 113. The common relative proportion between interest and mercantile profits inquired into, 114.

Was not lowered in consequence of the discovery of the American mines, 354. How the legal rate of, ought to be fixed, 357. Consequences of its being fixed too high or too low,

357–8. The market rate of, regulates the price of land, 358. Whether a proper object of taxation, 848.

Ireland, why never likely to furnish cattle to the prejudice of Great Britain, 459–60. The proposed absentee tax there, considered, 895. Ought in justice to contribute toward the discharge of the public debt of Great Britain, 944. Expediency of a union with Great Britain, ib.

Isocrates, the handsome income he made by teaching, 149–50.

Italy, the only great country in Europe, which has been cultivated and improved in every part by means of its foreign commerce, 426. Was originally colonized by the Dorians, 556.

J

Jamaica, the returns of trade from that island, why irregular, 943.

Jewels. See *Stones*.

Jurisdictions, territorial, did not originate in the feudal law, 415.

Justice, the administration of, a duty of the sovereign, 708–9. In early times a source of revenue to him, 715. The making justice subservient to the revenue, a source of great abuses, 716. Is never administered gratis, 718. The whole administration of, but an inconsiderable part of the expence of government, 719. How the whole expence of justice might be defrayed from the fees of court, ib. The interference of the jurisdictions of the several English courts of law, accounted for, 720. Law language, how corrupted, 721. The judicial and executive power, why divided, 722. By whom the expence of the administration of, ought to be borne, 814–15.

K

Kalm, the Swedish traveller, his account of the husbandry of the British colonies in North America, 240.

Kelp, a rent demanded for the rocks on which it grows, 161.

King, Mr. his account of the average price of wheat, 215.

King, under feudal institutions, no more than the greatest baron in the nation, 415. Was unable to restrain the violence of his barons, 418.

King, treasure trove an important branch of revenue to, 908. His situation how favourable for the accumulating treasure, ib. In a commercial country, naturally spends his revenue in luxuries, ib. Is hence driven to call upon his subjects for extraordinary aids, 909.

Kings and their ministers, the greatest spendthrifts in a country, 346.

L

Labour, the fund which originally supplies every nation with its annual consumption, 10. How the proportion between labour and consumption is regulated, ib. The different kinds of industry seldom dealt impartially with by any nation, 11. The division of labour considered, 13. This division increases the quantity of work, 17. Instances in illustration, 22. From what principle the division of labour originates, 25. The divisibility of, governed by the market, 31. Labour the real measure of the exchangeable value of commodities, 47. Different kinds of, not easily estimated by immediate comparison, 48. Is compared by the intermediate standard of money, 49. Is an invariable standard for the value of commodities, 51. Has a real, and a nominal price, ib. The quantity of labour employed on different objects, the only rule for exchanging them in the rude stages of society, 65. Difference between the wages of labour and profits on stock, in manufactures, 66. The whole labour of a country never exerted, 71. Is in every instance suited to the demand, 75. The effect of extraordinary calls for, 76. The deductions made from the produce of labour employed upon land, 83. Why dearer in North America than in England, 87. Is cheap in countries that are stationary, 89. The demand for, would continually decrease in a declining country, 90. The province of Bengal cited as an instance, 91. Is not badly paid for in Great Britain, ib. An increasing demand for,

favourable to population, 98. That of freemen cheaper to the employers than that of slaves, ib. The money price of, how regulated, 103. Is liberally rewarded in new colonies, 109. Common labour and skilful labour distinguished, 118–19. The free circulation of, from one employment to another, obstructed by corporation laws, 152. The unequal prices of, in different places, probably owing to the law of settlements, 156. Can always procure subsistence on the spot where it is purchased, 162. The money price of, in different countries, how governed, 209. Is set into motion by stock employed for profit, 266. The division of, depends on the accumulation of stock, 276. Machines to facilitate labour, advantageous to society, 287.

Productive and unproductive, distinguished, 330. Various orders of men specified, whose labour is unproductive, 330–1. Unproductive labourers all maintained by revenue, 333. The price of, how raised by the increase of the national capital, 353. Its price, though nominally raised, may continue the same, 355. Is liberally rewarded in new colonies, 565. Of artificers and manufacturers, never adds any value to the whole amount of the rude produce of the land, according to the French agricultural system of political œconomy, 667. This doctrine shewn to be erroneous, 675–6. The productive powers of labour, how to be improved, 676.

Labourers, useful and productive, every where proportioned to the capital stock on which they are employed, 11. Share the produce of their labour, in most cases, with the owners of the stock on which they are employed, 67. Their wages a continued subject of contest between them and their masters, 83–4. Are seldom successful in their outrageous combinations, 85. The sufficiency of their earnings, a point not easily determined, ib. Their wages sometimes raised by increase of work, 86. Their demands limited by the funds destined for payment, ib. Are continually wanted in North America, 88. Miserable condition of those in China, 89–90. Are not ill paid in Great Britain, 91. If able to maintain their families in dear years, they must be at their ease in plentiful seasons, 92. A proof furnished in the complaints of their luxury, 96. Why worse paid than artificers, 119. Their interests strictly connected with the interests of the society, 266. Labour the only source of their revenue, 279. Effects of a life of labour on the understandings of the poor, 781–2.

Land, the demand of rent for, how founded, 67. The rent paid, enters into the price of the greater part of all commodities, ib. Generally produces more food than will maintain the labour necessary to bring it to market, 162–3. Good roads, and navigable canals, equalize difference of situation, 163. That employed in raising food for men or cattle, regulates the rent of all other cultivated land, 168, 175. Can clothe and lodge more than it can feed, while uncultivated, and the contrary when improved, 178. The culture of land producing food, creates a demand for the produce of other lands, 192. Produces by agriculture a much greater quantity of vegetable, than of animal food, 206–7. The full improvement of, requires a stock of cattle to supply manure, 238. Cause and effect of the diminution of cottagers, 243. Signs of the land being completely improved, 245. The whole annual produce, or the price of it, naturally divides itself into rent, wages, and profits of stock, 265.

The usual price of, depends on the common rate of interest for money, 358. The profits of cultivation exaggerated by projectors, 374. The cultivation of, naturally preferred to trade and manufactures, on equal terms, 377. Artificers necessary to the cultivation of, 378. Was all appropriated, though not cultivated, by the northern destroyers of the Roman empire, 382. Origin of the law of primogeniture under the feudal government, ib. Entails, 384. Obstacles to the improvement of land under feudal proprietors, 385–6. Feudal tenures, 389. Feudal taxation, 394. The improvement of land checked in France by the taille, ib. Occupiers of, labour under great disadvantages, 395. Origin of long leases of, 421. Small proprietors, the best improvers of, 423. Small purchasers of, cannot hope to raise fortunes by cultivation, ib. Tenures of, in the British American colonies, 572; is the most permanent source of revenue, 821. The rent of a whole country, not equal to the ordinary levy upon the people, 822. The revenue from, proportioned, not to the rent, but to the produce, 823. Reasons for selling the crown lands, 824. The land-tax of Great Britain considered, 828. An improved land-tax suggested, 830. A land-tax, however equally rated by a general survey, will soon become unequal, 836. Tythes a very unequal tax, 837. Tythes discourage improvement, ib.

Landholders, why frequently inattentive to their own particular interests, 265. How they contribute to the annual production of the land, according to the French agricultural system of political œconomy, 664–5. Should be encouraged to cultivate a part of their own land, 832.

Latin language, how it became an essential part of university education, 765–6.

Law, Mr., account of his banking scheme for the improvement of Scotland, 317.

Law, the language of, how corrupted, 721. Did not improve into a science in ancient Greece, 778. Remarks on the courts of justice in Greece and Rome, 778–9.

Lawyers, why amply rewarded for their labour, 122–3. Great amount of their fees, 718.

Leases, the various usual conditions of, 831.

Leather, restrictions on the exportation of, unmanufactured, 654–5.

Lectures in universities, frequently improper for instruction, 763.

Levity, the vices of, ruinous to the common people, and therefore severely censured by them, 794.

Liberty, three duties only necessary for a sovereign to attend to, for supporting a system of, 687–8.

Lima, computed number of inhabitants in that city, 568.

Linen manufacture, narrow policy of the master manufacturers in, 643–4.

Literature, the rewards of, reduced by competition, 148. Was more profitable in ancient Greece, 149–50. The cheapness of literary education an advantage to the public, 151.

Loans of money, the nature of, analysed, 350–1. The extensive operation of, 351–2.

Locke, Mr. remarks on his opinion of the difference between the market and mint prices of silver bullion, 60. His account of the cause of lowering the rates of interest for money, examined, 353. His distinction between money and moveable goods, 430.

Lodgings, cheaper in London, than in any other capital city in Europe, 134.

Logic, the origin and employment of, 769–70.

Lotteries, the true nature of, and the causes of their success, explained, 125.

Luck, instances of the universal reliance mankind have on it, 124–5.

Lutherans, origin and principles of that sect, 807–8.

Luxuries, distinguished from necessaries, 869–71. Operation of taxes on, 871–2. The good and bad properties of taxes on, 895–6.

M

Macedon, Philip of, the superiority that discipline gave his army over those of his enemies, 701–2.

Machines for facilitating mechanical operations, how invented and improved, 20–1. Are advantageous to every society, 287–8.

Madder, the cultivation of, long confined to Holland, by English tythes, 838.

Madeira wine, how introduced into North America and Britain, 502–3.

Malt, reasons for transferring the duty on brewing to, 889. Distillery, how to prevent smuggling in, 890–1.

Manufactures, the great advantage resulting from a division of labour in, 14–15. Instances in illustration, 22–3. Why profits increase in the higher stages of, 68. Of what parts the gains of manufacturers consist, 70–1. The private advantage of secrets in manufactures, 77. Peculiar advantages of soil and situation, 78. Monopolies, 78. Corporation privileges, 79. The deductions made from labour employed on manufactures, 83. Inquiry how far they are affected by seasons of plenty and scarcity, 101. Are not so materially affected by circumstances in the country where they are carried on, as in the places where they are consumed, 103, 114. New manufactures generally give higher wages than old ones, 131. Are more profitably carried on in towns than in the open country, 142. By what means the prices of, are reduced, while the society continues improving, 260. Instances in hard ware, ib. Instances in the woollen manufacture, 261. What fixed capitals are required to carry on particular manufactures, 280.

For distant sale, why not established in North America, 378–9. Why manufactures are preferred to foreign trade, for the employment of a capital, 379. Motives to the establishment of manufactures for distant sale, 407–8. How shifted from one country to another, ib. Natural circumstances which contribute to the establishment of them, 408–9. Their effect on the government and manners of a country, 412. The independence of artisans explained, 420. May flourish amidst the ruin of a country, and begin to decay on the return of its prosperity, 445. Inquiry how far manufacturers might be affected by a freedom of trade, 469. Those thrown out of one business can transfer their industry to collateral employments,

470. A spirit of combination among them to support monopolies, 471. Manufacturers prohibited by old statutes from keeping a shop, or selling their own goods by retail, 529. The
use of wholesale dealers to manufacturers, 531. British restraints on manufactures in North
America, 580–2. The exportation of instruments in, prohibited, 659.

Manufacturers, an unproductive class of the people, according to the French agricultural system of political œconomy, 666. The error of this doctrine shewn, 674. How manufacturers
augment the revenue of a country, 677. Why, the principal support of foreign trade, 680.
Require a more extensive market than rude produce of the land, 682. Were exercised by
slaves in ancient Greece, 683. High prices of, in Greece and at Rome, 684–5. False policy to
check manufactures in order to promote agriculture, 686. In Great Britain why principally
fixed in the coal countries, 874.

Manure, the supply of, in most places depends on the stock of cattle raised, 238.

Maritime countries, why the first that are civilized and improved, 34.

Martial spirit, how supported in the ancient republics of Greece and Rome, 786. The want of
it now supplied by standing armies, 787. The establishment of a militia little able to support
it, ib.

Mediterranean sea, peculiarly favourable for the first attempts in navigation, 34.

Meggens, Mr. his account of the annual importation of gold and silver into Spain and Portugal, 226. His relative proportion of each, 229.

Mercantile system explained, 880.

Mercenary troops, origin and reason of, 695. The numbers of, how limited, ib.

Merchants, their judgments more to be depended on respecting the interests of their particular branches of trade, than with regard to the public interest, 266–7. Their capitals altogether circulating, 280. Their dealings extended by the aid of bankers notes, 299, 304–5.
Customs of, first established to supply the want of laws, and afterward admitted as laws,
309. The manner of negociating bills of exchange explained, ib. The pernicious tendency of
drawing and redrawing, 309.

    In what method their capitals are employed, 361. Their capitals dispersed and unfixed,
364. The principles of foreign trade examined, 372. Are the best of improvers, when they
turn country gentlemen, 411. Their preference among the different species of trade, how
determined, 454. Are actuated by a narrow spirit of monopoly, 462, 493. The several
branches of the corn trade specified and considered, 524. The government of a company of,
the worst a country can be under, 570. Of London not good œconomists, 613.

Merchants, an unproductive class of men, according to the present agricultural system of political œconomy in France, 668. The quick return of mercantile capitals, enables merchants
to advance money to government, 910. Their capitals, increased by lending money to the
state, ib.

Mercier de la Riviere, M. character of his natural and essential order of political societies, 679.

Metals, why the best medium of commerce, 38. Origin of stamped coins, 40. Why different
metals become the standard of value among different nations, 56. The durability of, the
cause of the steadiness of their price, 228. On what the quantity of precious metals in every
particular country depends, 253.

    Restraints upon the exportation of, 656.

Metaphysics, the science of, explained, 770–1.

Metayers, description of the class of farmers so called in France, 389.

Methodists, the teachers among, why popular preachers, 789.

Methuen, Mr. translation of the commercial treaty concluded by him between England and
Portugal, 546.

Mexico was less civilized than Peru, when first visited by the Spaniards, 221.

Militia, why allowed to be formed in cities, and its formidable nature, 403.

    The origin and nature of, explained, 698. How distinguished from the regular standing
army, ib. Must always be inferior to a standing army, 699–700. A few campaigns of service
may make a militia equal to a standing army, 701. Instances, 701–2.

Milk, a most perishable commodity, how manufactured for store, 244.

Mills, wind and water, their late introduction into England, 263.

Mines, distinguished by their fertility or barrenness, 182. Comparison between those of coal
and those of metals, 185. The competition between, extends to all parts of the world, ib.
The working of, a lottery, 187. Diamond mines not always worth working, 191. Tax paid to

the king of Spain from the Peruvian mines, 219. The discovery of mines not dependent on human skill or industry, 254.

In Hungary, why worked at less expence than the neighbouring ones in Turkey, 684.

Mining, projects of, uncertain and ruinous, and unfit for legal encouragement, 562.

Mirabeau, Marquis de, his character of the œconomical table, 679.

Mississippi scheme in France, the real foundation of, 317.

Modus for tythe, a relief to the farmer, 839.

Money, the origin of, traced, 38. Is the representative of labour, 47. The value of, greatly depreciated by the discovery of the American mines, 49. How different metals became the standard money of different nations, 56. The only part of the circulating capital of a society, of which the maintenance can diminish their neat revenue, 288. Makes no part of the revenue of a society, 289. The term money, in common acceptation, of ambiguous meaning, 290. The circulating money in society, no measure of its revenue, 291. Paper money, 292. The effect of paper on the circulation of cash, 292–3. Inquiry into the proportion the circulating money of any country bears to the annual produce circulated by it, 296. Paper can never exceed the value of the cash, of which it supplies the place, in any country, 300. The pernicious practice or raising money by circulation explained, 309.

   The true cause of its exportation, 340. Loans of, the principles of, analysed, 350. Monied interest, distinguished from the landed and trading interest, 351. Inquiry into the real causes of the reduction of interest, 354. Money and wealth synonymous terms in popular language, 429. And moveable goods compared, 430. The accumulation of, studied by the European nations, 431. The mercantile arguments for liberty to export gold and silver, ib. The validity of these arguments examined, 433. Money and goods mutually the price of each other, 435. Over-trading causes complaints of the scarcity of money, 437. Why more easy to buy goods with money, than to buy money with goods, 438. Inquiry into the circulating quantity of, in Great Britain, 442. Effect of the discovery of the American mines on the value of, 447. Money and wealth different things, 449–50. Bank money explained, 481. See *Coins*, *Gold*, and *Silver*.

Monopolies in trade or manufactures, the tendency of, 78. Are enemies to good management, 163.

   Tendency of making a monopoly of colony trade, 608. Countries which have colonies, obliged to share their advantages with many other countries, 628. The chief engine in the mercantile system, 630. How monopolies derange the natural distribution of the stock of the society, 631. Are supported by unjust and cruel laws, 648.

   Of a temporary nature, how far justifiable, 754. Perpetual monopolies injurious to the people at large, 755.

Montauban, the inequalities in the predial taille in that generality, how rectified, 836.

Montesquieu, reasons given by him for the high rates of interest among all Mahometan nations, 112–13.

   Examination of his idea of the cause of lowering the rate of interest of money, 353.

Morality, two different systems of, in every civilized society, 794. The principal points of distinction between them, ib. The ties of obligation in each system, 795. Why the morals of the common people are more regular in sectaries than under the established church, 796. The excesses of, how to be corrected, ib.

Morellet, M. his account of joint stock companies, defective, 755.

Mun, Mr. his illustration of the operation of money exported for commercial purposes, 431–2.

Music, why a part of the ancient Grecian education, 774. And dancing, great amusements among barbarous nations, 776.

N

Nations, sometimes driven to inhuman customs, by poverty, 10. The number of useful and productive labourers in, always proportioned to the capital stock on which they are employed, 11. The several sorts of industry, seldom dealt with impartially by, ib. Maritime nations, why the first improved, 34.

   How ruined by a neglect of public œconomy, 342. Evidences of the increase of a national capital, 343. How the expences of individuals may increase the national capital, 346–7.

Navigation, inland, a great means of improving a country in arts and industry, 35. The advantages of, 163. May be successfully managed by joint stock companies, 756–7.

Act of England, the principal dispositions of, 463–4. Motives that dictated this law, 464. Its political and commercial tendency, ib. Its consequences, so far as it affected the colony trade with England, 595–6. Diminished the foreign trade with Europe, 596. Has kept up high profits in the British trade, 598. Subjects Britain to a disadvantage in every branch of trade of which she has not the monopoly, 599.

Necessaries, distinguished from luxuries, 869–70. Operation of taxes on, 871. Principal necessaries taxed, 873–4.

Negro slaves, why not much employed in raising corn in the English colonies, 388. Why more numerous on sugar, than on tobacco plantations, 389.

Nile, river, the cause of the early improvement of agriculture and manufactures in Egypt, 35.

O

Oats, bread made of, not so suitable to the human constitution, as that made of wheat, 177.

Œconomists, sect of, in France, their political tenets, 663–79.

Ontology, the science of, explained, 771.

Oxford, the professorships there, *sinecures*, 761.

P

Paper money, the credit of, how established, 292. The operation of paper money explained, 292–3. Its effect on the circulation of cash, ib. Promotes industry, 294. Operation of the several banking companies established in Scotland, 297. Can never exceed the value of the gold and silver, of which it supplies the place, in any country, 300. Consequences of too much paper being issued, 301–2. The practice of drawing and redrawing explained, with its pernicious effects, 308–10. The advantages and disadvantages of paper credit stated, 320–1. Ill effects of notes issued for small sums, 322. Suppressing small notes, renders money more plentiful, 323. The currency of, does not affect the prices of goods, 324. Account of the paper currency in North America, 326–7.

Paper-money, expedient of the government of Pennsylvania to raise money, 326–7, 820. Why convenient for the domestic purposes of the North Americans, 940.

Paris, enjoys little more trade than is necessary for the consumption of its inhabitants, 336.

Parish ministers, evils attending vesting the election of, in the people, 808.

Parsimony is the immediate cause of the increase of capitals, 337. Promotes industry, 337–8. Frugal men public benefactors, 340.

Is the only means by which artificers and manufacturers can add to the revenue and wealth of society, according to the French agricultural system of political œconomy, 668.

Pasture land, under what circumstances more profitable than arable land, 165–6. Why it ought to be inclosed, 167.

Patronage, the right of, why established in Scotland, 809.

Pay, military, origin and reason of, 694–5.

Pennsylvania, account of the paper currency there, 326, 820, 940. Good consequences of the government there having no religious establishment, 793. Derive a revenue from their paper currency, 940.

People, how divided into productive and unproductive classes, according to the present French system of agricultural political œconomy, 664. The unproductive class, greatly useful to the others, 669. The great body of, how rendered unwarlike, 697. The different opportunities of education in the different ranks of, 784–5. The inferior ranks of, the greatest consumers, 887. The luxurious expences of these ranks ought only to be taxed, 888.

Persecution for religious opinions, the true cause of, 789.

Peru, the discovery of the silver mines in, occasioned those in Europe to be in a great measure abandoned, 185. These mines yield but small profit to the proprietors, 187. Tax paid to the king of Spain from these mines, 219. The early accounts of the splendour and state of arts in this country, greatly exaggerated, 221. Present state of, under the Spanish government,

ib. The working of the mines there become gradually more expensive, 232. Low state of arts there when first discovered, 568. Is probably more populous now, than at any former period, ib.

Philosophy natural, the origin and objects of, 767–8. Moral, the nature of, explained, 768–9. Logic, the origin and employment of, 769–70.

Physicians, why amply rewarded for their labour, 122.

Physics, the ancient system of, explained, 770–1.

Pinmaking, the extraordinary advantage of a division of labour in this art, 14–15.

Plate of private families, the melting it down to supply state exigencies, an insignificant resource, 441. New plate is chiefly made from old, 550.

Ploughmen, their knowledge more extensive than the generality of mechanics, 143–4.

Pneumatics, the science of, explained, 770–1.

Poivre, M., his account of the agriculture of Cochin China, 173.

Poland, a country still kept in poverty by the feudal system of its government, 256.

Political œconomy, the two distinct objects, and two different systems of, 428. The present agricultural system of, adopted by the French philosophers described, 663.
    Classes of the people who contribute to the annual produce of the land, 664. How proprietors contribute, 665. How cultivators contribute, ib. Artificers and manufacturers, unproductive, 666. The unproductive classes maintained by the others, 668. Bad tendency of restrictions and prohibitions in trade, 671–2. How this system is delineated by M. Quesnai, 672–3. The bad effects of an injudicious political œconomy, how corrected, 674. The capital error in this system pointed out, ib.

Poll taxes, origin of, under the feudal government, 398.
    Why esteemed badges of slavery, ib. The nature of, considered, 867.

Poor, history of the laws made for the provision of, in England, 152–3.

Pope of Rome, the great power formerly assumed by, 800. His power how reduced, 803–4. Rapid progress of the reformation, 805.

Population, riches and extreme poverty, equally unfavourable to, 96–7. Is limited by the means of subsistence, 97, 180.

Porter, the proportion of malt used in the brewing of, 889.

Portugal, the cultivation of the country not advanced by its commerce, 426. The value of gold and silver there, depreciated by prohibiting their exportation, 511–12. Translation of the commercial treaty concluded in 1703 with England, 546. A large share of the Portugal gold sent annually to England, 547. Motives that led to the discovery of a passage to the East round the Cape of Good Hope, 558. Lost its manufactures by acquiring rich and fertile colonies, 609.

Post-office, a mercantile project well calculated for being managed by government, 818.

Potatoes, remarks on, as an article of food, 176–7. Culture, and great produce of, ib. The difficulty of preserving them, the great obstacle to cultivating them for general diet, 177.

Poultry, the cause of their cheapness, 242. Is a more important article of rural œconomy in France than in England, ib.

Poverty, sometimes urges nations to inhuman customs, 10. Is no check to the production of children, 96. But very unfavourable to raising them, 97.

Pragmatic sanction in France, the object of, 804. Is followed by the concordat, ib.

Preferments, ecclesiastical, the means by which a national clergy ought to be managed by the civil magistrate, 798. Alterations in the mode of electing to them 799–800, 804.

Presbyterian church government, the nature of, described, 809. Character of the clergy of, 810, 813.

Prices, real, and nominal, of commodities distinguished, 51. Money price of goods explained, 63. Rent for land enters into the price of the greater part of all commodities, 67. The component parts of the prices of goods explained, 67. Natural and market prices distinguished, and how governed, 72–4, 104. Though raised at first by an increase of demand, are always reduced by it in the result, 748.

Primogeniture, origin and motive of the law of succession by, under the feudal government, 382–3. Is contrary to the real interests of families, 384.

Princes, why not well calculated to manage mercantile projects for the sake of a revenue, 818–19.

Prodigality, the natural tendency of, both to the individual and to the public, 339. Prodigal men enemies to their country, 340.

Produce of land and labour, the source of all revenue, 332. The value of, how to be increased, 343.

Professors in universities, circumstances which determine their merit, 810–11.

Profit, the various articles of gain that pass under the common idea of, 70. An average rate of, in all countries, 72. Averages of, extremely difficult to ascertain, 105.

Interest of money the best standard of, 105–6. The diminution of, a natural consequence of prosperity, 108. Clear, and gross profit, distinguished, 113. The nature of the highest ordinary rate of, defined, ib. Double interest, deemed in Great Britain, a reasonable mercantile profit, 114. In thriving countries, low profit may compensate the high wages of labour, ib. The operation of high profits and high wages, compared, ib. Compensates inconveniencies and disgrace, 118. Of stock, how affected, 128. Large profits must be made from small capitals, 129. Why goods are cheaper in the metropolis than in country villages, ib. Great fortunes more frequently made by trade in large towns than in small ones, 130. Is naturally low in rich, and high in poor countries, 266.

How that of the different classes of traders is raised, 362. Private, the sole motive of employing capitals in any branch of business, 374. When raised by monopolies, encourages luxury, 612.

Property, passions which prompt mankind to the invasion of, 709. Civil government necessary for the protection of, 710. Wealth a source of authority, 711–12, 714.

Provisions, how far the variations in the price of, affect labour and industry, 92, 100–1, 103. Whether cheaper in the metropolis, or in country villages, 129. The prices of, better regulated by competition than by law, 158. A rise in the prices of, must be uniform, to shew that it proceeds from a depreciation of the value of silver, 257.

Provisors, object of the statute of, in England, 804.

Prussia, mode of assessing the land-tax there, 834.

Public works and institutions, how to be maintained, 723. Equity of tolls for passage over roads, bridges, and canals, 724–5. Why government ought not to have the management of turnpikes, 727. Nor of other public works, 730.

Purveyance, a service still exacted in most parts of Europe, 394.

Q

Quakers of Pennsylvania, inference from their resolution to emancipate all their negro slaves, 388.

Quesnai, M. view of his agricultural system of political œconomy, 672. His doctrine generally subscribed to, 679.

R

Reformation, rapid progress of the doctrines of, in Germany, 805. In Sweden, and Switzerland, 806. In England and Scotland, 806–7. Origin of the Lutheran and Calvinistic sects, 807.

Regulated companies. See *Companies*.

Religion, the object of instruction in, 788. Advantage the teachers of a new religion enjoy over those of one that is established, 788–9. Origin of persecution for heretical opinions, 789. How the zeal of the inferior clergy of the church of Rome is kept alive, 789–90. Utility of ecclesiastical establishments, 791. How united with the civil power, 792.

Rent, reserved, ought not to consist of money, 52. But of corn, 53. Of land, constitutes a third part of the price of most kinds of goods, 67. An average rate of, in all countries, and how regulated, 72. Makes the first deduction from the produce of labour employed upon land, 83. The terms of, how adjusted between landlord and tenant, 160. Is sometimes demanded for what is altogether incapable of human improvement, 161. Is paid for, and produced by, land in almost all situations, 163. The general proportion paid for coal mines, 184–5. And metal mines, 185–6. Mines of precious stones frequently yield no rent, 191. How paid in

ancient times, 200. Is raised, either directly or indirectly, by every improvement in the circumstances of society, 264. Gross and neat rent distinguished, 286.

Rent, how raised and paid under feudal government, 334. Present average proportion of, compared with the produce of the land, ib. Of houses, distinguished into two parts, 840. Difference between rent of houses, and rent of land, 842. Rent of a house the best estimate of a tenant's circumstances, 843.

Retainers, under the feudal system of government, described, 413. How the connexion between them and their lords was broken, 418–19.

Revenue, the original sources of, pointed out, 69. Of a country, of what it consists, 286. The neat revenue of a society, diminished by supporting a circulating stock of money, 288. Money no part of revenue, 289. Is not to be computed in money, but in what money will purchase, 290.

How produced, and how appropriated, in the first instance, 332. Produce of land, ib. Produce of manufactures, ib. Must always replace capital, ib. The proportion between revenue and capital regulates the proportion between idleness and industry, 337. Both the savings and the spendings of, annually consumed, 337–8. Of every society, equal to the exchangeable value of the whole produce of its industry, 455–6. Of the customs, increased by drawbacks, 503.

Why government ought not to take the management of turnpikes, to derive a revenue from them, 727. Public works of a local nature, always better maintained by provincial revenues, than by the general revenue of the state, 730. The abuses in provincial revenues trifling, when compared with those in the revenue of a great empire, 731. The greater the revenue of the church, the smaller must be that of the state, 812. The revenue of the state ought to be raised proportionably from the whole society, 814. Local expences ought to be defrayed by local revenue, 815. Inquiry into the sources of public revenue, 817. Of the republic of Hamburgh, 817, 820. Whether the government of Britain could undertake the management of the Bank to derive a revenue from it, 818. The Post-office a mercantile project well calculated for being managed by government, ib. Princes not well qualified to improve their fortunes by trade, ib. The English East India Company good traders before they became sovereigns, but each character now spoils the other, 819. Expedient of the government of Pennsylvania to raise money, 820. Rent of land, the most permanent fund, 821. Feudal revenues, ib. Great Britain, ib. Revenue from land proportioned, not to the rent, but to the produce, 823. Reasons for selling the crown lands, 823–4. An improved land-tax suggested, 830. The nature and effect of tythes explained, 837. Why a revenue cannot be raised in kind, 839. When raised in money, how affected by different modes of valuation, ib. A proportionable tax on houses, the best source of revenue, 843. Remedies for the diminution of, according to their causes, 884. Bad effects of farming out public revenues, 902. The different sources of revenue in France, 904. How expended, in the rude state of society, 907.

Rice, a very productive article of cultivation, 176. Requires a soil unfit for raising any other kind of food, ib. Rice countries more populous than corn countries, 223.

Riches, the chief enjoyment of, consists in the parade of, 190.

Risk, instances of the inattention mankind pay to it, 125.

Roads, good, the public advantages of, 163.

How to be made and maintained, 724. The maintenance of, why improper to be trusted to private interest, 726. General state of, in France, 729. In China, 729.

Romans, why copper became the standard of value among them, 56. The extravagant prices paid by them for certain luxuries for the table, accounted for, 235–6. The value of silver higher among them than at the present time, 236.

The republic of, founded on a division of land among the citizens, 556. The agrarian law only executed upon one or two occasions, 557. How the citizens who had no land, subsisted, ib. Distinction between the Roman and Greek colonies, 558. The improvement of the former slower than that of the latter, 566–7. Origin of the social war, 622. The republic ruined by extending the privilege of Roman citizens to the greater part of the inhabitants of Italy, 624.

When contributions were first raised to maintain those who went to the wars, 694. Soldiers not a distinct procession there, 696. Improvement of the Roman armies by discipline, 703. How that discipline was lost, 704. The fall of the Western empire, how effected, ib. Remarks on the education of the ancient Romans, 774. Their morals superior to those of

the Greeks, 775. State of law and forms of justice, 778–9. The martial spirit of the people, how supported, 786. Great reductions of the coin practised by, at particular exigencies, 930–1.

Rome, modern, how the zeal of the inferior clergy of, is kept alive, 789. The clergy of, one great spiritual army dispersed in different quarters over Europe, 800. Their power during the feudal monkish ages similar to that of the temporal barons, 800–1. Their power how reduced, 803.

Rouen, why a town of great trade, 335–6.

Ruddiman, Mr. remarks on his account of the ancient price of wheat in Scotland, 203.

Russia, was civilized under Peter I by a standing army, 706.

S

Sailors, why no sensible inconvenience felt by the great numbers disbanded at the close of a war, 469–70.

Salt, account of foreign salt imported into Scotland, and of Scots salt delivered duty free, for the fishery, *Append.*, 950. Is an object of heavy taxation everywhere, 874. The collection of the duty on, expensive, 896.

Sardinia, the land-tax how assessed there, 835–6, 854, 934.

Saxon lords, their authority and jurisdiction as great before conquest, as those of the Normans were afterward, 416.

Schools, parochial, observations on, 785.

Science, is the great antidote to the poison of enthusiasm and superstition, 796.

Scipio, his Spanish militia, rendered superior to the Carthaginian militia by discipline and service, 703.

Scotland, compared with England, as to the prices of labour and provisions, 93. Remarks on the population of the Highlands, 97. The market rate of interest, higher than the legal rate, 107. The situation of cottagers there, described, 133. Apprenticeships and corporations, 138. The common people of, why neither so strong nor so handsome as the same class in England, 177.

Cause of the frequent emigrations from, 209. Progress of agriculture there before the union with England, 239. Present obstructions to better husbandry, 240. The price of wool reduced by the union, 252, 651–2. Operation of the several banking companies established there, 297. Amount of the circulating money there before the union, 298. Amount of the present circulating cash, 298. Course of dealings in the Scots bank, 299. Difficulties occasioned by these banks issuing too much paper, 303. Necessary caution for some time observed by the banks in giving credit to their customers, with the good effects of it, 305. The scheme of drawing and redrawing adopted by traders, 308–9. Its pernicious tendency explained, 310. History of the Ayr bank, 313. Mr. Law's scheme to improve the country, 317. The prices of goods in, not altered by paper currency, 324. Effect of the optional clauses in their notes, 325.

Cause of the speedy establishment of the reformation there, 807. The disorders attending popular elections of the clergy there, occasion the right of patronage to be established, 809. Amount of the whole revenue of the clergy, 813.

Sea service and military service by land, compared, 126.

Sects in religion, the more numerous, the better for society, 792–3. Why they generally profess the austere system of morality, 794.

Self-love, the governing principle in the intercourse of human society, 26–7.

Servants, menial, distinguished from hired workmen, 330. The various orders of men, who rank in the former class, in reference to their labours, 330–1; their labour unproductive, 675.

Settlements of the poor, brief review of the English laws relating to, 152. The removals of the poor, a violation of natural liberty, 157. The law of, ought to be repealed, 470.

Sheep, frequently killed in Spain, for the sake of the fleece and the tallow, 247. Severe laws against the exportation of them and their wool, 647–8.

Shepherds, war how supported by a nation of, 690–1. Inequality of fortune among, the source of great authority, 711–13. Birth and family highly honoured in nations of shepherds, 714. Inequality of fortune first began to take place in the age of shepherds, 715. And introduced civil government, ib.

Shetland, how rents are estimated and paid there, 161.

Silk, manufacture, how transferred from Lucca to Venice, 407.

Silver, the first standard coinage of the northern subverters of the Roman empire, 56. Its proportional value of gold, regulated by law, 57. Is the measure of the value of gold, 58. Mint price of silver in England, 60. Inquiry into the difference between the mint and market prices of bullion, ib. How to preserve the silver coin from being melted down for profit, 61. The mines of, in Europe, why generally abandoned, 185. Evidences of the small profit yield to proprietors in Peru, 186–7. Qualities for which this metal is valued, 189–91. The most abundant mines of, would add little to the wealth of the world, 192. But the increase in the quantity of, would depreciate its own value, 194. Circumstances that might counteract this effect, ib. Historical view of the variations in the value of, during the four last centuries, 195. Remarks on its rise in value compared with corn, 199. Circumstances that have misled writers in reviewing the value of silver, 199–200. Corn the best standard of judging of the real value of silver, 206. The price of, how affected by the increase of quantity, 207. The value of, sunk by the discovery of the American mines, 210. When the reduction of its value from this cause, appears to have been completed, 211. Tax paid from the Peruvian mines to the king of Spain, 219. The value of silver kept up by an extension of the market, 220. Is the most profitable commodity that can be sent to China, 224–5. The value of, how proportioned to that of gold, before and after the discovery of the American mines, 228–9. The quantity commonly in the market in proportion to that of gold, probably greater than their relative values indicate, 230. The value of, probably rising, and why, 232.

The opinion of a depreciation of its value, not well founded, 258. The real value of, degraded by the bounty on the exportation of corn, 509.

Sinking fund in the British finances, explained, 915. Is inadequate to the discharge of former debts, and almost wholly applied to other purposes, 920. Motives to the mis-application of it, 920.

Slaves, the labour of, dearer to the masters than that of free men, 98.

Under feudal lords, circumstances of their situation, 386–7. Countries where this order of men still remains, 387. Why the service of slaves is preferred to that of free men, 388. Their labour why unprofitable, 389. Causes of the abolishing of slavery throughout the greater part of Europe, 389–90. Receive more protection from the magistrate in an arbitrary government, than in one that is free, 587.

Why employed in manufactures by the ancient Grecians, 683–4. Why no improvements are to be expected from them, 684.

Smuggling, a tempting, but generally a ruinous employment, 128. Encouraged by high duties, 881–2. Remedies against, 884. The crime of, morally considered, 898.

Soldiers, remarks on their motives for engaging in the military line, 126. Comparison between the land and sea service, ib.

Why no sensible inconvenience felt by the disbanding of great numbers after a war is over, 469–70.

Reason of their first serving for pay, 694–5. How they became a distinct class of the people, 698. How distinguished from the militia, ib. Alteration in their exercise produced by the invention of fire-arms, 699.

South Sea company, amazing capital once enjoyed by, 741. Mercantile and stock-jobbing projects of, 745. Assiento contract, ib. Whale fishery, ib. The capital of, turned into annuity stock, 746, 914.

Sovereign and trader, inconsistent characters, 819.

Sovereign, three duties only, necessary for him to attend to, for supporting a system of natural liberty, 687. How he is to protect the society from external violence, 689, 707. And the members of it, from the injustice and oppression of each other, 708–9. And to maintain public works and institutions, 723.

Spain, one of the poorest countries in Europe, notwithstanding its rich mines, 256.

Its commerce has produced no considerable manufactures for distant sale, and the greater part of the country remains uncultivated, 425–6. Spanish mode of estimating their American discoveries, 429. The value of gold and silver there, depreciated by laying a tax on the exportation of them, 511. Agriculture and manufactures there, discouraged by the redundancy of gold and silver, 512. Natural consequences that would result from taking away this tax, 513. The real and pretended motives of the court of Castile for taking possession of

the countries discovered by Columbus, 561. The tax on gold and silver, how reduced, 562. Gold, the object of all the enterprises to the new world, 562. The colonies of, less populous than those of any other European nation, 568. Asserted an exclusive claim to all America, until the miscarriage of their invincible armada, 569. Policy of the trade with the colonies, 576. The American establishment of, effected by private adventurers, who received little beyond permission from the government, 589–90. Lost its manufactures by acquiring rich and fertile colonies, 609. The alcavala tax there explained, 899.

Speculation, a distinct employment in improved society, 21. Speculative merchants described, 130.

Stage, public performers on, paid for the contempt attending their profession, 124. The political use of dramatic representations, 796.

Stamp duties in England and Holland, remarks on, 860–1.

Steel-bow tenants in Scotland, what, 391.

Stock, the profits raised on, in manufactures, explained, 65–6. In trade, an increase of, raises wages, and diminishes profit, 105. Must be larger in a great town than in a country village, 106–7. Natural consequences of a deficiency of stock in new colonies, 109. The profits on, little affected by the easiness or difficulty of learning a trade, 120. But by the risk, or disagreeableness of the business, 128. Stock employed for profit, sets into motion the greater part of useful labour, 266. No accumulation of, necessary in the rude state of society, 276. The accumulation of, necessary to the division of labour, ib. Stock distinguished into two parts, 277–8. The general stock of a country or society, explained, 281. Houses, ib. Improved land, 282. Personal abilities, ib. Money and provisions, 282–3. Raw materials and manufactured goods, 283. Stock of individuals, how employed, 284–5. Is frequently buried or concealed, in arbitrary countries, 285.

   The profits on, decrease, in proportion as the quantity increases, 334–5. On what principles stock is lent and borrowed at interest, 350. That of every society divided among different employments, in the proportion most agreeable to the public interest, by the private views of individuals, 630. The natural distribution of, deranged by monopolizing systems, 631. Every derangement of, injurious to the society, 632–3.

   Mercantile, is barren and unproductive, according to the French agricultural system of political œconomy, 667. How far the revenue from, is an object of taxation, 847. A tax on, intended under the land tax, 849.

Stockings, why cheaply manufactured in Scotland, 134. When first introduced into England, 262.

Stone quarries, their value depends on situation, 179, 193.

Stones, precious, of no use but for ornament, and how the price of, is regulated, 191. The most abundant mines of, would add little to the wealth of the world, 192.

Subordination, how introduced into society, 710. Personal qualifications, ib. Age and fortune, ib. Birth and fortune two great sources of personal distinction, 714.

Subsidy, old, in the English customs, the drawbacks upon, 499–500. Origin and import of the term, 880.

Sugar, a very profitable article of cultivation, 173, 389.

   Drawbacks on the exportation of, from England, 500. Might be cultivated by the drill plough, instead of all hand labour by slaves, 586.

   A proper subject for taxation, as an article sold at a monopoly price, 893.

Sumptuary laws superfluous restraints on the common people, 346.

Surinam, present state of the Dutch colony there, 570.

Switzerland, establishment of the reformation in Berne and Zurich, 806. Taxes how paid there, 850–1, 860.

T

Taille, in France, the nature of that tax, and its operation, explained, 394, 854.

Talents, natural, not so various in different men as is supposed, 28.

Tartars, their manner of conducting war, 690. Their invasions dreadful, 692.

Tavernier, his account of the diamond mines of Golconda and Visiapour, 191.

Taxes, the origin of, under the feudal government, 397–8.

The sources from whence they must arise, 825. Unequal taxes, ib. Ought to be clear and certain, ib. Ought to be levied at the times most convenient for payment, 826. Ought to take as little as possible out of the pockets of the people, more than is brought into the public treasury, ib. How they may be made more burdensome to the people than beneficial to the sovereign, 827. The land-tax of Great Britain, 828. Land-tax at Venice, 830. Improvements suggested for a land-tax, 831. Mode of assessing the land-tax in Prussia, 836. Tythes a very unequal tax, and a discouragement to improvement, 837. Operation of tax on house rent, payable by the tenant, 841. A proportionable tax on houses, the best source of revenue, 842–3. How far the revenue from stock is a proper object of taxation, 847. Whether interest of money is proper for taxation, 847–8. How taxes are paid at Hamburgh, 850. In Switzerland, 850–1. Taxes upon particular employments, 852. Poll taxes, 857. Taxes, badges of liberty, ib. Taxes upon the transfer of property, 858. Stamp duties, 860. On whom the several kinds of taxes principally fall, 862. Taxes upon the wages of labour, 864. Capitations, 867. Taxes upon consumable commodities, 869. Upon necessaries, 870. Upon luxuries, 871. Principal necessaries taxed, 874. Absurdities in taxation, 874–5. Different parts of Europe very highly taxed, 875. Two different methods of taxing consumable commodities, 876. Sir Matthew Decker's scheme of taxation considered, 877. Excise and customs, 878. Taxation sometimes not an instrument of revenue, but of monopoly, 882. Improvements of the customs suggested, 883. Taxes paid in the price of a commodity little adverted to, 895. On luxuries, the good and bad properties of, 896. Bad effects of farming them out, 902. How the finances of France might be reformed, 904. French and English systems of taxation compared, 905. New taxes always generate discontent, 920–1. How far the British system of taxation might be applicable to all the different provinces of the empire, 933. Such a plan might speedily discharge the national debt, 938.

Tea, great importation and consumption of that drug in Britain, 223.

Teachers, in universities, tendency of endowments to diminish their application, 760. The jurisdictions to which they are subject, little calculated to quicken their diligence, 761. Are frequently obliged to gain protection by servility, 762. Defects in their establishments, 762–3. Teachers among the ancient Greeks and Romans, superior to those of modern times, 772. Circumstances which draw good ones to, or drain them from, the universities, 810. Their employment naturally renders them eminent in letters, 812.

Tenures, feudal, general observations on, 334. Described, 383.

Theology, monkish, the complexion of, 771–2.

Tin, average rent of the mines of, in Cornwall, 186. Yield a greater profit to the proprietors than the silver mines of Peru, 187. Regulations under which tin-mines are worked, 188.

Tobacco, the culture of, why restrained in Europe, 174. Not so profitable an article of cultivation in the West Indies as sugar, ib.

The amount and course of the British trade with, explained, 372–3, The whole duty upon, drawn back on exportation, 500. Consequences of the exclusive trade Britain enjoys with Maryland and Virginia in this article, 594.

Tolls, for passage over roads, bridges, and navigable canals, the equity of, shewn, 724–5. Upon carriages of luxury, ought to be higher than upon carriages of utility, 725. The management of turnpikes often an object of just complaint, 726. Why government ought not to have the management of turnpikes, 727, 894.

Tonnage and poundage, origin of those duties, 879–80.

Tontine in the French finances, what, with the derivation of the name, 917.

Toulouse, salary paid to a counsellor or judge in the parliament, of, 720.

Towns, the places where industry is most profitably exerted, 142. The spirit of combination prevalent among manufacturers, 142, 145.

According to what circumstances the general character of the inhabitants, as to industry, is formed, 335. The reciprocal nature of the trade between them and the country, explained, 376. Subsist on the surplus produce of the country, 377. How first formed, 378. Are continual fairs, ib. The original poverty and servile state of the inhabitants of, 397. Their early exemptions and privileges, how obtained, 398. The inhabitants of, obtained liberty much earlier than the occupiers of land in the country, 399. Origin of free burghs, 400. Origin of corporations, ib. Why allowed to form militia, 403. How the increase and riches of commercial towns contributed to the improvement of the countries to which they belonged, 411.

Trade, double interest deemed a reasonable mercantile profit in, 114.

Four general classes of, equally necessary to, and dependent on, each other, 360. Wholesale, three different sorts of, 368. The different returns of home and foreign trade, ib. The nature and operation of the carrying trade examined, 370-1. The principles of foreign trade examined, 372. The trade between town and country explained, 376. Original poverty and servile state of the inhabitants of towns, under feudal government, 397. Exemptions and privileges granted to them, 398. Extension of commerce by rude nations selling their own raw produce for the manufactures of more civilized countries, 407. Its salutary effects on the government and manners of a country, 412. Subverted the feudal authority, 418. The independence of tradesmen and artisans, explained, 421. The capitals acquired by, very precarious, until some part has been realized by the cultivation and improvement of land, 426. Over trading, the cause of complaints of the scarcity of money, 437. The importation of gold and silver not the principal benefit derived from foreign trade, 446. Effect produced in trade and manufactures by the discovery of America, 448. And by the discovery of a passage to the East Indies round the Cape of Good Hope, ib. Error of commercial writers in estimating national wealth by gold and silver, 449-50. Inquiry into the cause and effect of restraints upon trade, 450. Individuals, by pursuing their own interest, unknowingly promote that of the public, 456. Legal regulations of trade, unsafe, ib. Retaliatory regulations between nations, 467. Measures for laying trade open, ought to be carried into execution slowly, 471. Policy of the restraints on trade between France and Britain considered, 474. No certain criterion to determine on which side the balance of trade between two countries turns, 475. Most of the regulations of, founded on a mistaken doctrine of the balance of trade, 488. Is generally founded on narrow principles of policy, 493. Drawbacks of duties, 499. The dealer who employs his whole stock in one single branch of business, has an advantage of the same kind with the workman who employs his whole labour on a single operation, 530. Consequences of drawing it from a number of small channels into one great channel, 604. Colony trade, and the monopoly of that trade, distinguished, 607. The interest of the consumer constantly sacrificed to that of the producer, 660. Advantages attending a perfect freedom of, to landed nations, according to the present agricultural system of political economy in France, 670. Origin of foreign trade, 671. Consequences of high duties and prohibitions, in landed nations, 671-2. How trade augments the revenue of a country, 677. Nature of the trading intercourse between the inhabitants of towns and those of the country, 686.

Trades, cause and effect of the separation of, 15. Origin of, 26, 27.

Transit duties explained, 894.

Travelling for education, summary view of the effects of, 773.

Treasures, why formerly accumulated by princes, 445.

Treasure trove, the term explained, 285. Why an important branch of revenue under the ancient feudal governments, 908.

Turkey company, short historical view of, 735.

Turnpikes. See *Tolls*.

Tythes, why an unequal tax, 837. The levying of, a great discouragement to improvements, ib. The fixing a modus for, a relief to the farmer, 839.

U

Universities, the emoluments of the teachers in, how far calculated to promote their diligence, 760. The professors at Oxford have mostly given up teaching, 761. Those in France subject to incompetent jurisdictions, 762. The privileges of graduates improperly obtained, ib. Abuse of lectureships, 763. The discipline of, seldom calculated for the benefit of the students, 764. Are, in England, more corrupted than the public schools, ib. Original foundation of, 765. How Latin became an essential article in academical education, 765-6. How the study of the Greek language was introduced, 766. The three great branches of the Greek philosophy, ib. Are now divided into five branches, 770. The monkish course of education in, 771. Have not been very ready to adopt improvements, 772. Are not well calculated to prepare men for the world, 773. How filled with good professors, or drained of them, 810-11. Where the worst and best professors are generally to be met with, 811. See *Colleges* and *Teachers*.

V

Value, the term defined, 44.

Vedius Pollio, his cruelty to his slaves checked by the Roman emperor Augustus, which could not have been done under the republican form of government, 587–8.

Venice, origin of the silk manufacture in that city, 407–8. Traded in East India goods before the sea track round the Cape of Good Hope was discovered, 558. Nature of the land-tax in that republic, 830, 832.

Venison, the price of, in Britain, does not compensate the expence of a deer park, 241.

Vicesima hæreditatum among the ancient Romans, the nature of, explained, 859.

Villages, how first formed, 378.

Villenage, probable cause of the wearing out of that tenure in Europe, 389.

Vineyard, the most profitable part of agriculture, both among the ancients and moderns, 170. Great advantages derived from peculiarities of soil in, 172.

W

Wages of labour how settled between masters and workmen, 83. The workmen obliged to comply with the terms of their employers, 84. The opposition of workmen outrageous, and seldom successful, 84–5. Circumstances which operate to raise wages, 86. The extent of wages limited by the funds from which they arise, 86. Why higher in North America, than in England, 87. Are low in countries that are stationary, 89. Not oppressively low in Great Britain, 91. A distinction made here between the wages in summer and in winter, ib. If sufficient in dear years, they must be ample in seasons of plenty, 92. Different rates of, in different places, ib. Liberal wages encourage industry and propagation, 99. An advance of, necessarily raises the price of many commodities, 104. An average of, not easily ascertained, 105. The operation of high wages and high profits compared, 114. Causes of the variations of, in different employments, 116. Are generally higher in new, than in old trades, 131, 151. Legal regulations of, destroy industry and ingenuity, 157.
    Natural effect of a direct tax upon, 864.

Walpole, Sir Robert, his excise scheme defended, 886.

Wants of mankind, how supplied through the operation of labour, 37. How extended, in proportion to their supply, 178. The far greater part of them supplied from the produce of other men's labour, 276.

Wars, foreign, the funds for the maintenance of, in the present century, have little dependence on the quantity of gold and silver in a nation, 441.
    How supported by a nation of hunters, 689–90. By a nation of shepherds, 690. By a nation of husbandmen, 692–3. Men of military age, what proportion they bear to the whole society, 693. Feudal wars, how supported, 694. Causes which in the advanced state of society, rendered it impossible for those who took the field, to maintain themselves, 694–5. How the art of war became a distinct profession, 697. Distinction between the militia and regular forces, 698. Alteration in the art of war produced by the invention of fire-arms, 699, 707. Importance of discipline, 700; Macedonian army, 702; Carthaginian army, 702–3; Roman army, 703. Feudal armies, 705. A well-regulated standing army, the only defence of a civilized country, and the only means for speedily civilizing a barbarous country, 705–6. The want of parsimony during peace, imposes on states the necessity of contracting debts to carry on war, 909, 919–20. Why war is agreeable to those who live secure from the immediate calamities of it, 920. Advantages of raising the supplies for, within the year, 925–6.

Watch movements, great reduction in the prices of, owing to mechanical improvements, 260.

Wealth and money, synonymous terms, in popular language, 429, 449. Spanish and Tartarian estimate of, compared, 429
    The great authority conferred by the possession of, 711–12.

Weavers, the profits of, why necessarily greater than those of spinners, 68.

West Indies discovered by Columbus, 559. How they obtained this name, 560. The original native productions of, ib. The thirst of gold the object of all the Spanish enterprizes there, 562. And of those of every other European nation, 564. The remoteness of, greatly in favour

of the European colonies there, 567. The sugar colonies of France better governed than those of Britain, 586.

Wheat. See *Corn.*

Window tax in Britain, how rated, 846. Tends to reduce house-rent, ib.

Windsor market, chronological table of the prices of corn at, 272–5.

Wine, the cheapness of, would be a cause of sobriety, 492. The carrying trade in, encouraged by English statutes, 501

Wood, the price of, rises in proportion as a country is cultivated, 183. The growth of young trees prevented by cattle, ib. When the planting of trees becomes a profitable employment, ib.

Wool, the produce of rude countries, commonly carried to a distant market, 246. The price of, in England, has fallen considerably since the time of Edward III, 248. Causes of this diminution in price, 248–9. The price of, considerably reduced in Scotland, by the union with England, 252.

Severity of the laws against the exportation of, 647–8. Restraints upon the inland commerce of, 649. Restraints upon the coasting trade of, 650. Pleas on which these restraints are founded, 651. The price of wool depressed by these regulations, ib. The exportation of, ought to be allowed, subject to a duty, 653.

Woollen cloth, the present prices of, compared with those at the close of the fifteenth century, 261. Three mechanical improvements introduced in the manufacture of, 263.

FINIS